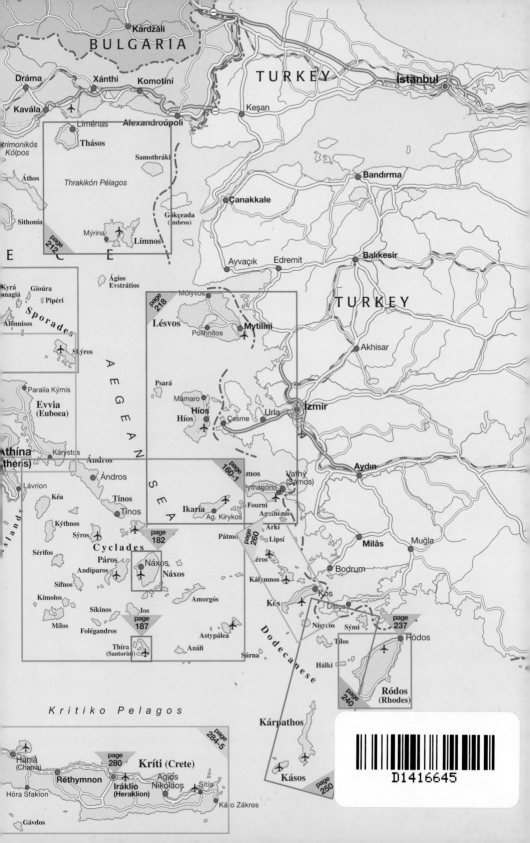

INSIGHT GUIDES
GREEK ISLANDS

APA PUBLICATIONS L
Part of the Langenscheidt Publishing Group

INSIGHT GUIDE

GREEK
ISLANDS

Editorial
Project Editor
Alexia Georgiou
Art Director
Ian Spick
Picture Manager
Steven Lawrence
Series Manager
Rachel Fox

Distribution

UK & Ireland
GeoCenter International Ltd
Meridian House, Churchill Way West
Basingstoke, Hampshire RG21 6YR
sales@geocenter.co.uk

United States
Langenscheidt Publishers, Inc.
36–36 33rd Street 4th Floor
Long Island City, NY 11106
orders@langenscheidt.com

Australia
Universal Publishers
1 Waterloo Road
Macquarie Park, NSW 2113
sales@universalpublishers.com.au

New Zealand
Hema Maps New Zealand Ltd (HNZ)
Unit 2, 10 Cryers Road
East Tamaki, Auckland 2013
Tel: (64) 9 273 6459
sales.hema@clear.net.nz

Worldwide
Apa Publications GmbH & Co.
Verlag KG (Singapore branch)
38 Joo Koon Road, Singapore 628990
Tel: (65) 6865 1600

Printing

Insight Print Services (Pte) Ltd
38 Joo Koon Road, Singapore 628990
apasin@singnet.com.sg

©2010 Apa Publications GmbH & Co.
Verlag KG (Singapore branch)
All Rights Reserved

First Edition 1990
Fourth Edition 2010

CONTACTING THE EDITORS
We would appreciate it if readers
would alert us to errors or out-
dated information by writing to:
Insight Guides, P.O. Box 7910,
London SE1 1WE, England.
insight@apaguide.co.uk

www.insightguides.com

ABOUT THIS BOOK

The first Insight Guide pioneered the use of creative full-colour photography in travel guides in 1970. Since then, we have expanded our range to cater for our readers' need not only for reliable information about their chosen destination but also for a real understanding of the culture and workings of that destination. Now, when the internet can supply inexhaustible (but not always reliable) facts, our books marry text and pictures to provide those much more elusive qualities: knowledge and discernment. To achieve this, they rely heavily on the authority of locally based writers and photographers.

Insight Guide: Greek Islands is structured to convey an understanding of the region and its people as well as to guide readers through its many attractions:

◆ The **Features** section, indicated by a pink bar at the top of each page, covers the natural and cultural history of the region as well as illuminating essays on religion, music, architecture, cuisine, outdoor pursuits and wildlife.
◆ The main **Places** section, indicated by a blue bar, is a complete guide to all the sights and areas worth visiting. Places of special interest are coordinated by number with the maps.
◆ The **Travel Tips** listings section, with a yellow bar, provides full information on transport, hotels, activities from culture to shopping to sports, an A–Z section of essential practical information, and a handy phrasebook with Greek words and expressions. An easy-to-find contents list for Travel Tips is printed on the back flap, which also serves as a bookmark.

LEFT: the Greek islanders' relationship with the sea goes back for millennia.

Significant portions of text remain from the specialist writers whose in-depth knowledge made past editions of the book so valuable to readers over the years. Writer, tour leader and botanist **Lance Chilton** has published numerous guide books on Greece and Cyprus. He supplied the material on island wildlife, wild flowers and the Palace of Knossós. Journalist **Stephanie Ferguson** contributed pages on religious festivals and the cuisine photo feature. Contributors have also included **Rowlinson Carter** (history), **Mark Mazower** (history), **Marcus Brooke** (Ancient Delos, Lindos and Crete), **John Chapple** (Italian Architecture), **Rhoda Nottridge** (Corfu), **David Glenn** (Sailing), **Kerin Hope** (Athens), **Carol Reed**, **John Carr** (Cruising), **Anthony Wood** (Working the Land), **Jane Cocking**, **Nile Stanton**, **Anita Peltonen** (Cyclades and Northeast Aegean) and **Diana Farr Louis** and **Nikos Stavroualakis**.

Many of the stunning photographs in this latest edition are the output of award-winning photographer **Britta Jaschinski**, German-born and based in London. Out-of-house designer **Louise Boulton** worked on the layout.

Thanks also go to **Neil Titman** who proofread the guide and to **Isobel McLean** who brought the index up-to-date.

Map Legend

▬ ▪▪	International Boundary
▬ ▬ ▬	Province Boundary
▬ ▪ ▬	National Park/Reserve
▬ ▬ ▬	Ferry Route
⊖	Border Crossing
✈ ✈	Airport: International/Regional
🚍	Bus Station
Ⓜ	Metro
❶	Tourist Information
∴	Archaeological Site
✝ ✝ ✝	Church/Ruins
✝	Monastry
☾	Mosque
✡	Synagogue
∩	Cave
🗿	Statue/Monument
★	Place of Interest
⚑	Beach
⌂	Lighthouse
🏰	Castle (ruins)
☼	Viewpoint

The main places of interest in the Places section are coordinated by number with a full-colour map (eg ❶), and a symbol at the top of every right-hand page tells you where to find the map.

The contributors

This new edition of *Insight Guide: Greek Islands* was put together by Insight Guides editor **Alexia Georgiou**. It builds on earlier editions by **Jeffery Pike** and **Martha Ellen Zenfell**, with the addition of new features on People and Identities, Religion, Food and Drink, Aegean Architecture, Outdoor Pursuits, and New Immigrants, as well as extensive revisions to existing sections, all written by **Marc Dubin** – a well-travelled resident of London who has a house on Sámos. A Best Of the Greek Islands feature has been added, pointing out the Top Attractions and including an Editor's Choice, our handpicked recommendations for getting to grips with the Greek archipelago. The Travel Tips have been reworked in a new style for ease of reference, with hotel and restaurant listings completely updated.

Contents

LEFT: glimpse of St John's Monastery, Pátmos, Dodecanese.

Maps

Inside front cover: Greece: Political. **Inside back cover**: Greece: Physical and Main Ferry Routes

THE BEST OF THE GREEK ISLANDS: TOP ATTRACTIONS

From elegant Old Towns, dizzyingly perched cliffside monasteries and ancient sites steeped in history, to a reviving dip in a thermal spring and basking on the deck of your own yacht

△ Eminently strollable **Corfu Old Town** is indisputably Greek – but Latinate in style with its slatted Venetian shutters, canal-tile roofs, intimate squares and celebrated arcades, nestled between two giant fortresses. *See page 126*

▽ The juxtaposed colonnades of the Classical **Temple of Aphaea** on Aegina seem straight out of an M.C. Escher drawing; the piney hilltop site is everything you'd expect for an ancient sanctuary. *See page 148*

△Improbably perched **Panagía Hozoviótissa Monastery**, on a cliff above Amorgós's southeast coast, greatly impressed Le Corbusier on his 1911 visit. It is still the spiritual centre of the Cyclades. *See page 179*

△ An unusual combination of the Ottoman and Venetian distinguishes the stage-set **Haniá Old Port**, a double bay with ample eating, drinking and people-watching opportunities. *See page 293*

◁ Only explored and opened after 1985, the **Sykiás Olýmbon Cave** on Híos has delicate formations which evolved between 150 and 50 million years ago. *See page 222*

△ Elegant yet lived in, contrasting marble pavements with colourful houses, Unesco-recognised **Ermoúpoli** on Sýros was founded by Hiot refugees and is the Cyclades' tip-of-the-hat to the Belle Epoque. *See page 165*

△ Flotilla-sailing between the **Ionian islands** is the best choice for novices; conditions are milder than in the open Aegean, but the scenery is every bit as gorgeous, and characterful anchorages are close together. *See pages 80 and 306*

△ Exquisitely preserved **Skópelos Hóra** seems to exist in a 1980s time-warp, but in the best sense: old-fashioned shops, atmospheric arcades and a generous sprinkling of churches. *See page 197*

▷ Fortified **Agíou Ioánnou toú Theológou Monastery** on Pátmos, founded in 1088, transcends the cruise-ship crowds besieging it with vivid frescoes, a rich treasury and unique architecture. *See page 271*

◁ Lésvos has more **thermal springs** than any other Greek island, thanks to its volcanic core; the Ottoman-era and domed Loutrá Géras on the eponymous gulf is the most user-friendly of several. *See page 217*

THE BEST OF THE GREEK ISLANDS: EDITOR'S CHOICE

The Greek Islands' museums, festivals, culinary specialities, beaches and hiking trails... here, at a glance, are some recommendations to help you plan your journey

BEST MUSEUMS

● **Museum of Modern Greek Art, Rhodes**. The most important collection of 20th-century Greek art outside of Athens. *See page 237*

● **Vathý Archaeological Museum, Sámos**. Exquisite small Archaic-era objects from the local Hera sanctuary, plus an enormous *kouros. See page 226*

● **Museum of Cycladic Greek Art, Athens**. Honorary island location by virtue of its contents – stop over en route to the Cyclades. *See page 116*

● **Theóphilos and Thériade Museums, Lésvos**. Over 50 works by Naïve local artist Theóphilos, next door to Greece's finest modern art collection, amassed by his patron Thériade. *See page 219*

● **Iráklio Archaeological Museum**. Showcases the best Minoan frescoes and artefacts; due to reopen after renovation in 2010. *See page 278*

ABOVE: Easter, a spiritual time in the Islands.
LEFT: exhibit at the Iráklio Archaeological Museum.

BEST FESTIVALS

See pages 48–9, 58–9 and 344–5, 346

● **Easter on Hydra**. Fishermen carry the *Epitáfios* (Bier of Christ) into the water to bless the boats and ensure calm seas.

● **15 August at Ólymbos, Kárpathos**. Exemplified by tables for communal feasting and music on *lýra, tsamboúna* and *laoúto*.

● **Rhodes Ecofilms, late June**. Not just environmental documentaries, but new features and classic films from around the Mediterranean, Europe and Asia.

● **Carnival on Skýros**. Derived from pagan

revels, this features outrageously costumed revellers performing the "Goat Dance" over four weekends preceding Lent.

● **Santoríni International Music Festival, Firá**. Two weeks of classical music in September, by top-notch international performers.

LEFT: the Museum of Cycladic Art. **ABOVE:** Easter eggs.

BEST LOCAL SPECIALITIES

See pages 71–4, 76–7 and 327–9

● **Pickled caper greens, Nísyros.** The "national shrub" of this volcanic islet gets the vinegar treatment, thorns and all.
● **Genuine thyme honey**. Scrub-covered islands like Kálymnos, Foúrni

and certain Cyclades produce the purest – dark and strongly aromatic.
● **Tsitsíravla, Sporades**. Pickled wild pistachio shoots, gathered in spring – superb by themselves or in a salad.
● **Kalatháki féta, Límnos.** Small, drum-shaped sheep-milk cheese with telltale wire-mould marks; blissfully creamy.
● **Gávros marinátos, Léros.** Marinated anchovy fillets, headed and boned; an ideal *oúzo* partner. There's also *koliós marinátos* (mackerel), equally delicious.

LEFT: marinated anchovy fillets. **ABOVE:** Samariá Gorge.

BEST HIKES

● **Egiáli to Hóra on Amorgós.** This five-hour traverse takes in Hozoviótissa Monastery and sweeping sea views en route. *See page 179*
● **Northwest coast, Sámos**. A path along this verdant coast links Potámi Bay and Drakéï village via the Seïtáni beaches, still home to monk seals. *See page 227*
● **Gorge of Samariá**. It slashes through the White

Mountains and its descent is an unmissable part of Crete. *See page 295*
● **Bare, craggy Kálymnos** has some of the best walking in the Dodecanese, with old paths linking villages and remote chapels. *See page 264*
● **Alónnisos** in the Sporades offers loop-walks through Kastanórema ravine from coastal Agios Dimítrios, or around Melegákia with its country chapels. *See page 198*

BEST BEACHES

● **Egremní, Levkáda.** This west-coast paradise just pips two adjacent rivals for the Ionian crown. *See page 133*
● **Pláka, Náxos.** Dune-backed and part naturist, this stretches for 5km (3 miles) to other, wilder beaches. *See page 183*
● **Soúda, Crete.** The most protected and

scenic of many beaches near Plakiás, fed by a palm-tree-lined stream. *See page 289*
● **Evgátis, Límnos**. Stream-fed fine blonde sand framed by volcanic pinnacles, and with Agios Evstrátios islet to look at. *See page 215*

MONEY-SAVING TIPS

● Travel from late May to late June, or during September. You won't have the full range of sea transport, but air schedules are much the same as high summer, hotel rates may be little more than half of peak season prices, and taverna food and service are better.
● Book domestic air tickets well in advance. Aegean, Athens and

Olympic airlines are largely web-only airlines with tiered fare structures. Early birds can find seats cheaper than a ferry cabin berth to the same island destination. *See pages 302–3.*
● Book rental cars in advance, online. Even in peak season it's possible to secure rates of under €160 per week from airports and

major towns. *See pages 305–7.*
● Don't order expensive main courses. Instead, assemble a meal from *mezédes* (starters) – six to eight of these dishes will satisfy most dining couples. *See pages 71–4, 76–7 and 327–9.*

THE GREEK ARCHIPELAGO

The Greek islands have fascinated European travellers since the Grand Tourists passed through in the 18th century

The Greek islands rank among the most alluring realms in the Mediterranean – indeed the world. Clean, cobalt-hued seas, beaches of all sizes and consistencies, the availability of a range of sophisticated water sports and up to nine reliably sunny months a year ensure a winning combination. With recent infrastructure changes and a sharpening up of the tourism "product", the vivid, rough-and-ready country which first attracted large numbers of artists, writers and the generally bohemian during the 1960s has finally come of age.

Thankfully, even with development, the Greek islands will never become a type of Switzerland-on-Aegean. Despite inducements from the EU, of which Greece has been a member since 1981, the islanders stubbornly inisist on their right to be Greek. Modernity, as manifested by proper Gaggia coffee machines and bank ATMs, is often only superficial. Pride in traditions is still evident to varying degrees. This goes hand in hand with an awareness of politics and history to put to shame that in most of jaded Northern Europe.

Indeed, a healthy historical consciousness comes with the territory due to all the islands having had a turbulent past. Never powerful enough – except, briefly, Crete – to rule themselves, but too strategically sited to be ignored by adventurers en route to richer pickings, the islands were fated to suffer a dizzying succession of invaders and foreign rulers, each of whom was to leave an indelible legacy in terms of monuments, cuisine, language and culture in general.

Perhaps the biggest surprise for new visitors to the archipelago – "leading sea", the age-old term for the Greek islands – is the sheer variety of what, from the map, looks like a homogeneous portion of the Mediterranean. Ranging from the small, arid islets of the central Aegean, with their poster-cliché Cubist houses, to the fertile, forested giants, whose high mountains even carry a frosting of snow in the right season, there is no such thing as a stereotypical Greek island. ❏

PRECEDING PAGES: Emborió Harbour, Hálki; an Orthodox priest on his way to work; on Hydra, where road vehicles are banned, donkeys do the hauling. **LEFT:** Náousa Harbour, Páros; **FROM TOP:** tending the olive groves at Petaloúdes, Páros; catch of the day on Tílos; *bouzoúki* player in Skiáthos Town.

ISLAND MENTALITY

Greece has over 100 permanently inhabited islands.
Despite their superficial similarities, each has a distinct
identity and an often idiosyncratic history

I t's one of those words that psychiatrists might
use to trigger an automatic response from a
patient stretched on the couch. Say "island"
and childhood recollections of *Robinson Crusoe*
may spring to mind. Often, islands are associated
with escape from a complex universe into a private, more manageable world that offers individuals control over their own destiny. Crusoe
becomes comfortable in his prelapsarian paradise, and it's a surprise, when rescue is at hand,
that he doesn't tell his saviours to push off.

"Greek island" would probably add some
specific touches to the imagery: a cluster of daz-
zlingly white buildings against a shimmering sea,
donkeys bearing their burdens against a backdrop
of olive groves, small circles of weather-beaten
fishermen bent over their nets, jolly tavernas full
of *retsína, moussakás*, shattered plates and background music from *Never on Sunday* and *Zorba
the Greek*. Accurate as far as it goes, perhaps, but
any generalisation about the Greek islands – anything more ambitious than the staringly obvious
– would almost certainly be wrong.

Inter-island relations

Although islands are classified as members of
one group or another, each has a strong sense of
separate identity and invariably an idiosyncratic
history to back it up. Often, neighbouring islands
exhibit mutual resentment bordering on loath-
ing (though islands separated by two or three
intervening ones are at least neutral about each
other if not actively cordial). Visitors would seldom be aware of this unless they made a point
of going down to the local café and chatting to

the men entrenched there. Conditioned by long
winter nights when nothing much happens, they
have developed the knack of holding forth on
any subject under the sun, and a new audience
is welcome. Taxi drivers, ticket agents and your
landlords can be similarly garrulous.

The reasons for fraught inter-island sentiments
may be current, as in smaller islands (eg Ikaría)
perceiving the inhabitants of a larger, favoured
provincial neighbour (Sámos, in the case of Ikaría)
as overbearing. Or they may be of long-standing
bad blood that has arisen from a variety of causes:
rivalry in fishing or sponge-gathering (think Kar-
pathians' views on the Kalymnian fleets); abduc-
tions and forced marriages generations back; or

LEFT: flying the flag at the Castle of the Knights, Kós.
RIGHT: *Óhi* Day celebrations on Skópelos.

participation in a long-ago rebellion against the Ottomans, at their neighbour's behest, with disastrous consequences (as happened to the Hiots). Even a proven historical incident will be given a different spin or even disputed by neighbours. Skiathots proudly describe the burning of much of their main port in August 1944 as German reprisal for persistent, patriotic resistance activities; tell that to a Skopelot and the reply might be "They have to find some excuse for why their town is so ugly!"

Almost everywhere, you will be assured that "those people" (just on or over the horizon) are untrustworthy, inhospitable or worse, that the – an outgrowth of centuries of self-sufficiency enforced by neglect or outright abuse by overlords. Since Neolithic times, the islands have been tossed around like loose pebbles in the cultural tides that have surged to and fro through the eastern Mediterranean, and none has emerged from that experience quite like any other.

Intruders

Momentous events were taking place on Crete and some of the Cyclades as early as 3000 BC. The golden age of Athens under Pericles lay as far in the future then as, for us, it now lies in the past – more than two millennia either way. Settlers from

climate is unhealthy, the houses barely fit even for animals, the water undrinkable, the beaches uncomfortable. For example, many Corfiot jokes revolve around the supposedly dim, slow Paxiots to the southeast. You shouldn't take such stories or opinions too seriously (often those propounding them don't): they are great fun, and the opportunity to move between neighbouring islands in order to compare notes should be savoured. It is sometimes said that if two islands were to strike the curious visitor as being practically identical, those islands would necessarily be at opposite ends of the Aegean.

Apart from the natural tendency for small island communities to be staunchly independent, there is a historical basis for their individualism

FOREIGN OCCUPIERS

The history of Corfu is a typical saga of occupation by foreign powers, each of whom left some mark. From the 11th century, the island was ruled successively by Greeks (the Byzantine Empire), Normans, Sicilians, Venetians, Greek Orthodox once more ("the despotate of Epirus"), more Sicilians, Neapolitans and then the Venetians again – this time for 400 years. Then the procession of foreign rulers resumed: France, Russia, Britain and then Greece. Italy occupied Corfu briefly in the 1920s and again during World War II. After Italy capitulated in autumn 1943, Germany became the last foreign occupier, until the German surrender in 1944.

the Middle Eastern coast landed with the skills which developed into the Minoan civilisation.

To look at the history of Corfu, for instance, merely from the 11th century AD, is to pick up the chronicle of invasions a long way down the line. Nevertheless, the record from that date reveals an amazing cavalcade of intruders to the island (*see panel opposite*). All of them have left a mark, even if finding traces today would require more diligent research than most visitors care to conduct while on holiday. Dedicated scholars could probably assemble a jigsaw, with pieces extant on Corfu, that would reflect each and every one of these waves.

unwanted outside attention as Corfu. Piracy was a perennial problem, hence the number of collective fortifications (*kástra*) to which the island population retreated when danger threatened. The defences did not always keep determined pirates like Khair-ed-din Barbarossa out, but they did mean that the pirates had to make an effort instead of lazily helping themselves to 10 years of stored harvests or all the eligible virgins when they happened to be cruising by.

Stepping stones

Crete, Límnos, Sámos, Kós and Rhodes have the richest and most thoroughly documented sites

The evidence does not necessarily consist of archaeological ruins or excavated objects. Corfu extrapolated from one small chapter of its convoluted history an abiding passion for cricket. It is still played on the square in the middle of the town, albeit with local variations which would raise the eyebrows of traditionalists in England. The same epoch bequeathed to both Corfu and its tiny neighbour Paxí a taste for *tzíntzi býra* (ginger beer) – though again, scarcely recognisable as such to an Edwardian Englishman.

Other islands received almost as much

for historically minded visitors, but on any island there is bound to be something to pick over, even if it isn't mapped. A good tip for amateur archaeologists would be to ask themselves where, taking into account security, prevailing winds, terrain, water supply etc, they themselves would have chosen to build something – and then start looking for evidence of past peoples.

The topographical differences among the islands are worth considering. If some islands look like mountain peaks, it is because, basically, they are – much of the area now covered by the Aegean was once a solid land bridge between the Balkan peninsula and Asia Minor, which became submerged completely only at the end of the last Ice Age, leaving only the summits

---

LEFT: a street seller peddles his wares in Skiáthos Town, from herbal teas to dried fruits. **ABOVE:** café life is very much a part of island social interaction.

exposed. The seabed around the islands can drop precipitously to 3,500 metres (11,600ft) in places, for example east of Crete. Closer to Asia Minor, the sea is generally much shallower, but even here the Aegean, quiet and bather-friendly one moment, can be transformed into a lethal cauldron within the space of an hour or two.

Anyone hiring a boat on holiday should never leave port without consulting the islanders. For thousands of years, lives have depended on accurate weather predictions, and local lore handed down is often more reliable than official forecasts on meteorological websites or via other electronic media.

ILLEGAL SUBSTANCES

The apparently tolerant attitude towards tourist behaviour in Greece does not extend to recreational drug use, and islands with a youth clientele or counter-cultural reputation like Íos, Ikaría or Crete are subject to close undercover surveillance. Although laws against prescription or over-the-counter compounds containing codeine are no longer enforced and customs searches of EU arrivals very rare, it's wise to err on the side of extreme caution in other respects. The legal system is largely based on a presumption of guilt, with up to a year in remand until charges are brought, and typical sentences for even small amounts of cannabis for personal use can be two to three years.

Ways and means

If the purpose of a visit to the islands is nothing more than to settle on a stretch of agreeable beach and live (relatively) cheaply, visitors should be lucky on both counts. Greece has nearly 10,000 (mostly uninhabited) islands altogether, and these, plus the mainland shores, add up to technically the longest coastline of any country in Europe. Basic commodities, including certain accommodation categories, taverna meals and ferry tickets, have regulated prices; though the adoption of the euro in early 2002 led to stiff hikes well beyond inflation, the 2008–9 crisis saw prices in many areas frozen at summer 2008 levels, comparing well to other Mediterranean destinations.

Expensive exceptions include Zákynthos, Rhodes, Mýkonos and Santoríni. Whatever the local businesspeople may think in private of the antics of their visitors, they tend to be stoical about them in public and continue to pocket the money. Zákynthos (ground zero for youth boozing) and Mýkonos (a gay mecca) in particular would not have been allowed to develop as they have under the puritanical 1967–74 dictatorship, when even topless sunbathing was discouraged. However, since the 1980s if not earlier, what bathers choose to wear or discard has been a matter of personal choice, and there is usually at least one beach on every island where nudity is tolerated, if not officially so.

The best way to enjoy the islands is to arrive with a certain attitude. By all means, begin by uncritically enjoying the vistas seared into the senses by island holiday brochures – the white buildings set against a shimmering sea, the donkeys on a backdrop of olive groves, and so on. Then, when the novelty wears off, or perhaps earlier, examine each island as if it were an onion, and start stripping off the skins. If not a long-standing dispute about fishing rights, some other unexpected aspect is certain to be revealed.

How to strip the onion is a large part of what this book is about. It hopes to show by example, as no book will ever be written that says everything about 10,000 (or even 100) islands. The learned Helidoros once tried to set down everything of note about Athens's Acropolis, as it existed in the 2nd century BC. Fifteen volumes later… ❏

LEFT: informal signage daubed on a wall in Skópelos Town. **RIGHT:** preparing the evening meal of *hórta* – wild greens.

DALMATIÆ PARS

ALBANIA PARS ILLYRIDIS

MACEDONIA

Sintica

Orbeli

Iori

Migdonia

Bisaltica

Odomantice

Iamboli

Amphaxitis

Paraxia

Chalcidica

Pelagonia

Astræi

Pæonia

Lincheste

Emathia

Bottiaa

Golfo di Salonichi

Albani

Tamoriza

Fordei

Comenolitari

Dassaretii

Douriopes

Macedonia

Pieria

Elymiotæ

Parthia

Orestia

Stymphalis

Poncessa

Pelagonia Tripolitis

Pelagoitis

Magnesia

Canina

Elyma

TESSALIA

Estiæots

Iannala

Chimera o Chilonia

Tympha

Pindus M.

Phtiotis

EPIRO

Parorei

Hellopes

Dolopes

Larta

Thessalious

Pindus M.

Isola di Negt

Cassiopei

Molossi

Dryopes

Dors

Phocis

Beotia nunc Stramulipa

Pachru o Paxu I.

Agræi

Perrhebi

Amphilochi

Athamanes

Livadia

Locri Ozolæ

Corfu I. et Coreyra

Santa Maura I. et Leucas Insula

Acarnania

A Despotato

Ætolia

Golfo di Lepanto et Cirreus, et Corynthiacus sinus

Ducato di

Cefalonia I. et Cephalenia

Val di Compre

Golfo di Patrasso

Achaia

Clarenza

Stolu ogi Saccania

Zante I. o Zacynthus

Golfo d'Arcadia o Sinus Cheloanes

PELOPONNESVS

Arcadia

MOREA

Elide

Izaconia

Braccio di Maina

Belvedere

Messenia

Lacedia

Strivali I. Strophades Insulæ

Sapienza I. et Sphagia

MARE DI SAPIENZA

MARE IONIO O DI GRECIA

Ponente

MARE IONIO

LA GRECIA
VNIVERSALE ANTICA
Paragonata con la Moderna da
Giacomo Cantelli da Vignola
Con le direttioni delle Carte Migliori é de più accre-
ditati Scrittori di Geografia. data in luce da Gio.
Giacomo Rossi in Roma alla Pace l'anno 1689.
con Priu. del S. Pont.

DECISIVE DATES

3000 BC
First Bronze Age cultures in Crete and the Cyclades.

2600–1500 BC
Minoan civilisation flourishes on Crete until tsunami from huge volcanic eruption on Santoríni devastates north coast. Subsequently, many Cretan palaces destroyed by fire.

c.1450 BC
Mycenaeans occupy Crete and Rhodes, establish a trading empire, devise Linear B – the first written Greek.

12th century BC
"Sea Peoples" from beyond the Black Sea invade islands, destroying Mycenaean civilisation but bringing Iron Age technology with them.

1150–720 BC
"Dark Ages": cultural and economic stagnation. Refugee Mycenaeans (known as Ionians) settle on Aegean islands, in Asia Minor and in Attica.

750 BC onward
Rise of first city-states, foremost among them Athens.

c.770 BC
Contact with Etruscans, Phoenicians and Egyptians spurs a revival of Greek cultural life. Phoenician alphabet adopted.

c.725 BC
The *Odyssey* and the *Iliad* are written down for the first time.

546–500 BC
Persian Empire expands to control Ionian Greek cities on Asia Minor's west coast. Under Darius the Great, Persians conquer many Aegean islands.

499–479 BC
Persian invasions of Greek mainland repulsed by united Greeks led by Spartan army and Athenian navy. Ionian cities freed from Persian rule.

CLASSICAL AND HELLENISTIC AGES

477–465 BC
Athens establishes Delian League comprising islands and cities in Asia Minor. Islands attempting to secede are brutally suppressed by Athens.

454 BC
The League's treasury is moved from Delos to Athens. Effectively, the islands are now part of an Athenian Empire. "Golden Age" of Classical Athens.

431–404 BC
Peloponnesian War leaves Athens defeated and weakened.

338 BC
Greek city-states defeated by Philip II of Macedon.

336–323BC
Philip succeeded by son Alex-

ander, who extends an empire as far as India.

323 BC
On Alexander's death, this empire is divided between his generals. Greek islands mostly run by Egyptian Ptolemies.

ROMANS AND BYZANTINES

197–146 BC
Romans defeat Macedonian Antigonids and annex Greece.

3rd century AD
Christianity spreads; barbarian raids from north.

330
Constantine establishes Byzantine Empire with Constantinople as its capital.

391–5
Theodosius I outlaws paganism and Olympic Games banned. Roman Empire splits into two, Latin West and Byzantine East.

827–961
Arabs occupy Crete until Emperor Nikiphoros Phokas retakes island.

1081
Normans from Sicily invade Greek islands.

1204
The Fourth Crusade: Constantinople temporarily taken by Latins. Venetians claim the Ionians and other islands.

1309
Knights Hospitallers of St John occupy and fortify the Dodecanese, especially Rhodes.

1344–1478
Genoese assume control of north Aegean islands.

1453
Ottoman Turks capture Constantinople, renamed Istanbul and made capital of Ottoman Empire.

1523
Dodecanese islands taken over by Ottoman Turks.

1649–69
Ottoman sieges of Crete, which the Venetians lose to the Turks.

1797–1814
Napoleonic French occupy Ionian islands.

1815–64
British rule in Ionian islands.

INDEPENDENCE AND AFTER

1821–9
War of Independence against Ottomans.

1830–32
At peace conferences, Ottomans cede Évvia to Greeks, but

PRECEDING PAGES: 17th-century map of ancient Greece. TOP LEFT: the owl, symbol of goddess Athene's wisdom, appeared on early Athenian coins. ABOVE: British troops liberate Athens in 1944. RIGHT: police gathered outside the Parliament (former Royal Palace) in Athens.

keep Dodecanese, northeast Aegean and north mainland.

1834
Athens becomes capital of Greece, replacing Návplio.

1864
Ionian islands ceded to Greece.

1896
First modern Olympics held in Athens.

1897
Crete becomes an independent principality within the Ottoman Empire.

1909–10
Army revolts against political establishment in Athens allow Elefthérios Venizélos to form new government. Venizélos intermittently PM until 1935.

1912–13
Balkan Wars: Greece takes Crete, northeast Aegean islands and Macedonia. Italy occupies Dodecanese.

1917
Greece belatedly enters World War I on Entente side.

1919–22
Asia Minor campaign ends in catastrophic defeat. Expulsion of Greek civilians from Turkey.

1940–1
Greece rebuffs Italian invasion and fights with Allies until invaded by Nazi Germany.

1944
Greece is liberated by Allies.

1946–9
Civil War between Greek government and Communists opposed to restoring monarchy.

1947
Dodecanese joined to Greece.

1967–74
Greece ruled by junta of right-wing colonels; King Constantine in exile.

1974
Colonels deposed; republic established.

1981
Andréas Papandréou's PASOK party forms first leftist government. Greece becomes full member of EEC (now EU).

1996
Kóstas Simítis replaces Papandréou.

2002
Greece adopts the euro.

2004
Centre-right New Democracy wins elections; Athens hosts the Olympic Games.

2008–9
Riots in response to police killing of an Athens youth. George Papandréou leads PASOK to crushing victory in snap October 2009 elections.

WAVES OF INVADERS

The history of Greece, and especially its islands,
is inextricably linked to the sea. It is largely
a chronicle of foreign conquerors and occupiers

What distinguishes the course of Greek history from that of her Balkan neighbours is the impact of the sea. The sea diffuses cultures, transfers peoples and encourages trade – and until our own times it was invariably a swifter means of transmission than overland. Nowhere in Greece is the sea as inescapable as on the islands.

The poverty of the arid island soil has forced inhabitants to venture far afield for their livelihood. At the same time, the islands have been vulnerable to foreign incursions, whether by Arab pirates, Italian colonists or modern tourists. All have played their part in transforming local conditions; some have had an even wider impact. Phoenician traders, for example, appear to have brought their alphabet to Crete in the early Archaic period, which the Greeks then adopted and changed. At the same time, Egyptian influence was leading island sculptors to work in stone. It is no coincidence that the earliest examples of monumental Greek sculpture are all to be found on the islands.

On Crete, the Bronze Age had produced the first urban civilisation in the Aegean: this was the age of the Knossós and Festós palaces, erected in the centuries after 2000 BC. Other islands such as Thera (today Thíra) also flourished at this time. Thucydides' account of how King Minos of Crete established his sons as governors in the Cyclades and cleared the sea of pirates certainly suggests considerable Cretan control of the Aegean. The Aegean was not to be dominated by a single sea power for another millennium until the rise of the Athenian Empire.

LEFT: a marble figure from the early Cycladic era. **RIGHT:** an inaccurate artist's view of the Colossus of Rhodes.

Economic growth

Before this, however, communities of Greeks had begun to flourish on most of the islands, exploiting local quarries and mines, and developing indigenous political systems. Some communities achieved considerable wealth, notably on Sífnos, whose gold and silver mines had made her inhabitants reputedly the richest citizens in the Cyclades by the 6th century BC. Some reflection of this wealth can be seen in the ruins of the marble treasury which Sifniots dedicated to Apollo at Delphi.

It was in the 6th century, too, that the inhabitants of Thera began to mint their own coinage, a physical manifestation of the island's powerful status in the Aegean. At one point Thera's influence was to extend not only to Crete, Mílos, Páros and Rhodes, but as far west as Corinth and as far east as Asia Minor.

During the 5th century BC, the islands' independence was curtailed as Athens used anti-Persian fears to manipulate the Delian League. This had been formed in 478 BC as an alliance between equal partners to form a strong naval power in the Aegean. But Athens soon controlled the League and used its resources in a series of wars against rivals such as the naval city-state of Aegina (Égina). It was Athenian intrigues with the Corinthian colony on Corfu, however, that

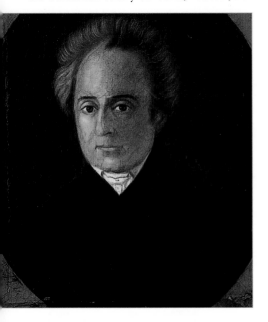

led to the Peloponnesian War which was ultimately to cripple – and break – Athens for ever.

During the Hellenistic period the islands remained turbulent backwaters, prone to internecine struggles which made them easy prey for their more powerful neighbours. By the middle of the 1st century BC, Rome had established herself in the Aegean; Crete became the centre of a province which included a part of North Africa.

Under Roman guidance roads were laid, aqueducts constructed, new towns and grand buildings erected. Despite this prosperity, the Aegean as a whole remained in the background in Roman times. Little is known of conditions of life in the islands either then or after AD 395, when they passed under the control of the East-

ern Roman Empire. Only with the onset of the Arab raids in the 7th century does the historical record become more complete.

With the decline of Roman power in the Mediterranean, the islands faced a long period of instability: for more than a millennium they were attacked by invaders from all points of the compass. From the north, briefly, came the Vandals and Goths; from the south, the Arabs, who established themselves on Crete in 827 and proceeded to plunder the rest of the Aegean for over a century. From the west came Normans in the 11th century, followed by the Genoese and Venetians; finally, from the east came the Ottoman Turks, who succeeded in dominating almost all of the islands in the Aegean between the 15th and 18th centuries.

Other groups, too, played minor roles – quite apart from powers such as the English, French and Russians, who all shared an interest in the Greek islands. The impact of these various peoples on the islands was complex and tangled, making it awkward to generalise about the historical experiences of the islands themselves. Only by considering the main island groups individually may things fall into place.

The Ionian islands

On the eve of the 1821 Greek uprising, an English traveller to Corfu noted: "The natural weakness and position of the Ionian islands, and all their past history, demonstrate that they must ever be an appendage of some more powerful state; powerful at sea and able to protect them as well as to command." Close to the Greek mainland, vital staging-posts on the voyage from Western Europe to the Levant, it was inevitable that the Ionian islands should be a focus of constant conflict.

Corfu had suffered brief attacks during the 5th century from Vandals and Goths, the destroyers of the Roman Empire in the West, but it was not until the Eastern Empire lost its possessions in southern Italy that the Ionian islands again became vulnerable to invasion. This time the predators were the Normans. At the time when William the Conqueror was establishing Norman control over England, Robert Guiscard, Duke of Apulia, defeated the Byzantine army and its emperor, before dying of a fever at Kefaloniá. His nephew Roger, King of Sicily, occupied Corfu in 1146 and held it for six years. As the Byzantine hold over the islands weakened, the Venetians came in as reluctant allies.

These allies soon proved to have territorial ambitions of their own. The islands were situated on important trade routes to the eastern Mediterranean, and commercial interests led to the desire for political control. After the sack of Constantinople in 1204 during the Fourth Crusade, the Ionians were divided into fiefdoms among noble Venetian families. Not until 1387, however, were the islands brought under direct Venetian rule, which continued through a succession of Ottoman attacks (which intermittently captured Levkáda) down to 1797, when

uninhabited in the late 15th century, vigorous resettlement policies soon created the basis for new prosperity. Zákynthos had only 36 families in 1485, but 752 families by 1516, and her revenues increased forty-fold in 30 years thanks to the introduction of these valuable crops.

By the 18th century Venice had lost her possessions in the Aegean and the Peloponnese; in the Ionian Sea, the Venetian-held islands were ravaged by pirates operating from Paxí and the Albanian coast; internally, blood feuds and political assassination made life precarious.

The end of Venetian rule was bloodless: when the French invaders arrived, they discovered the

under the new order created by Napoleon's conquests, the islands went to France.

During these four centuries, the Ionian islands were ruled by local nobility and by administrators sent out from Venice. The influence of the Republic was felt in the introduction of cash crops such as olives and currants, in the repressive regime under which the peasants worked and in the Italian language which the nobility affected to speak. At first Venetian rule was energetic – so that, for example, after Ottoman raids had left Zákynthos virtually

LEFT: Dionýsios Solomós, the Ionian poet whose *Hymn to Freedom* was adopted as the national anthem after Independence. **ABOVE:** a watercolour of Itháki harbour.

BRIBERY AND CORRUPTION

By the end of the 18th century, the Venetians' last remaining stronghold in the Ionian islands was thoroughly corrupt. In 1812, the British Whig politician Henry Holland wrote of the Venetian rulers of Corfu: "The governors and other officers sent to the island were usually of noble family and often of decayed fortune; men who undertook the office as a speculation of interest and executed it accordingly. Bribery and every mode of illegal practice were carried on openly; toleration for a crime might easily be purchased; and the laws, in many respects imperfect themselves, were rendered wholly null by the corruption of the judges."

fortress guns rusting and the garrison without any gunpowder. Napoleon himself had written in 1797 that "the great maxim of the Republic ought henceforth to be never to abandon Corfu, Zante…" However, British troops managed to establish a foothold in the minor islands in 1809. After Napoleon's defeat this was extended and the new Septinsular Republic was placed under British protection.

Sir Thomas Maitland, the first Lord High Commissioner, in the words of a Victorian historian, "established a Constitution which, possessing every appearance of freedom, in reality left the whole power in his hands". But it could

not satisfy the islanders' desire for freedom from foreign rule, a desire which intensified after the creation of the Kingdom of Greece in 1832. In 1864 Britain relinquished control and the Ionian islands became part of the modern Greek state, a condition stipulated by the new King George I for taking the throne.

The Cyclades, Sporades and Saronic Gulf islands

The Cyclades, unlike the Ionian islands, were a commercial backwater: main trade routes passed through Crete and the eastern Aegean islands to Smyrna and Aleppo. While they remained a lure to pirates, they were never of comparable interest to major powers. Until the

rise of the seafaring Italian city-states in the 11th century, most trade in the Aegean was in the hands of Greeks.

However, the weakness of the Byzantine navy was underlined by a series of Arab raids against the islands and the Greek mainland. By the 12th century a British chronicler noted that piracy had become the curse of the Aegean: many of the islands were abandoned, while others – Skýros in the Sporades, for example – became pirate lairs.

The sack of Constantinople in 1204, which brought the Ionian islands under Venetian control, also brought new masters to the Aegean. The unimportance of this group of islands to them meant that the Venetians were content to leave the task of occupying them to minor nobility. Of these, the most successful was Marco Sanudo, a nephew of the Doge Enrico Dandolo, who equipped eight galleys at his own expense and sailed to the Aegean where he founded the Duchy of Náxos in 1207.

Náxos itself became the capital of a fiefdom of 10 surrounding islands, and on it Sanudo built a castle, erected a Catholic cathedral and provided solid fortifications for the town. Other adventurers helped themselves to islands such as Andhros and Thíra (Santoríni). The Ghisi family obtained Tínos and Mýkonos, as well as the islands in the Sporades, establishing a dynasty which clashed with the Sanudi until both were overwhelmed by the Ottoman navy in the 16th century. The Duchy of Náxos lasted over 350 years and only ended with the death of Joseph Nasi, the Sephardic Jewish favourite of Selim II, upon

BACKWARD PRIESTS AND BAD ROADS

When the British took control of the Ionian islands in 1815, they found a society very different to their own. Wheeled transport was virtually unknown on several islands owing to the appalling roads, and the priests opposed the introduction of the potato to the islands on the grounds that this was the apple with which the serpent had tempted Eve in the Garden of Eden. At the same time, the inhabitants of the islands were demanding the amenities of Western Europe. The British obliged by bringing improved roads, drainage schemes and, with a touch of the public-school love of team sports, the game of cricket.

whom the sultan had bestowed the islands after their capture.

But the exceptional longevity of the Duchy of Náxos should not obscure the turbulence of life in the Aegean in these centuries. Piracy had increased in the late 13th century, with Greek corsairs from Monemvasiá or Santoríni, Sicilians and Genoese – and had caused, for example, the inhabitants of the island of Amorgós to emigrate en masse to Náxos, whose fertile interior was relatively inaccessible.

In the 14th century Catalan mercenaries, brought in for the conflict between Venice and Genoa, ravaged some of the islands, raided others and even occupied Aegina (Égina) for some decades. Ottoman troops landed on Náxos and took 6,000 captives. The Ottoman forces often consisted of recent converts to Islam, and were led by renegade Aegean Greeks such as the notorious brothers from Lésvos, Khair-ed-din and Amrudj Barbarossa.

Local rulers began to complain of depopulation: Andros had to be resettled by Albanian mainlanders; Íos, virtually uninhabited, was replenished by families from the Peloponnese. Astypálea was repopulated in 1413 by Cycladic colonists, abandoned in 1473 and only inhabited once more after 1570. During the 16th century, the islands suffered a series of attacks by the Turkish navy and by mid-century Venetian influence was on the wane. Within 50 years, most of the islands had been brought under Ottoman rule, though Tínos only succumbed as late as 1715.

Conditions of life did not improve under Ottoman rule. Piracy, famine and fatal disease remained the perennial problems. In the 18th century the plague decimated the islands on four separate occasions, continuing into the next century, well after this scourge had died out in most of Europe. Thus the Ottomans, like their predecessors, were forced to repopulate.

Often the new colonists were not Greeks. The Frenchman Joseph Pitton de Tournefort reported in the early 18th century that most of the inhabitants of Andíparos were descended from French and Maltese corsairs. He also noted that villages on Andros were "peopled only by Albanians, dressed still in their traditional style and living their own way, that is to say with neither creed nor law".

It was the Albanians who were to play a major role in the struggle for Greek independence. Waves of Albanians had been colonising the islands of the Aegean since the 14th cen-

Italianate family names provide linguistic evidence of Venetian rule in the Cyclades, while Catholic communities have also survived: Náxos has many small, double-naved country churches for both Catholic and Orthodox use.

tury. They were concentrated on the Saronic islands – the eminent Koundouriótis family, for example, moved from Epiros to Hydra around the year 1580. By the late 18th century, Hydra, with a largely Albanian population, possessed one of the largest and most powerful shipping fleets in the Aegean, which played a prominent role in the War of Independence.

The importance of these islands was underlined by the choice of Aegina (Égina), for a short time, as the first capital of the new Greek state. Refugees flocked here when it was the seat of government, only to leave again when it was replaced by Návplion, on the mainland. When Edouard About visited the town in 1839 he reported it "abandoned – the homes that had

LEFT: detail of an embroidery from Skýros, probably from the 17th century. **RIGHT:** a 1795 watercolour showing the unfinished Temple of Apollo, Náxos.

been built tumbled into ruins, the town once more became a village; its life and activity fled with the government".

The northeast Aegean islands

Although the east Aegean islands shared the experience of Arab raids with the Cyclades, the two areas developed differently as the rivalry between Venice and Genoa increased after the Fourth Crusade. As allies of the resurgent Byzantine Empire against her Latin enemies, the Genoese were given trading rights in the Black Sea and granted permission to colonise (and garrison) the eastern Aegean.

A Genoese trading company controlled the mastic plantations of Híos from 1346, that year also seeing occupation of Ikaría and Sámos. In 1355 Lésvos passed into the hands of the Gattelusi family, who eventually extended their control to Thássos, Límnos and Samothráki. However, as in the west Aegean, the power of the Ottoman navies simply overwhelmed these local potentates, and with the fall of Híos in 1566 all the islands of the east Aegean passed into Ottoman hands.

Lésvos had been conquered by the Ottoman Turks as early as 1462, and most of the inhabitants emigrated. In 1476 the inhabitants of Sámos fled to Híos, but returned to the deserted island in the 1550s. Belon du Mans,

who visited the island around 1546, wrote: "It is striking that an island like Sámos must remain deserted. The fear of pirates has rendered her uninhabited so that now there is not a single village there, nor any animals" (an exaggeration, as a few primitive hamlets remained in the mountains). Despite these islands' proximity to the mainland, they attracted only a small number of Muslim colonisers, and the bulk of the population remained Greek, supplemented by immigrants from the Balkans and Anatolia. Only on Lésvos were Muslim settlers to be found farming the land; elsewhere they stayed close to the towns.

The 1821 insurrection sent shock waves through the islands. Sámos was first. The unrest then spread to Híos where, in 1822, the Ottomans brutally suppressed a rather half-hearted revolt. Fustel de Coulanges wrote in 1856: "Any person aged more than 32 years whom one meets today on Híos was enslaved and saw his father slaughtered".

It was little consolation to know that the massacre on Híos had aroused the attention of European liberals, and strengthened philhellenic sentiment. Refugees fled westwards, transporting the island's traditional *loukoúmi* industry (the making and selling of Turkish delight) to Sýros in the Cyclades, whose port of Ermoúpoli became the busiest port in the new Greek state. Other refugees settled in Alexandria, Trieste, Marseilles and as far north as Amsterdam.

Elsewhere in the east Aegean, the changes were just as great. The Ottoman authorities were only able to suppress the uprising with the aid of Mehmet Ali and his Egyptian mercenaries, who had as little respect for the local Muslim notables as they had for the Greeks: many Turkish landowners sold up and emigrated to Anatolia, while their properties were bought by middle-class Greeks who became an increasingly powerful force in the ageing Ottoman Empire.

By the end of the century the Ottoman hold had become tenuous: Sámos, for example, from 1832 onwards, had an autonomous regime under an appointed Christian "prince". And on Thássos the Oxford don Henry Tozer found in 1884 that there were no Muslims apart from the governor himself and a few soldiers. Since the islanders had to pay neither the "head tax" – universal elsewhere in the Ottoman Empire

– nor Ottoman trade duties, it is not surprising that they appeared content with their system of government.

The Muslim islanders, on the other hand, continued to leave for the mainland. Even before the Greco-Turkish population exchange

> When the Arabs occupied Rhodes from AD 653–8, they broke up the remains of the famous 3rd-century BC Colossus, which had collapsed in 227 BC, and sold the bronze for scrap to a Jewish merchant from Mesopotamian Edessa.

in 1923, the Turkish communities on Híos, Lésvos and Límnos had dwindled considerably. Their place was filled by a mass of Greek refugees from Anatolia.

The Dodecanese

These 18 islands, misleadingly known as the Dodecanese (*dódeka* means "12"), suffered as elsewhere from the collapse of Roman authority. They were repeatedly attacked and plundered. The Byzantine hold remained firmer here than it did in the West, but after 1204 many of the islands were ceded to Frankish adventurers in return for nominal acknowledgement of Byzantine sovereignty.

By the beginning of the 14th century, Venice had helped herself to those two crucial stepping stones to the East, Kássos and Kárpathos. At the same time, Rhodes was captured from the Genoese by the Knights of St John, a military order which, after the loss of Jerusalem in 1187, had been based in Cyprus since 1291. Foulques de Villaret, the first Grand Master of Rhodes, reconstructed the city.

Although the Knights of St John were able to withstand a siege by the Ottomans in 1480, they could not hold off the Ottoman threat indefinitely. In 1522 they were outnumbered by a massive Ottoman force nearly 200,000 strong, and after a siege lasting five months the starving defenders were forced to capitulate. With the fall of Rhodes, the position of neighbouring islands became untenable, and by 1541 they had all been incorporated into the formidable

Ottoman Empire, Venetian-held Astypália being the last to surrender.

Rhodes's Orthodox inhabitants were compelled to leave the Old Town and settle outside the walls. But because the Ottomans never made up more than a quarter of the Rhodian population, their overall influence was never that strong. Since the land on many islands was difficult to farm, the islanders looked elsewhere for their livelihoods.

Many became seamen, while on Kálymnos, Hálki and Sými the sponge-fishing trade prospered. In 1523, the islanders of Kálymnos paid homage to conquering Sultan Süleyman with

sponges and white bread to demonstrate that "sponge-fishers do not cultivate corn, but buy flour – and only of the best quality". During the 19th century, the sponge-fishers went international, opening agencies in London, Frankfurt and Basle.

But these developments, typical of the growing Greek middle class, did not lead to union with Greece until late in the day. These islands had been intended for the new Greek state in 1830, but were retained at the last minute by Turkey in return for the central island of Euboea (Évvia). Liberation from the Ottoman Empire came unexpectedly through the occupation of the islands by the Italians during their war with the Turks in 1912.

LEFT: the sea battle of Sámos, one of the first clashes in the War of Independence; watercolour from 1824.
RIGHT: 19th-century drawing of a Kássos woman.

At first, the islanders welcomed the Italians. A congress on Pátmos passed a resolution thanking the Italian nation for delivering them from the Turkish yoke. However, another resolution at the same congress calling for unification of the islands with Greece was less satisfactory to the local Italian commander, who broke up the congress and forbade such public meetings.

The Italians did not intend to hold the islands permanently but, with the dismemberment of the Ottoman Empire, their dreams of establishing a foothold in Asia Minor led them to renege on a promise made in 1915 to return these islands (except Rhodes) to Greece. Mus-

Strategic Crete

The "Great Island" has had the most violent history of all, thanks to its strategic position, agricultural riches and, not least, its inhabitants' fierce tradition of resistance to foreign oppression. Since before AD 827, when it was conquered by Arab freebooters from Andalucía, who made it the centre of the slave trade and a base for pirate raids throughout the Aegean, the strategic importance of Crete has been obvious.

From 2600 BC onwards, a prosperous civilisation spread its influence throughout the Aegean. The Minoans left proof of their archi-

solini sent groups of zealous administrators to turn the islands into a Fascist colony. But the process was brought to an abrupt halt by World War II. Once Italy surrendered in 1943, the islands were taken over by the Germans who managed, in the course of their brief and very brutal occupation, to exterminate the ancient Jewish population, against the evident wishes of the islanders, the Italians and even some of their own soldiers.

Of the 2,093 Jews deported from Kós and Rhodes, only about 160 returned from Auschwitz. Just a few months after the Jews had been deported, the islands were occupied by the British, who finally handed them over to Greece in March 1947.

IMPERIALISM IN ACTION

The Italian occupation of the Dodecanese under Mussolini imposed the draconian prohibitions of an imperialist regime, intent on "Italianising" the islands and islanders. An extensive secret-police network guarded against nationalist activity; the Orthodox religion had no official status from the late 1920s; the blue-and-white colours of the Greek flag were prohibited in public; and only Italian could be used in public from 1936 – slogans such as *Viva il Duce, viva la nuova Italia imperiale!* were daubed on the walls of recalcitrant shopkeepers. During the 1930s, many islanders emigrated to the Greek mainland, Egypt, southern Africa and America.

tectural genius in the ruined palaces of Knossos and Phaestos. Though they were daring soldiers, they appear to have preferred commerce to agriculture. They established outposts in the Peloponnese and made contact with the Egyptians.

By 1650 BC, Minoan civilisation had reached its zenith. But then Crete was shaken by a series of disasters: a stupendous volcanic eruption on the island of Thíra (Santoríni) in about 1500 BC unleashed tidal waves that damaged settlements along the north coast. Then, barely a generation later, most of the important sites in central and southern Crete were destroyed by fire. But the causes of the wider disintegration of Minoan

exiles fleeing the Turks, and briefly became the centre of a renaissance of Byzantine culture: Cretan artists such as Domínikos Theotokópoulos, otherwise known as El Greco, helped to enrich the Renaissance in Western Europe.

Though the Venetians developed the towns and fortresses on the north coast, they knew how little they were loved by the Cretans. In 1615 a certain Fra Paolo Serpi warned that "the Greek faith is never to be trusted", and he had recommended that the people "must be watched with more attention lest, like the wild beasts they are, they should find an occasion to use their teeth and claws. The surest way is to

control remain a mystery. Only Knossos continued to be inhabited as Cretan dominance in the Aegean ended.

In the early 13th century AD, Venice and Genoa tussled to wrest the island away from the waning Byzantine Empire. Although Venice ultimately turned Crete into a prize possession, Byzantine influence remained strong. The old Greek noble families survived, while ties with Constantinople were reflected everywhere in church art and secular literature.

This strong Byzantine tradition became crucial after 1453, when the island gave refuge to

keep good garrisons to awe them". Under such a regime the peasants were probably worse off than under the Turks on the mainland.

Occasionally, as in 1263 and 1571, there were major uprisings which the Venetians harshly put down. After one such revolt, 300 people were executed and many exiled, their villages burnt and razed, their property confiscated and other severe penalties exacted. In 1538 the coasts were laid waste by the pirate Khair-ed-din Barbarossa. On top of all this, the inhabitants faced other, natural terrors, such as the famine of 1626 which reduced Crete's population by one-fifth. In these circumstances it is no surprise that the Venetian presence on the island remained small and that Roman Catholicism never became widespread.

LEFT: oil painting of the 1866 Cretan Revolt.
ABOVE: Iráklio at the turn of the 20th century.

Venice kept its hold on Crete long after most of her other Aegean possessions had been surrendered. But, in 1645, the town of Haniá fell to the Turks and, in 1669, after a siege lasting two years, Iráklio fell too and the entire island came under Ottoman rule. By this time, Ottoman administration had lost much of its early vigour: in the early 18th century one commentator described Iráklio as "the carcass of a large city... little better than a desert".

In an effort to escape the burdens of Ottoman rule many Cretan families converted to Islam, especially during the 18th century, on a scale unknown elsewhere in the Aegean. But

these converts continued to speak Greek, drink alcohol and had names such as Effendákis and Mehmedákis, which were linguistic hybrids of Greek and Turkish elements. Villages continued to be called by their Greek names even after all their inhabitants had converted.

From 1770, a series of revolts broke out against Ottoman rule. But it required more than a century to bring about independence; nevertheless, these insurrections altered the balance of power on the island, as many Muslim farmers sold out to Christians before moving, first to the coastal towns – Réthymno became one-third Muslim – and then, after 1923, away from the island altogether. These revolts also had a catastrophic effect on the island's econ-

omy. Passing through the interior shortly after the 1866–9 insurrection, Henry Tozer noted: "Every village that we passed through, and all that we could see along the hillsides, had been plundered, gutted and burnt."

In 1896, when the next major revolt broke out, the inadequacies of Ottoman rule were so evident that the European powers stepped in. For example, on the whole of the island there was just one short stretch of carriage road which went from from Haniá to Soúda Bay; and as William Miller reported in 1897, in Iráklio, the largest town on the island, there were no carriages at all, "for the two that used to exist were last employed for the conveyance of the admirals on the Queen's Jubilee last year, on which occasion the bottom of both vehicles fell out, and the distinguished officers had to walk inside the bottomless machines". Troubles in Ottoman Crete in 1897 provoked a wave of sympathy on the mainland. Greek naval forces were sent to the island while the army marched northwards– only to be crushed by Ottoman forces who pushed back down into Thessaly. This defeat was humiliating for the Greeks, but it proved only to delay the future enlargement of the kingdom for a while.

In 1898 Crete was made an independent principality under Ottoman sovereignty. The new prince, George, was significantly a member of the Greek royal house; the writing was on the wall, and by 1913 union with Greece had finally been achieved.

A new revolt

In 1909, junior army officers staged a revolt against the political establishment in Athens and, at their invitation, a new politician with a radical reputation, Elefthérios Venizélos, came to Athens from Crete to form a new government. A consummate diplomat and a man of great personal charm, Venizélos channelled the untapped energies of the Greek middle class into his own Liberal Party, which governed Greece for 13 of the next 25 years. It also marked the first time that leadership in Greece was held by someone from the islands, breaking the previous monopoly on power excercised by Peloponnesians and central mainlanders. ❏

LEFT: watercolour of urban Cretan costume.
RIGHT: a Naïve painting of Elefthérios Venizélos.

THE ISLANDS TODAY

The 20th century was a political roller-coaster for Greece and its islands, alternating between monarchy, military dictatorship and republicanism

The islands did not all become part of independent Greece at the same time. Only the Cyclades, the Sporades and Évvia (Euboea) formed part of the original state after the peace treaties of 1830–2. At the insistence of about-to-be King George I, a Danish prince (and – more to the point – because they were no longer considered of strategic value), the Ionian islands were ceded by Britain to Greece in 1864.

The other major additions resulted from war. Crete and the northeast Aegean islands became part of Greece in 1913 after the First Balkan War, except for Samothráki which was joined in 1920. The Dodecanese islands were freed from Italian occupation by World War II and formally incorporated into Greece in 1948 after a year's Greek military government. Since several of the islands were wealthy ports at a time when Athens was still a village, it is scarcely surprising that their influence on cultural developments in the new state was disproportionate to their size and overall population.

In politics, the Hydriot families of Voúlgaris and Koundouriótis, the Metaxás clan in the Ionians, the Samian Themistoklís Sofoúlis, not to mention the Cretan Eleisthérios Venizélos – in many ways the founder of the modern Greek state – all typified the vigour which the islanders brought to the political scene. Greek literature and music were marked by the Ionian islands' close links with Italy – personified in poet Dionýsios Solomós, whose *Hymn to Freedom* became the words of the national anthem – while many Aegean islands were the birthplace

of musical stars in rebetic and folk genres (*see page 63*). Skiáthos bred the important fiction writers Aléxandros Papadiamántis and his cousin Aléxandros Moraítis; Lésvos has produced the Nobel Prize-winning poet Odysséas Elýtis, the regional writer Stratís Myrivílis and the Naïve painter Theóphilos; while Crete, not to be outdone, produced in literature and letters a figure to match Venizélos – Níkos Kazantzákis.

The islands' economic influence has also been profound, especially before the Balkan Wars of 1912–13 added the fertile regions of northern Greece to the impoverished state, and again in recent decades with the increasing traffic in tourists. The shipping fleets of the Aegean islands,

LEFT: a Cretan peasant in traditional dress, around 1950. **RIGHT:** a pelican once started an inter-island feud between Mýkonos and Tínos.

exports of currants from Zákynthos and Kefaloniá, olive oil from Lésvos and Crete, salted fish from various east Aegean islands, and emigrant remittances from islanders scattered across the globe – from Canada to Australia to Florida – have all helped bolster the country's economy.

Islands for outcasts

But islands have long had other uses, too. Límnos, under Ottoman rule, was used as a place of exile for political offenders. Henry Tozer, who visited the island in 1884, learnt that a former grand vizier had been living there for eight years and was "almost forgotten at the capital", while

**MADE
IN
GREECE**

1967-74

an extreme instance of isolation was Gávdos islet off Crete. According to Spratt, an English vice-admiral distinguished for his *Travels and Researches in Crete* who visited in 1865, its inhab-

> The fortress islet of Spinalónga, off the northeast coast of Crete, after a long career as Venetian citadel and Muslim village, was used as a leper colony until the late 1950s.

itants did not see a boat for months on end, while he himself disembarked among naked swimmers who, to his Victorian eye, were "primitive in their habits and ideas… a mixed and degenerate race".

The Greek central government also found the islands useful as prisons, both for regular criminals in large compounds on Aegina (Égina) and Corfu and, more ominously, at certain times for political opponents. On Aegina, what was built as an orphanage under the new Kapodístrias government in the late 1820s soon became an important prison (now closed pending restoration as a potential museum), and the originally British-built jail on Corfu, now well short of humane requirements, is still used.

During the 1930s the Metaxás dictatorship sent its political opponents – as well as social misfits like the *rebétes (see page 65)* – to forbidding, isolated islands such as Folégandros, Síkinos and Amorgós. During the Civil War (1946–9), in which the left-wing forces which had strongly resisted the occupying Nazis and Fascists were suppressed, the uninhabited island of Makroníssos just off the southeastern coast of Attica was home to a vast, bleak prison camp for political detainees, as were Ikaría, neighbouring Foúrni, Límnos and its tiny satellite Ágios Evstrátios.

The colonels, who ruled Greece with a heavy, sometimes brutal hand from 21 April 1967 until 24 July 1974, continued the tradition, incarcerating their political opponents in Makroníssos, Yioúra, Léros and Amorgós, as well as the regular prisons on Aegina and Corfu. On occasions, particularly on Amorgós and Corfu, the islanders managed to circumvent military security and give the political prisoners some support.

Incoming and outgoing

Since the late 1950s most islands have experienced the erratic but inexorable growth of tourism, a trend initiated when Greek shipowners began to acquire islands for their own private use. When Stávros Niárhos and Aristotle Onassis continued their competition by respectively buying the islands of Spetsopoúla just off Spétses in the Saronic Gulf and Skórpios beside Levkáda in the Ionian Sea, they set an ideal which innumerable tourists have tried to follow in finding their own island paradise.

Mýkonos, Rhodes, Skiáthos and Corfu were the first to see large numbers of summer visitors, but the trend has spread to virtually all the inhabited islands. If a ship goes there, there will be tourists, and the luxury of what they will find varies more or less according to the island's

constrained by the availability of transport and their own awareness of the wider world, and, in the case of islands like the northeast Aegean group and the Dodecanese, by citizenship status (Ottoman, Italian) which made obtaining passports and permission to enter countries such as the US awkward.

Moreover, several islands prospered after being incorporated into the Greek state. Sýros, for example, became the most important port and manufacturing centre in Greece in the first few decades after 1830. Even after the rise of Piraeus (Pireás) it remained an important centre, whose standing may be gauged by the fine

accessibility. For both visitors and island residents, the biggest changes since the 1970s have been the increasing availability of hydrofoils and catamarans or "high-speed" ferries, more expensive but far faster vessels, as well as multiplied and/or improved airports and airlines.

The counter to this influx has been a steady flow of emigration from the islands. Between 1880 and 1920 or thereabouts, most Greek emigrants were from the mainland. For various reasons, large numbers of islanders did not follow until the 1950s: would-be island emigrants were

LEFT: a poster protesting at the military regime.
ABOVE: a café frequented by the locals of Plomári, Lésvos's second town.

19th-century villas and warehouses of its capital Ermoúpolis. On other islands, such as Ándros and Náxos, the late 19th century was a period of rapid exploitation of mineral resources.

By World War I, however, much of this activity had slowed down, and emigration both to Athens and abroad was increasing, taking advantage of improved transport and communications. In Athens and Piraeus, newcomers from islands formed closely knit communities, each with its own affinity clubs and cafés – recreated islands of familiarity in the urban sprawl. With the collapse of international trade between the world wars, the trend slowed for several decades, but gathered pace once more with the European "miracle" of the post-war years. Many islanders moved to Sweden, France, Holland and West Germany, as well as to South Africa, Rhodesia, Australia and North America.

Improved communications

By the 1960s, road and rail links between Greece and Western Europe began to be modernised. So too were links between the islands and the mainland: the first seaplane connection with Rhodes had been established as early as 1927 by the Italians, but it was only in the 1960s that aerial links between Athens and the Aegean became significant; many airports on the border islands were built in the mid-1960s amidst

the first major Cyprus Republic crises, and doubled as military airbases. At the same time, relatively modern, faster car ferries were introduced, replacing vintage rust-buckets which could take almost twice as long for the same trajectory. On the islands themselves, dirt – then paved – vehicle roads appeared, often for the first time, in some cases displacing local boat services (such as, for instance, Haniá to villages of the southwestern Cretan coast).

Improved communications not only opened up the closed island societies, but also exposed their local economies – which had survived World War II mostly by subsistence farming – to a new world of export and import. Trucks could now be loaded with agricultural produce on Crete, say, or Rhodes, and then be driven directly up from Piraeus to markets in northwestern Europe. The return flow was (and still is) consumer delights: household appliances, cars, motorbikes, clothes and inevitably plastic junk from the Far East.

A new balance has been established since about the 1970s. During the warm months at least, many islands appear to be thriving, what with the crowds disembarking from boats and clogging the village streets, and with their actual and official populations (compiled from voter registration rolls) more or less matching. With the advent of modern transport, weekend visits by internally emigrated islanders (or second-home owners) have become feasible almost year-round. But the bustle is often illusory.

Limits to full-time life

The stark reality is that keeping Greece's islands viable for year-round habitation – especially the smaller, remoter ones – is an uphill task, inevitably involving subsidies EU or national, getting difficult to come by in the current political and economic climate. Financial assistance can mean everything from preferential VAT rates (13 percent in the Dodecanese and most east Aegean islands), to state-of-the-art fibre optic cables, to intrinsically uneconomical ferry routes. Despite the optimistic picture of improved transport painted above, it's a constant battle to maintain links with the mainland; even before its 2009 liquidation-and-reformation, Olympic Airways was steadily reducing flight frequencies to secondary islands, with competitors not taking up the slack. Shipping companies also cherry-pick the most profitable routes to the largest islands, grudgingly providing often irrational schedules

POST-JUNTA POLITICS

After the colonels were deposed in 1974, a referendum terminated the monarchy. The new prime minister was Constantine Karamanlís, a conservative who negotiated entry into the EEC. Greece became a member in 1981, the year that Andréas Papandréou's PASOK party won elections to form Greece's first socialist government. Financial and personal scandals brought defeat in 1989, but with no effective alternative offered by centre-right Néa Dimokratía (ND), PASOK regained power in 1993 and prevailed until 2004 when ND, led by Kostas Karamanlís, again took office. Ongoing scandals plus the world economic crisis paved the way for the PASOK's re-election in 2009.

(see page 304) to other destinations while trousering large subsidies for the privilege. Eastern border islands like Sámos or Lésvos once flourished as trans-shipment points within the Ottoman Empire, but in more recent times indeed languish literally and figuratively at the end of the line, a status only likely to be relieved in the improbable event that Turkey joins the EU.

But this logistical summary can only hint at the everyday feeling of being marooned in the Aegean, so pleasant to short-term visitors but evidently irksome to islanders who have found it increasingly difficult to resist the black-hole-like gravitational pull of Athens (and to a lesser extent

hospital in favour of the vastly superior teaching hospital attached to Ioánnina University on the mainland. Before the advent of helipads suitable for medical evacuations on the smaller islands, those taken suddenly, severely ill were as good as doomed.

There are decent universities on Crete (Réthymno), Corfu and the east Aegean, where the University of the Aegean has its faculties deliberately scattered over Lésvos, Híos, Sámos, Léros and Rhodes to spread employment opportunities and inject life into communities during winter. But again they're competing with the higher-learning colossi of Athens, Thessaloníki,

Thessaloníki, Pátra and Vólos). On a smaller scale, this proves true within large islands too – the four major coastal towns of Crete have done a good job of emptying the villages of their hinterlands in recent decades.

The main three reasons for leaving can be summarised as employment opportunities (severely reduced outside of the tourist season), health care and educational facilities. With some sterling exceptions, state hospitals on the islands leave much to be desired – for instance, if they can manage it Corfiots, shun their own

Pátra, Ioánnina and Vólos. Most mainland-bred doctors and public-school teachers consider island positions a short-term, hardship posting (paid extra as such) away from the bright lights – even if there are those conscientious and/or eccentric exceptions, repeatedly signing up to staff a clinic on a *vrahonisída* (rocky outcrop). As for bright, ambitious islanders who have worked and studied abroad or on the mainland, they rarely return unless forced to by economic or family circumstances.

Left-leaning politics

In national politics, on average the islands are slightly left of centre (in the case of Lésvos, Ikaría and some of the Ionians, communist or

---

LEFT: Sókratous, the main commercial artery in Rhodes' Old Town. **ABOVE:** compare and contrast the islands by hopping from one to the other.

nearly so). Besides his native Crete, Venizélos received staunch initial support from all the northeast Aegean plus Corfu, this political affiliation still reverberating four generations on. The Cyclades and Dodecanese, as permanent net beneficiaries for every sort of subsidised programme, have generally plumped for PASOK as the party most likely to provide them. But despite their illustrious contributions to Greek leadership and territorial aggrandisement, today's islands are unlikely ever to swing a close election – these are typically decided in suburban precincts of Athens or Thessasloníki – and their relative (un)importance was aptly

> On the larger forested islands, wildfires remain a constant fear – and temptation to unscrupulous developers and their hired arsonists.

islands, to such a degree that the tanker-boat is a routine sight in summer. Despite the economic downturn, purpose-built villa projects pitched at both Greeks and foreigners proliferate, the worst-planned ones amounting to visual pollution as well as putting pressure on water resources.

The future of the islands is, much as some Greeks might resent it, bound up with foreign-

symbolised by the late 2007 subsuming of the Ministry of the Aegean into that of the merchant marine. Even during the late 2008/early 2009 youth rioting, which convulsed Athens following the shooting of an unarmed 15-year-old boy by an Athens policeman, barely a ripple registered in most island towns other than some anti-establishment graffiti.

Coming together over conservation

One concern which most islands do share with the mainland – in fact to an enhanced degree owing to fragile ecosystems – is conservation and development policy. Limited water supplies are constantly outstripped, especially on the smaller

ers. Ignoring for the moment landed refugees (*see page 56*), settled immigrants – for the most part Albanians – make up an increasing proportion of the workforce, especially in the building trades (they also outnumber the native-born population in some neighbourhoods). Yet since the millennium direct, non-charter, all-year air links between Northern Europe and Corfu, Iráklio and Rhodes – with more destinations likely to appear – attest to the burgeoning numbers of expats and holiday-home owners who also help keep local economies going. ❑

ABOVE: a potter plies his trade in eastern Lésvos.
RIGHT: the bustling ferry harbour in Náxos, largest of the Cyclades.

MIXING PIETY WITH PLEASURE

Greek religious festivals – and there are many – celebrate saints' days and other events in the religious calendar with devotion and high spirits

Greek island life is punctuated year-round by saints' days and religious festivals, or *panigýri*. As there are about 150 major saints in the Orthodox calendar, there's an excuse for a party most weeks of the year.

Easter is the most important festival, seven weeks after the pre-Lenten carnival, and make for a great time to visit. Colourful and noisy, traditional services mark the Resurrection everywhere, from humble chapels to mighty monasteries.

During *Megáli Evdomáda* (Holy Week), churches are festooned in black velvet. On Maundy Thursday, Pátmos monks re-enact Christ's washing of his disciples' feet prior to Gethsemane. On Good Friday an *Epitáfios* (Bier of Christ) is decorated by women in each parish and paraded solemnly through the streets at dusk.

On Easter Saturday churches are decked in white and red. At midnight all is plunged in darkness as the priest lights the first candle from the holy flame representing the light of the world, and intones: *"Hristós anésti"* (Christ has risen) as the flame is transmitted to the entire congregation to light their candles. The moment is marked by deafening, potentially dangerous fireworks and more – on Kálymnos they throw dynamite from the cliffs, on Híos rival parishes rocket each other's steeples. Back at home, everyone plays a form of conkers with eggs dyed red on Maundy Thursday, then breaks the Lenten fast with *magirítsa* soup made from lamb's offal, lemon, rice and dill.

On Easter Sunday there's great rejoicing as a lamb or kid is barbecued outdoors over coals (or baked in domed ovens on some islands), with the usual music and dancing. Celebrations can continue into Easter Monday, and in some islands an effigy of Judas is filled with fireworks and burnt.

LEFT: hard-boiled eggs, dyed red to symbolise the blood of Christ, are cracked in a conkers-like game at Easter.

ABOVE: in the early hours of Easter Sunday after the midnight service, churchgoers, here on Aegina, head home in candlelit processions.

BELOW: *militínia*, Cycladic Easter cakes with goat's cheese filling.

CELEBRATING ALL YEAR ROUND

Greeks mix piety and pleasure with gusto for all their festivals, from the most important to the smallest fair. The biggest religious event after Easter, the Dormition of the Virgin *(Kímisis tis Panagías)* on 15 August, draws Greeks home from across the globe. After a liturgy on 14 August evening, the icon of the Virgin is paraded – often with brass bands playing funeral dirges – prior to a communal feast which can last for days. Celebrations are especially spectacular in Olymbos, Kárpathos, with dazzling costumes, special dances and traditional songs.

Seasonal festivals on the islands honour everything from sponges to sardines to snakes, and national holidays like *Óhi* ("No") Day (28 October) have patriotic parades marking Greece's reply to Mussolini's surrender ultimatum.

Celebrations usually occur the night before the actual feast day; everyone in the community attends, from babies to grannies. The main liturgy is on the day, at churches hung with pennants and decked in cut foliage.

ABOVE: icons are paraded during the celebrations for Lambrí Tríti (Easter Tuesday) in Olymbos, the remote mountain village on Kárpathos, in the Southern Dodecanese.

LEFT: resplendent in their ceremonial garb, Greek Orthodox priests on Pátmos come together for the Easter ceremony.

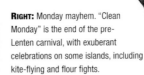

RIGHT: Monday mayhem. "Clean Monday" is the end of the pre-Lenten carnival, with exuberant celebrations on some islands, including kite-flying and flour fights.

PEOPLE AND IDENTITIES

Attachment to the ancestral village, seasonal and diurnal
rhythms dictated by climate, and an assumed identity
between Orthodoxy and Greekness typify islanders

Roughly 10 percent of Greece's population resides in the islands, nearly half in towns of over 5,000 souls – which means that the stereotypical rural idyll, even (or especially) in the remotest spots, is fading fast.

Historically, Greeks rarely moved far from their *patrída*, or home province. But the mid-20th century saw a sort of seasonal transhumance established between one's native village and the big city, usually Athens, for this reason nicknamed *To Megálo Horió* (The Big Village). If the island in question is close enough to the town migrated to, weekend visits are feasible; otherwise, the *patrikó spíti* (ancestral family home) may only be occupied in high summer, typically from late July until the new school term around 11 September. On arrival, dead bugs and dust are swept out, paint brushes and awnings deployed, repairs commissioned, barbecues lit, and positions taken on plastic terrace chairs, all with remarkable speed.

Work and leisure

Until spiralling debt and expenses plus the current economic crisis dictated more nose-to-the-grindstone attitudes, most Greeks reckoned that they worked to live, not the other way around. Even in winter, when there is less need for a siesta, the midday *mikró ýpno* time is still sacred, to be spent over a long lunch with family, friends or business associates. The summer climate, meanwhile, dictates that people who work outdoors, in agriculture or the building trade, begin a single shift just after dawn and knock off by 3pm.

Nationwide and regional chains may be spreading rapidly – specifically supermarkets, travel agencies, homewares, computers and electronics – but many island businesses are still small-scale, family-owned and staffed. This helps disguise unemployment as underemployment, and allows for various fiddles concerning pension contributions.

Sunday remains very much a day of rest, and at weekends warm weather prompts a mass exodus towards the beaches, which often have lively "all-day" bars complete with loud music. Despite recent laws dictating that these should close by 2am, at weekends at any rate this is widely winked at: nights in island towns are long and loud, with motorcycle traffic in particular, and with yet more noise (from car horns especially) when a

LEFT: waiting for custom in Parikía, Páros.
RIGHT: taking refreshment at Iráklio's market, Crete.

favoured athletic team, or political faction, wins a contest. Earlier, at dusk, the local military band might march down the quay playing tunes not necessarily martial, and not necessarily in tune either, prior to lowering the flag.

Even in these pinched times, every sizeable island makes an effort to organise some sort of summer festival. This will include folk dance, theatre and above all concerts with big-name stars, pitched as much at seasonally returned islanders as at foreigners (or more so). But the most authentic entertainments arguably won't be experienced at such organised events but at tavernas. These can serve as informal showcases

early on, children are inculcated into the routine of late nights out at the taverna, either as toddlers asleep in a pram parked by the chairs, or as older kids playing tag around the tables. They are spoken to – and expected to converse up to their abilities – as adults, which accounts in part for the tremendous (over-)confidence of kids and teenagers. Not too many shrinking violets here: in an often rough-and-tumble culture like that of Greece, assertiveness is a survival skill.

Individual families tend to be small. Like Spain and Italy, Greece has negative native population growth, with a birth rate well

for Greek music and lyrics, the latter stemming from a rich mid-20th century tradition in poetry which spawned two Nobel laureates, Odysséas Elýtis and George Seféris. A small group of men (or women), maybe a bit tipsy, will interpret well-loved songs accompanied by unamplified *bouzoúki*, guitar and accordion: the intimate *ta tragoúdia tis paréas* (songs with one's oldest friends).

Children, families, gender roles

Children are adored – arguably spoilt, especially boys – and expected to behave like children; yet at the same time they are not allowed to determine adults' schedules, or kept segregated, as so often happens in Anglo-Saxon countries. Very

> Progonoplixía *(ancestor fixation), crediting all and everything to the ancient Greeks – neatly embodied by dad Gus in* My Big Fat Greek Wedding *– is the flip side to* xenomanía, *a fetishisation of foreign consumer goods, music and foodstuffs.*

below replacement level at roughly 1.4 kids per couple. Much of this is a reaction to impoverished times before the 1960s when four or five siblings growing up in a single room was the norm. Now it's considered shameful to have more offspring than you can properly educate and set up with a house of their own (the D-word, "dowry", is used circumspectly since the practice of demanding it per se was outlawed in the 1980s). Abortion is widely resorted to, with surprisingly little comment from the Orthodox Church.

Nipagogía (crèches) certainly exist, a worthwhile legacy of the first PASOK government, but one suspects they are used to full capacity only in the biggest towns and cities and by the most harassed of working parents. Elsewhere, grandmothers are perennially available childminders, a role assumed with relish. Throughout the day there will be to-ing and fro-ing with foodstuffs and/or child in hand between the houses of the various generations.

Food symbolism – and consequences

Food and eating is not just a pretext for sociability, or proof of maternal virtue, but is highly symbolic and integral to a sense of identity. *Kólyva* (food for the dead, made up of varying proportions of grain, breadcrumbs, nuts, pomegranate seeds and raisins), for instance, forms an essential part of periodic memorial services for the departed, symbolically keeping the deceased linked to the living. Food-related terms are used as diagnostic, affectionate or insulting tags: an older relative will scoop up an adorable infant and exclaim *"Ná sé fáo!"* ("Good enough to

The legal status of women was significantly upgraded by PASOK reforms, and many women (like long-serving foreign minister Dóra Bakogiànni and Communist Party head Aléka Paparíga) are now prominent in public life. Most, however, are still caught up in the bind of both having to work – if only in a family business – and fulfil traditional mother and wife roles. That said, men's attitudes have changed since the relatively recent, macho 1970s: happily seen in public pushing a pram or carrying children, they've even been rumoured to change a nappy or two.

LEFT: taking a wander in Skiáthos Town.
ABOVE: triangles of sticky *baklavá* are boxed up for a customer at this Ionian delicatessen in Levkáda Town.

eat!"); sleek, spoilt children (especially male), presumably overfed from infancy in the belief that a plump toddler is a healthy one, are dubbed *voutyrópeda* ("butter-kids"); coddled, 20-something offspring of either gender, still taking their laundry to be done at the parental home (actually they will probably still be living there until marriage or a job in another town), are deemed *mamóthrefti* ("mother-fed"). Since their attempted 1940 invasion, Italians are *makaronádes* ("macaroni-eaters" – though the Greeks eat just as much), while Asia Minor refugees were long derided as *giaourtovaptisméni* ("yoghurt-baptised", after that Anatolian staple little known in Greece before the 1920s).

You'll notice that many people are, to put it

diplomatically, plump. Greece perennially jostles in EU statistics with Malta and the UK for the crown of Most Overweight Population. This is a consequence, in part, to uncomfortably close memories of hunger, especially during World War II and the Civil War, as well as a diet enjoining the consumption of bread *and* potatoes/rice/pasta *and* oil with every meal.

Mortified by this ranking (especially in the run-up to hosting the 2004 Olympics), the country is now well sown with gyms and rather more dubious slimming salons; while increasing numbers of Lycra-clad cyclists and joggers sporting MP3 players brave the hazardous road verges.

war and after the 1953 earthquake. Refugees from Asia Minor were far less important than on the mainland – in the Ionian islands their settlement was actively resisted – although these communities are a noticeable factor on Thásos, Límnos, Lésvos, Híos, Sámos and espe-

> *Bread is fraught with symbolism – chunks of leavened loaves comprise the* andídoron, *blessed and distributed to church congregations, and to refuse it at a taverna or shared table is considered deviant at best.*

Orthodoxy, Hellenism and minorities

Before the recent influx of immigrants (*see pages 56–7*), Greece, the islands included, was remarkably homogeneous, not to say parochial, in being Greek Orthodox in religious affiliation. About the only exceptions were a significant community of Armenians in Iráklio, Crete – who have been there since they accompanied Nikiphoros Phokas on his reconquest of the island from the Arabs in AD 961 – and the Catholics of the Cyclades (concentrated in Sýros and Tínos).

In 1944, the numerous Jewish communities of the islands were wiped out with the exception of those on Zákynthos, though they elected to depart en masse for Israel after the

cially Crete, where most north-coast towns had large Muslim populations before 1923.

Even for those who rarely set foot in a church, "Orthodox" is inextricably synonymous with "Greek", and vice versa; there seems no place in the national discourse for Jews, Catholics and Protestant sects such as the Jehovah's Witnesses, let alone Muslims, who are all considered at least faintly suspect. The 50,000 native Catholics (plus about 150,000 foreign resident ones) are particularly vociferous on the severe legal disadvantages of being a *xénon dógma* or foreign creed, unrecognised in contrast to the Established Church. ❏

ABOVE: baptismal font at Ekatonpylianí Church, Páros.
RIGHT: island communities are largely Greek Orthodox.

New Immigrants

With its frontier islands doubling as a gateway to Europe, Greece is struggling to control the mounting tide of illegal immigration.

An August evening on tiny Agathonísi, remotest of the Dodecanese, and the ferry quay hosts 150 people preparing to bed down rough for the night: the last three days' worth of illegal immigrants, landed here after a clandestine

sea-crossing from Turkey, guarded by just two gendarmes. Mostly comprised of men but also some women and children, they are not apt to cause trouble – which explains the lack of guards – for they have so far got what they want: entry into Europe.

The crowd is largely from the Middle East and the Indian Subcontinent, but some sub-Saharan Africans also make up their number. The migrants don't talk much to strangers, but if they do it's probably to ask to change US dollars for euros, or else enquire where they can buy a phone card to call relatives back home. Despite appearances, they are rarely completely destitute – money is usually held back from the rapacious people-smugglers who demand thousands to get each individual to, through, and out of Turkey.

Every summer, the *akritiká nisiá* or frontier islands off the Turkish coast act as an irresistible magnet for illegal immigration until winter storms halt the passage. Greece has demanded that Turkey stem the flow, and accept for deportation illegal immigrants proved to have come from Turkey. But given the low pay of most Turkish port officials, bribes from captains for turning a blind eye to departing boats have the desired effect – when the local police aren't themselves moonlighting as smugglers. In 2008, Turkey accepted just over 10 percent of the 57,000 Greek applications to return illegal migrants.

Survival of the fittest

Walking across Agathonísi, you'll spot discarded lifevests and synthetic drip-dry clothing inappropriate to summer conditions, plus the occasional deflated rubber raft on the shore: unscrupulous captains, wary of being detained by the Greek coastguard, may dump their human cargo in international or Greek waters, well short of Agathonísi, and hightail it back to Turkey. An alternative is launching the migrants in overloaded rafts with just a compass and a baulky engine, leaving West Africans who know something of the sea in charge. Refugees have become aware of these tactics, and are prepared to paddle or swim for land if close enough, or else wait to be fished out of the Aegean by the Greeks as required by law. Drownings occur regularly even in good weather, but it's amazing that there aren't more, considering that the coastguard is just as likely to swamp the rafts or drive them back into Turkish waters. What you won't find amongst the debris, or on the migrants themselves, are any ID, SIM cards, clothing labels or bus tickets that would prove where they're from or where they have passed through – making it impossible for Greek authorities to repatriate them legally.

The next afternoon the *Nísos Kálymnos*, the local ferryboat serving the northern Dodecanese, departs with all 150 refugees sitting quietly at the back of the upper sun-deck, cordoned off from holiday-makers by a length of marine rope. On arrival at Pátmos, they're lodged temporarily in and around the police station – figures on its roof silhouetted against the night sky – until the midnight mainline ferry arrives from Rhodes to take them away to Athens and further processing. Many locals resent even this brief stopover – *"Dióhni ton tourismó"* ("It drives out tourism"), they say – on their smart island much more used to cruise-ship passengers than ragged refugees.

"Processing" means shelter, meals and medical examinations for just three days at a dozen receiving centres scattered across Greece – soon to be upped to 17, against strenuous local opposition – after which migrants are served with a deportation order giving them a month to leave the country. Some disappear into the huge refugee underground, with little to fear if caught, as the police merely lock them up for 90 days and then release them again. Others apply for political asylum, giving them six to 24 months' residence while their case is reviewed. Rather scandalously, less than 1 percent are accepted; Greece views asylum-seeking as economic migration by the back door.

The EU's highest immigration ratio

Versus a native population of about 10.4 million, Greece has around 1.4 million immigrants – only about 600,000 of them legalised through various amnesties between 1998 and 2005. This is the highest ratio in the EU, in what previously had been a monochrome culture, and unsurprisingly immigrants have become a major social issue.

Most established and numerous are the nearly 1 million Albanians, who arrived mostly in the early 1990s; but there are also Bengalis, Afghans, Pakistanis, Chinese, Somalis, Lebanese, Iranians, Syrians, Egyptians, Filipinos, Iraqis, West Africans and nationals of various non-EU Central European states (to name only the largest groups). While violent responses as seen elsewhere in Europe have been relatively few so far – notwithstanding clashes between right-wing demonstrators and immigrants in Athens during May 2009 – racist or discriminatory attitudes and laws are common. In particular, non-EU immigrants hoping to be self-employed must invest in that aim and spend 60,000 euros in any business, no matter how small – an unrealistic figure. Thus many refugees never escape being roving pedlars of fake designer bags, sunglasses and pirate CDs. As one pro-immigrant NGO's (non-governmental organisation's) leaflet ironically put it, "Our grandparents refugees, our parents emigrants, and we – xenophobes and racists?"

There were 146,000 recorded illegal migrants in 2008, 30 percent up from 2007 and a 50 percent gain on 2006, with perhaps a quarter of these

entering via the border islands. Greece has received a 13.7 million euro grant from the EU to secure its frontiers, including 3.2 million euros to beef up the coastguard, but it's doubtful whether the country will get help upgrading reception facilities – or would want to, as many Greek police say this will just attract more migrants. Had the Agathonísi group's landfall been instead Sámos just to the north, they would have been lodged in a designated holding centre, opened there in 2008 at the behest of the UNHCR (the UN refugee agency), which had condemned as inhumane the prior detention facility in an old officers' club. The sun-baked, hillside camp, built on a former army firing range and

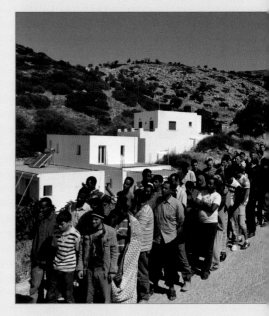

dubbed "Guantánamo" locally, is already overflowing with 600 residents, who in July 2009 went on hunger strike to protest against the transfer of some to northern Greek camps prior to expulsion.

Overall, the official response to the illegal immigrants has been substandard, often in breach of various UN and EU regulations. Given the worldwide economic crisis, the Greek construction and agricultural industries no longer need cheap undocumented labour, one result of which has been, near the docks of Pátras and Igoumenítsa, impromptu camps (cleared in July 2009) of immigrants hoping to stow away on boats to Italy. "Greece is not really Europe," many say, their sights set firmly on Italy, Spain, Sweden or England, where they often already have relatives in residence. ❑

LEFT: an illegal immigrant and his child arrive on Crete following rescue by the Greek coastguard.
RIGHT: immigrants wait in line outside a police station on Agathonísi in May 2009, some of over 1,200 immigrants so far that year to have landed on the shores of the island (population: 150) with its desperately over-stretched facilities.

RELIGION

The degree of religious faith in the countryside contrasts
sharply with opinions on the all-too-human Church itself

The Orthodox Church still exerts a noticeable influence over contemporary Greek life, especially on the smaller islands, and even the most worldly, sceptical of families will have religious services for the critical rites of marriage, baptism and funerals. Yet there's a marked disconnect between private devotion and beliefs (some little changed since pagan times), and public disparagement of the Church, which has suffered a sharp loss in prestige since the 1960s.

Historical background

In 1833, the Church in newly independent Greece was detached from the Constantinople Patriarchate and made autocephalous, but controlled by the Ministry of Education and Religion, which paid the salaries of priests and bishops (both ministry and this civil-servant status endure). As Greece expanded, territories incorporated after 1912 remained subject to the Ecumenical Patriarchate, which at times produced friction with the Athenian archbishop. Although the Church in the mid-20th century ran charitable programmes for refugees and war orphans, its reputation suffered badly under the junta, which most clerics endorsed (with a few honourable exceptions). After the 1974 restoration of democracy, the Church was downgraded from state institution to just Greece's established religion; and during the first PASOK term, civil marriage was legalised.

Despite notional subordination to a secular ministry, however, no government ever managed to bring Orthodox institutions to heel. The most serious attempt, during 1987–8, saw incumbent minister Andónis Trítsis make a stab at thorough reforms, specifically urging lay participation in elections for all Church offices and the expro-

priation of surplus ecclesiastical property. When thwarted by Andréas Papandréou himself, Trítsis resigned on principle – from the party as well – and was soon elected Mayor of Athens as an independent.

The next kerfuffle occurred in 2002 when, in accordance with EU directives, the government proposed to omit religious affiliation from identity cards. Led by combative, controversial Archbishop of Athens and All Greece, Khristódoulos, the faithful unavailingly marched in the streets against this godless innovation; a compromise bill to make declaration of creed optional went nowhere.

But this was as nothing compared to the consecutive scandals which erupted during late

2004 and early 2005, so lurid you couldn't make them up: monasteries as hotbeds of homosexual intrigue; embezzlement by the Archbishop of Attica (jailed for six years and defrocked); smuggling of rare icons; bribing of judges (one of whom absconded). Greek media comics like Lákis Lazópoulos and Tzímis Panoúsis mercilessly satirised the clerical foibles; all of which made the attempted prosecution by a Church deacon (with Khristódoulos' connivance) of veteran musicologist and folk musician Dómna Samíou, for singing bawdy carnival songs in public, that much more pathetic a diversion.

Still rumbling on are scandals emanating from two Mount Athos monasteries: Esfigménou's refusal to recognise the current patriarch and a resultant long-running campaign by other Athonite monks and the Greek state to eject its tenants, and a rigged real-estate swap between Vatopedíou and the government, greatly to the latter's detriment. Some might say parishioners are getting poor value from their tax-paid clerics.

A bedrock of belief

The old adage that organised religion need not have much to do with spirituality or belief is amply borne out by Greek everyday life, especially in rural areas. Out in the countryside, you will notice numerous hillside chapels and roadside shrines (proskynitária), many built by a family or by individuals in fulfilment of a vow of thanks (for supernatural assistance) to the patron saint. Inside are more votive offerings: the támmata, flat metal or 3D wax images representing the exact nature of the favour granted – a longed-for baby, healed body part or returned relative.

Saints are considered intercessors for the faithful, real, hovering personages in contrast with the remote deity. Icons, which form the core of Orthodox worship, are not just two-dimensional images hung with támmata but conduits to the "other side" which the saint inhabits. They are emblems of the parish, village or island, paraded with honour on feast days to bestow blessings and receive homage in return. The unseen world is contiguous in both its benevolent and menacing aspects: saints are occasionally still glimpsed in or near their chapels by the pure of heart, while priestly sermons advise the wearing of crucifixes

around the neck, considered particularly vulnerable to demonic attack.

Though birthday parties for children are on the increase, traditionally Greeks only marked giortés (saints' namedays), which celebrate Orthodox baptismal names. Even people named for pagan

> Priests have long been the focus of a superstition at odds with their social status. Meeting one on the street was supposed to be exceedingly unlucky; there were men who dispelled the jinx by discreetly touching their testicles.

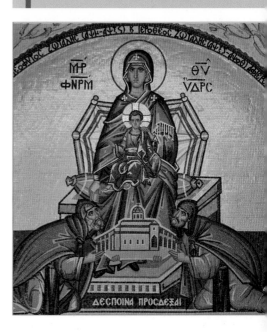

or mythological personalities have a "Christian" moniker, and a baby is usually christened after one of its four grandparents. Someone will say "Giortázo símera" (I'm celebrating today) – which in the case of a popular name like Ioánnis or Eléni can mean a quarter of the village holding open house for friends to drop by – to which the proper response is "Hrónia pollá" (Many years, or in other words, many happy returns).

Devotional fasting may be on the wane in towns, but it is still prevalent in rural areas, especially during the days of "Great Lent" (before Easter), the first two weeks of August, and "Little Lent" (before Christmas). A whole range of foodstuffs is forbidden then, which has had a marked effect on Greek cuisine (see pages 71–7). ❑

LEFT: colouring the everyday – devotional architecture in Firá, Santoríni.
RIGHT: Monastery of the Panagía, Hydra.

DEBUNKING THE BOUZOÚKI

Like the islands themselves, Greek music has been influenced by many other cultures, which give it a richness and complexity worth seeking out

The visitor is ambling along some photogenic island harbour at sunset, looking forwards to a meal of grilled octopus washed down with a little *oúzo*. What better way to complete the image than with some background music on the *bouzoúki*? After all, isn't *bouzoúki* music the quintessence of all things Greek?

Well, yes and no. Those familiar soundtracks for Mános Hatzidákis's *Never on Sunday* and Míkis Theodorákis's *Zorba the Greek*, sold ad nauseam in instrumental cover versions from resort souvenir stalls, have effectively closed foreign minds to anything else of value in Greek music.

What the big record companies push on inexperienced foreigners, in catalogue sections cynically labelled *"Touristiká"*, is merely the tip of the iceberg, a snapshot of a brief period in the early 1960s which coincided with Greece's emergence as a mass-tourism destination. While the original compositions, arrangements and recordings skilfully distilled elements of Greek music into a cinema-friendly form, the offcut remixes – adulterated for foreign tastes and with titles like *Disco Bouzouki My Love* (*sic*) – are another matter.

Diverse influences

Greece amply deserves the cliché image of a musical crossroads and collecting-basket, with a range of diverse influences inside a deceptively small country; even a small selection of CDs will give some idea of Greece's rich musical traditions. The *bouzoúki* stereotype has obscured the Aegean music hidden away behind *skyládika* (roadhouse-type venues) with their heavy amplification. Acoustic *nisiótika* or island music has

PRECEDING PAGES: fishing boat lights. **LEFT:** mixing the new and the traditional. **RIGHT:** the ubiquitous *bouzoúki*.

an altogether cleaner, gentler sound, and against the odds has mounted a mild comeback since the 1980s. In the Cyclades especially (of all Greek territories the least affected by the invaders – *see pages 32–3*), it's very much *sui generis*, displaying only some Italian influence.

Rhythms, often in unconventional time signatures, are lilting and hypnotic; melodies, traditionally executed on violin, bagpipes and *laoúto*, the fretted folk lute, are exquisite. The lyrics, tokens of a more innocent time, grapple with eternal island concerns – the sea that claimed a loved one, the mother who wonders if her sons will ever return from exile, fishing or farming days interrupted by the festival of a beloved saint – but occasionally verge on the poetically surreal.

Various members of the Náxos-born Konitópoulos clan are the ones you're most likely to hear, but a younger performer with frankly better musicanship and new original compositions is fiddler Níkos Ikonomídis, a native of Skhinoússa, near Amorgós. Particularly prized are archival recordings of Anna and Emilía Hatzidáki, a mother-daughter team from the Dodecanese, and singing sisters from Kós, Anna Karabesíni and Efi Sarrí. In the Ionian islands, the Italian heritage is evident in Neapolitan-style *kantádes*, sung in four-part harmony, and often accompanied by mandolin, violin and guitar tuned to Western scales.

Compositions and instrumentation (the *sandoúri* or hammer dulcimer, or brass bands) of Asia Minor enrich the repertoire of the northeast Aegean islands and the Dodecanese. Meanwhile, the long vocal introductions to Cretan songs carry traces of North African and Arab music.

Structure and social context

Most traditional Greek music is either pentatonic (five notes in the scale) or based on a modal system used in musics of the Middle East. The *októehos* system at the basis of Byzantine ecclesiastical chant, however, was not (as many nationalists assert) descended from ancient Greek music, but from the modes of Jewish or secular melodies

from ancient Palestine; its greatest composer was 5th-century Syria's Romanos O Melodos.

Greece's lyrics were never divorced from music as in the West, where for example opera librettos were commissioned separately. Since antiquity both have been inseparable, and in recent decades musical settings of poetry – or high-quality if purpose-written lyrics – have constituted some of Greece's most powerful music. The enthusiastic Greek website www.stixoi.info contains tens of thousands of songs and poems, including translations into foreign languages. Instrumental music remains a relative rarity, while unaccompanied voice still features in women's laments, *tis távlas* (table songs), *tis strátas* (road songs) and the epics such as the medieval Cretan *Erotókritos*.

Like all folk music, *nisiótika* were not originally conceived as entertainment but were integral to religious festivals, weddings, funerals or work. Unfortunately, on the more touristed islands it's become almost impossible to hear genuine acoustic music – count yourself lucky if you're invited to a soirée with traditional instrumentation.

Rhythms – and blues?

Unlike Western metres in units or multiples of two, three or four beats, the Greeks seem to have matched their musical rhythms to the cadences of their poetry since the age of the Homeric hexameter; catchy 5/8, 7/8, 9/8 and even 11/8 time signatures are common in Greek traditional music. The composer Mímis Pléssas (1924–), a former jazzman also responsible for numerous Greek movie soundtracks, remembers a 1953 jam session with American jazz trumpeter Dizzy Gillespie. Pléssas had no trouble fingering a nim-

> Some modes do not start with do–re–mi (C–D–E), like the Western major scale, but do–do sharp–mi (C–C#–E). Violins on the islands are still sometimes tuned à la Toúrka, D-A-D-G, rather than the standard tuning with E on top.

ble 7/8 rhythm on the piano – and promptly lost Dizzy. "I can't do it, something's missing," said the great jazzman. Less convincingly, Pléssas claimed: "Imagine the field cry of the black man transported to Greece – that's what Greek music is."

Pléssas was not the first to have simplistically found similarities between the American blues and Greek song – especially *rebétika*, the genre foreigners are most likely to gravitate towards. Originally, this was the semi-clandestine music of a particular segment of the Anatolian refugee population which flooded into Athens, Piraeus and Thessaloníki after the disastrous 1919–22 Greco-Turkish War, and the compulsory exchange of religious minorities between the two nations.

Hard-core urban *rebétika* superficially resembles the blues in origins and preoccupations – poverty and social exclusion, disease, the allure of drugs and idleness, faithless women, thwarted love – and its practitioners (the *rebétes*) and lyrics were persecuted and censored during the 1930s. Westernising Greeks despised, and still despise, its "oriental" roots, but one can safely say that *rebétika* existed in some form around the east Aegean coast and the Black Sea for decades before that. By the 1950s, however, *rebétika* became "domesticated" and incorporated into mainstream Greek music. In 1953 Manólis Hiótis marked the demise of the original rebetic style by adding a fourth string to the *bouzoúki*, allowing it to be tuned tonally rather than modally – thus spawning *laïkó* and *elafrá*, the urban "popular" music heard on the radio countrywide.

This was just one aspect of the ongoing post-war Westernisation of Greece, with the local musical scene arrayed in two opposing camps: adherents of traditionally derived styles versus those who forsook roots music for imported jazz/cabaret, symphonic and rock models.

The state of the art

Then-Communist Theodorákis, after his 1965 *Zorba* outing, shunned Byzantine/rebetic/traditional sources completely in favour of Western quasi-symphonic works and film music. Generally, the political Left historically condemned apolitical, escapist styles such as *rebétika* and *laïkó*, attempting at one point to "raise mass consciousness" with recycled *andártika*, wartime resistance songs.

More thoughtful musicians attempted to bridge the high–low culture gap with hybrid styles: the *éntekno* or "artifice" music of Crete-born Yánnis Markópoulos, where traditional instruments and themes were used within large-scale compositions of great emotive power; a succession of guitarist singer-songwriters, led by Dionýsis Savvópoulos, who challenged the supremacy of the

ubiquitous *bouzoúki* with modern lyrics too, giving rise to Greek folk-rock; and revivalists such as Cretans Haínides and Loudovíkos ton Anogíon, who countered rock-drum-kit-and-electrification of live traditional performances with updated, rearranged standards and original compositions.

> There is substantial overlap between nisiótika and rebétika: many composer-musicians hailed from the islands, including Márkos Vamvakáris of Sýros and Giórgos Katsarós from Amorgós, with inevitable cross-pollination between the genres.

Rebétika enjoyed a revival after the fall of the junta, which had tried to ban it like much else, although the fad – most pronounced among urban intellectuals – has long since waned. Re-issue recordings now mainly target a foreign audience, many first exposed to the genre by Stávros Xarhákos's soundtrack to the 1983 film *Rebétiko*.

But "pure" *laïkó* and *nisiótika*, despite being looked down on by educated Greeks (especially overseas students), refuses to die. It's a perennial scenario in Greece, where a Westernised cultural elite keep busy attempting unsuccessfully to banish "low-class" habits. Unruly cosmopolitanism continues to be the the the nemesis of nationalists and reformers in search of an illusory "purity". ❑

LEFT: an evening's entertainment.
RIGHT: fine-tuning a *lýra*.

AEGEAN ARCHITECTURE

Traditional architecture and town planning on Aegean
islands is a response both to the environment and
local history between the 13th and 19th centuries

The development of both architecture and town profiles across the Aegean was spurred by several factors. By the late 12th century, Byzantine power had declined considerably, and the Venetians took advantage of this to divert the Fourth Crusade to Constantinople in 1204, smashing the central authority which until then had ruled all the islands. The Cyclades and Sporades in particular were parcelled out to Venetian nobles and adventurers, while in the course of the following centuries the crusading Knights of St John and the Genoese established themselves in the Dodecanese and northeast Aegean respectively. After various attempts, the Venetian Republic acquired sovereignty of the Ionian islands in 1386, and the main towns that evolved on Zákynthos, Corfu and Kefaloniá conformed very much to the example of Venice itself, with high, tottering, shuttered townhouses as well as Baroque churches giving onto vast piazzas.

Anti-piracy measures

Piracy became rife in the Aegean, and most coastal settlements were abandoned in favour of inland or at least elevated towns known as the *hóra* ("the place"), from which hostile ships could be sighted from a distance and appropriate measures taken. Cycladic and Sporadic villages featured zigzagging lanes and cul-de-sacs, with the purpose not only of acting as wind baffles, but so as to confuse intruders, who (not knowing the maze-like street plan) could more easily be trapped and dispatched.

The ultimate anti-raider defence was the *kástro*, a usually rectangular compound with gated access, the backs of the contiguous

The doorways of kástra *all faced inwards, with upper storey doorways reached by arpeggios of parallel staircases.*

houses substituting for conventional curtain walls. Some, but not all, *kástra* are originally Venetian-planned and -built; others are adapted from Byzantine or even ancient sites. The best examples, still inhabited, are located on Andíparos, Sífnos, Náxos, Folégandros and Síkinos. The *kástra* at Kímolos (which were founded by a Greek Orthodox trader under Ottoman rule) and Astypálea were effectively abandoned after World War II, while Skáros on Santoríni and Kástro on Skiáthos were both deserted by the mid-19th century, after the Barbary corsairs had been suppressed by the French in 1833.

The Dodecanese and northeast Aegean had no *kástra* per se – except arguably the mastic villages on Híos – but towns grew up at the

> Rhodes Old Town is an instance of Western military engineering and grid planning based strongly on the ancient city, and doesn't really count as vernacular architecture.

ity. Steps and walkways were also outlined in whitewash to aid night-time travel – invaluable before the era of streetlamps. Flat roofs served both for drying crops like figs or grapes, and to collect rainwater for cisterns; in the *kástra* they served a military purpose, as defenders could move rapidly on them from one threatened side of the settlement to another. Given a lack of deciduous hardwood, these flat roofs (and any upper floors) were supported by intertwined *fíthes*, gnarled but extremely strong trunks of a local juniper species, covered with a perpendicular series of canes and finally a layer of *pateliá*, special earth tamped down with a roller.

base of proper Genoese or Knights' castles, or on Pátmos around a fortified monastery.

Materials, styles, structures

Construction of houses both humble and grand was drystone (without mortar), using local rock, though recycling ancient masonry was common, and plaster rendering the rule on village-centre dwellings. On small islands, walls were (and still are) whitewashed regularly for hygienic reasons, to impart texture with built-up coats, and to enhance heat reflectiv-

---

LEFT: the benefits of whitewashing, here on Páros, include heat reflectivity. ABOVE: Crusader architecture – the 15th-century Knights Hospital in Rhodes Old Town.

Wooden balconies and railings are typical of many ports in the Cyclades and Dodecanese; during former times this was often *katráni*, a durable cedar imported from Asia Minor – now it is probably tropical hardwood. Ornate, wrought-iron fanlights and railings are a feature of many islands, particularly Kálymnos, Léros and the northeast Aegean.

Houses on the larger Dodecanese, and most of the northeast Aegean, tended to eschew whitewashing, opting either for bright colour (especially on Kálymnos), pointed bare masonry (Lésvos and Límnos) or painted lath-and-plaster upper storeys – notably on Sámos and Thásos – identical to that found across the mainland Balkans.

Building for all purposes

Multi-room, courtyarded houses emerged in the 19th century, replacing the one- or two-room modular houses typical of *kástra*; Cretan townhouses with courtyards date from the Venetian occupation. Neoclassical ornamentations and methods – including pitched roofs with canal- or pan-tiles, as well as the ironwork noted previously *(see page 67)* – became common after Greek independence.

Churches, many of them diminutive and incorporated seamlessly into the fabric of a village, were built in a similar style to secular buildings (though usually with vaulted roofs).

Monasteries, especially isolated rural ones, had similar architecture but were always walled – both in accordance with Orthodox doctrine, in other words to mark them apart from "the world", and as a practical measure to deter piracy. Belfries and bell-walls, the star of many a postcard, are relatively recent, Western-influenced introductions: during Ottoman times there were restrictions on the ringing of church bells lest they offend Muslim sensibilities, though this held less true in homogeneously Christian islands like the Cyclades.

Certain communal constructions were vital to a largely self-sufficient rural economy: domed ovens suitable for bread and roast meat alike, windmills to process the summer grain harvest

(when the *meltémi* wind was conveniently at its height) and watermills – found on Kéa, Andros, Skiáthos, Skýros, Náxos and Kýthnos, as well as islands with more obvious, strong streams like Sámos, Lésvos, Ikaría and Crete.

Some watermills have ended up outlasting windmills in terms of usage, working right up until the 1980s. Their profile, usually with a sluice preceding a staged descent tower, is unmistakable. Windmill construction and repair was a special trade, and hardwood tree trunks suitable for the main shaft had to be imported from mainland forests; walls might be over 1 metre (3ft) thick to support the tre-

> *Churches often owed their existence to a private vow, and they remained in the same family for generations.*

mendous stresses imparted through the masts.

Rectangular dovecotes, introduced by the Venetians as a feudal privilege, are restricted to Tínos (which has almost 1,200 of them), Andros, Mýkonos and Sífnos. Stone-slab niches and vents in geometric designs adorn a leeward side of the structure.

Improved conditions within the Ottoman Empire from the late 18th century onwards fostered the growth of a Christian bourgeoisie, something evident in the sumptuous shipowners' mansions on Hydra and Spétses, plus others on a less grand scale at Límni, Évvia and on Andros. The same era saw the appearance of multi-storey, semi-fortified tower-mansions around Mytilíni (Lésvos), structures with few parallels on other islands, though plenty on the mainland.

The 19th-century industrial warehouses of the larger east Aegean islands like Lésvos, Híos and Sámos, typically devoted to the olive-milling, leather-tanning or distilling trades, constitute a special case in both style – derived from similar structures in Asia Minor, just across the water – and size, with typically 80cm (2½ft) thick walls

– deemed cramped, dark and insanitary – are left to those nostalgic Athenians and foreigners foolish enough to purchase them for renovation. When locals deign to remain in an old house, they typically deface it with mass-produced aluminium windows and doors, and flanged, so-called *romaïká* tiles which arguably

> Rarely are there any subsidies available to support those islanders who do wish to employ the invariably more expensive, labour-intensive traditional techniques.

rather the 50cm (1½ft) thickness almost universal for dwellings across the Aegean.

Modern adulterations

Sadly, none of the foregoing seems to interest many of today's islanders, especially those on the larger islands. Like most Greeks, their dream is of a modern rural villa or at least free-standing house amidst gardens or fields, with wraparound balconies, fireplaces doubling as space heaters and, above all, easy car access and parking. Traditional village-centre houses

make many communities look like a southeast Asian slum when seen from above (unless the settlement has been declared *diatiritéo* – under a conservation order).

A stab at checking the spread of inappropriate styles and materials was made in 2001 when then-Minister of the Aegean, Níkos Sifounákis, promulgated rules for building on the smaller, more picturesque islands – but not on any of the larger ones, where too many voters would have been antagonised. These restrictions, even where still in force, have been more or less substituted by those of the very powerful state archaeological service, which effectively controls areas like the Cycladic *kástra*, Sými and Rhodes Old Town.   ❑

FAR LEFT: Panagía tou Pýrgou church, a diminutive landmark of Skópelos. **LEFT:** the Achilleion Palace, Corfu. **ABOVE:** the Aquarium – Italian architecture on Rhodes.

FOOD AND DRINK

Renewed pride in traditional regional recipes, a change in restaurant cooking habits and the advent of a quality wine industry have all done wonders for Greek cuisine

Greek restaurant fare long had a poor reputation amongst foreign visitors. Casserole dishes *(magirevtá)* were saturated in oil, overcooked and served lukewarm; resinated wine was likened to paint stripper; leafy greens and seafood were severely limited in summer. Unless they travelled off-season, or were invited to eat by a family, visitors were apt to form a frankly libellous impression of local cuisine.

Eating in Greece at the dawn of tourism was constrained by the interrelated factors of poverty, religious strictures and the unforgiving Mediterranean environment, not to mention feelings of shame about "peasant" culture. Until the 1960s, most people ate meat just a few times a month and at major holidays – not just for financial reasons, but because of Church-mandated abstention from meat and cheese which, for the devout, could total several months of the year. A range of *nistísima* or fasting foods had evolved, many of them the so-called *laderá* or "oily" dishes comprising stewed

> The apparent variety of beers in Greece is deceptive: one holding company controls 95 percent of the market. The best label from this near-monopoly is Alfa; worthy independents are Vergina, brewed in Komotiní, and Craft microbrewery in Athens.

or rice-stuffed fresh vegetables, and pulses; those ladles of olive oil, along with chunks of bread, also conveniently quelled hunger pangs. Piping-hot food was actively believed to be bad

LEFT: bringing in the catch in Livádia harbour, Tílos.
RIGHT: a simple classic, the Greek salad, or *horiátiki*.

for you. Bread was made partly or wholly from barley, easy to grow on the more barren islands, and equally easy to turn into long-keeping *paximádia* (rusks).

Snails emerging from hibernation after the first rains, *volví* (bitter wild hyacinth bulbs), various kinds of *hórta* (radicchio, notchweed and chicory) gathered from a hillside, purslane sprigs weeded from the summer garden: such were the wild foods much sought after by resourceful country-dwellers. But this kind of "granny" fare collided head-on with returning Greek emigrants and their Western, fast-food tastes, and a simultaneous tendency to give tourists what they seemed to want, not threatening "ethnic" food. Thus *kalamári* and chips ruled unchallenged for decades.

Slow food redux

The late 1980s saw a rehabilitation and upgrading of traditional Greek cooking. Increased prosperity and travel or study overseas had broadened culinary horizons, while under the post-junta PASOK governments there was certainly an anti-Western backlash and increased pride in Greekness. But growing nostalgia for the *patrída* (rural homeland), and the loosening of country cooking's association with grinding poverty, were more powerful forces. Crete, with its long grow-

The basics

Despite the waning of strict fasting and more disposable income, vegetables remain the backbone of island cuisine. Tasty *nistísima*-compliant standards include all manner of *hórta* drizzled with oil and lemon juice, fresh *koukiá* (broad beans – abundant during Lent), *angináres alá políta* (artichoke hearts, carrots, dill and potatoes), *briám* or *tourloú* (ratatouille) of courgettes, aubergine, tomatoes, garlic and onion, and stewed lentils or chickpeas. Potatoes, hand-cut daily into chips or medallions, are still thought of as a hallmark of a good restaurant; Belgian pre-pack chips are considered

ing season and rich wild flora, became a main focus for this renaissance. Cookbooks multiplied – Myrsíni Lambráki's *Hórta*, telling one what to do with every variety of edible wild plant, went through dozens of printings – while celebrity TV chefs emerged. Restaurants and *ouzerís* began to update home-style recipes, emphasising fresh, locally sourced, seasonal ingredients, sensible cooking times and a minimised use of oil, and allowing intrinsic food flavours to emerge. The most *nouvelle* restaurants were (and are) dubbed *koultouriárika* – "highbrow" – sometimes a bit precious in their menus, slimline portions and prices. But those that succeeded in providing value, and which survived, left a lasting mark on the eating-out scene.

THE IDEAL VS THE REAL

While researching *Heirs to the Greek Catastrophe*, her classic 1970s study of an Asia Minor refugee community near Piraeus, anthropologist Renée Hirschon learned that a "good" girl's or housewife's worth was demonstrated by her reliable presence in the kitchen, slaving over labour-intensive dishes involving lots of rolling out of phyllo dough, stuffing and baking – slow food *avant la lettre*. Quick, mostly fried or grilled dishes were dismissed by her informants as *to faï tis poutánas* or "whore's food", the sort of skillet-snacks that a prostitute could be expected to whip up between clients. Ironically, perhaps, such recipes are largely the staples of many contemporary *ouzerí* menus.

for tourists only. Minced meat appears in such *magirevtá* as *lahanodolmádes* (stuffed cabbage leaves), *giouvarlákia* (rice-and-mince-balls in egg-lemon sauce) and *yaprákia* (stuffed vine leaves) – though the last also has a vegetarian version called *gialantzí* ("liar's") *dolmádes*. *Píttes* (turnovers) can similarly be stuffed with *nistísima* or a meat/cheese filling.

Mezédes or *orektiká* (starters) are frequently meat-free, with pulses popular: *fáva* is the bean of that name puréed, then served with chopped onions, lemon wedges and olive oil – a much-esteemed, cool-weather comfort food – while *mavromátika* (black-eyed peas)

carrot early in winter, followed by medleys of lettuces, rocket, radishes, spring onions and dill.

Perhaps surprisingly, Greeks are Europe's top per capita cheese-eaters. *Féta* – for which Greece has secured European court rulings protecting its "registered trademark" status

> Certain shellfish must be eaten alive to avoid food poisoning, including petalídes *(limpets)*, gialisterés *(smooth Venus)*, kydónia *(cockles)*, kténia *(scallops)* and petrosolínes *(razor clams)*. If they twitch when drizzled with lemon juice, they're alive.

are boiled and then served chilled, garnished with onion and parsley. *Taramosaláta*, *tzatzíki* and *melitzanosaláta* will be familiar from a thousand overseas kebab houses, but in the islands no outfit with an eye to its reputation will decline to make these in-house to a notably chunky consistency; pre-purchased catering packs are for touristy tavernas or "snack bars" only.

Although *horiátiki*, or peasant's salad, is the summer mainstay, between October and April salads are more diverse – cabbage with grated

– is the most famous of numerous varieties, which range from soft to hard, sweet to sharp. Cow, goat or sheep milk are the raw ingredients, alone or in unpredictable combinations. Hard cheeses (like *kefalograviéra*) are for grating, grilling or frying, crumbly (like *dermatísio*) for stuffing, soft (like the sweet *myzíthra*) for spreading or spooning. *Saganáki* is any suitable cheese, fried, or alternatively any cheese-based sauce.

Meat and fish

Budget meat options mean the ubiquitous *souvláki* (traditionally pork-based from November to April, lamb-based otherwise), *loukániko* (thick, coarse-grained sausage) and *gýros* (pork

LEFT: atmospheric dining in Skiáthos Town. **ABOVE:** starters of *féta* cheese and *fáva*, which is made from puréed yellow peas and similar to pease pudding.

slices cut from a dense-packed, side-cooked cylinder). A step up gets you *brizóla* (chops, usually pork) and *pansétta* (spare ribs, not belly bacon as elsewhere). On bigger islands with extensive flocks, there may be local *soúvla* or *exohikó*, various spit-roasted cuts of lamb, goat or pork.

Non-farmed scaly fish is as expensive in Greece as elsewhere in the Mediterranean. You're usually better off setting your sights on humbler, seasonally available species than on the bream and sea bass familiar from Northern-European supermarket counters. East Aegean and Dodecanese islands near the

Washing it all down

Another driving force in the makeover of Greek cuisine was the emergence from the late 1980s onwards of a quality wine industry, overseen by foreign-educated Greek oenologists. Owing to limited bottling capacity – many micro-wineries don't exceed 15,000 bottles annually – most premium wines are unknown outside of Greece, but they can be as good (and expensive) as French, Italian or southern hemisphere rivals. The best island wines are reckoned to hail from Límnos, Rhodes, Sámos, Santoríni, Ikaría, Kefaloniá and, of course, Crete. Conversely, the Greek culinary renaissance included new-found

nutrient-rich river mouths of Anatolia and Dardanelles outflow, have the best choice. The profile changes from spring, with the last of the shrimp and sole, to early summer's swordfish and *marídes* (pickarel), to the deliciously flash-fried *atheřína* (sand smelt) and *gávros* (anchovy), plus grillable *sardélles* (sardines) and *koliós* (mackerel), on the cusp between summer and autumn. The last two also make excellent marinated *mezédes*. Other affordable seafood includes grilled or stewed octopus and cuttlefish prepared with rice and greens. Once poor people's food, now trendy and expensive, are sea urchin roe and *foúskes*, a bizarre invertebrate of the Dodecanese which tastes much like oysters.

esteem for bulk wines, which had nearly disappeared. Some is great, some barely quaffable, but bulk wine will rarely break the bank.

Oúzo, the national aperitif, is distilled from grape-mash residue left over from winemaking, and then flavoured with aniseed or fennel; strength is typically 40–48 percent alcohol. The best island labels come from Lésvos, Híos and Sámos. Unflavoured variants of *oúzo* include *tsípouro* (on Thássos and the Sporades), and *rakí* or *tsikoudiá* (Crete). ❏

ABOVE LEFT: try the humbler, seasonally available species of fish. **ABOVE:** a *frappé*, icy cold coffee whipped up in a shaker. **RIGHT:** the covered market, Rhodes New Town.

Eating Your Way Round the Islands

Traditional Greek food is better than its reputation, especially if you ignore what's offered for tourists and seek out traditional local dishes

Anyone who has experienced tourist menus of chicken and chips or microwaved *moussakás* can be excused for believing that Greece isn't the place for culinary delights. So for a taste of real Greek cooking, follow the locals to backstreet tavernas. The food at such traditional places, geared for a lunch-hour clientele, more than compensates for any lack of fancy decor. If communication is a problem, take a look at what's cooking and point at what you want. Ordering this way is accepted practice.

You'll soon find there's more to Greek cuisine than kebabs and *taramosaláta*. Vegetables like fresh green beans, okra or butter beans, cooked in olive oil and tomato; hearty fish soups; cheese, leek or spinach pies with a feather-light filo pastry; cuttlefish with spinach or rabbit stew; courgette flowers stuffed with rice and fried in batter – the islands offer dishes for all tastes. There are plenty of vegetarian options because of the many fast days in the Orthodox calendar. But fish is usually expensive, whether sold by weight or by portion.

Regional variations reflect island history, and many dishes have strong Italian and Turkish influences from past occupations. You'll find pastas and pilafs, plus vegetable recipes like *briám* and *imám baïldí*, their foreign names absorbed into Greek menus.

From the *krasotýri* of Kós, the *sofríto* (veal casserole) of Corfu to the *froutála* omelettes of Andros, every island has its speciality. Some may seem strange – *foúskes* (a marine invertebrate) or *kokorétsi* (spit-roasted offal) are not for the faint-hearted – but most island food is delicious. If all else fails, *horiátiki*, the classic Greek village salad, with feta, olives, peppers, cucumber and tomato, takes some beating.

ABOVE: the informal taverna is the m[ost] common form of eatery, often with tables outside and music at night. For [a] wider menu, look for an *estiatório*.

LEFT: yet-to-be-ripe figs on the branc[h]

LEFT: *loukánika*, home-made sausages to a traditional recipe.

RIGHT: the fish and seafood of the Aegean is delicious but scarce, so prices can be high.

AND SOMETHING TO DRINK?

You can drink anything in Greece from cocktails to local firewater. *Oúzo*, the national aperitif, is flavoured with aniseed and turns milky when water is added. It's usually drunk with olives or other starters *(mezédes)*. If you prefer wine, *retsína* (white or rosé wine flavoured with pine resin, *right*) is an acquired taste, ranging from lightly to heavily scented.

Popular inexpensive wines include Cambas Attikos and Rhodian CAIR, available in reds, whites and rosés, but if you want something better, go for Emery's crisp white Villaré, Tsantalí Agiorítiko in white and red, or anything from Límnos. Try local wines like Gentilini Robola white from Kefaloniá or boutique labels such as Papaïoánnou or Skoúras. Over half a dozen varieties of beer are available, mostly lager.

After dinner try Greek brandy, Metaxá, which comes in three starred grades. Any *kafenío* (coffee bar) will serve up Greek coffee – *skéto* (without sugar), *glykó* (sweet) or *métrio* (medium). Decent espressos or filter coffees are steadily displacing a prior fixation with bad instant formulas.

ABOVE: *Retsína* is usually better from the barrel, but bottled brands like Liokri, Malamatína and Georgiádi are fine.

BELOW: restaurants may come up with their own variations on the classic *horiátiki* salad, but Greek law dictates that any salad going by that name should contain a generous helping of *féta*.

OVE: a *psistariá* (grill house) ers spit-roasts and charcoal-led meat – lamb, kid, pork, l, chicken – by weight.

HT: *kataífi* is made from a micelli-like pastry of edded filo dough, filled 1 chopped nuts and nched in honey syrup.

CRUISING ROUND THE ISLANDS

Greeks have sailed between the islands for thousands of years. Today it is possible to follow in their wake, on anything from day-trips to all-inclusive luxury cruises

Having around 100 inhabited islands means having ships to serve them, and Greece has a long shipping tradition. Anyone who has sailed the Aegean, where white cruise-ship superstructures rival the dazzling sun itself, knows the affinity Greeks have for their boats.

The giants of the past, such as Aristotle Onassis and Stávros Niárhos, are no longer with us, and their successors keep a much lower profile. They are there, however: hundreds of Greek shipping companies operating out of 1 sq km (0.4 sq miles) of office blocks in the port city of Piraeus and overlooking the seafront at Aktí Miaoúli, where international bankers in pinstriped suits rub shoulders with burly crewmen headed for the NAT (seamen's social fund) building.

Despite economic turmoil, owners remain emotionally committed to their businesses. In terms of satisfaction, little can equal gazing out of one's air-conditioned headquarters and watching one's ship come in. The same feeling must have prompted the great 18th-century captains of Hydra and Spétses to build their *arhondiká*, or mansions, facing out to sea.

The transportation of goods to and from the Greek islands is fundamental to their economies. For visitors to the country, however, best is the pleasure of being cargo, the joys of cruising.

Which cruise to choose?

The most frequent voyages in Greece are one-day cruises, most of them operating out of Piraeus or the Flísvos marina at Paleó Fáliron, just outside Athens, and taking you to the islands of Aegina, Hydra and Póros; some one-day cruises depart from Iráklio, Crete, bound for Santoríni.

There are also three, four, seven, nine- and ten-day cruises, most of them operating out

ONE-DAY WONDERS

A typical one-day cruise from Piraeus or Fáliron is an excellent introduction to the Greek islands. You will visit the 5th-century BC Temple of Aphaea *(Aféa)* on Aegina, one of the finest in all Greece; at Póros you will pass through the narrow straits with the town's tile-roofed houses towering above the ship on one side and extensive lemon groves on the other, mainland side; in Hydra you will stroll through the beautiful little town arrayed around the harbour. There are also one-day cruises from Iráklio, Crete, to Santoríni – sailing into that remarkable caldera is one of the highlights of Aegean travel.

of Piraeus, though some worthwhile one-week cruises (Variety Cruises; www.varietycruises.com), on pleasantly intimate small boats, visit Santoríni, Mýkonos, Spétses and Monemvasiá from Iráklio and Réthymno on Crete. Variety Cruises' subsidiary Zeus does more excellent, small-ship,

> Examine itineraries carefully before you book. Ideally you should be covering long stretches of open sea after dark, with overnights or late-night stays only in interesting ports like Návplio, Mýkonos or Pátmos. Many cruises are simply too rushed.

one-week cruises confined to a chosen island group: the Dodecanese (out of Rhodes), the Ionians (out of Kefaloniá or Zákynthos) and, of course, the Cyclades from Piraeus.

It is wise to opt for a longer cruise on a reputable Greek line such as Variety, Louis (www.louiscruises.com) or Royal Olympic Cruises (www.royal-olympic-cruises.com), because their ships – while perhaps not up to the luxury standards of transatlantic or Caribbean cruises – are usually small enough (capacity under 1,000 passengers) to manoeuvre into most chosen harbours, and do not dwarf their destinations like the towering new generation of gin palaces. They constitute the best way to see the most interesting ports in the eastern Mediterranean and Black Sea, in reasonable comfort and with good food.

A typical three-day cruise starts from Piraeus, taking in Mýkonos, Kuşadası (Ephesus) in Turkey, Pátmos, and either Rhodes or Crete; four-day cruises will definitely include all of the ports just noted, plus Santoríni, whereas a one-week cruise will stretch up to Istanbul too. Ten-day cruises forsake Turkey (except for Ephesus) in favour of add-ons to Katákolon (for ancient Olympia), Sicily and Genoa in Italy, plus Marseilles. It's also possible to circle much of the Black Sea coast in nine days, stopping at Varna (Bulgaria), Yalta (Russia), Trabzon and Samsum (Turkey) as well as Istanbul and Kavála in northern Greece. Much less frequently, there are seven-day cruises taking in the best of Cyprus, Egypt and Israel, with stops in Santoríni and Mýkonos.

LEFT: cruising in the Cyclades.
RIGHT: Santoríni's black volcanic cliffs make a dramatic backdrop to a cruise.

Politics at sea

As with all things Greek, there is a political dimension, hingeing on the word *cabotage*. Cabotage is an international legal term meaning, as far as Greek shipping companies are concerned, a monopoly on all lines connecting Greek domestic ports. Many foreign ships cruise Greek waters with passengers they bring from outside, and return to some port outside Greece, but cabotage has until now protected Greek cruise companies from foreign competition in Greek waters.

By decree of the European Union, this nautical monopoly was supposed to cease, for EU ships at least, in 2004. Since then, in theory,

the market has been incrementally opened, with many existing Greek ships improved and brand-new ships brought into service to stave off competition. It has certainly brought about a number of mergers and rationalisations to enable survival in trying times.

Greek governments are fond of imposing regulations, often impenetrable, usually expensive, upon every aspect of life imaginable, including Greek shipping. Many Greek shipowners have responded by registering their ships under a cheaper flag of convenience (usually Malta, Liberia or the Caymans). This was fine for international routes but, with cabotage in force despite EU mandates, foreign-registered ships still cannot cruise between the Greek islands. ❑

THE SAILING SCENE

Sailing is a rewarding way of exploring this country
of islands, whether in your own yacht, in a chartered
boat or as part of a flotilla

W hile the package holidaymaker and the independent island-hopper are forced to rely on the ferries and their often idiosyncratic timetables in order to travel among the islands, the yachtsman can enjoy a remarkable degree of independence – except, of course, from the winds. Sailing around Greece is not over-complicated by bureaucracy, but some paperwork, unfortunately, is unavoidable.

To sail into Greek waters in your own yacht, you need customs clearance in one of 29 designated entry ports (the list can be obtained from tourist boards or your country's national sailing authority) to obtain a Transit Log for yachts over 12 metres (39ft), or a Temporary Duty-Free Admission booklet for smaller yachts. Usually, both these documents are valid for six months and enable a crew to sail freely throughout the country. A visiting yacht should be officially registered in its country of origin and its skipper should make sure that each member of the

> Occasionally the hot, damp, southeasterly sirókos wind, often carrying reddish dust from North Africa, will blow hard across the southern Aegean and Ionian – but it doesn't last long.

crew has a valid passport. It's worth writing out a crew list with passport numbers so that any official check can be made easier.

Chartering, now a fundamental part of the sailing scene in Greece, began throughout the islands in the mid-1970s; it was the idea of an enterprising group of British boat-owners who decided that they had had enough of miserable English summers and wanted holidays in the sun. This type of sailing is increasingly prevalent and has done much to encourage the development of marinas and improved facilities. Increasing numbers in recent years have seen a spread of poorer-quality boats, but most reputable charter companies supply yachts that are renewed every five years or so. They are designed for holidays in the sun and equipped to a luxurious standard with deep freezes, deck showers, snorkelling equipment and even a pair of gardening gloves to handle the anchor chain.

Making the right choice

It's important to match experience with the correct type of charter. Inexperienced sailors should select a flotilla holiday where a group of yachts cruise as a fleet, under the instructive eye of a lead boat crew. If you are an experienced sailor, you may want to arrange a "bare boat" charter, in which you act as your own skipper. If you can afford a crewed charter, you can simply relax on deck and leave all the sailing, boat handling, cooking and bureaucracy to paid hands.

Whether you're taking your own yacht to Greece or chartering, the range of sailing areas is large and your choice should take account of varying local weather conditions.

The recognised sailing season is from April to October, when the skies are mostly clear; temperatures vary between 25° and 35°C (80s

must take care not to be caught on a lee shore, and should be aware that the *meltémi* can cause an extremely uncomfortable steep, short sea.

In the northern Aegean the *meltémi* blows from just east of north and, further south towards the Cyclades and Crete, predominantly from true north. By the time it reaches Kárpathos, Rhodes and other southerly Dodecanese, this wind has gathered even more strength and is from the northwest. Its local violence has persuaded some charter companies to classify the Dodecanese as the most difficult waters in which to sail.

Sailing in the Dodecanese has the additional problem of the nearby Turkish maritime

and 90s Fahrenheit) in July and August. Winds throughout the Aegean Sea tend to be from the north. The most talked-about weather phenomenon is the *meltémi*, a steady north wind which can affect the entire Aegean, and can reach Force 7 to 8 on the Beaufort scale in midsummer. It's a capricious wind, typically appearing around mid-June and dying down in late September. Usually the *meltémi* arises just before or after midday and calms with sunset, but can arrive without warning and blow for as little as one hour or for as long as one week. Yachtsmen

LEFT: yachting offers a high level of independence.
ABOVE: when choosing a sailing area, bear in mind the varying local weather conditions.

border. The Turks insist that anyone sailing in their waters must clear customs at one of their ports of entry. The border is policed at sea and it is therefore unwise to enter Turkish waters unless you intend to enter Turkey officially.

Weather-reporting in Greece is generally good. If you have a weather fax you can get up-to-date information whenever you need it, as you also can from VHF channels 16 and 25. Virtually every Greek evening newscast is followed by a weather report which someone can translate for you, and the port authorities will be well informed. If you have a laptop and proximity to a wi-fi zone (increasingly common in marina cafés), log on

MARINAS AROUND THE ISLANDS

The biggest concentration of marinas is on the coast near Athens and Piraeus, though these are not particularly aesthetic. Other major marinas among or near Greek islands are at Kalamariá, just outside Thessaloníki; at Gouviá, about an hour's sail north from Corfu Town; and at Corfu Town itself. The recently enlarged marina at Levkáda is right in town, just off the canal. In the Dodecanese, there's a large marina at Mandráki on Rhodes, which is more suited to larger yachts, plus smaller ones on Kálymnos and Léros. The 2008-inaugurated one at Pythagório (Sámos) is enormous and ideal as an end point for a one-way itinerary. All these marinas make excellent staging posts/charter bases.

to www.meteo.gr or www.poseidon.ncmr.gr, the latter with useful wind-and-waves graphic profiler; www.sailingissues.com is another useful site.

The Saronic Gulf and the Ionian Sea offer the gentlest sailing conditions, mainly because the islands are relatively close to each other (and to the mainland) and because the *maístros*, the more northwesterly variant of the *meltémi* in the Ionian, is usually far weaker. The *maístros* tends to blow only in the afternoon, when the heat of the Greek mainland accelerates the wind off the sea.

Despite this variety of local winds, Greek seas are often quite windless, so yachtsmen should be prepared to motor. Whatever the conditions, you should always protect yourself against the sun and the increased glare off the water – which can produce temporary blindness.

The greatest appeal of the Greek islands is the solitude offered by their remoteness. The green islands of the Ionian are a frequent first-choice venue for a number of reasons. The shelter among the many islands offers safe cruising, but if you want more lively conditions, a trip in the open waters to the west of Levkáda (Léfkas) and Kefaloniá will provide marvellous sailing. Easy anchorages and safe village moorings are within a few hours' sail of each other throughout these islands. The best time to sail here is definitely during spring and autumn: August sees Italian yachtsmen pouring over from Italy, clogging up the numerous but small harbours.

The Saronic Gulf is a favourite haunt of yachtsmen because it is so close to Piraeus. The little island of Angístri, off Aegina, has some lovely coves; Póros, Hydra and Spétses have attractive town harbours as well as quieter anchorages; and the east coast of the Peloponnese is unjustly underrated. In mid-season it will be difficult to find a berth at the town quays where, almost without exception, mooring is stern or bow to the quay.

Moving east from the Saronic Gulf, the influence of the *meltémi* becomes stronger, and it is not until you travel north of Évvia to the Sporades that you find dependable shelter in any weather – each island here has a protected, south- or southeast-facing harbour. Beyond Skýros to the northeast lies the open, and generally wild, Aegean, with little casual sailing owing to the great distances involved. From the Sporades, most skippers make for the inlets and peninsulas of the Halkidikí peninsula, east of Thessaloníki. ❏

Island-Hopping

The pleasures of travelling from one island to another using Greece's interlinking ferry routes are numerous, but it pays to be prepared.

First there's the never-ceasing view – a bas-relief pattern on a blue base of low, mysterious summits. Then, a chance to mingle with the Greeks themselves, who pile on board with food, children and, as often as not, a *bouzoúki* or two. Plus, a unique opportunity to visit other islands not on the itinerary – 15 minutes observing a port from the top deck can reveal much about a place and its people. A bustle of activity occurs just below the rear railing: reunions, farewells and the redistribution of a warehouse's worth of goods. Is that a piano or an ice-cream freezer being offloaded? Is that cheeping coming from an embarking truck with a battery farm of chickens?

Without thorough advance checking, however, it's easy to experience the worst aspects of island-hopping in the form of missed connections, being stranded, or even sailing straight past the intended island and then having to make a two-day journey to reach it again. Even ferry journeys that go according to plan can be lengthy, not to mention nerve-racking rather than restful: if the boat reaches your small, remote destination at 2am, it's your responsibility to wake up – set your alarm – and get off. However, a hasty departure in darkness has deposited more than one traveller on the wrong island altogether.

Weather is an overriding factor. The *meltémi* is a fact of Greek summer life, unaffected thus far by global climate change. When winds are too strong, ships are delayed or kept in port. If you are depending upon ferries to take you back to Athens for your flight home, leave at least one full day's leeway. Athens has its pleasures; missing your flight home does not.

Among the most renowned ferry routes are the central Cyclades circuit (Mýkonos, Páros, Náxos, Íos and Santoríni), the Argo Saronic line (Póros, Hydra, Spétses), and that serving the major Dodecanese (Pátmos, Léros, Kálymnos, Kós and Rhodes). Less popular, and thus more satisfying, are the western Cyclades arc (Kýthnos, Sérifos, Sífnos and Mílos), the main Sporades islands (Skiáthos, Skópelos, Alónnisos), and the link between Rhodes and Crete via

Hálki, Kárpathos and Kásos. In the Ionian islands, it's easy to travel between Levkáda, Itháki and Kefaloniá. Besides Piraeus, the most important mainland ports are Lávrio, Rafína, Thessaloníki, Kavála, Vólos and Pátra; on the islands, Páros, Sámos, Rhodes and Kós are useful regional hubs.

Hydrofoils and larger catamarans which carry cars play a significant role in inter-island travel. They are twice as fast as conventional ferries – ideal if time is limited – but also twice as expensive, and not without other disadvantages. Both "cats" and hydrofoils provide practically no view, and both are far more sensitive to bad weather than conventional boats. A good compromise is the newer generation of *tahyplía*

or "high speed" ferries (especially Blue Star's), which cost little more than the old tubs but sail a good deal more quickly. Hydrofoils have also been known to stay in port rather than depart simply because there were not enough passengers to justify the trip.

The most comprehensive, up-to-date source of ferry schedules is the website of the Greek travel agents' manual, *Greek Travel Pages* (www.gtp.gr). You'll notice that peripheral, subsidised lines – the so-called *agonés grammés* – often have user-hostile schedules, either with uncivilised departure/arrival hours, unhelpful frequencies (departures on two consecutive days, then nothing for five), or both. The ministry which pays shipowners handsome subsidies does not in exchange seem to stipulate the provision of rational, tourist-friendly timetables. ❑

LEFT: private craft moored in Páros harbour.
RIGHT: island-hopping in the major Dodecanese.

MANAGING THE TOURISTS

Mass tourism has not brought many destination islands what they wanted. Diverse remedies have been attempted, but there is still quite some way to go

Greece supports a permanent indigenous population of 10.4 million. Yet every year – even in a very bad one like 2009 – at least as many foreign tourists descend on the country, while over 13 million appear in good seasons. Tourism has been the second-largest or largest foreign-exchange earner for Greece since the early 1970s, and accounts for 20 percent of gross domestic product.

Accordingly, Greece's first Ministry of Tourism was put in charge of EOT (the Greek National Tourism Organisation) in 1987 to address long-neglected crises in the industry. After being sub-sumed by PASOK governments into the ministries of Development and Economy on two occasions, it was revived by the ND government in 2004 as the Ministry for Touristic Development. But over the years ambitious ministry initiatives have had little effect, not least because most ministers have no experience in tourism and are anyway rotated in cabinet shuffles every 18 months. EOT, devoting most of its energies to dubious marketing slogans like "Greece, the authentic experience", or "5,000 years of history you can afford", has argu-ably outlived its usefulness and might be better off divided into lean, mean regional entities, as has been done in Spain.

Growing pains, theoretical remedies

Touristic Greece had, by 1987, become a victim of its own success – and of unplanned growth, beginning under the junta, when easy credit was extended to build hotels and *domátia* (pri-vate rented rooms). Popular islands teemed with

thousands of summer visitors; streets designed for a donkey and two passers-by became rivers of slow-moving gawpers; hotels were booked far in advance, disappointing foolhardy travellers who arrived on spec. Arid, smaller islands, supplied by tanker, had to ration water for visitor showers.

Beaches were packed with sun-worshippers lying only inches apart, including nude sun-bathers inimical to the sensibilities of conser-vative native islanders. Still less popular were thousands of penniless backpackers arriving without pre-reserved accommodation: they would often indulge in petty crime, and ended up sleeping rough on rooftops or beaches.

Ferryboats were consistently overcrowded at

LEFT: sun, clean seas and sand (or shingle) have made for a winning tourist formula. **RIGHT:** easy riders.

high season, and the craft themselves – retired from more demanding North Sea or Baltic services, pending relegation to Southeast Asia, or the wrecker's yard – were nothing to write home about either. Seats on island-hopping aeroplanes had to be booked two months in advance, and transitting cramped 1960s airports approximated the Black Hole of Calcutta.

The ministry's late-1980s response was to promote quality clientele over quantity. Impecunious backpackers were to be discouraged in favour of specialised, high-spend tourism, and the necessary infrastructure projects built. An initial measure forbade admission to charter-flight passengers with no accompanying room reservation, so as to quash "hooliganism" among young tourists. Athens also put a theoretical halt to licensing C-class hotels and B-class rooms on islands over-supplied with them, while granting more permits for A- and luxury-class hotels, with generous incentives for facilities such as golf courses, tennis courts and convention halls.

But with the connivance of seat-only operators, the accommodation requirement was easily circumvented. Required vouchers soon became dummies, or were valid only for the first night, and anyway could not be enforced for EU nationals after 1993. Local bribes frequently neutralised national or urban controls on hotel-building permits.

Reality bites

Restored spas on Lésvos, a new marina on Híos where few yachters go – a more useful one on Sámos took 17 years to finish – and proposed golf courses in a perennially water-short environment: such "solutions" seemed like shuffling deckchairs on the *Titanic*, so inadequate was Greece's chaotic infrastructure.

Uneven accommodation distribution was the main bugbear. By early 1998 there were almost 1 million licensed beds in hotels and *domátia* – up to nearly 1.4 million in 2008 – with several provinces (such as Sámos and Iráklio) suffering from vast excess capacity, while other spots remain under-supplied; 1970s-vintage room quality reflected a cheap and cheerful mentality, ignoring the fact that travellers now had some better-value choices – though necessary renovations accelerated from the 1990s onwards.

The ferryboat scandals of 1996, when boats were loaded to double safe capacity, were confronted by theoretically mandatory computerised booking and ticketing. Numerous exceptions were finally winkled out by the September 2000 wreck of the *Express Samira*, which glaringly exposed the ongoing shortcomings of Aegean shipping. Many rust-buckets were subsequently junked, but by no means all – shipowners have repeatedly wangled exceptions to the EU law ordering disposal of 30-year-old craft. Reputable companies now do order purpose-built, state-of-the-art boats rather than relying on cast-offs from Northern Europe; but high-speed boats, with their enormous fuel consumption, only financially break even when three-quarters full of passengers – which happens during summer only.

BARBARIANS AT THE GATES – AGAIN

Louts, especially British ones, returned in a big way to resorts like Faliráki (Rhodes) and Kávos (Corfu) either side of the millennium, drawn by a pub-crawl culture where tour company reps got illegal backhanders from bars and clubs. In August 2003, a young English lad was fatally stabbed outside a Faliráki club and others arrested on charges of public lewdness. Rhodian authorities reacted sternly, succeeding in turning Faliráki into a ghost town after dark. The party merely shifted to more amenable locales on Crete and Zákynthos, where islanders who thought they'd seen everything with nude hippies on the beaches in the 1980s were treated to the spectacle of public sex.

Private competitors to Olympic Airways have emerged – and survived – since the 1990s deregulation of domestic aviation, and Olympic Air (as it is now named) itself liquidated and reformed as a private entity in October 2009. Popular peripheral flights such as Rhodes–Sámos or Corfu–

> A vast cultural gap yawns between Greeks in all walks of life, and young British ravers on Crete and the Ionians. Said one Zakynthian policeman, "When we get drunk, we get merry and maybe louder. We don't wreck the place."

Zákynthos – the subsidised PSO (Public Service Obligation) routes – have to be run by somebody under law; but Olympic's concession for these expired end 2009, and it is debatable whether the re-tendering process will result in fares cutomers are happy to pay, or a government subsidy that the EU would approve. Even on profitable main routes, frequencies and seat availability remain stubbornly inadequate in high season.

Hopes and prospects

A budget, studio-based package in Greece compares in price to one in competing Mediterranean destinations such as Turkey, Croatia or Tunisia. A higher-quality Greek holiday costs nearly the same as the exotic delights of Cuba, Goa or Florida. Individuals who love Greece, have a connection with a particular place and speak a bit of the language continue to return regularly; but the country overall hasn't been trendy since the 1970s and stacks up poorly against Spain and Italy in food, wine and service quality and value. While Greece does have resorts as exclusive as any in the world, for the most part professionalism and a service ethic are lacking, especially on the agricultural islands – an ingrained farming mentality doesn't easily assimilate notions like training and investment.

The mountain to climb in terms of attracting new visitors and keeping old customers is a huge one, but it can be done through addressing weak areas and playing to the islands' strengths: clean seas, a high degree of personal safety, characterful inland villages, affordable low-impact

LEFT: after its beaches, the largely tasteful nightlife of Skiáthos is its big draw. **RIGHT:** the islands are the setting for a range of wallet-friendly, low-impact sports.

sports *(see page 88)*. Little headway has been made in extending the tourist season – in fact, more and more places are making their main living from mid-July to late August – and to be fair, Greece is vulnerable to forces beyond its control: a strong euro, the economy of Northern European countries, Schengen Zone rules and uproar in the aviation industry. Nonetheless, there is scope for improvement even within the new realities; for example, weekend visits by Turks to the border islands could be encouraged by reducing visa fees. (On many islands the tourist "crop" has already changed character, with nationalities unseen a decade ago now

prevalent: Slovenians, Czechs, Poles, Russians.)

A worrisome development belying a supposed commitment to upscale tourism is the spread of all-inclusive resorts. These are paid a risible per-passenger sum by the contracting overseas companies, and the full board they offer has devastated nearby tavernas – a far cry from when a taverna outing used to be a quintessential part of the island experience. Potentially more positive is the upswing in residential tourism, repeat visitors who have bought island property and help keep shops and businesses going. And much more can still be done with Greece's abundant medieval ruins and historic buildings: boutique hotel proprietors report nearly 100 percent occupancy even in lean years. ❑

OUTDOOR PURSUITS

With over seven months of clement weather annually, the Greek islands are an obvious venue for all manner of sporting activities, from leisurely rambles to the adrenalin-rush-inducing thrills of newer sports

Time was – not so long ago – that all an island had to offer was a few patches of beach (whether sandy or pebbly), some bars or cafés as meeting points, and a reasonable choice of food and accommodation, and it was likely to have met the expectations of its prospective clientele. More energetic pastimes meant hiking inland and uphill from the beach onto the network of trails which still existed, largely intact, until the 1990s. No longer: visitors, especially younger ones, now expect to be tempted by a range of often high-tech options which have pretty well eclipsed walking and the modest commitment of those who remembered to tuck a mask and snorkel into their luggage.

On land

Despite destructive nibblings by bulldozers since the 1970s, a considerable portion of historic paths and exquisitely engineered *kalderímia* (cobbled lanes) – many centuries old and the only link between villages in pre-vehicle days – survives. Perhaps counter-intuitively, the biggest, greenest islands are not always the best choices for hiking; ongoing agriculture means that many old paths have been widened into muddy, tractor-width lanes. Reliable islands for quality trail-walking (best during the cooler months) include Níssyros, Sými, Kálymnos and Tílos in the Dodecanese; Anáfi, Andros, Tínos, Sífnos and Amorgós in the Cyclades; Alónisos in the Sporades and Hydra in the Argo-Saronic. The granddaddy of small-island walks is the five-hour lengthwise traverse from Hóra to Egiáli on Amorgós, an island – with its protected network of *kalderímia* and profuse documentation – that has done more than most others to promote walking.

Honourable exceptions to the big-island rule are western Sámos around mounts Kérkis and Karvoúnis, Corfu with its marked and maintained 200km (125-mile) Corfu Trail, and Crete, with two mountain ranges rising to over 2,400 metres (7,874ft): the westerly White Mountains cradling the Samariá Gorge.

Besides a surprisingly extensive trail network, Kálymnos has some of the best big-wall climbing in the Mediterranean on its limestone cliffs, especially in the north – again, an off-season activity unless you fancy baking against the sheer faces.

On the sea

With gold or silver medallists at the last three Olympics, windsurfing has the cachet in Greece

> The best topographical hiking maps, covering most islands listed, are published by Anávasi (www.anavasi.gr) in Athens; otherwise local maps and guide booklets exist.

that cycling has in France. While it might seem windy – and boards are on offer – almost everywhere, only certain resorts have the right combination of exposure and onshore topography to be world-class. Indeed, sites like southern Kárpathos, Prassonísi on Rhodes and Vassilikí on Levkáda do host annual European tournaments; but Kamári

Amorgós; many tours are organised here by SwimTrek (www.swimtrek.com). Sea kayaking is a slightly less strenuous way of covering much the same territory and visiting otherwise inaccessible coastal formations. The rewards are subtle but tangible, like glimpsing brightly hued kingfishers perching on sea-level rocks in autumn.

Under the sea

Scuba-diving has been slow to take off in Greece, owing to historical restrictions on the practice: so much archaeological wealth is assumed still to be submerged that the government has generally denied applications to authorise new dive zones

on Kós, Agios Geórgios on Náxos, Kokkári on Sámos and Paleohóra on Crete will be more than enough for beginners and intermediates. Kitesurfing, where devotees standing on a small board are propelled very quickly by a parabolic kite controlled with four lines, is like windsurfing on steroids. Frequently launched into the air, kitesurfers are the skateboarders of the sea.

Just about every island visitor gets into the Aegean, though perhaps not quite to the extent of inter-island swimmers, who think nothing of an afternoon's crawl back and forth amongst the smaller Cyclades lying between Náxos and

for fear of antiquity theft. In 2007, after years of lobbying, existing schools managed to have the list of allowable venues greatly expanded, especially around Rhodes, Skiáthos and Alónisos, and more venues should be opened once the painfully slow process of archaeological surveying is completed. The most reputable schools are on Skiáthos, Alónisos, Léros, Kálymnos, Mýkonos, Náxos, Mílos, Corfu (Paleokastrítsa), Kefaloniá, Sámos and Rhodes. Don't expect a tropical profusion of fish – the Aegean is far too exploited for that. The attraction lies rather in caves, tunnels and other formations, as well as in sedentary marine life. Léros, with its World War II wrecks and debris from the battle of autumn 1943, is arguably the most interesting spot. ❏

LEFT: kitesurfing on Levkáda. **ABOVE:** trails snake across the caldera floor of Níssyros's dormant volcano.

ISLAND WILDLIFE

The diverse island landscapes support a varied collection of flora and fauna. Birds in particular, both resident and migrant, bring delight to ornithologists

Arrive at a mid-Aegean island in the heat of summer and you may feel you've inadvertently stumbled upon a little-known outpost of the Sahara. Arid brown countryside sheds clouds of dust each time the hairdryer wind blows, and the only surviving plant life is in carefully nurtured village window-boxes.

Visit in spring, however, and the picture is an entirely different one. Lush greenery and brightly coloured flowers cover the plains and hillsides, and even waste ground becomes garden.

The first seedlings and bulbs sprout shortly after the first autumn rains. Growth gathers pace through the cool but partly sunny winters; a few weeks into the new year, flowers start to bloom in the far southeast. Rhodes, Kárpathos and eastern Crete are followed in succession by western Crete, then the Cyclades and the eastern Aegean. Spring arrives in the Ionian islands and the north Aegean as summer appears in Rhodes.

As plants lead, so other wildlife follows. The number of insects increases, and the insect-eaters flourish; food chains gear up for a spring and early summer of proliferation.

Plants a-plenty

Before mankind first settled in the region, the Greek islands had a mixture of forest, some tall, impenetrably dense *maquis* vegetation, and much *garrigue*. The latter consists of low shrubby bushes which are often spiny, resisting both the grazing of animals and the bare legs of walkers. Mixed together with the shrubs are fragrant herbs, colourful annuals and, enjoying protection under those spines, fragile orchids.

It's a myth that man and his flocks destroyed a verdant Greek Eden of continuous woodland: some larger islands had populations of wild plant-munching animals – such as deer – long before any human arrivals. Native grazers led to the flora's evolution of discouraging defences – spines, foul tastes – which armed it well for the comparatively recent introduction of domesticated sheep and goats. *(See also pages 94–5.)*

Reclusive mammals

Wild mammals occur on the islands, but most are secretive. Crete has its ibex-like wild goat or *agrími* (also called the *krí-krí*), a shy inhabitant of the White Mountains. Amid fears of its

LEFT: the domesticated goat.
RIGHT: a stone marten clambers atop a fallen branch.

demise from over-hunting, some animals were transferred to the island of Día, near Iráklio, where they flourished and multiplied – eliminating the rare native plants.

Elsewhere, the largest mammals are the badger, and the jackal of the eastern Aegean and Corfu, but the one you are more likely to see is the stone marten. This resembles a dark-brown ferret, long, slim, agile and fast-moving, sighted both during the day and in headlights crossing roads at night. They are frequent victims of the taxidermist's art, and many tavernas have one stuffed on display.

Most other mammals are small: field rats (common on Corfu and Sámos), rabbits or hares, wild

crossing. Both black and white storks migrate through Greece, nesting on the way. Individual flamingos may turn up anywhere there is a salty coastal pool, but you should visit Lésvos, Sámos and Límnos to see them nesting in quantity.

Much smaller, but most colourful, are the crested pink, white and black hoopoe, the bright blue and brown roller, and the multicoloured bee-eater. For many ornithologists, raptors – hawks, falcons, eagles and vultures – prompt the biggest thrill, although the most frequently sighted species is the common buzzard.

Larger species inhabit mountain areas, where gorges and cliffs provide secure nesting and the

mice, and a variety of bats that can move from island to mainland and vice versa.

The National Marine Park northeast of Alónnisos is an important haven for the Mediterranean monk seal – the most endangered of all the world's seals. About 55 of a total world population of under 400 live here. Between islands, look out for common dolphins shadowing ferries.

Twitchers' territory

While mammal-watchers may find themselves underemployed, the birdwatcher should not be. The spring migration brings a variety of species from Africa. Their final destination will probably be much further north, but the Greek islands may be their first landfall after the Mediterranean

> On Skýros there is a very small wild horse, a unique breed thought to be that depicted on the frieze of the Parthenon; less than 150 pure-bred specimens survive.

requisite isolation. Golden eagles may be the most romantic, but vultures are undoubtedly the most spectacular. Griffon vultures, sometimes in flocks of up to 20, patrol the skies in search of dead livestock, soaring effortlessly on broad wings the size of a door and then some. The scarcer lammergeier has narrow wings, the ultimate flying machine in its search for bones – or tortoises – to drop onto rocks and break open.

Reptiles and insects

The most abundant reptiles are lizards, some 21 species, of which the Balkan green lizard is perhaps the most conspicuous. Bolder and more stockily built is the iguana-like agama, sometimes called the Rhodes dragon, though it's also found on Corfu and several Aegean islands. Unlike others, this greyish rough-skinned lizard, when disturbed, will often stay around for a few minutes to check out the danger.

Tortoises occur on many islands, though surprisingly not on Crete. Once gathered in tens of thousands for the pet trade, they now lead safer lives wandering noisily through the under-

of being bitten. Poisonous vipers do occur on some of the Ionian, Cycladic and east Aegean islands – they usually have a zigzag pattern down the spine, and move rather lazily.

Mosquitoes may seem the commonest insects at night, but Corfu is noted for its springtime fireflies, little flashing beacons that drift over damp fields and hedges after dark. Paler lights in the hedgerows are wingless glow-worms. During the day, butterflies are obvious, often in great quantity and variety. Some of the large hawk-moths may be seen during the day – the hummingbird hawk-moth, like its namesake, relies on superfast wingbeats to hover at flowers as it feeds.

brush, especially during spring migration. Their freshwater aquatic relatives, the terrapins, favour streams with bare muddy banks for sunbathing.

Marine loggerhead turtles are decreasing in numbers as their nesting beaches are lost to tourism. They used to breed until the 1980s on Crete, Kós and Rhodes – now they are restricted to a few beaches on Kefaloniá and Zákynthos.

Snakes often cause alarm, but most are harmless, and all prefer to be left alone. Locals tend to overreact and attack any snake they see, though this is actually the best way to increase the chance

Noisier are the huge, glossy blue-black carpenter bees which spend much of their time looking for suitable nesting sites, usually a hollow cane. Noisiest of all is the cicada, basically an overgrown aphid, which perches – usually on a pine tree – and keeps up a deafening racket. Despite their size and volume, they are surprisingly hard to see. African locusts are really giant grasshoppers, though they never pillage in devastating swarms this side of the Mediterranean.

Praying mantids keep their barbed forearms in a position of supplication until an unwary insect moves nearby – then the mantid becomes a hungry atheist. Even the male of the species is devoured as he romances the female, his substance helping to nourish the next generation. ❏

LEFT: the white pelican, or *Pelecanus onocrotulus*. **ABOVE:** locusts, large but harmless. **ABOVE RIGHT:** the once-endangered tortoise.

THE ISLANDS IN BLOOM

The Greek islands are at their most colourful in spring and early summer, when every hillside and valley is bedecked with glorious flowers

Greece in spring is a botanist's (and photographer's) dream. Some 6,000 species of wild plant grow in mainland Greece and the islands, and in the spring (February to May) visitors may enjoy a magnificent cornucopia of flowers and fragrances.

Hillsides resemble giant rock gardens, while brilliantly coloured patches of untended waste ground outdo Northern Europe's carefully tended herbaceous borders with ease. Winter rains, followed by a bright, warm, frost-free spring, produce a season's blooming compressed into a few spectacular weeks before the summer's scorching heat and drought become too much. By late May or early June the flowers are done, the seeds for next year's show are ripening, and greens are fading to brown to match the tourists on the beaches.

Except in the cooler, higher mountains, most plants go into semi-dormancy to survive the arid summer. The first rains of autumn, as early as mid-September, but usually mid-October, tempt a few autumn bulbs into flower but also initiate the germination of seed plants that will grow and gather strength during the winter in preparation for the following spring when their flowers will again colour in the waiting canvas of the hills and valleys.

The richness and diversity of the flora are due in part to the islands' location between three continents – Europe, Asia and Africa – partly to the Ice Age survival in temperate Greece of pre-glacial species, and partly to the wonderful variety of habitats. Limestone, the foundation of much of Greece, is a favoured home for plants, providing stability, minerals, water supply and protection.

ABOVE: the hills are alive – sunshine, colour and quantity mark spring flowering of the islands, as here in the mountains of Crete, mid-April.

LEFT: the startling reds of *Anemone* coronaria mark the arrival of spring, and represent the spilt blood of the dying Adonis.

BEETLES, BEES AND BUTTERFLIES

The profusion of flowers and plants provides food for an equal profusion of insects. Butterflies are conspicuous from spring to autumn, including the swallowtail (above), whose equally colourful caterpillars feed on the leaves of common fennel. Its larger, paler and more angular relative, the Scarce swallowtail, despite its name, is even more abundant.

Look for clouded yellows and paler cleopatras, reddish-brown painted ladies and southern commas, white admirals and a myriad of smaller blue butterflies.

Butterflies, bees and day-flying hawk-moths tend to go for flowers with nectar, while beetles and flies go for the pollen. Some bugs even take advantage of the heat accumulated in the solar cup of many flowers in order to warm up their sex lives.

The leaves of plants feed armies of insect herbivores, which themselves are eaten by more aggressive insects. Some of the omnivorous Greek grasshoppers and crickets are as happy munching through a caterpillar, or even another grasshopper, as the grass it was sitting on.

RIGHT: wild artichokes are painfully spiny to prepare for the pot, but their delicate flavour is much prized by Greek country folk – over the spineless cultivated variety – and they are gourmet items in tavernas.

ᴠᴇ: the long flowering period of the native oleander makes it lar on city streets and as an ornamental roadside crash-barrier.

: according to legend, fire was brought to earth by Prometheus n in the smouldering stem of a giant fennel *(Ferula communis)*.

ISLANDS OUT OF SEASON

The onset of winter and the disappearance
of tourists bring a sudden and dramatic
change to the smaller Greek islands

It is only when the charter flights have ceased for the year that the real character of a small island staggers out of its unseasonable hibernation. Larger islands can absorb a deluge of visitors without having to adopt an entirely different identity. A visitor arriving in Crete in October would not discover, as may happen on a smaller island, that the post office was working a nine-hour week, matching boat arrivals, with daily operation not set to resume until the following spring. It is difficult to overstate the disfiguring impact that occurs when an island population measured in hundreds is swamped by four or five times as many people simultaneously.

Quick change

Superficially, the change into hibernal uniform is swift. Migrant waiters, kitchen staff and scooter-hire personnel depart to look for winter jobs elsewhere. Awnings over quayside cafés are rolled up and stowed, chairs and tables dragged away, tourist-geared shops boarded up; beaches are suddenly bereft of their loungers and umbrellas.

A good sign that the islanders have literally found their feet again, after the grinding hours put in during the season, is the resumption of the evening promenade or *vólta*, a quasi-formal ritual stroll in which small groups file from one end of a locally prescribed route to the other, and back again. Among them are the elderly and handicapped, seldom seen in public during the season. However, in a few large, untouristed towns, such as Híos port, the *vólta* continues year-round.

Winter visitors who join the throng are bound to attract curious glances from the traf-

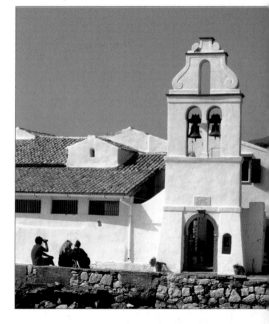

fic going in the opposite direction. The process of acceptance as an honorary member of the community is a ritual in itself. First, perhaps, a half-cocked eyebrow; later, a nod; then ultimately, triumphantly, a stop for a chat.

The *vólta* is a chance to observe all kinds of island machinery in motion. Orthodox priests, symbols of a notional propriety largely eclipsed by the summer heathens, reassert their magisterial presence among the faithful. Office-holders and petitioners in island politics fall into step beside the mayor for a peripatetic conference.

If municipal elections (usually in October) are imminent, the preliminary promenade-plotting will explode into campaigns complete with

LEFT: a *kafenío* on Aegina staying open during the cooler months. **RIGHT:** low-season Corfu.

mobile sound trucks and launching of fireworks by the winners. The party manifestos may commend or deplore, as the case may be, the state of the town drains, but the winner's powers of patronage are such that the outcome is regarded as a matter of economic life or death. Visitors can skip politics, however, and still feel that they are part of local life. Various religious festivals involve street processions, the mayor and priests conspicuously linked in secular-clerical solidarity at the head of an enthusiastic brass band.

The locals have to buy food and other supplies, so corresponding shops remain stocked (if not always with the same product lines as in sum-

mer). But no island is completely self-sufficient, and storms can play havoc with already reduced ferry services. Consequently, shelves go temporarily bare, and gas canisters for stoves and heaters may run out because the tanker-boat can't safely anchor opposite the fuel depot.

In calm seas, the fishermen sail at dusk and return at dawn but, for the rest of the male population, the longer nights are the cue to bring out the playing cards (or occupy themselves in other ways… Kastellórizo in particular has a huge quota of children, about 40 for its small adult population of about 200). Officially, no money changes hands, but substantial fractions of the summer takings surge back and forth. That said, the days when islanders in the seasonal tourism trade could spend all winter gambling away the proceeds in the *kafenío* are long gone: living costs have rocketed, and now everybody has to have a second enterprise to tide them over until spring.

Winter residence

Landlords don't expect to earn rent in winter, so out-of-season visitors will find prices negotiable. Prime accommodation near the sea may be worth a slight premium while the water is still at a tolerable temperature, although after September and before May many beaches can be annexed and occupied as private property. It's worth asking about vacant farmhouses; these have the simultaneous advantages of privacy, as well as neighbours popping around with eggs, greens and a bottle of local wine.

If outdoor conditions are an important criterion, southerly islands like Crete and Rhodes are marginally warmer. All across the Aegean, however, winter winds can cut to the bone, and houses not built specifically for the summer trade are more likely to have some form of heating. On more vegetated islands, the shriek of chainsaws in autumn heralds the stockpiling of firewood, the best of which are olive prunings. A basic, cast-iron wood stove is affordable; oil-fuelled radiators almost non-existent; catalytic gas heaters uneconomical. Even assuming a cosy interior, when the rain runs in muddy torrents down the village streets for hours on end, many expats discover the limits of their love for Greece.

An insider's view

The English novelist Simon Raven spent the winter of 1960 on Hydra looking into "what goes on when winter comes, when the last epicene giggle has hovered and died in the October air". He decided he was among a bunch of atavistic pirates who, happily engaged in making money during the summer, reverted in winter to the old distrust of strangers who used to come only to spy on their illicit booty.

Hydra has since acquired a considerable number of full-time expats and, assuming the Hydriots never read what Raven wrote, he would probably feel more comfortable among them now. But one of his conclusions stands the test of time: only in winter can one discern what the island is really like.   ❑

LEFT: an ancient provider of winter warmth on Ikaría.
RIGHT: January storm clouds over Hydra harbour.

PLACES

A detailed guide to all the island groups,
with their principal sites clearly
cross-referenced by number to the maps

The poet Odysséas Elýtis once said: "Greece rests on the sea." It's an observation that few countries could claim with such authority. Some 25,000 sq km (10,000 sq miles) of the Aegean and the Ionian seas are covered by islands, the exact number of which has, in characteristic Greek fashion, been subject to dispute. There may be 3,000 islands and islets, of which 167 are inhabited; a more realistic total is 2,000, with fewer than 90 inhabited.

The definition of "inhabited" is open to interpretation, too. Does a tiny *vrahonisída* (rocky islet), bare save for one shepherd and 20 goats, count as uninhabited? Can an island that is totally deserted except for pilgrimages made annually to a small chapel at its summit claim to be inhabited?

The truth is perhaps immaterial; both visitors and inhabitants are more interested in sea and sky than in facts and figures. What is indisputable, however, is the sheer variety of landscape and experience behind the familiar images.

This is what we attempt to show here; islands with an ancient past and a modern outlook, the complex choices and the pure, simple pleasures. In

order to accommodate everything implied in the phrase "a Greek island", we have devoted space to islets such as Agios Evstrátios and Télendos, as well as to well-known giants like Crete and Rhodes and holiday favourites such as Corfu and Mýkonos. We do not ignore the familiar, popular islands, but explore them with typical Insight thoroughness, to grasp the true heart of the place behind the tourist clichés.

So welcome aboard the ferry – and don't be fazed by spelling variations you will encounter on notices or road signs. We have tried to be consistent in transliterating place names, but the Greeks themselves are notoriously variable when rendering their language into Roman characters. For more on the Greek language, see the *Travel Tips* section at the back of this book. ❑

PRECEDING PAGES: Pythagório harbour, Sámos; reflections in Avithos Lake, Kefaloniá; lunchtime on Corfu. **LEFT:** Emborió harbour on Hálki, the island's only settlement. **FROM TOP:** day-trippers departing; Hydra felines; the cove of Lalária, Skiáthos.

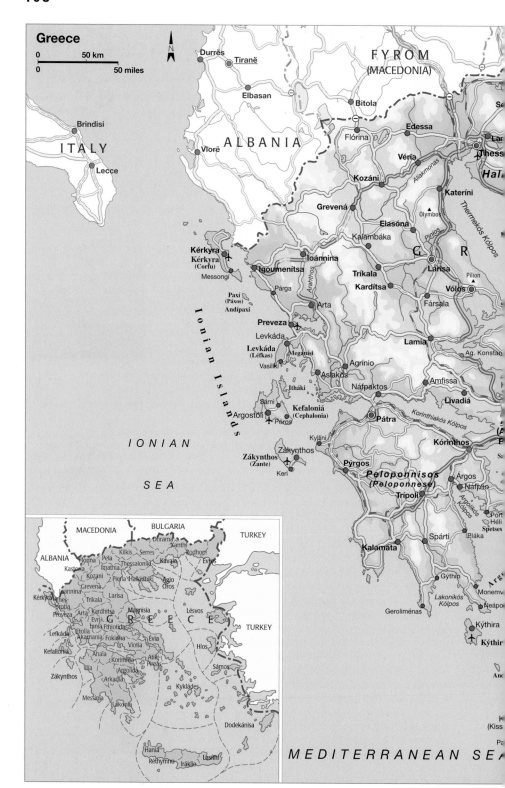

ATHENS STOPOVER

Large and hectic, often spectacular, always exhilarating, Athens can be simply exhausting. But if you have a day or two to look around, there's plenty to see

Athens was suddenly designated capital of the new Greek state after the War of Independence, and despite diligent Bavarian attempts at town planning – largely disregarded – it never mellowed into a venerable old age. Since the post-1923 influx of refugees, Athens has grown haphazardly and rapidly, with incongruent juxtapositions of old and new, such as a faded neoclassical mansion, still with a garden, ensconced between modern office blocks, its windows hermetically closed against the traffic roar. A whole raft of infrastructure projects completed before the 2004 Olympics – most notably the efficient metro system – have made this brash, sometimes plain ugly capital much more liveable.

Branching off from the frenzied central arteries are the less congested minor veins of the city; most apartment blocks have balconies or full-sized verandas, where you glimpse half-clad Athenians emerging from their afternoon siesta to read the paper, water their plants, or prepare and eat their evening meal. The hot weather makes open-air life a necessity, or at least open-window life, as prime-time television draws folk indoors.

Ancient Athens

If your time in Athens is limited, it makes sense to start with the premier monuments dating from Ancient Athens's "Golden Age", the 5th century BC. Seen from the right angle, driving or walking along below, the **Acropolis ❶** (daily, summer 8am–7pm, winter 8.30am–4.30pm; charge) can still make the grimy concrete fade into insignificance. Climb up in the early morning, when crowds are thinnest, and a strip of blue sea edged with grey hills marks the southwestern horizon.

The **Propylaia**, the official entrance to the Acropolis built by Mnesikles around 430 BC, was cleverly designed with imposing columns to impress people coming up the hill. Parts of its coffered stone ceiling, once painted

---

Main attractions
PARTHENON
TEMPLE OF OLYMPIAN ZEUS
PLÁKA QUARTER
NEW ACROPOLIS MUSEUM
GOULANDRÍS CYCLADIC MUSEUM
BYZANTINE AND CHRISTIAN
  MUSEUM
NATIONAL ARCHAEOLOGICAL
  MUSEUM

LEFT: looking past the Acropolis out to sea (viewed from Lykavitós hill).
BELOW: shopping around Sýndagma.

Supporting the porch of the Erechtheion, the Caryatids' faces still bear the pigments of ancient "make-up".

and gilded, are still visible. On what was once the citadel's southern bastion, from which King Aegeus legendarily threw himself off when his son Theseus forgot to change his signal-sail from black to white, is the small, square temple of **Athena Nike**, finished in 421 BC, and recently completely rebuilt.

The scaffolded **Parthenon** looks a bit like a stonemason's workshop, just as it must have done in the 440s BC when it was under construction as the centrepiece of Pericles' giant public works programme. Some of his contemporaries thought it extravagant, accusing Pericles of dressing his city up like a harlot. In fact, the Parthenon celebrates Athena as a virgin goddess and the city's protector. Her statue, 12 metres (39ft) tall, and made of ivory and gold plate to Phidias' design, used to gleam in the dim interior. In late antiquity it was taken to Constantinople, where it disappeared.

The **Erechtheion**, an elegant, architecturally complex repository of ancient cults going back to the Bronze Age, was restored around the millennium. Completed in 395 BC, a generation after the Parthenon, it once contained the supposed tomb of King Kekrops, mythical founder of the ancient Athenian royal family. The Caryatids now supporting the porch are modern copies; four surviving originals (one is missing, one is in the British Museum) are prize exhibits in the **New Acropolis Museum** (*see page 115*).

On the south side of the Acropolis lies the **Theatre of Dionysios ❷** (daily, summer 8am–7pm, winter 8.30am–3pm; charge). Surviving marble seating tiers date from around 320 BC and later, but scholars generally agree that plays by Aiskhylos, Sophokles, Euripides and Aristophanes were first staged here at 5th-century BC religious festivals. A state subsidy for theatregoers meant that every Athenian citizen could attend these events.

Herodes Atticus, a wealthy Greek landowner and Roman senator, built another theatre on the south slope of the Acropolis in the 2nd century AD: the steeply raked **Herodes Atticus Theatre ❸** (aka the Iródio), which is now used during the Hellenic Festival

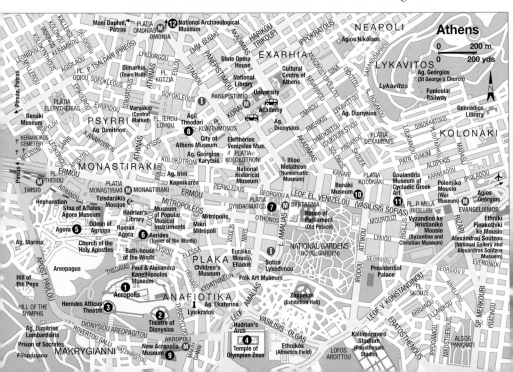

for performances of popular music, opera and ballet.

Earlier in the 2nd century, Roman Emperor Hadrian, a fervent admirer of classical Greece, erected an ornate **arch** marking the spot where the classical city ended and the provincial Roman university town began. Little of this Roman city can be seen beneath the **National Gardens**, or the archaeological area behind the towering columns of the **Temple of Olympian Zeus** ❹ (Stíles Olymbíou Dioú; daily, summer 8am–7pm, winter 8am–3pm; charge), but recent excavations indicate that numerous Roman buildings stood in this area, at least as far as the **Panathenaic Stadium** (Kallimármaro), refurbished by Herodes Atticus. Work on the temple had been abandoned in around 520 BC when funds ran out, but Hadrian finished the construction and donated a statue of Zeus as well as one of himself.

As the Acropolis was mainly used for religious purposes, while the ancient Greek **Agora** ❺ (daily, summer 8am–7pm, winter 8.30am–3pm; charge) was employed for most other public activities – commercial, political, civic and educational. Today it looks like a cluttered field of ruins, but the reconstructed **Stoa of Attalos**, a 2nd-century BC shopping mall, is a refreshingly cool place to linger and houses a worthwhile museum of Agora finds. The completely intact **Hephaestion**, the Doric temple opposite (often misnamed the Thisseion), is rather clunky compared to the Parthenon.

A 1st-century BC astronomer, Andronikos of Kyrrhos, designed the picturesque **Tower of the Winds** ❻ (Aerides; daily 8.30am–3pm), a well-preserved marble octagon within the scanty remains of the **Roman Agora** (daily, summer 8.30am–7.30pm, winter 8.30am–3pm; charge). The tower is decorated with eight relief figures, each depicting a different breeze, and once contained a water-clock.

One block north of the tower stand the remains of what is known as **Hadrian's Library** (daily, summer 8am–7pm, winter 8am–3pm; charge), and is actually an enormous multi-purpose cultural centre built around a colonnaded courtyard.

In Ottoman times, the Erechtheion was used by the city's Ottoman military commander as a billet for his harem.

BELOW:
view to the
Erechtheion.

Restoring the Parthenon

Conservators have levered down hundreds of blocks of marble masonry from the Parthenon, to replace the rusting iron clamps inserted in the 1920s with non-corrosive titanium ones (rust made the iron clamps expand, which cracked the stone). The restorers have also succeeded in collecting and identifying about 1,600 chunks of Parthenon marble scattered all over the hilltop. Many of these pieces were blown off in the 1687 explosion caused by a Venetian artillery shell igniting Ottoman munitions stored inside the temple. Once they have been painstakingly replaced, about 15 percent more of the building will be on view. New blocks cut from near the ancient quarries on Mount Pendéli, which supplied the 5th-century BC constructors, will be used to fill the gaps.

The Tomb of the Unknown Warrior, by Sýndagma Square, is guarded by Evzónes, *elite soldiers in traditional mountain costume.*

BELOW: the Féthiye Tzamí, an Ottoman mosque on the edge of the Roman Forum. **BELOW RIGHT:** art souvenirs in Pláka.

City streets

The heart of the modern city lies within a triangle defined by **Platía Omónias** (Omónia Square) in the north, **Platía Syndagmátos** ❼ (Sýndagma Square) to the southeast and **Monastiráki** to the south. Except for a few small cross-streets, this is a car-free area, which has taken on a new lease of life. **Ermoú** is now a long pedestrian walkway with reinvigorated shops, enlivened by pavement buskers and push-carts. Many buildings have been refurbished, while the new lighting makes this an attractive area to wander in the evening.

The entire area is a huge warren of shops, more upmarket towards Sýndagma Square. **Monastiráki** has a market selling a weird assortment of objects, where collectors of kitsch will find much to interest them. The old **Varvákio covered market**, a 19th-century gem roughly halfway between Monastiráki and Omónia, is the city's main meat and fish market, crowded with shoppers milling between open stands displaying fish, seafood and every variety of poultry and meat you could imagine.

Pláka, the old quarter clustering at the foot of the Acropolis, has been refurbished and restored to its former condition (or rather, to a fairly good reproduction of it), with motor vehicles prohibited (for the most part), 19th-century houses restored and streets tidied up. It has become a delightful, sheltered place in which to meander, full of small beauties: look out for half a dozen Byzantine churches, two Ottoman mosques, several museums and the 4th-century BC **monument of Lysikratos**.

Byzantine Athens is fairly well represented with mostly 11th-century churches – besides a dozen in Pláka, there are several others huddling below street level in the shadow of the city's tall, modern buildings. They are still in constant use: passers-by slip in to light a yellow beeswax candle, cross themselves and kiss an icon in near-darkness before returning to the noise outside. One of the most handsome is **Agii Theodóri** ❽, just off Klavthmónos Square, built on the site of an earlier church, in characteristic cruciform shape with a tiled dome and a

terracotta frieze of animals and plants. **Kapnikaréa** in the middle of Ermoú has frescoes by the distinguished neo-Byzantine painter Fótis Kóntoglou; while the 12th-century **Mikrí Mitrópoli** (Small Cathedral) next to its garish successor features extensive external bas-relief masonry recycled from all previous eras. The huge, domed **Church of Sotíra Lykodímou** on Filellínon Street was bought by the Tsar of Russia in 1847 and refurbished inside to serve the city's growing Russian Orthodox community.

Athens's museums

Top of the agenda for rushed visitors is likely to be the **New Acropolis Museum** ❾ (Tue–Sun 8am–8pm; charge), a few hundred metres south of and below the Acropolis rock. While decidedly retrograde-modern when seen from the outside, inside the building is arrayed to duplicate the experience of ascending the Parthenon's various levels. A ramp – reproducing the approach to the Propylaia – leads up from the ground floor to an intermediate one, home to all the free-standing statuary (and much more) displayed in the cramped old museum, including the four original Caryatids still in Greece (plus bits of the fifth), revealing an Archaic ideal of femininity in their earrings, tresses and crinkled, close-fitting dresses. The top floor has been built exactly to mirror the arrangement of the friezes of the Parthenon, clearly visible through windows – those originals that Greece retains pointedly abut plaster casts of the roughly 60 percent residing in the British Museum, with the clear implication that they ought to be returned.

The **Benaki Museum** ❿ (Mon and Wed–Sat 9am–5pm, Thur until midnight, Sun 9am–3pm; charge), at the National Gardens' northeast corner, houses an eclectic collection of treasures from all periods of Greek history – including jewellery, costumes, the recreated interiors of two rooms from a Kozáni mansion, and two icons attributed to El Greco in the days when he was a Cretan painter called Doménico Theotokópoulos. The beautifully laid-out galleries make this one of the most attractive museums in the city.

The main tourist information office (EOT) is at Amalías 26, just off Sýndagma Square (tel: 21033 10392; daily). It provides free maps of Athens and the islands, ferry timetables and museum schedules. There's also a branch in the airport.

BELOW: inside the New Acropolis Museum.

Socialising over a frappé (iced coffee) – and the obligatory mobile.

BELOW: stunning displays at the Byzantine and Christian Museum.

The privately endowed **Goulandris Museum of Cycladic Greek Art ⑪** (Mon and Wed–Fri 10am–4pm, Sat 10am–3pm) nearby features the beautiful prehistoric white marble figurines dismissed as barbaric by Belle Epoque art critics but numbering Picasso and Modigliani among their admirers. They come from graves in the Cycladic islands, but scholars are still uncertain of their purpose (*see also page 162*). There are also numerous worthwhile temporary exhibits, some held in the adjoining neoclassical Eléna Stathátou mansion-annexe.

The **Byzantine and Christian Museum** (Tue–Sun 7.30am–7.30pm) across busy Vassilísis Sofías, partly occupying a mock-Florentine mansion built by the eccentric philhellene Duchess de Plaisance, has just emerged from a long refit that showcases better than ever a brilliant array of icons, frescoes and church relics.

The **National Archaeological Museum ⑫** (summer Tue–Sun 8.30am–7.30pm, Mon 1–7.30pm, winter Tue–Sun 8.30am–3pm) holds the city's most important collection of ancient artefacts. Highlights include the stunning gold work of the Mycenaean trove, more prehistoric Cycladic art, the Andikythera mechanism (an intricate astronomical computer 15 centuries ahead of its time), the Akrotiri frescoes (*see page 186*) and major bronze sculptures, including the wonderful Poseidon found off the coast of Évvia.

Of the many small Pláka exhibitions the best two are the **Folk Art Museum** (Tue–Sun 9am–2pm; charge) at Kydathinéon 17, with a reconstructed house full of murals by Naïve Lésvos artist Theóphilos; and the **Museum of Popular Musical Instruments** (Tue and Thur–Sun 10am–2pm, Wed noon–6pm; free), in a fine neoclassical mansion at Diogénous 1–3. The collection here, curated by Greek ethnomusicologist Fívos Anoyanákis, features just about every traditional instrument ever played in Greece, with archival photos and listening posts to round out the experience. The museum shop sells CDs of folk recordings, particularly of island music.

Athens by night

The night is long in this city. Athenians fiercely resist sleep, or make up for lost night-time sleep with a long afternoon siesta (*never* telephone an Athenian between 2.30pm and 6pm). Cafés and bars stay open until the small hours, providing music (usually loud), drink and snacks (usually expensive).

Three o'clock in the morning, and the traffic still won't give up. Groups linger on street corners; goodnights take for ever. The main streets are never entirely deserted, which makes Athens one of the safer cities in which to walk at night, although metro pickpocketing and car break-ins are on the rise. But the "unquiet generation" does finally go to bed; balconies go dark, cats prowl undisturbed, climbing jasmine smells stronger – and all the conflicting elements in the patchwork city seem momentarily resolved in the brief summer night. ❏

Coping with Piraeus

Most visitors only go to Piraeus if they have a ferry to catch, but there are some interesting things to see in this bustling port.

The port of Athens, Piraeus, is a city in its own right. Although unabashedly industrial, with few concessions to the large numbers of tourists who pass through every year, it is an easy place to idle away a few hours while waiting to catch a ferry, even if there are few echoes of *Never on Sunday* these days. (The underworld moved to Athens during the puritanical colonels' dictatorship. Since then, successive mayors have been elected on a "smarten up Piraeus" ticket.)

If you are going to catch one of the Piraeus ferries, get there one hour before sailing time so that you have half an hour to find the right quay – often very remote, although a shuttle bus does run – in good time: ships really do leave promptly. You also need to allow time to buy a ticket, now a requirement to board; if you have a car or want a sleeping berth, you should organise it days (in season, a week or more) in advance.

The easiest way to get to Piraeus from central Athens is on the metro (line 1; allow around 45 minutes' journey time from Sýndagma). Alternatively, bus no. 40 leaves from Sýndagma, but this can be very slow. From Athens Airport, express bus X96 takes about 90 traffic-free minutes to the main quay at Piraeus.

In the right quay

Your ticket agent will be able to tell you which quay your ferry departs from. They are numbered E1 to E10 going around the main basin clockwise. As a general guide: boats to the Cyclades depart from quays E5–E7 opposite the metro station; direct boats to Crete leave from E4, along Aktí Kondýli on the northern side of the port; catamarans and hydrofoils to the Argo-Saronic islands depart from E9, along Aktí Miaoúli, while slow car ferries to the same destinations go from E8 next to Karaïskáki Square; while the Dodecanese are served both from E10, at the far end of Aktí Miaoúli, and from E1, way across the harbour.

The radical cosmopolitan atmosphere for which Piraeus was famous 2,500 years ago still exists – immigrants are conspicuous, and Communist deputies are regularly returned to parliament – but few remains survive. A stretch of elegant 4th-century BC wall runs beside the coast road beyond Zéa Marína, and an amphitheatre backs onto the **Archaeological Museum** (Tue–Sun 8.30am–3pm; charge) at Hariláou Trikoúpi 31, which is well worth visiting if you have time before your boat leaves, although it is a very long walk from the docks. Its prize exhibits are two bronze statues found by workmen digging a drain in Piraeus: a magnificent 6th-century BC *kouros* (idealised figure of a young man), that is known as the Piraeus Apollo; and a 4th-century helmeted Athena, looking oddly soulful for a warrior goddess, plus another 4th-century BC bronze of Artemis. All may have come from a shipment of loot overlooked by raiding Roman general Sulla in 86 BC.

Just beyond, **Zéa Marína** is crowded with yachts and schooners of all sizes, a veritable floating campsite in summer. Sadly, there are few restaurants worth recommending; those are at the next harbour southeast, Mikrolímano, much closer to the Fáliro metro station and tram terminus than the Pireás station. ❑

ABOVE RIGHT: Zéa Marína.
RIGHT: statuary at the Piraeus Archaeological Museum.

THE IONIAN ISLANDS

Corfu, Paxí, Levkáda, Itháki, Kefaloniá, Zákynthos, Kýthira

The islands of the Ionian Sea just west of Greece are dubbed the *Eptánisa* – "seven isles". However, the seventh, Kýthira, lies south of the Peloponnese and, while sharing history, culture and architecture, remains isolated from the other six islands.

During the 8th and 7th centuries BC, colonists from Corinth occupied the most northerly Ionian islands; two centuries later Corfu's rebellion against Corinth helped start the Peloponnesian War. The Ionians have since had many overlords, but the Venetian period left the most indelible mark. Artists, craftsmen and poets were sent to Venice for their education, returning home with a cosmopolitan perspective. Today, thanks to regular links with Italy, the islands still have a distinctly Italian flavour – and not just in the pizzerias jostling for space with harbour-front tavernas.

Heavy rainfall makes the Ionians among the greenest of Greek archipelagos. Olive groves and vineyards are reminders that agriculture still plays a role in the economy. But this same unsettled weather has ruined many a holiday: from mid-September until mid-May, storms can wash out beach outings without warning. But escape to the mainland (or neighbouring, sunnier islands) is easy. There are several daily buses to Athens, regular seasonal ferries between Levkáda, Kefaloniá and Zákynthos, and flights between Athens and the four largest islands (as well as peripheral flights between them).

Today the Ionians are beset not by invaders (other than tour companies) but by earthquakes, the most recent serious one in 1953. Casualties were high and the beautiful Venetian-built capitals of Kefaloniá and Zákynthos were flattened. Reconstruction began almost immediately, though with different emphases. The Zakynthians recreated their Venetian town plan, albeit in reinforced concrete, while Ithacans rebuilt houses faithfully in the old style. Except in the central business district, the pragmatic residents of Argostóli in Kefaloniá put up makeshift buildings; a few unmodernised ones still remain. ❏

PRECEDING PAGES: Assos, Kefaloniá; roadside shrine on Levkáda. **LEFT:** Cape Skinári, Zákynthos. **FROM TOP:** north Itháki; in an Ionian deli; waiting patiently for that lift.

CORFU

Few places have been exploited for tourism as much as Corfu. Yet away from the package-tour resorts there is much to savour in this beautiful verdant island

S trategically poised where the Ionian Sea becomes the Adriatic, just off the mainland, Corfu (Kérkyra) has always been coveted, with a turbulent history and a long catalogue of invaders and rulers. There's evidence of habitation dating back 50,000 years, but Corfu enters history as "Korkyra" in the mid-8th century BC, when it was colonised by ancient Corinth. By the 5th century BC, Korkyra was a major, independent naval power, siding with Athens against Sparta (and Corinth) in the Peloponnesian War. After 229 BC, the island fell under relatively uneventful Roman dominion.

Nearly eight centuries of Byzantine tenure from AD 395 brought stability and prosperity, but latter years saw incursions and periods of domination by various groups: "barbarians", the Norman-Angevin Kingdom of the Two Sicilies, the Despotate of Epirus, and the Venetians. Weary of misrule and pirate raids, the Corfiots themselves asked to be put definitively under the protection of Venice, which obliged in 1386 – and stayed for 411 years, successfully defying four Ottoman sieges and leaving a rich legacy of olive groves. Napoleon dissolved what remained of the Venetian Empire in 1797, and the French held the island until 1814 except for the brief reign of the Ottoman/Russian-controlled "Septinsular Republic"). The British took over in 1814, staying for 50 years until all the Ionian islands were ceded to Greece as

a sweetener for Giorgos I's ascent of the Greek throne.

During World War I, Corfu was the final destination of a retreating, defeated Serbian army; memorials and two cemeteries from that era remain. In the next world war, the city suffered extensive damage in 1943 under a German bombardment to displace the Italian occupiers, who had surrendered to the Allies; during their brief but brutal stay, the Nazis rounded up and deported Corfu's significant Jewish community, resident here since Venetian times.

Main attractions
LISTÓN
NÉO FROÚRIO
ARCHAEOLOGICAL MUSEUM
VLAHÉRNA ISLET
PALEÁ PERÍTHIA
ANGELÓKASTRO
MYRTIÓTISSA BEACH

LEFT: the Angelókastro.
BELOW: relaxing at Aqualand.

A multicultural capital

Corfu Town, known as **Kérkyra ❶**, occupies a peninsula on the east coast. The name is a corruption of *koryfo*, or "peak", there being two such on a Byzantin-fortified outcrop much altered as the **Paleó Froúrio** (daily, summer 8am–7.30pm, winter 8am–3pm; charge) by the Venetians during the 15th and 16th centuries, when they cut a canal to make the citadel an island. The more complete **Néo Froúrio** to the west (same hours; charge) is strictly Venetian, and offers superb views over the tiled roofs of the town, cradled between the two forts.

With its tottering, multi-storeyed Venetian-style apartments, and maze-like lanes ending in quiet plazas, the old town constitutes a *flâneur*'s paradise; it was tidied up prior to hosting a 1994 EU meeting, but you wouldn't know it. Vacant bomb sites still yawn near the Néo Froúrio, and many main thoroughfares are blighted by touristic tat, but the backstreets are surprisingly unspoilt, festooned with washing-lines and echoing to pigeon coos. The elegant counterpoint to this is the **Listón**, built by the French as a replica of the Rue de Rivoli in Paris. The name refers to local aristocrats listed in the Venetian *Libro d'Oro*, with sufficient social standing to frequent the arcades.

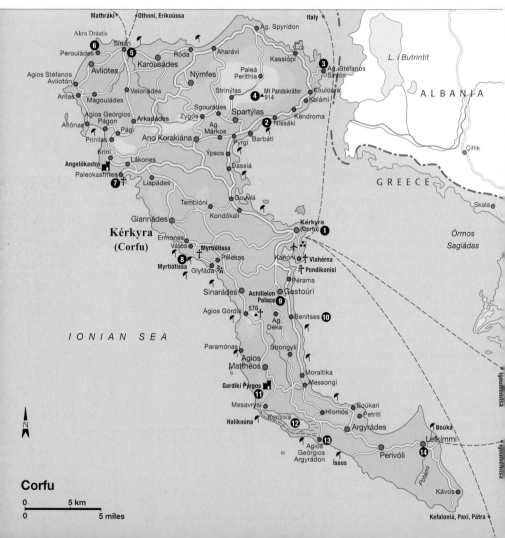

Corfu

0   5 km

0   5 miles

The Listón faces the Spianáda, a large and grassy open space cleared by the Venetians to deprive attackers of cover. At pricey Listón cafés you can order *tsintsíbira* (ginger beer), an enduring British legacy; other such linguistic legacies include cricket, played idiosyncratically on the Spianáda, and the Victorian cemetery at the edge of town, still used by the 7,000-strong expat community.

The Spianáda is also the focus for Orthodox Easter celebrations, which are among the best in Greece. On Good Friday eve, each parish parades its *Epitáfios* (Christ's Bier) accompanied by uniformed brass bands, playing funeral dirges. On Saturday morning the relics of local patron saint Spyrídon go walkabout, and then the tunes get jollier as townspeople shower special pots and crockery from their balconies to banish misfortune. The Saturday midnight Resurrection Mass finishes with fireworks launched from the Paleó Froúrio.

Both music and Saint Spyrídon are integral parts of Corfiot life. Until destroyed by Nazi incendiary bombs, Corfu had the world's largest opera house, after Milan's La Scala, and premières of major works took place here; there are still regular opera performances and thriving conservatories. Spyrídon, after whom seemingly half the male population is named "Spyros", was actually an early Cypriot bishop whose relics ended up here after the fall of Constantinople. Credited with saving Corfu from several disasters, his casket is processed four times yearly from his 16th-century shrine a block back from the Listón.

Unmissable sights

The town's two unmissable indoor sights are the **Asiatic Museum** (Tue–Sun 8am–7.30pm; charge), a collection housed (together with changing exhibits) in the British-built Palace of Saints George and Michael, plus the **Archaeological Museum** (Tue–Sun 8.30am–3pm; charge), south of the Spianáda, with superb late Archaic art. Pride of place goes to the massive Gorgon pediment from a temple of Artemis at Paleopolis, but the more detailed pediment of a Dionysiac symposium, complete with the god, acolyte and lion, equals it. Both came from excavations in **Mon Repos estate** (daily 8am–7.30pm; free), where there are not only other ruined temples and an early Christian basilica, but the **Paleópolis Museum** (same hours; charge), which holds worthwhile exhibits. Just south of this at **Kanóni** are the photogenic islets of **Vlahérna**, with a little monastery and causeway to it, and **Pondikonísi**, said to be a local ship petrified by Poseidon in revenge for the ancient Phaeacians helping Odysseus.

The north of the island

Northwest of town are busy resorts such as **Kondókali**, Komméno, Dassiá and Ypsos, used by both Greek and foreign visitors, though **Barbáti** is probably the first beach you would stop for. The coast between **Nissáki** ❷ and **Agios Stéfanos Sinión** ❸ fancies itself a mini-Riviera, with smart villas – there are hardly any hotels – and secluded pebble coves lapped by turquoise water. But mass tourism takes over again at **Kassiópi**,

The White House at Kalámi, where Lawrence Durrell wrote Prospero's Cell, *is now accommodation (top floor) and a taverna (ground floor).*

BELOW: the Paleó Froúrio.

The Achilleion Palace is stuffed with over-the-top statuary.

BELOW: Theotókos Monastery near Paleokastrítsa.

important in antiquity but now with only a crumbled castle. Up the slopes of 914-metre (2,300ft) **Mount Pandokrátor** ❹ nestles **Paleá Períthia**, a well-preserved Venetian-era village. Back on the coast, little-frequented beaches between Kassiópi and **Aharávi** are pleasant alternatives to overdeveloped **Róda** and **Sidári** ❺. From Sidári ply the most reliable boats to the three small inhabited Diapóndia islets: **Mathráki, Othoní** and **Erikoússa**. Mathráki is the wildest and least developed, Erikoússa the most visited, thanks to its sandy beaches.

West-coast beaches beyond Sidári are superior, beginning at quieter **Perouládes** ❻, continuing through **Agios Stéfanos Avliotón**, Arílas and **Agios Geórgios Págon**. Beyond **Kríni** looms the shattered but still impressive Byzantine-Angevin **Angelókastro**, guarding the approach to the beautiful double bay of **Paleokastrítsa** ❼, now oversubscribed; best admire it from above, at the namesake monastery, or from the cafés in **Lákones** village.

Beyond here, beaches resume at **Érmones**, but either **Myrtiótissa** ❽, small but beloved of naturists, or big

Glyfáda, with lots of amenities, are better, while **Agios Górdis** is a backpackers' paradise. Inland, **Pélekas** has famous coastal panoramas and sunsets, which prompted Kaiser Wilhelm II to build a special viewing tower.

The south of the island

Inland and south of Kérkyra, near Gastoúri, stands the pretentious **Achilleion Palace** ❾ (daily, summer 8am–7pm, winter 8am–4pm; charge), built in 1890 for Empress Elisabeth of Austria, then acquired by Kaiser Wilhelm II. It once housed a casino, has hosted EU meetings, and is now a museum of kitsch. **Benítses** ❿ has seen its heyday come and go, though the village itself is quite attractive; **Moraïtika** and **Messongí** are by contrast unsightly, but local beaches are better.

Inland, roads visit what is seemingly another island, winding around **Agii Déka** hill (576 metres /1,890ft), with a tiny inhabited monastery near the summit. Due west of Messongí is the **Gardíki Pýrgos** ⓫, a crumbling octagonal Angevin castle in a curious lowland setting. The castle road continues to the fine Halikoúna beach at the northwest end of the **Koríssia lagoon** ⓬, a protected nature reserve and a magnet for birdwatchers. From the nearby hill village of **Agios Matthéos**, you can reach another sandy beach, Paramónas.

Back on the main trunk road, Argyrádes gives access to the north-coast villages of Boúkari and Petrití, which have been protected from exploitation by a lack of beaches. In the opposite direction lies **Agios Geórgios Argyrádon** ⓭, developed during the 1990s for what is delicately called "low-quality tourism", and with only splendid Íssos beach to its credit. The Corfiots have deliberately quarantined the Club 18–30 set at **Kávos**. The underrated, second largest town on Corfu, **Lefkímmi** ⓮ goes about its business just inland, seemingly oblivious to its raucous neighbour: the Lefkimians visit the beach at Boúkar the mouth of the river picturesquely bisecting Lefkímmi.

Working the Land

Traditional farming methods are still used on Corfu, but the exodus of young people to the towns means that things are changing.

The silver-leafed olive trees that grace the Ionian landscape form an integral part of island life. For centuries olive oil has formed a staple part not only of the Greek diet, but the local economy. Even urban families have olive groves, gathering their own olives to take to a local mill. Depending on the variety and the locale, harvesting – either raking from the trees or collecting from black mesh nets that are also a feature of the scenery – is between October and December, with pruning (the wood is a highly prized fuel) soon after.

Even for most full-time island farmers, agricultural produce is for domestic use only, with non-mechanised methods enforced by hilly terrain, though roto-tillers have now replaced ploughing teams. The striking visual aspect of irregular fields results from the system of splitting up the land to form inheritances and marriage dowries. A typical farming community consists of 10 to 100 close-packed houses, their small yards containing chickens and the occasional pig being fattened for Christmas. Most villages now have at least dirt-road access, power lines (or solar panels) and perhaps some fixed phones (definitely universal mobile subscription), but water supply can be a problem.

A large-scale goat- or sheep-herder may have 100 to 500 animals, with supplemental feed such as maize, millet or pressed cake purchased when springtime pasture is exhausted; he concentrates on producing kids or lambs for the peak periods of Easter and summer. By contrast, there's the elderly widow with a few goats and fields, working them on her own. Small-scale farmers supplement the family diet with lentils, broad beans and chickpeas, fruit and vegetables.

In the cooler months, most herders collect wild foliage from the hills and bring it down by pickup or (rarely) donkey for both bedding and fodder. In spring, animals are taken to graze in fairly remote pastures. During spring and summer, the ubiquitous vegetable patches produce (in this order) potatoes, beans, tomatoes, courgettes, peppers, melons and aubergines – in return for considerable investment in time and effort, but not always pesticides or fertilisers. Subsistence farmers unable to spend on these products often make a virtue of necessity by producing de facto organic crops.

During early summer, grain – especially barley – is still reaped by hand with a sickle, laid out in the fields to dry, then transported to be threshed. This is usually done by machine, but on a few more remote, rugged islands, a team of mules or donkeys is still walked over the crop strewn on the threshing *cirques* or *alónia* to smash the husks with their hoofs, prior to winnowing and sieving. On larger islands like Rhodes, Kós and Límnos, mechanised reaping and baling is universally practised.

Traditional farming methods are quickly disappearing, sporadic EU subsidies notwithstanding. The youth exodus from the villages to towns or the mainland to find work, plus competition with other EU farmers, have spelt doom for labour-intensive methods, as numerous overgrown fields and crumbled terraces attest. The only hope for much of the rural economy is to increase value through official organic certification – difficult when your olive groves are aerially sprayed without your consent against the destructive *dákos* fly – or the marketing of speciality cash-crops such as almonds, pine-nuts and kumquats. ❑

RIGHT: the oil-producing olive grove, at the heart of both the local economy and of the Greek diet.

SOUTHERN IONIAN ISLANDS

Everything here, from architecture to food, has been influenced by the Italians, who continue to arrive in large numbers each August. Yet every Ionian island has its own character

Paxí (Páxos), the smallest of the seven main islands of the Ionian archipelago, is 90 minutes by conventional boat from Kérkyra (Corfu). Hilly and green, it has rugged west-coast cliffs, several sea-caves and various pebble beaches. Paxí figures little in ancient history and mythology, when it was uninhabited, though Tim Severin in *The Ulysses Voyage* identifies the Homeric spring and dell of Circe as the modern one beside the late Byzantine **church of Ypapandí**, in the far north. Paxí acquired extensive olive groves and served as a hunting reserve for the Corfiot Venetian aristocracy, but was only systematically populated as of the 15th century. The gnarled olive trunks, their shimmering leaves like coins tossed in the breeze, are emblems of the island, and provided the main livelihood before tourism – Paxí oil ranks among the best in Greece, and has won many international medals. Dwellings, from humble cottages to baronial mansions, are tucked into hollows out of sight, and out of reach of the *maístros*, the prevailing northwest wind; only during modern times have coastal view villas appeared.

All boats dock at the small capital, **Gáïos ❶**, arrayed fan-like around its main square and sheltered by the two islets of **Agios Nikólaos** and **Panagía**, with, respectively, a Venetian castle and small monastery. Gáïos preserves narrow streets and a few grand 19th-century buildings with Venetian-style

balconies and shutters, plus most island shops, though tavernas are undistinguished.

Paxí's single main road meanders northwest, through the olive groves and tiny hamlets consisting of a few houses, and perhaps a *kafenío* at main junctions. Locally sold walking guides point you along a maze of old walled paths, dirt tracks and paved lanes, which provide the best way to see the island. Reached by a side road, **Longós** on the northwest coast is the most exclusive resort, flanked by the popular beaches

Main attractions
ANDÍPAXI BEACHES
RONIÉS WATERFALLS
PÓRTO KATSÍKI BEACH
ODYSSEUS TRAIL
KIÓNI BAY
KORGIALÉNIOS MUSEUM
PLATIÁ AMMOS
ASSOS
MELISSÁNI CAVE
MUSEUM OF POST-BYZANTINE ART
VASILIKÓS PENINSULA
SHIPWRECK BAY

LEFT: Agios Dionýsios in Zákynthos. **BELOW:** ferry to Zákynthos.

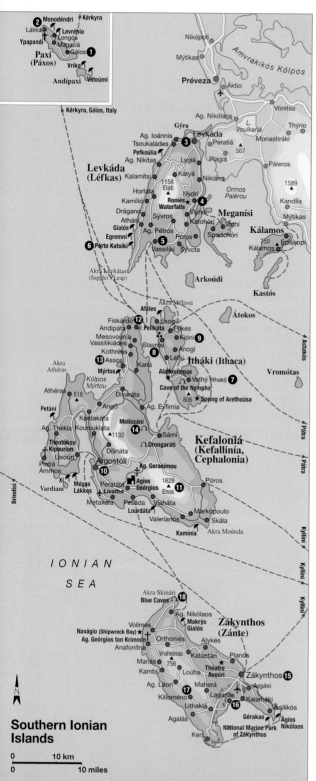

Southern Ionian Islands

```
0        10 km
0            10 miles
```

of **Levréhio** and **Monodéndri**, the latter with road access. The "motorway" ends at **Lákka** ❷, beloved of yachts and the majority of landbound tourists, with a better choice of food and lodging; small beaches like **Orkós** lie within walking distance.

The northeast coast of **Andípaxi** (Andípaxos) islet shelters the two excellent beaches of **Vatoúmi** and **Vríka**, well known to day-trippers in summer but idyllic off-season. Only in summer, when three tavernas operate do a dozen people live here; Andípaxi's vineyards produce a heavy red wine favoured for local festivals, and a lighter tawny white.

Levkáda (Léfkas)

Like Évvia, Levkáda is barely an island, joined to the mainland by a floating drawbridge over a canal. Greeks seasonally crowd the place, glad to find an island exempt from the prices and weather-whims of a ferry crossing. Yet Levkáda feels like the Ionian, with standard Venetian influences on speech and cuisine, the imposing fort of Santa Maura by the bridge, plus spear-like cypress and bright yellow broom in May carpeting the steep hillsides. Kefaloniá may be higher, but Levkáda has a more rugged landscape, which has preserved rural lifestyles in the hill villages; the older women still wear traditional dress, while local crafts and foodstuffs are avidly promoted.

Levkáda Town ❸ faces the canal and the lagoon enclosed by the Gýra sandspit; local topography provides safe mooring for numerous yachts on the southeast quay. Of all Ionian capitals, it's the most pedestrian-friendly; much of the central area is off-limits to cars. The municipal axis is Ioánnou Melá, which beyond lively Platía Agíou Spyrídonos becomes Wilhelm Dörpfeld, in honour of the early 20th-century German archaeologist who attempted to prove that Levkáda was in fact Homeric Ithaca. He is again duly revered in the excellent **Archaeological Museum** (Tue–Sun 8.30am–3pm;

charge), with well-labelled exhibits on ancient religion and daily life. Also notable are several ornate Italianate churches dating from the late 17th or early 18th century, where arched windows and Baroque relief work sit oddly beside post-earthquake belfries modelled on oil derricks.

Levkáda is the homeland of 20th-century poet Angelos Sikelianós, and Lafcádio Hearn, a 19th-century short-story writer born here to American missionary parents, who immortalised supernatural Japan. There are cultural links between the island and Japan, and streets commemorate both men.

Heading down Levkáda's east coast, the little port-resorts of **Lygiá** and **Nikiána**, with pebble coves and fish tavernas, are the first places to prompt a stop. They are calmer and quieter than **Nydrí** ❹, 20km (12 miles) south of Levkáda opposite a mini-archipelago of four islets. The view out to them is the reason Nydrí has been earmarked for package-tourist development, since local beaches are frankly mediocre. Until the 1970s it was a tiny fishing village, where Aristotle Onassis used

to pop over for dinner from Skorpiós, his private island; there's a statue of the man on the quay now named for him, but no trace of exclusivity lingers.

The one conventionally inhabited satellite island, **Meganísi**, accessible by daily ferry, is an increasingly ill-kept secret; yachters already appreciate its quiet bays and attractive villages. The best escape for landlubbers lies 3km (2 miles) inland, where the **Roniés Waterfalls** prove suprisingly impressive, and indicative of abundant water at the heart of Levkáda.

Beyond Nydrí, Dörpfeld excavated extensively at Stenó, and is buried on the far side of sumpy **Vlyhó** bay. The island ring road curls past Mikrós Gialós pebble bay and Sývota yacht harbour before descending to **Vassilikí** ❺, 40km (25 miles) from town, one of Europe's premier windsurfing resorts. Boat tours are offered around Cape Levkátas – where Sappho legendarily leaped to her death – to spectacular west-coast beaches, also accessible by roads of varying steepness. Southern-most **Pórto Katsíki** ❻ stars on every third postcard of Levkáda; **Egremní**

The church of Agios Minás in Levkáda Town has a unique clock tower made of steel girders.

BELOW: fishermen on Levkáda

and **Gialós** are less frequented, while panoramic **Atháni** village has the closest tourist facilities. Further on, **Drymónas** is the most architecturally preserved settlement on the island, while **Kalamítsi** has an eponymous beach and "shares" **Káthisma**, Levkáda's longest, with **Agios Nikítas** (Aï Nikítas). The only port actually on the west coast has become a relatively upmarket resort, though worth avoiding in peak season. Beyond Agios Nikítas's own little beach, **Pefkoúlia** stretches north to the headland dividing it from **Agios Ioánnis**, the nicest section of Gýra beach, with its abandoned windmills.

Journeys inland thread through the half-dozen **Sfakiótes** hamlets occupying a fertile upland, where churches with Venetian belfries may be seen. The usual destination is **Karyá**, even higher and cooler, with a thriving crafts tradition and a vast central *platía* shaded by several giant plane trees.

Itháki (Ithaca)

Evidence that Itháki actually was the ancient home of Odysseus, wander-

ing hero of Homer's *Odyssey*, is hardly conclusive, but this hasn't discouraged a local Homeric "heritage industry", with numerous streets and businesses named for characters in the epic, and modest archaeological sites assiduously signposted as putative locales for various episodes.

Most ferries dock at the cheerful capital, **Vathý** ❼, occupying the head of a long bay. Though badly damaged by the 1953 earthquake, many buildings survived, while others were tastefully rebuilt with traditional architectural elements. There are more tavernas and *kafenía*, especially along the quay, than in any other port town of this size. Several pebble beaches, pleasant, if not Itháki's best, lie close by; this is an island ideally sized for scooter exploration and walking.

Itháki is almost pinched in two by an isthmus barely wide enough for the main corniche road. The northern half has more lush vegetation and better beaches; below **Léfki** village the secluded pebble bays of **Agios Ioánnis** and **Koutoúpi** grace the west coast. **Stavrós** ❽, 16km (10 miles)

from Vathý, is Itháki's second town, with another small museum devoted to finds from local sites with a better claim to being Odysseus' possible home. These are a citadel on **Pelikáta** hill and, more intriguing, an excavation marked as "**School of Homer**" off the road to Exogí. Walls and foundations, a few Mycenaean graves, steps carved into the rock and a vaulted cave-well lie exposed. In size and position, the place feels just right to be the base of a minor chieftain like Odysseus. **Exogí**, the highest village on the island, is seasonally occupied but offers superb views northeast. From Platrithiás village a paved drive goes to **Afáles** bay with excellent sand-and-pebble patches, while another road loops through Agii Saránda and Lahós, partly spared by the earthquake, en route to **Fríkes**. There are ferries here (to Kefaloniá and Levkáda) and many yachts, although most visitors continue, past attractive pebble coves, to **Kióni** ❾, Itháki's most upmarket resort, where again various houses survived the quake. At either port, free rooms are rare items during high season.

From Kióni you can walk up the cleared and profusely waymarked old path to Anogí, a three-hour round trip; it's the best hike on the island, with only the last 20 minutes spoilt by the heliport and its access road. In half-deserted **Anogí**, there's a medieval church of **Kímisis tis Theotókou** (Dormition of the Virgin), with heavily retouched Byzantine frescoes and a Venetian belfry. Some 4km (2½ miles) south, the **Monastery of Katharón** is by contrast a post-quake barracks-like structure, flanked by modern antennae, but the views are unsurpassed.

Stavrós is one of several places in Itháki claiming to be the site of Odysseus' castle, and marks its claim with this bust of the Homeric hero.

Kefaloniá (Kefallinía, Cephalonia)

Kefaloniá is the largest and second-most mountainous Ionian island, its population famous for a studied (often creative) eccentricity. It has mixed feelings about being typecast as "Captain Corelli's Island", since political opinions expressed in Louis de Bernières's locally set blockbuster novel are not popular here.

The capital town of **Argostóli** ❿, levelled by the 1953 earthquake, was

BELOW: hiking Mount Enos, Kefaloniá.

The Odysseus Trail

Odyssean sites near Vathý include the **Bay of Phokrys** (now **Fórkynos**), the **Cave of the Nymphs**, the **Spring of Arethoúsa**, and ancient **Alalkomenae** (Alalkoméni). Having landed at Phokrys, it is said, Odysseus climbed up to the cave and hid various gifts given him by King Alkinous of the Phaeacians. Next, Odysseus met his loyal swineherd Eumaeos and son Telemakhos at the Arethoúsa spring; the track-and-path walk from Vathý takes 90 minutes, challenging but with good views. Alalkomenae occupies a hillside 5km (3 miles) west of Vathý, above the road between Fórkynos and the secondary port (and a good pebble beach) of **Píso Aetós**; Heinrich Schliemann excavated here, but most of the finds (now in Vathý's museum) clearly do not date from the Homeric era.

Argostóli's museum tells the recent history of Kefaloniá and its earthquakes in photographs.

BELOW: looking out from the Agios Theodóros lighthouse.

rebuilt in utilitarian style and has a workaday feel, epitomised by meat and produce markets perched right on the commercial quay near the pedestrian-only, British-built **Drápano** stone bridge across the lagoon. The quay's names honour two islanders: Ioánnis Metaxás, 1930s dictator and defier of the Italians, and Andónis Trítsis (1937–92), innovative architect, maverick politician and ultimately Mayor of Athens. The heart of town is **Platía Vallianoú**, ringed by hotels and *kafenía*, though trendy cafés have sprouted on pedestrianised, relatively elegant **Lithóstroto**, beside its smart shops. Specific sights are limited to three museums, of which the **Korgialénios Historical and Folkloric Museum** (Mon–Sat 9am–2pm; charge) is the most interesting, with pictures of Argostóli before and after the quake, and thorough coverage of traditional daily life. Northwest of town, near the Doric rotunda of **Agios Theodóros** lighthouse, the "sea mills" at **Katavóthres** used to grind grain and generate electricity; salt water pouring down sinkholes here emerges three weeks

later near Sámi, but the 1953 disaster reduced the flow to a trickle.

To the east looms **Mount Enos ⓫** (Ainos), at 1,628 metres (5,340ft) the highest peak in the islands and still partly covered with native firs *(Abies cephallonica)*; two small reserves protect the remaining trees, much reduced by fires and loggers. The inclined south coastal plain at the base of the mountain, **Livathó**, is punctuated by a conical hill bearing the Venetian capital of **Agios Geórgios**, inhabited from Byzantine times until the 17th century. The impressive summit castle (unreliable opening hours) has wonderful views. Aristocratic associations linger at certain Livathó villages: pre-quake stone walls enclose vast estates; Lord Byron lived at nearby Metaxáta in 1823; and Keramiés still harbours dilapidated pre-quake mansions and a huge olive mill. The largest beach in the area, with resort amenities, is **Lourdáta**.

On the west shore of Argostóli gulf, reached by frequent ferries used by drivers and pedestrians alike to avoid the tedious journey by road, **Lixoúri** has long been eclipsed by rival Argostóli, but it's a pleasantly sleepy town with views to Zákynthos. Beyond, southwest on the peninsula, lie the busy red-sand beaches of **Mégas Lákkos** and **Xí**; en route you'll see how the fertile, grain-and-grape-planted terrain was heaved and buckled by the force of the quake. Beyond Xí, **Kounópetra** (Rocking Stone) no longer does so since 1953. Northwest of Lixoúri is the long, fine-pebble beach of **Petáni**, exposed but spectacular, although much the best beach near Lixoúri is the lonely, and facility-less, **Platiá Ammos**, reached by 300 steps from near Theotókou Kipouríon monastery.

Northern Kefaloniá was less damaged by the earthquake, and surviving medieval houses in various states of repair, especially at **Vassilikiádes** and **Mesovoúnia**, serve as poignant reminders of a lost architectural heritage. But the port resort of **Fiskárdo ⓬** emerged almost unscathed, and ruth-

lessly exploits the fact despite a lack of beaches. The atmosphere is very pukka, if not precious, and yachts congregate in force, dodging the occasional ferry to Levkáda or Itháki. "Fiskárdo" is a corruption of the name of Norman leader Robert Guiscard, who made Kefaloniá his headquarters, but died here in 1085.

On the west coast, the perfect horseshoe harbour of **Assos** ⓭ sees only fishing boats and is the better for it; there's good swimming from the isthmus joining this partly preserved village to a pine-covered bluff, with its fine late 16th-century Venetian fort. A bit further south, **Mýrtos** is among the most famous – and overrated – beaches in the Ionians: coarse-pebbled and downright dangerous if a surf is up.

The water is calmer and the pebbles smaller at **Agía Evfimía**, a fishing village on the east coast; between here and the functional ferry port of **Sámi** lies the **Melissáni cave** ⓮ (daily 8am–7pm; charge), containing an underground lake with its roof partly open to the sky. Nearby, another cave, **Drongaráti** (Apr–Oct daily 9am–8pm;

charge) offers multicoloured stalactites and stalagmites, and is the occasional venue for concerts.

Beyond Sámi, a good road threads attractively through vegetated scenery to underrated **Póros**, another ferry/yacht port with a backdrop of green cliffs. From here you loop around the coast to busy **Skála**, with its superb sand-and-gravel beach fringed by pines, and extensive mosaic flooring in a Roman villa (daily 10am–2pm and 5–8pm; free); and then around Cape Moúnda to the all-sand **Kamínia** beach, Kefaloniá's principal turtle-nesting venue.

Zákynthos (Zánte)

Zante, Fior di Levante, said the Venetians, and its central plain – the most fertile in the Ionians – and eastern hills support luxuriant vegetation. The southeastern coasts shelter excellent beaches: some are almost undeveloped, others are home to notoriously unsavoury tourism. Zákynthos also has some of the most dangerous roads in the islands, so you should take extra care when driving.

Kefaloniá is noted for its honey (thyme-scented), quince jelly and a local speciality called riganáta – feta cheese mixed with bread, oil and oregano.

BELOW: peering down over the partly exposed lake of Melissáni cave.

BELOW: Shipwreck Beach, Zákynthos.

At the once-elegant harbour town of **Zákynthos** , ferries dock by Platía Solomoú, named for native son Dionýsios Solomós, a 19th-century poet who wrote the words to the Greek national anthem. At the rear of his *platía*, the **Zákynthos Museum of Post-Byzantine Art** (Tue–Sun 8am–3pm; charge) features icons rescued from quake-blasted churches, as well as numerous 17th–19th-century religious paintings of the Ionian School, founded by Cretan artists fleeing the Ottoman conquest, who met local artists strongly influenced by the Italian Renaissance. In medieval times people lived above the present town in **Bóhali** district, inside the huge *kástro*, which is mostly Venetian but with Byzantine foundations. Here, several tavernas provide superb views.

Unfortunately, most of the 700,000 annual visitors don't stray far from adjacent **Laganás/Kalamáki** ⑯ beach resorts, whose explosive growth since the late 1970s is endangering the survival of loggerhead turtles (*see opposite*), which have nested here for millennia. Luckily, the tourist tat is easily skirted,

and Zákynthos shows its best side in the more remote corners. The **Vasilikós peninsula**, lying beyond forgettable Argási, has the island's best, most scenic beaches, culminating in **Agios Nikólaos** and **Gérakas**, nearest the east cape.

Start a tour of the unspoilt western hill villages from **Kerí** at the far south cape, with its lighthouse; next stop would be **Kilioméno** ⑰, which survived 1953 largely intact. Tourists are coached to **Kambí** to watch the sunset, but **Éxo Hóra** and **Mariés** have more character, with pre-quake churches and wells, vital in this arid region. Still further north, **Anafonítria** village offers an eponymous 14th-century monastery with a daunting gate-keep; plaques recall the local legend that 1578–1622 abbot St Dionýsios forgave and sheltered his brother's murderer here. Nearby, the 16th-century monastery of **Agios Geórgios ton Krimnón** has a round lookout tower in its well-tended courtyard; just beyond is the overlook for **Shipwreck (Navágio) Bay**, the most photographed in the Ionians, where a rusty freighter lies half-buried in sand. Boat trips, the only access, visit from **Pórto Vrómi**, below Mariés.

From Shipwreck, head east through grain fields, and the two **Volímes** villages noted for their honey, textiles and cheese, to reach the east coast near **Makrýs Gialós** pebble beach and the bleak port of **Agios Nikólaos**, with daily ferries to Kefaloniá and excursion boats to the **Blue Caves** ⑱, interconnecting grottoes with spectacular light effects at the right hour.

Back towards town, you wind through **Alykés** (the calmest beach resort), past secluded bays favoured by Greeks, before hitting mass tourism again at **Planós**. A welcome antidote to this, set in the hills between Planós and Tragáki, is Dimítris Avoúris's exemplary stone-built **Skaliá Cultural Centre/Théatro Avoúri** (tel: 26950 62973 or email: skalia@zakynthos-net.gr for information and programmes). ❏

Turtles vs. tourists

The survival of the loggerhead turtles of Zákynthos is under threat from the undesirable effects of mass tourism.

A loggerhead turtle crawls out of the sea onto the moonlit beach of her birthplace, the island of Zákynthos. She has crossed the Mediterranean to return, at last, to this spot. Summoning all her strength, the 90kg (200lb) reptile selects a place in the sand where she digs a nest with her rear flippers. In it she lays 100 soft eggs, each the size of a ping-pong ball, covers them with sand and returns exhausted to the sea to rest in the shallows. However, her labour may have been in vain, for thoughtless tourism is threatening these ancient creatures with extinction.

The survival of the loggerhead (Caretta caretta) is endangered before she even reaches the beach. It has been estimated that nearly half the females basking in the shallows may be maimed or killed by the propellers of speedboats taking waterskiers and paragliders out to sea. Carelessly discarded litter creates another hazard, as turtles suffocate trying to swallow plastic bags which they mistake for jellyfish, a favourite food.

For the female turtle, hazards increase when she slips ashore. Disorientated by the glittering lights of hotels and the strange noises coming from the tourists and bars, she may scurry back to the surfline, uncertain where to deposit her eggs. Those that try to continue their labours may suffer the indignity of ignorant spectators brandishing torches and flashing cameras, frightening the turtles back into the sea where the eggs may be released, never to hatch.

Eggs successfully laid are often crushed by thoughtless quad-bikers, horse-riders and motorists who drive across the sand, packing it down so that it is impossible for the hatchlings to emerge. Beach umbrellas are unwittingly driven into nests, piercing the eggs. Tamarisk trees, planted to shade sunbathers, pose another problem, as hatchlings become tangled up in the roots. Even sandcastles may create holes that become shallow graves for the young turtles.

Hatching takes place from early August to late September – precisely when most tourists arrive. The 6cm (2½in) hatchlings may emerge from their hazardous 50-day incubation and, instead of heading instinctively to starlight on the horizon line at sea, frequently wander confused up the beach to hotel and bar lights – an error that brings death from exhaustion or dehydration.

Zákynthos formerly had one of the greatest concentrations of nesting turtles in the Mediterranean. Laganás Bay was a particularly favourite spot but, confused by the combination of boats, lights and noise that tourism has brought, the turtles have abandoned these busy sands. The majority now nest in the more secluded beaches of Sekánia, Gérakas and Dáfni, where there is barely room for the activities of the bewildered reptiles. Fewer than 800 turtles now breed annually on Zákynthos, barely half the number found in the early 1980s.

The Greek Sea Turtle Protection Society (www.archelon.gr), locked in frequent, sometimes violent conflict with unscrupulous developers, succeeded in the 1999 creation of the National Marine Park of Zákynthos (www.nmp-zak.org), encompassing the whole gulf between the capes of Gérakas and Kerí. Three levels of control restrict boating and land access; all affected beaches have dawn-to-dusk curfews. Volunteers are on hand during the season to help inform visitors, and monitor nests. ❑

RIGHT: welcome sign for a turtle information centre on the Vasilikós peninsula, Zákynthos.

KÝTHIRA

Geographically nearer to Crete than to the Ionian group, this is one of Greece's quietest islands. Most visitors are Greeks from Athens – or Greek Australians returning home

BELOW:
Kapsáli harbour
seen from Hóra
high above.

In legend Kýthira, suspended off Cape Maléa in the Lakonian Gulf, was one of the birthplaces of Aphrodite (the other, stronger contender is in Cyprus). A bleak, thyme-covered plateau slashed by vegetated ravines, the island forms part of a sunken land bridge between the Peloponnese and Crete, from where many Venetian refugees arrived in the 17th century.

It has two names (Tsérigo was its Venetian alias); a history of Venetian and British rule, but today governed from Piraeus along with the Argo-Saronics; an architecture that's a hybrid of Cycladic and Venetian; a pronounced Australian flavour, courtesy of remittances and personal visits from emigrants Down Under – and ubiquitous eucalypts.

Kýthira (also spelled Kýthera and Kíthira) does not put itself out for outsiders. Accommodation is expensive and difficult to secure in summer; good tavernas are thin on the ground. Rough seas, which can play havoc with ferries from Cape Maléa, prompted the construction of an all-weather harbour at Diakófti in 1997. Despite all that, Kýthira has become a popular haunt of trendy Greeks, thanks to its appearance in Theo Angelópoulos's 1984 film *Taxídi sta Kýthira* and a more recent television series shot on the island.

Hóra ❶ (also called Kýthira) is one of the finest Aegean island capitals. Imposing, flat-roofed mansions in the lower town date from the 17th to 19th centuries, though the Venetian *kástro* above is of earlier vintage. An elaborate domed cistern system is still intact, while a few rusty cannons guarding a church seem superfluous, given the incredibly steep drop to the sea at **Kapsáli** yacht harbour, where most tourists stay, though the beach is mediocre.

Around the island

Much better beaches lie east of Hóra at **Halkós**, south of **Kálamos** village, and at **Fyrí Ammos**, east of Kálamos, with sea-caves to explore. North of

Fyrí Ammos, and easier to get to, more excellent beaches dot the east coast: **Kombonáda**, **Kaladí** with a rock monolith in the surf at one end, and two – **Asprógas** and **Paleópoli** – to either side of Kastrí Point with its Minoan settlement, which was explored by Heinrich Schliemann in 1887.

The beachy strip ends at the fishing anchorage of **Avlémonas** ❷, where seemingly half the island's population comes for weekend lunches at the main fish taverna. The diminutive octagonal Venetian fort is scarcely more than a gun emplacement. There's a better, 16th-century castle, complete with a Lion of St Mark, at **Káto Hóra**, just outside the attractive village of **Mylopótamos** ❸, with a waterfall and abandoned mill in a wooded canyon. This fortress was not a military stronghold but a civilian pirate refuge, with derelict houses inside.

Some 2.5km (1½ miles) west of Káto Hóra, perched above the surf-lashed west coast, the black-limestone cavern of **Agía Sofía** ❹ (June–Sept Mon–Fri 3–8pm, Sat–Sun 11am–5pm; charge) is the best of several namesake caves

on Kýthira. A 13th-century hermit adorned the entrance with frescoes of Holy Wisdom personified, and three attendant virtues. (Locals insist that Aphrodite slept here, but today the only endemic life is a minute white spider.) About one-sixth of the cave, with marvellous stalactites and stalagmites, is open for visits.

The ghost village of **Paleohóra** ❺ in the northeast failed the pirate-proof test in 1537, when the notorious Barbarossa sacked it. The ruins, including six frescoed (and locked) churches, cover the summit of a high bluff plunging to the confluence of two gorges that unite as **Kakí Langáda**, reaching the sea at a small lake.

Potamós ❻, 2km (1¼ miles) north of the Paleohóra turning, is Kýthira's largest village, notable for a Sunday farmers' market. **Agía Pelagía**, the disused former ferry port, has come down in the world since **Diakófti** started working. More rewarding is **Karavás** ❼, the northernmost and prettiest of the ravine oasis-villages, which meets the sea at **Platiá Ammos** beach; pebbly **Foúrni** cove lies adjacent. ❑

So many Kýthirans (possibly 60,000) have emigrated to Australia that the post office in Hóra contains a Sydney telephone directory.

BELOW:
sailing the waters around Kýthira, which legend links to Aphrodite.

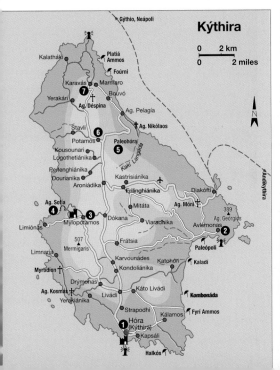

ISLANDS OF THE
SARONIC GULF

Salamína, Aegina, Póros, Hydra and Spétses

The five islands of the Saronic Gulf could be described as "commuter" islands – although that doesn't sound very romantic. As they lie within a short ferry ride (or an even shorter hydrofoil trip) from Piraeus, the temptation exists to treat the islands as an extension of the mainland or, more specifically, suburbs of Athens.

Entrepreneurs have been quick to exploit the islands' proximity. The one-day cruise from Piraeus calling at Aegina, Hydra and Póros remains a popular atraction for tourists visiting Athens (it is rivalled only by Delphi as a day-trip destination), although numbers have been down of late. When the cruise ships mingle with the ferries, the hydrofoils and the catamarans, there is often a virtual traffic jam on the waters, and foreign visitors temporarily outnumber Greeks.

In spite of all this, the Argo-Saronics are definitely Greek islands, not Athens suburbs – distinctive in character, rich in history and, behind the crowds and the chichi boutiques, remarkably attractive places. Salamis (Salamína), the largest of these islands, is renowned for the epoch-making naval battle in 480 BC, which decided the outcome of the Persian Wars. Aegina (Égina) is home to the beautiful Doric Temple of Aphaea, which is one of the most important antiquities to be found on any Greek island.

Póros and its channel have been immortalised by American author Henry Miller (1891–1980) in *The Colossus of Maroussi*, and forested Spétses (thinly disguised as Phraxos) by John Fowles in his celebrated 1966 novel *The Magus*. Not to be outdone, since the early 1960s Hydra (Ýdra) has attracted artists, filmmakers, well-heeled Athenians, trendy French and Italians, movie stars and other international celebrities. ❏

PRECEDING PAGES: view from Póros towards Gálatas, on the Peloponnesian mainland. **LEFT:** bougainvillea blazing a trail in the afternoon sun.
FROM TOP: Greek worry beads, or *kobolói*; icon at the Monastery of the Panagía, on Hydra; kiosk seller.

ARGO-SARONIC ISLANDS

These six islands all lie within easy reach of the mainland, and thus are popular destinations. Nevertheless, they are distinctive, rich in history and remarkably attractive

L ow, flat Salamína (ancient Salamis) is invariably overlooked by island-hoppers intent on more glamorous hangouts. It's the largest Saronic Gulf island, but so close to Athens (and so frequently connected from Pérama port) that most Athenians regard it as a commuter dormitory.

Salamína

Salamína is best known for the naval battle in 480 BC in which the outnumbered Athenian ships routed Xerxes' Persian fleet, the Greek ships being the "wooden walls" that the Delphic Oracle had predicted would save Athens. Today the island is decidedly workaday, especially the port of **Paloúkia**, with its naval base; **Selínia**, 6km (4 miles) southwest, has tavernas and two hotels.

Most islanders live in the busy capital, **Salamína ❶** (or Kouloúri), which has an archaeological and a folk museum, and decent tavernas. The 13th-century **Faneroméni Convent ❷** overlooks the northwest coast, 6km (4 miles) from Salamína; it now houses 5 nuns and has vivid 17th-century frescoes. **Eándio**, a pleasant village on the west coast, has a good hotel. From here you can reach the southeast coast resort of **Peráni** and the small but very pretty little harbour of **Peristéria**.

Aegina and Angístri

An hour and a half by ferry from Piraeus, or 45 minutes by the hydrofoil, Aegina (or Aigina or Egina) has

little trouble attracting visitors. Long a favourite Athenian weekend retreat, it remains more popular with them than among foreign tourists or other Greeks. Shaped like an upside-down triangle, Aegina's south is punctuated by the magnificent cone of **Mount Oros**, the highest (532 metres/1,745ft) peak in the Argo-Saronic islands, visible on a pollution-free day from the Acropolis in Athens. The centre and eastern side of the island is mountainous; a gently-sloping fertile plain runs down to the northwestern corner

Main attractions
FANEROMÉNI CONVENT
HRÍSTOS KAPRÁLOS MUSEUM
TEMPLE OF APHAEA
PALEOHÓRA CHURCHES
ZOÖDÓHOU PIGÍS
HYDRA TOWN
LÁZAROS KOUNDOURIÓTIS MUSEUM
AGIOS NIKÓLAOS BEACH
BOUBOULÍNA MANSION
PALEÓ LIMÁNI
AGÍA PARASKEVÍ BEACH

LEFT: Agios Nektários, Aegina.
BELOW: Aegina's marketplace.

Bishop Nektários was born Anastásios Kefalás in 1846 in Silívria, Thrace, died in 1920 and was canonised in 1961 – the first modern saint of the Orthodox Church. The church honouring him is the largest in all Greece.

BELOW: fishing boats in Aegina harbour.

where Aegina Town (Egina) partly overlays the ancient capital.

From 1826 until 1828, Aegina served as the first capital of the modern Greek state. Elegant **Aegina Town ❸** has numerous 19th-century buildings constructed when the country's first president, Ioánnis Kapodístrias (1776–1831), lived and worked here. In Livádi suburb, just north, a plaque marks the house where **Níkos Kazantzákis** lived during the 1940s and 1950s, and wrote his most celebrated book, *Zorba the Greek*. The modern harbour, crowded with pleasure craft and fishing-boats, abuts the ancient harbour, now the shallow town beach north of the main quay. Aegina's main produce is pistachio nuts, sold all along the quay. The **Archaeological Museum** (Tue–Sun 8.30am–3pm), about 10 minutes' walk from the ferry quay, features exquisite Middle Bronze Age pottery with squid or octopus motifs. It stands in the precinct of the ancient Temple of Apollo (built 520–500 BC), of which only a single column – **Kolóna** – remains, a landmark for approaching boats. Continuing 3km (2 miles) north from here

brings you to the **Hrístos Kaprálos Museum** (June–Oct Tue–Sun 10am–2pm and 6–8pm, Nov–May Fri–Sun 10am–2pm; charge), housed in the studio of this prominent sculptor and painter (1909–93), heavily influenced by Henry Moore. There's a replica of his famous *Monument of the Battle of the Pindus*, the original frieze adorning the Greek Parliament building.

Aegina's main attraction is the exceptionally beautiful **Temple of Aphaea ❹** (Aféa; daily, summer 8am–7pm, winter 8am–5pm; charge), in the northeast, on a pine-tufted hilltop commanding a splendid view of the gulf. Built around 490 BC in the Doric order, it is the only surviving Greek temple with a second row of small, superimposed columns in the interior of the sanctuary, and one of the most completely preserved – it's well worth waiting for any crowds to disperse to enjoy it in solitude. A short distance below lies the beach resort of **Agía Marína**, now perking up after some very lean years, though there are much better tavernas – if not swimming – at quieter **Pórtes**, 8km (5 miles) south.

On the way to the temple you will pass the **Convent of Agios Nektários** (*see margin note opposite*); a steady stream of pilgrims approaches his tomb in expectation of miracles. Across the ravine from Agios Nektários is the abandoned medieval **Paleohóra** (Old Town), established after the island was sacked by pirates in the late 9th century, and inhabited until 1827. About 30 churches and little monasteries remain more or less intact, but only around seven – Agios Geórgios Katholikós, Tímios Stavrós and Metamórfosis are usually unlocked – retain frescoes of any merit or in recognisable condition; a helpful map near the site entrance (always open) helps locate them.

The west coast of the island is quite gentle, with serviceable beaches at **Marthóna** and shaded **Eginítissa**, though the sea – as around much of Aegina – is often not that clean. Perhaps a better target in this direction are several fish tavernas along the inlet-harbour of **Pérdika** ❺, from where there are several daily boat trips to uninhabited limestone **Moní** islet, a nature reserve with swimming in pristine waters.

Angístri is the small, pine-covered, low-key island opposite Aegina Town. Like most of the Argo-Saronics, it was resettled by medieval Albanians, but in recent decades was colonised by Germans and Athenians, who bought up houses in the villages of hillside **Metóhi** and coastal **Mýlos**, which bracket the port, sandy beach and main package resort of **Skála**. Larger boats stop at Skála, while smaller speedboats call at Mýlos. Tourism is mixed and increasing: young Greek trendies camping on the pebbly beaches, plus British and Scandinavian package-holiday vistors. A path heads south from Skála for clothing-optional **Halikiáda** beach, while the paved road from Mýlos passes scenic **Dragonéra** cove en route to the southerly hamlet of **Limenária**.

Póros

Póros is separated from the Peloponnese by a narrow channel, which gives the island its name – *póros* in Greek means "ford". As you sail down the 350-metre/yd wide passage from its northwest entrance, **Póros Town** ❻ comes into view, presiding over one of

Lemonódassos, opposite Póros on the mainland, is a huge lemon grove with 30,000 trees – and a taverna selling delicious fresh lemonade.

BELOW: the unique two-layered Temple of Aphaea.

> *Suddenly the land converges on all sides and the boat is squeezed into a narrow strait from which there seems to be no egress... To sail slowly through the streets of Póros is to recapture the joy of passing through the neck of the womb. It is a joy too deep almost to be remembered.*
>
> Henry Miller
> *The Colossus of Maroussi*, 1942

BELOW: the homogeneous rooftops of Póros Town.

the most protected anchorages in the Aegean, with scores of yachts berthed in a row. From an approaching boat, the sight of the pyramidal, orange-roofed town culminating in a blue-and-white hilltop clock tower is one of the iconic images of the Argo-Saronics. **Galatás** village on the mainland opposite is dull by comparison, aside from flanking lemon groves, but sends constant passenger shuttles (and regular car barge-ferries) across. Póros Town, built on several hills, occupies most of the little sub-islet of **Sferiá**, attached to the bulk of Póros (called Kalávria) by a narrow isthmus cut by a disused canal. Whichever route you choose to climb to the clock tower, you'll probably lose yourself in narrow lanes overhung with vines and flowers. Down on the waterfront, pride of place is given to a busy meat and seafood market similar to Aegina's, and a small but worthwhile **Archaeological Museum** (Tue–Sun 8.30am–3pm; charge) with finds from the island and mainland opposite.

Despite mediocre beaches on Kalávria (the best of these are **Monastiríou** in the east and **Megálo Neório**

to the west), Póros sees far more package tourism than its neighbours, along with Athenian weekenders and second home owners. The island has never been fashionable, but has had a naval connection since 1846 when a cadet training station was established just beyond the isthmus bridge.

The main inland sights are both on Kalávria. The early 19th-century **monastery of Zoödóhou Pigís ❼** (Virgin of the Life-Giving Spring), home to four monks, sits on a wooded hillside (20 minutes from town by bus), next to the Argo-Saronics' only natural spring. From here, the paved road winds further inland through the pines to the 6th-century BC **Sanctuary of Poseidon** (daily 8am–3pm; free), near the island's summit. It's currently being re-excavated by a Swedish team, though there isn't much to see yet beyond foundations – and a superb view. Much of the masonry was carted off to Hydra during medieval times.

Hydra

The island of Hydra (or Ydra, the ancient Ydrea, "the well watered")

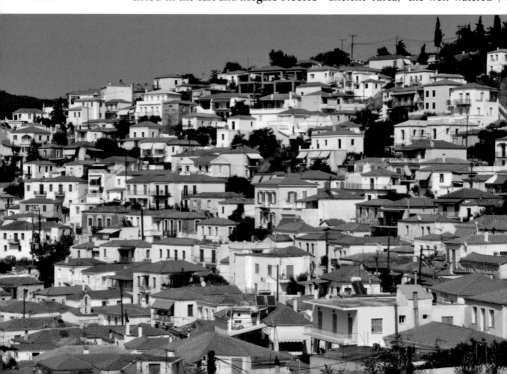

today mostly a long, barren rock with a few stands of pine. But the postcard-perfect harbour bracketed by grey-stone mansions and Byzantine-tiled vernacular houses is incomparable, attracting the artistic and the fashionable since the 1950s, and many others ever since. It is one of the few islands declared an Architectural Heritage Reserve, which has helped Hydra retain its original beauty through strict building controls and the banning of most motorised transport – the donkeys you see are working freight-carriers, not just photo opportunities.

The central port-town, also called **Hydra ❽** (Ydra), is a popular destination, packed out during summer and at weekends most of the year. The harbour, girded by a slender breakwater, forms a perfect crescent, its two ends flanked by 19th-century cannons. Overhead, white-plastered houses climbing the slope are accented by massive grey *arhondiká*, mansions built by shipping families who made fortunes in the 18th and 19th centuries. Some of these imposing *arhondiká* are open for visits, for example the gorgeously restored **Lázaros Koundouriótis Museum** (Tue–Sun 9am–4pm; charge), on the western slope, and the **Historical Archives** (daily 9.30am–4pm; charge) on the east quay, also displaying costumes, engravings and nautical paraphernalia. Just back from the quay, with its multiple gift shops aimed at cruise passengers, is a wonderful marketplace and the belfry-studded, 18th-century cathedral of **Kímisis tis Theotókou**, built largely of stone from Póros's Poseidon temple.

The higher reaches of the town and the hills beyond, accessed by narrow alleys and steep stairways, remain surprisingly untouched, charming and full of Greek colour. The uniformity of white walls is broken again and again by a century-old doorway, a bright-blue window frame, a flight of striking scarlet steps, or a dark-green garden fence. An hour's walk upwards and inland leads to **Agía Evpraxía Convent** and the **Profítis Ilías Monastery**, while **Zoúrvas Monastery** stands at the extreme eastern tip of Hydra. Island beaches, however, are less impressive. **Mandráki ❾**, northeast of town,

Tourism to Hydra was given a boost by the 1957 film Boy on a Dolphin, starring Sophia Loren, which was set on the island.

BELOW: daily life in the streets of Hydra Town.

Laskarína Bouboulína

The national heroine of the War of Independence, Laskarína Bouboulína was a wealthy Spetsiot woman who took control of the local fleet after her seafaring husband was killed. A colourful figure, she was said to have seduced her lovers at gunpoint, and ended up being murdered in 1825 by the father of a girl with whom her son had rashly eloped. The now defunct 50-drachma note showed her on her flagship *Agamemnon*, directing the gunnery crew; on land, she organised a ruse to deter an Ottoman landing by perching fezes atop thistles on the shore, to simulate a massed army. Her mansion behind the Dápia (daily Mar–Oct 9.45am–8pm, guided tours only; charge), still belonging to her family, is now a museum dedicated to her life and works. Her bones are kept in Spétses Museum.

On an island where most motor vehicles are banned, Hydra's mules and donkeys perform all haulage.

has the only all-sand beach. It's more interesting to follow a wide path tracing the coast southwest to the hamlets of **Kamíni** and **Vlyhós**, with a 19th-century stone bridge. There are some good tavernas in both places, and water-taxis to get you back to town. Better beaches are found in the far southwest at **Bísti** and **Agios Nikólaos**, with boat access only; the hardy can walk an hour and a quarter to **Limnióniza** bay on the southeast-facing shore.

Spétses

Spétses (or Spétsai) is the southwesternmost of the Argo-Saronic Gulf islands. In antiquity it was known as Pityoússa (Piney Island), and despite devastating fires in 1990 and 2001 it is still marginally the most wooded of this island group, and with the best beaches. Tourist development here is far more extensive than on Hydra but less than on Póros or Aegina; building in **Spétses Town** ⑩, much the largest in extent, is controlled, though not quite as strictly as on Hydra, and while private cars are banned within town limits, scooters and taxis are not.

Like Hydra, Spétses was one of the main centres of activity during the Greek War of Independence, using its fleet for the Greek cause. It is distinguished for being the first in the archipelago to revolt against Ottoman rule in 1821, and the fortified **Dápia** harbour still bristles with cannons. Although Spétses's fleet declined after that war, with the emergence of Sýros then Piraeus, as the main seaports, ship-building traditions continue, especially in the east end of town at **Baltíza** inlet, where a few boatyards continue to build caiques the old way. The local **museum** (Tue–Sun 8.30am–2.30pm, charge) in the imposing *arhondikó* of Hatzigiánnis Méxis, a late 18th-century shipowner, contains painted ship-prows of the revolutionary fleet, and the bones of heroine Laskarína Bouboulína (*see panel page 151*). Passed en route to Baltíza, the **Paleó Limáni** (Old Harbour) still radiates a gentle grace thanks to the 18th-century mansions where wealthy Athenian families spend the summer. Above, the courtyard of **Agios Nikólaos** church has a particularly outstanding pebble mosaic, a highly developed Spetsiot art.

Out of town in the opposite direction (west), in more modest **Kounoupítsa** district, stands the **Anargyríos and Korgialénios College**, a Greek version of an English public school where John Fowles taught, memorialising institution and island in his 1966 novel *The Magus*. Like the Edwardian waterfront Hotel Possidonion, it was founded by local benefactor Sotírios Anárgyros; neither hotel nor school operates any longer, though the latter is occasionally used for conferences and children's summer programmes.

A paved road circles the island, giving access to several fine beaches. Heading anticlockwise, the first tempting stop is sandy **Zogeriá**. Next is pine-backed **Agía Paraskeví**, the most scenic on Spétses, then **Agía Anargyrí**, the longest, sandiest and most developed. Solitude-seekers will prefer less crowded **Xylokériza** pebble cove to the west.

THE CYCLADES ISLANDS

Andros, Kéa, Tínos, Kýthnos, Sýros, Mýkonos, Sérifos,
Sífnos, Andíparos, Páros, Náxos, Mílos, Kímolos,
Folégandros, Síkinos, Íos, Amorgós, Santoríni, Anáfi

The 24 inhabited Cyclades evoke visions of sun-drenched seascapes. The famous white Cubist houses have inspired many modern architects, Le Corbusier among them. The beaches are dazzling, the food fresh, fellow-travellers companionable, and seagoing connections allow you to take in more than one "small paradise" on a short holiday.

For many people the Cyclades *are* the Greek islands; other groups are mere distractions from this blue Aegean essence. The scenic high point is probably dramatic, southernmost Santoríni, created by a volcanic explosion about 3,500 years ago, and there is nothing like it. The spiritual centre remains Apollo's ancient Delos: "Cyclades" means a cycle around Delos.

There are several basic ferry or catamaran routes. The eastern one from Rafína takes in Andros, Tínos and Mýkonos, sometimes extending to pivotal Sýros, itself served on main lines from Piraeus, continuing to Páros, Náxos, Íos and Santoríni. Another route carries on past Náxos to the "back islands" like Skhinoússa and Koufonísi before winding up at Amorgós and Anáfi. A westerly service arcs by Kýthnos, Sérifos, Sífnos, Kímolos and Mílos, with onward catamarans stretching via Folégandros and Síkinos to meet up with the central line at Santoríni.

The Cyclades were inhabited as early as 6500 BC. By the third millennium a flourishing culture had emerged, with beautiful crafts and lively commerce, as anyone who visits the Goulandrís Museum of Cycladic Art in Athens will appreciate. This museum is the world's first devoted to Cycladic art, most famous for its marble female figurines. High culture continued through Roman-era decline, and while this may not be evident amid the hedonistic jet-setters of Mýkonos or youthful merrymakers of Íos, one sunset over the Vale of Klíma, the valley in Mílos where the Venus de Milo was discovered, will convince you.

As Greek Nobel laureate poet Odysséas Elýtis, wrote: "Íos, Síkinos, Sérifos, Mílos – each word a swallow to bring you spring in the midst of summer." ❏

PRECEDING PAGES: Ía's windmill, Santoríni. **LEFT:** Agios Konstandínos, Parikía, Páros.
FROM TOP: ocean's bounty; detail from the Vamvakáris Museum, Sýros; Firá, Santoríni.

THE CYCLADES

From the hectic nightlife of Mýkonos and Ios to the rugged beauty of Mílos and Sérifos or the unspoilt seclusion of tiny Kímolos and Anáfi, there is something for all tastes to be found on these islands

lorious beaches, Bronze Age art, almond orchards, gleaming white villages and the archaeological marvels of ancient Delos are just some of the reasons visitors return to the Cyclades again and again.

Andros

The reddish Andros soil makes everything glow sienna at sunset, especially in the heights of the north, settled centuries ago by Orthodox Albanians; their basic stone huts contrast with the whitewash and red tile of the other, wealthier villages. Farmland is still divided by painstakingly built stone walls, the *frákhtes*, unusual for the pattern of triangular slates incorporated into them.

The port town in the northwest, Gávrio, also doubles as a serviceable resort, though **Batsí 1**, 6km (4 miles) south, is more conventionally picturesque, with even more development and an attractive beach. On the east coast, **Andros Town 2** (Hóra) has more upmarket tourism and a significant contingent of Athenians with weekend homes here. The Goulandrís shipping family has created the excellent **Museum of Contemporary Art**, a few steps north of the main square (June–Sept Wed–Mon 10am–2pm and 6–8pm, Oct–May Sat–Mon 8am–2pm; charge), featuring works by top-notch figures like Matisse and Kandinsky, as well as temporary exhibits and an exquisite sculpture garden. The prize

exhibit in the **Archaeological Museum** (Tue–Sun 8.30am–3pm; charge; closed until 2010) is the Hermes of Andros, a 2nd-century copy of Praxiteles' statue.

Between Batsí and Andros Town extends a long, deep valley, with terraces all the way up its sides towards the island's highest mountain range, which rises to 994 metres (3,261ft). Plane, mulberry and walnut trees are nourished by a series of springs that whirl down from the mountain tops, most notably at **Ménites**, with its church of **Panagía Koúmoulos**. Its multi-

Main attractions
MUSEUM OF CONTEMPORARY ART
PÝRGOS MARBLE-CARVING
ERMOÚPOLI
MÝKONOS NIGHTLIFE
ANCIENT DELOS
VATHÝ BAY
ANDÍPAROS CAVE
NÁOUSA PORT
FOLÉGANDROS KÁSTRO
HOZOVIÓTISSA MONASTERY
ANÁFI BEACHES

LEFT: Hrysopigí Monastery, Sífnos. **BELOW:** windsurfing on the Aegean.

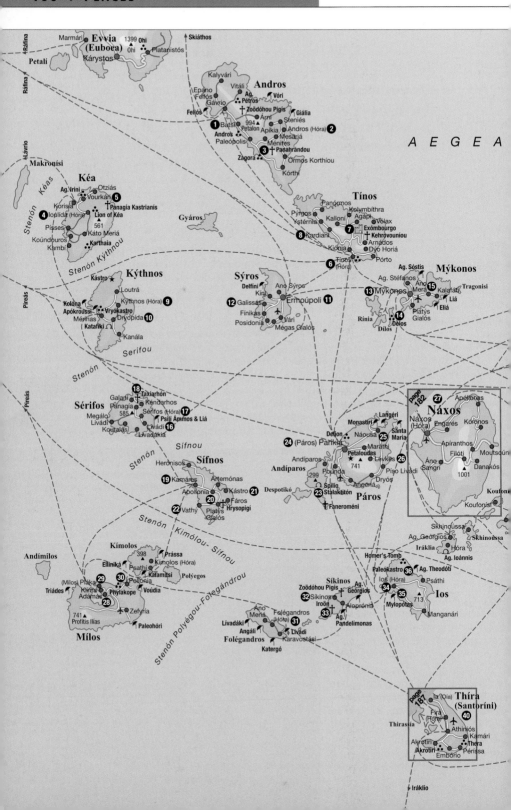

Rafína
Marmári ● **Évvia** 1399 **Ohi** ↑ Skiáthos
(Euboea) ▲ **Ohi** ∴ Platanistós
Petalí **Ohi**
Kárystos ●
Rafína

Kalyvári
Épano Vitáli ● **Andros**
Fellós Gávrio ● Vóri ●
Ag. ∴
● **Pétros**
Fellós ✝ Zoödóhou Pigis ● Giália
Árni ● Stenies
① Batsí 994 ▲ Apíkia ● Andros (Hóra) **②**
Andros Petalon
Paleópolis Mesariá
Ménites
Zágora ✝ **③** ✝ Panahrándou
Órmos Korthíou
Kórthi

A E G E A

Makronísi
Kéa Otziás
Ag. Irini ● Vourkári
Kórisia ✝ Pánagía Kastrianís
④ Ioplída (Hóra) **⑤** Lion of Kéa **Tínos** Kolymbithra
Pisses 561 Panórmos Agápi
Koúndouros Káto Meriá Pyrgos ● Kallóni ● Vólax
Kambí ▲ Karthaía Ystérnia ● Exómbourgo
Gyáros **⑦** ✝ Kehrovouníou
Kárdianí Arnádos
⑧ Kiónia ● Dyó Horiá
Kýthnos Tínos ● Pórto
Kástro ★ **⑥** (Hóra)
Loutrá Ag. Sóstis
Sýros Ano **Mýkonos**
Delfíni Ano Sýros Ag. Stéfanos Merá ● **⑮**
Kolóna Kíni ● ● Ano Kalafáti
Apókroussi Vryokastro **Ermoúpoli** **⑪** **⑬** Mýkonos ● Liá
Méríhas Dryopída **⑫** Galissás ● Eliá
Katafíki ☊ **⑩** Finikás Vári Plátys Giálos
Kanála Posidonía Mégas Gialós Rínia ● **⑭**
Dílos
Serífou Délos

Pireás

Galaní **⑱** ✝ Taxiarhón
Sérifos Panagía Kéndarhos **Náxos** **㉗** Apóllonas
Megálo 585 ▲ Sérifos (Hóra) **⑰** Langéri Náxos ● Engarés Koronos
Livádi Livádi Monastíri ★ (Hóra) Apíranthos
Koútalas Livadákia **⑯** Delion ● Santa Ano ▲ Moutsoúni
Sífnou Maria Sángri 1001 Danakós
Náousa **㉕**
Sífnos (Páros) Paríkia Maráthi Léfkes **㉖**
Heronísos **㉔** ✝ Petaloúdes Koufoní
⑲ Kamáres Artemónas Andíparos ● 741 ▲ Píso Livádi Koufonísi
Apollonía **⑳** Kástro **㉑** Pounda ● Dryós
㉒ Vathy Fáros **Andíparos** 299 ● Angeriá Skhinoússa
Plátys Hrysopigí Despotikó Spiliá ● Ag. Geórgios ●
Gialós **㉓** Stalaktitón **Páros** Iráklia ● Skhinoússa
Stenón Kimólou-Sífnou ✝ Faneroméni Ag. Ioánnis
Homer's Tomb ● Hóra

Kímolos Paleókastro **㊱** Ag. Theodóti
Andímilos 398 ▲ Prássa Ios (Hóra) Psáthi
Ellinikó ● Kímolos (Hóra) **㉞**
Psáthi Kalamítsi Polýegos Síkinos Ag. **㉟** ▲ **Ios**
㉙ ㉚ Pollónia Zoödóhou Pigis ✝ Geórgios Mylopótas 713
(Mílos) Pláka ✝ Voúdia **㉜** Síkinos Ioraón Aloprónia Manganári
Triádes ✝ Klíma Phylakope Meniá ● Aloprónia
Adámas **㉘** Ano **㉝** ✝ Pandelímonas
741 ▲ ✈ Zefyría Merá Folégandros
Profítis Ilías Lívadáki (Hóra) **㉛**
Paleohóri Angáli ● Lívadi
Mílos Folégandros ● Karavostási
Katergó

Stenón Polýegou-Folegándrou

page 187
la (Oía)
Thíra
(Santoríni)
Thirassía Fyra
(Hóra)
✈ **㊵**
Athiniós
● Kamári
Akrotíri ▲ **Théra**
Akrotíri ● Périssa
Emboríó

↓ Iráklio

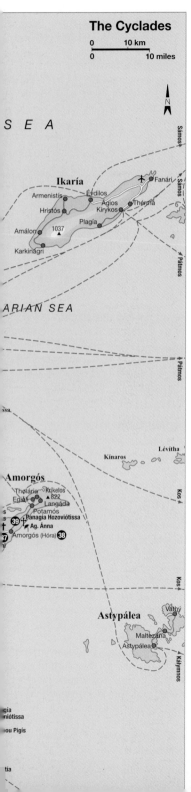

The Cyclades

0   10 km

0   10 miles

↑ N

S E A

Sámos

Ikaría

Armenistís   Évdilos

Hristós   Ágios   Thérma
              Kírykos

Amálon 1037   Plagía

Karkinágri

Fanári

Sámos

Pátmos

ARIAN SEA

ssa.

Pátmos

Kínaros   Lévitha

Amorgós

Tholária Krikelos
Egiáli   ▲822
          Langáda
s   Potamós
s   39   Panagia Hozoviótissa
t   ↑ Ag. Ánna
7 Amorgós (Hóra) 38

Kos

Kos

Astypálea   Vathy

Maltezána

Astypálea

gía
niótissa

ou Pigís

tia

Kálymnos

spouted spring is considered sacred; possibly there was once a big temple to Dionysos sited here. The centre of Andros is good walking country, with some of the 12 waymarked local trails hereabouts.

The **Monastery of Zoödóhou Pigís** (Life-Giving Spring) also claims a sacred site by its eponymous spring. Situated in the hills northeast of Batsí, the monastery is looked after by nuns guarding a library of precious sacred manuscripts. Three km (2 miles) east of Gávrio, the purpose of the remarkable, round Hellenistic tower of **Agios Pétros** remains a mystery.

South of the Paleópolis–Hóra road is the most spectacular of Andros's fortified Byzantine monasteries, cliffside **Panahrándou ❸** – more than 1,000 years old, it was founded in 961. The round trip on foot lasts about three hours from **Mesariá**, a green valley town with the Byzantine Taxiárhis (Archangel) church.

Paleópolis, the ancient capital, doesn't give much hint of its past, but the Hermes statue in the archaeological museum was discovered here. A bit further south, the **Zagora** promontory is the site of a walled city-state that flourished in the 8th century BC, Homer's time. It is fenced, and excavation work has stopped.

Andros has many fine beaches; the easiest to get to are **Nimbório** north of Hóra, the string of beaches between Gávrio and Batsí, and **Giália** (near Steniés, north of Andros Town). More remote coves worth the extra effort include **Fellós**, beyond Gávrio, and **Vóri** on the north coast.

Kéa

During the 19th century there were a million oaks on Kéa, and many still survive. Since ancient times, the island has also been noted for its almonds, though olive trees are curiously lacking. Traces of four ancient cities – Koressia, Ioulis, Karthaia and Poiessa – testify to the island's one-time importance. Kéa (popularly Tziá, in ancient times Keos)

The Cycladic Bronze Age

Numerous artefacts illuminate the Bronze Age culture of the Cycladic islands, shedding light on the way the ancient people lived and died.

B
ronze Age Cycladic peoples left behind many beautiful artefacts, most famously their stylised marble sculptures, that provide evidence of an organised and flourishing culture. Settlements and cemeteries excavated on a number of Cycladic islands are generally considered to be the first complex, organised, settled communities in Europe.

The Early Cycladic Bronze Age is thought to have begun close to 3200 BC, and to have lasted until around 2000 BC. The later Bronze Age in the Cyclades falls into two general periods, referred to by scholars and archaeologists as Middle and Late Cycladic respectively. These periods increasingly display the influence of the Minoan culture of Crete and the move towards urban settlement. In general, the term "Cycladic culture" refers to the Early Cycladic era, and it is during this period that the individuality of the culture of the Cycladic islands is most evident.

Early Cycladic settlements were small, numbering around 50 people, comprising densely packed stone-built housing, usually of only one storey. Accompanying the settlements, outside the residential area, are cemeteries of small cist graves (rectangular graves lined with stone) and chamber-tombs, clustered in family groups; the dead were inhumed in a contracted (foetal) position, along with everyday objects. Much of the evidence we have of how Early Cycladic society functioned comes from these cemeteries.

The often stark differences in grave goods between tombs provides evidence of a stratified society. While some graves contain an extremely rich variety of artefacts, including gold and silver jewellery, others have very little, often only a single marble figure. How these differences between rich and poor were manifest in practice is a matter of conjecture, but many artefacts display a high degree of skill in their manufacture, indicating the presence of skilled craft workers.

Besides hunting, fishing, animal husbandry and agriculture, much trade was carried out from the Cycladic islands, pointing to the existence of a merchant class, presumably among the wealthier members of society. The Cycladic peoples were skilled sailors and had contact with the Greek mainland, Crete, Anatolia and even the distant Danube Basin.

White marble figurines

Of all the items left by these peoples, the marble figurines are both the most famous and, perhaps, most intriguing. Their importance is such that they are used as a "diagnostic" tool by scholars to delineate the Cycladic Culture. The predominantly female figures are generally around 20cm (8in) in length (although a very few near life-sized sculptures have been discovered) and are made of white marble. Almost two-dimensional in their execution, they have flattened oval heads and arms folded below schematically rendered breasts; many features would have been painted onto marble (on the face, only the nose is rendered in stone). It is conjectured, from the position of the feet, that the figures were intended to lie horizontally, but there is no conclusive evidence for this, just as there is no firm consensus about their function. Explanations from scholars range from their being apotropaic (intended to ward off evil), to divinities, to ancestors, to symbolic companions for the deceased. ❑

LEFT: mysterious Cycladic figurines in the Santoríni Archaeological Museum.

has long been popular with Athenians. Regular Kéa-bound boats leave from Lávrio, some 50km (30 miles) from Athens, and land at **Korisía**; perhaps once a week there is a continuation to other Cyclades.

Kéa's main town, **Ioulída ❹** (Hóra), covers a rounded ridge overlooking the island's northern reach; home to most islanders, it was a spot chosen precisely because it was inaccessible for pirates. Unlike most Cycladic villages, its houses have pitched, tiled roofs. The **Archaeological Museum** (Tue–Sun 8.30am–3pm; free) contains abundant finds from the four towns of ancient Keos; the most interesting antiquity is the 6th-century BC **Lion of Kéa**, a 15-minute walk northeast of Hóra. Carved from granite, almost 6 metres (19ft) long, it represents a real lion brought in to eat malicious Nereids.

The scalloped coast has surprisingly few accessible beaches; **Písses**, at the mouth of a fertile valley, **Koúndouros** with Athenians' villas and **Kambí** with a good taverna are among the exceptions. Close to Korissía is the bayside village of **Vourkári ❺**, popular with

yachts, and with a notable concentration of fish tavernas. Further around the same bay stands **Agía Iríni**, the ruins of a Minoan-era palace. A short distance north, **Cape Kéfala** is the site of the oldest Neolithic settlement in the Cyclades.

Northeast of Agía Iríni, a paved road leads to **Otziás**, a sandy but exposed bay, and continues to **Panagía Kastrianís** monastery, focus of a 15 August pilgrimage, and with an inexpensive hostel available at other times.

Tínos

Tínos receives many thousands of visitors annually – but they are mostly Greek pilgrims bound for the church of **Panagía Evangelístria** (Annunciation). In 1822, the nun Pelagía dreamt of an icon of the Virgin; it was duly unearthed and the church was built to house it. The icon's healing powers have made **Tínos Town ❻** (Hóra) the Lourdes of Greece. Women fall to their knees upon arrival, and crawl painfully to the church (the marble steps are carpeted). Healing miracles are said to occur. On the Virgin's feast days – 25

According to legend, the water from the spring at Ménites turned to wine each year on Dionysos' feast day. Today the Sáriza spring in nearby Apíkia does the next best thing, supplying sparkling water that is sold in bottles throughout Greece.

BELOW: a modern café on Sýros.

Intricately designed stone dovecotes are a feature of Tínos, where the Venetians were the first to embark on the systematic breeding of pigeons.

BELOW: journey's end for pilgrims to Tínos – the Panagía Evangelístria.

March (Annunciation) and 15 August (Dormition) – thousands of Greeks pour off the boats for the procession of the little icon, which is carried downhill in an ornate baldachin over the kneeling supplicants. The church complex is full of marble, precious votive offerings (especially silver boats), and contains several museums. Like nearby Sýros, the island is, ironically, actually half Catholic in population.

The site of the Temple of Poseidon and Amphitrite at **Kiónia** beach, one of the few ancient sites, is neglected, though the town's **Archaeological Museum** is worth a look (Tue–Sun 8.30am–3pm; charge). Among the exhibits are a Roman-era marble sundial from Kiónia that shows the time, the equinoxes and solstices; and a large number of artefacts from excavations at Exómbourgo.

Tínos is renowned for marble work – especially fanlights and bas-relief plaques – and there is still a marble-sculpture school and many active workshops in the village of **Pýrgos**. Tínos's other speciality is Greece's most elaborate dovecotes. There are hundreds of

them inland, a tradition started by the Venetians. Their pattern of triangular windows is mimicked over doorways, on fences and in window shapes. It is a pliant symbol, which seems to represent anything from the shape of a sail to the Holy Trinity.

For an insight into Catholicism on Tínos, visit the peak of **Exómbourgo** ❼, 643 metres (2,110ft) high, with a ruined Venetian fortress, and the surrounding villages, which are mostly Catholic. Xinára at its base is the seat of the local Catholic bishop, and there are Catholic monasteries and convents in nearby villages. Tínos was the last island to fall to the Turks, in 1715. **Vólax** village, famous for its basket-weavers, is surrounded by weird, mushroom-shaped, wind-sculpted rocks; the climate up here is cool year-round, and potatoes flourish.

Kardianí ❽ on the Pýrgos-bound road is exceptional among Orthodox villages, a spectacularly set oasis settlement with views across to Sýros. From Ystérnia, a bit beyond, a mostly surviving marble-paved *kalderími* or cobbled path, among the finest of several on the island, leads down to Órmos Ysterníon. Southeast of Exómbourgo, the well-watered, arcaded villages of **Arnádos** and **Dýo Horiá** are equally handsome, and have attracted outsiders looking for second homes. Just above looms the Byzantine **Convent of Kehrovouníou**, where Pelagía had her vision of the icon.

Kolymbíthra in the north is Tínos's best beach, though **Agios Romanós, Agios Sóstis** and **Pórto** on the south coast, closer to the Hóra, are fine, if more commercialised.

Kýthnos

Unfashionable with foreigners, and among the quietest of the Cyclades, Kýthnos appeals – like Kéa – mostly to Athenian weekenders of more modest means. Native Kythniots are mainly dairy and livestock farmers belying the apparent infertility of the dun-coloured, undulating countryside

Elderly and/or unwell visitors frequent the thermal spa at **Loutrá** (the island's medieval name was Thermiá), on the northeast coast; about 90 minutes' walk northwest is the medieval **Kástro**, once home to thousands but abandoned by the 1700s.

Mérihas port on the west coast has most of the island's accommodation. In summer, taxi-boats run from Mérihas to **Episkopí, Apókroussi** and **Kolóna** beaches, the last a stunning sand-spit tethering **Agios Loukás** islet to the rest of Kýthnos. Near Apókroussi, **Vryókastro** is an ancient 10th-century BC town where a huge hoard of artefacts was uncovered in 2002.

Landlocked **Kýthnos** ❾ (Hóra) 6km (4 miles) northeast of Mérihas, is exquisite. Whereas most Cycladic towns crawl spider-like over local topography, Hóra adheres mostly to a rectangular plan. Wood-beamed arches span narrow streets to join two sides of one house; in the passages underneath, pavements are playfully decorated in whitewash with fish, stylised ships, or flowers. There is a small main square, around which are the better island tavernas

(though not much lodging). Fields at the back of town rise gently from the ravine to the south, dotted with farmhouses and tile-roofed chapels.

A stream bed splits into two **Dryopída** ❿, successor to Kástro as medieval capital; the chambered **Katafíki** cave here is linked in legend with the Nereids. The town itself presents, like Ioulída on Kéa, an appealing red-roofed spectacle, especially seen from above.

Sýros

When Sýros was overtaken as Greece's premier port by Piraeus in the late 1800s, it was left, as one writer put it, "a grand but old-fashioned lady who lives on her memories of the good old days and on her half-forgotten glories". This is a shame, for with its excellent inter-island ferry links and low-key but useful facilities, Sýros – still capital of the Cyclades – makes a pleasant and rewarding place to stay.

Just one large shipyard survives at the port-capital, **Ermoúpoli** ⓫, which doesn't help its resort image, but hasn't prevented the elegant neoclassical town from being designated a Unesco

Much of Kýthnos's electricity is supplied by a "wind park" just east of Hóra and a "solar park" on the road to Loutrá.

BELOW LEFT: local colour. **BELOW:** Dryopída, the blue domes of its church stark among the red roofs.

Heritage Site. The congested quay with its scent of roasting octopus doesn't give much away, but head inland and you'll see why Unesco bestowed the honour.

The marble-paved main square, **Platía Miaoúlis**, is lined with imposing buildings, some housing lively bars and cafés, and hosts a buzzing evening *vólta*. The Apollon Theatre, on nearby Platía Vardáka, is modelled after La Scala in Milan; its 1980s renovation is still a point of pride. Beyond the Apollon, the imposing dome and twin belfries of **Agios Nikólaos** mark the beginning of the **Vapória** quarter, where the wealthiest 19th-century shipowners and merchants built sumptuous mansions with painted ceilings and the like.

Ermoúpoli is dominated by two hills, each capped by a church. On the lower, **Vrontádo**, stands the Greek Orthodox **Church of the Resurrection** (Anástasis). On the higher is **Ano Sýros**, the medieval Catholic quarter – like Tínos, Sýros is approximately half Catholic – dominated by **Agios Geórgios** cathedral and 16th-century Capuchin monastery (adjacent is a

British World War I cemetery). One of Greece's greatest *rembétika* musicians, Márkos Vamvakáris, was born an Ano Sýros Catholic, and the **Vamvakáris Museum** (daily 10.30am–1pm, 7–10pm; charge), duly honours him. The worthwhile **Industrial Museum** on the road to Kíni (Mon and Wed–Sun 10am–2pm, Thur–Sun 6–9pm; charge), commemorates the island's now vanished shipping and mining enterprises.

The south of Sýros is gentler and greener than the rugged, empty north and has good beaches, especially near **Galissás** ⑫, a sizeable youth-oriented resort. Further up the west coast **Kíni** and lonelier **Delfíni** bay offer more good bathing. South of Galissás **Fínikas** and **Posidonía** – the latter immortalised by Vamvakáris, along with other Syrian locales, by its alternative name, Dellagrázia, in his overplayed standard *Frangosyriani* – are more mainstream resorts. Pythagoras' teacher, Pherekydes, the inventor of the sundial, hailed from here, and several caves bear his name. The southerly loop road continues east through

Mégas Gialós and Ahládi towards Vári, the most protected of the local coves. During the colonels' junta, political prisoners were interned on Gyáros, the barren island to the northwest.

Mýkonos

Mýkonos represents an emphatic victory of style (and self-promotion) over intrinsic substance. This rocky, treeless, gale-force windy, dry island, with admittedly excellent beaches and a Cycladic-cliché port town of dazzling beauty, receives close to a million visitors in a good year. They are drawn by a deserved reputation for big-city-standard shopping, sexy nightlife and (lately) some of the most luxurious accommodation in the islands – all of which makes Mýkonos the most expensive of the Cyclades, rivalled only by Santoríni.

Mýkonos Town ⓭, like the island overall, is one of the world's premier gay (male) resorts, with legendary clubs around Platía Mavrogénous, some including live drag shows in their repertoire. Cruise ships are also very much part of the picture, with passengers shipped ashore for some retail therapy, then horn-blasted reluctantly back aboard, clutching purchased designer clothing and jewellery.

It is possible to eschew all this and still enjoy Mýkonos. The Folklore Museum (Apr–Oct Mon–Sat 5.30–8.30pm, Sun 6.30–8.30pm; free) and the Archaeological Museum (Tue–Sun 8.30am–3pm; charge), at different ends of the quay, are full of interesting objects, including grave stelae and a Hellenistic copy of a 5th-century cult statue of Herakles. And the town is among the most photogenic and most solicitously preserved in the Cyclades, with wooden balconies loaded with flowers, red-domed chapels and irregular whitewashed surfaces. The odd-shaped Panagía Paraportianí (Our Lady of the Postern Gate) is probably Greece's most photographed church. "Little Venice" (officially Alefkándra), a row of arcaded buildings hanging

over the open sea west of the port, offers superb sunsets from its numerous classy bars and art galleries.

The town mascot has long been a pelican called Pétros. The original one settled on the island in 1955 after being blown off course by a storm. After various adventures, including an alleged kidnapping by a fisherman from Tínos, the original Pétros was killed when he was hit by a car in 1985. His replacement, who still inhabits the quayside, scattering his pink feathers, was donated in 1986 by a German businessman, although there are now actually three pelicans in residence.

Caiques depart from Mýkonos town for ancient Delos ⓮ (modern Dílos), the sacred island that is the hub of the Cyclades (see page 168). Or you could strike inland to Ano Merá ⓯ 7km (4 miles) east, the only real village on the island, which is less spoilt by tourism. Its main attraction is Tourlianí Monastery, with red domes and an ornate marble belfry. It houses some fine 16th-century Cretan icons and embroidery. On the road leading to Panórmos Bay and Fteliá hamlet lies the 12th-century

The Alefkándra district, known as "Little Venice" because of the balconies jutting out over the sea, is the artistic quarter of Mýkonos.

BELOW: one of Mýkonos Town's resident pelicans.

Ancient Delos

The archaeological wonders of Delos, first excavated in the late 19th century, make the choppy boat trip well worthwhile.

The tiny island of Delos (Dílos in modern Greek) is an archaeological mecca. Extensive Greco-Roman ruins occupying much of Delos's 4 sq km (1½ sq miles) make the site as extensive as Delphi or Olympia.

The morning voyage southwest from Mýkonos may take only 45 minutes but, as the caique heaves and shudders in the choppy sea, it can seem 10 times that long. Dress appropriately for the likely breezes, and have a dry-biscuit breakfast – a classic sea-sickness preventative. Better yet, try to ignore the physical and concentrate your mind on the metaphysical – although this is easier said than done.

It was on ancient Delos that the nymph Leto, pregnant by Zeus, supposedly gave birth to the divine twins Apollo and Artemis – although interestingly, an equally compelling legend (and elaborate sanctuary) places the momentous event in Lycia on the Asia Minor coast. Delos, until then just a floating rock, was honoured when four diamond pillars stretched up and anchored it in the heart of the Cyclades.

On arrival at Delos, orientate yourself to avoid getting lost among the ruins. Most of these occupy the two arms of a right angle. Ahead of you (the southern arm) are the theatre and mainly domestic buildings. To the left is the sanctuary to which pilgrims from all over the Mediterranean came with votive offerings and sacrificial animals.

For nearly 1,000 years, this sanctuary was the political and religious centre of the Aegean and host to the Delian Festival every four years. This, until the 4th century BC, was Greece's greatest festival. The Romans turned it into a grand trade fair and made Delos a free port. It also became Greece's slave market, where as many as 10,000 slaves were sold on one day.

By the start of the Christian era, the power and glory of Delos was waning, with frequent raids for plunder, and soon afterwards the island fell into disuse. During the next two millennia the stones were silent; then, with the arrival of French archaeologists in 1872, they began to speak.

The Sanctuaries of Apollo and Dionysos

Follow the pilgrim route to a ruined monumental gateway leading into the Sanctuary of Apollo. Within are three temples dedicated to Apollo – there is also a temple of Artemis – and parts of a colossal marble statue of Apollo which was destroyed when a massive bronze votive palm tree fell on it during a storm. Close by is the Sanctuary of Dionysos with several phalli (now mutilated) standing on pedestals and Dionysiac friezes.

Continue to the stunning Lion Terrace, where five scrawny, Archaic lions squat, apparently ready to pounce. They are replicas; some of the originals are in the site museum, but one was looted and taken to Venice in the 1600s. Below this is the Sacred Lake and the palm tree that marks the spot of the divine twins' birth.

Most visitors delight in that part of Delos which was occupied by artisans rather than gods. Their houses, close to the port, are a regular warren of narrow lanes lined by drains dating right back to 2,000 years ago, with niches for oil lamps which illuminated the streets. The main road leads to the theatre, which seated 5,500. It is unimpressive, but there are superb views from the uppermost of its 43 rows. Close to the theatre are grander houses with colonnaded courtyards and exquisite floor mosaics. ❑

LEFT: one of the guardians of the Lion Terrace.

Paleokástro (Dárga) convent; the nearby reservoir lake attracts thousands of migrating birds.

Mýkonos is famous, indeed notorious, for its all-night bars and all-day south-coast beaches. For bars, you must enquire when you arrive; the scene changes constantly. For beaches, **Paradise** is straight nude, **Super Paradise** partly gay nude, and both are beautiful; **Eliá**, **Kalafáti** and **Liá**, all reached via Ano Merá, are respectively partly gay/ nudist, popular with windsurfers, and a relatively quiet retreat. **Platýs Gialós** and **Psaroú** in the west are more family-oriented. With the exception of **Pánormos** and **Agios Sóstis** beaches on **Pánormos Bay**, the north coast is too exposed and windy for bathing.

Sérifos

Only at the last minute do approaching ferries round the long peninsula concealing the bay of **Livádi** , the harbour and main resort of Sérifos, along with its annexe **Livadákia** just south. Livádi is a pleasant base, with most of Sérifos's tourist facilities and good beaches to either side, including **Karávi**, **Liá**, **Agios Sóstis** and **Psilí Ammos**, accessible by paved roads and/or paths.

Sérifos Town ⑰ (Hóra) spills precipitously like scattered dice from the mountain above, contrasting with higher, gaunter ridges behind. Buses ascend to Hóra regularly, but the long flights of old stone steps (a 40-minute climb) make a more satisfying approach.

Hóra has two parts: Káto (Lower) and Ano (Upper). The upper, with arcaded passageways and incongruous neoclassical town hall, is the more interesting; its ridge leads in the west to the ruined *kástro*. The view of Livádi Bay and other islands is spectacular – and in the old days, eminently functional, as no pirate ship could approach without being seen long in advance.

A paved road system circles the heart of the island, but it's better to walk north on the remains of a wide *kal-*

derími (cobbled path), beginning from Ano Hóra's main square, designated "No.1" of half a dozen local paths. Numerous small bays with tiny, empty beaches lie below. Habitation is sparse, and there are just a few small farms along the way. After a good 90-minute walk, the village of **Kéndarhos** (Kállitsos) appears at the far side of a steep valley. Though there are no tavernas, a fresh-water fountain – despite appearances, Sérifos has abundant water – will refresh you. From here you must take the paved road west to the fortified medieval **Taxiarhón Monastery** ⑱, a half-hour distant. There are no longer any monks in residence, but a warden may be on hand to show you the ornate icon-screen, vivid frescoes and such rare treasures as lamps from Egypt and Russia and an ivory-inlaid bishop's throne.

From the nearest village, **Galaní**, the numbered path system resumes, taking you down to **Sykaminiá Bay** and then up to **Panagía** village. Scattered, tiny vineyards in this region produce the tawny-pink, sherry-like wine Sérifos is famous for – ask for it at local *kafenía*.

Most of the Cyclades islands that grew their own grain have windmills, but the majority have fallen into disuse.

BELOW:
Sérifos Town.

Rich pickings for this butterfly on Sýros – not to be confused with the Jersey tiger moths of Páros (see page 173).

(see page 173).

BELOW:
gloriously clear
waters on Sífnos.

Panagía's original 10th-century church is infamous for its 16 August feast day (*Xylopanagía*), when boys and girls used to rush in pairs to be the first to dance around the adjacent olive tree: the first couple to complete the dance would be allowed to marry during the year. Jealousy often prompted pitched battles, so nowadays the parish priest always goes first.

From Panagía scenic trails lead back to Hóra; those with vehicles can continue to southwestern Sérifos for isolated beaches. **Megálo Livádi** is relatively the most developed, with two tavernas; once an iron- and copper-mining centre until the deposits became uneconomical in the 1960s, it has a monument to four workers killed during a 1916 strike. Other, south-facing beaches on the way back to Livádi – some of this along dirt road – include **Koutalás**, **Gánema** and **Káto Ambéli**.

Sífnos

Noticeably greener than Sérifos or Kýthnos, and speckled with an improbable number (even by Cycladic standards) of churches and monasteries, Sífnos has long been a favourite of wealthier Athenians and French visitors, and at peak season can be nearly as crowded as Mýkonos or Santoríni. The harbour, **Kamáres** ⓭, at the base of two opposing dinosaur-back ridges, is relatively picturesque, and with ample facilities should you want to stay there.

The main road climbs a steep, deep valley from Kamáres 5.5km (3½ miles) to **Apollonía** ⓴, the capital, the slopes on the right culminating in the peak of Profítis Ilías with its atmospheric monastery, the most worthy hiking target of several paths. Pick of Apollonía's many churches is **Agios Athanásios**, with frescoes and a carved wood icon screen. There are fine examples of local weaving in Apollonía's **Folklore Museum** (Tue–Sun 9.30am–2pm and 6–10pm; charge); the other island crafts are jewellery, a legacy of ancient times when Sífnos was rich in gold and silver; and most notably **pottery**, with an equally long tradition. In Kamáres, Fáros, Platý Gialós and isolated **Herónisos**, potters still set out long racks of earthenware to dry in the sun prior to glazing.

Contiguous with Apollonía, **Artemónas** (the towns take their names from Apollo and Artemis, both of whom had temples in the vicinity) is Sífnos's wealthiest settlement, with mansions and more old churches, such as multi-domed **Kóhi** (Nook), in whose court-yard cultural events are sometimes held in summer. Down the block a plaque marks the house where mourn-ful poet Ioánnis Grypáris (1871–1942) was born.

Perched 100 metres (328ft) above the sea and 3km (2 miles) east of Apollonía is **Kástro ㉑**, the former capital originally established atop the ancient acropolis by a renegade Cata-lan Knight of St John in 1307. It soon passed by marriage of his heirs to the Venetians, who elaborated the elon-gated ground plan along the ridge top. A former Catholic church in the town centre shelters the **Archaeological Museum** (Tue–Sun 8.30am–2.30pm; free), mostly containing Hellenistic and Roman finds.

Sífnos's south-shore settlements make tranquil seaside bases, although beaches – as at **Fáros** and **Apókofto** – are not always the best the island has to offer. Just beyond the latter looms **Hrysopigí** (Golden Well) **Monastery**, built in 1653 on an islet reached by a footbridge. It is no longer in monastic use, but its main festival, 40 days after Easter, is well attended.

Still further southwest, **Platýs Gialós** has the longest – if windiest – beach on the island, and ample (perhaps too ample) development. Just above it is the glorious rural monastery of **Panagía tou Vounoú**, while the old trail west short-cuts the paved road to the almost landlocked bay of **Vathý ㉒**, which can also be reached by a more adventurous and scenic marked path from **Kataváti** just south of Apollonía. Caiques make the trip from Kamáres to the little hamlet here in summer, and there are tavernas and modest rooms on the excellent beach that sit some-what at odds with a new luxury hotel. (You can walk along a path to another beach, **Fykiádas**, at the far south tip of Sífnos). The visually arresting hallmark of Vathý is little **Taxiárhis** (Archangel) **Monastery**, poised with its feet in the sand as though ready to set sail.

Hrysopigí Monastery has an icon with allegedly miraculous powers: it once destroyed the stone bridge to the islet, saving the monastery (and the virtue of several young girls) from pirate attack; then later saved Sífnos from plague (1675) and locusts (1928).

BELOW LEFT:
Hrysopigí
Monastery, Sífnos.

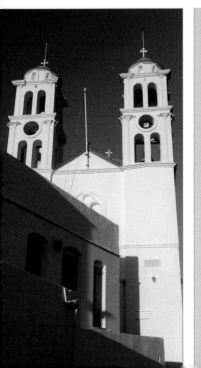

Underground Tourism

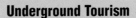

The Cave of the Stalactites (summer daily 10.45am–3.45pm; charge), the principal sight on Andíparos, was discovered during the reign of Alexander the Great, around 330 BC, and has been attracting visitors ever since. Despite the depredations of souvenir-hunters, who have broken and removed stalactites and stalagmites for centuries, it is still a fantastically spooky chamber, full of weird shapes and shadows.

Almost as impressive as the formations are the inscriptions left by past visitors, including King Otto of Greece and Lord Byron. The oldest piece of graffiti has sadly been lost – a note from several individuals stating that they were hiding in the cave from Alexander the Great, who suspected them of plotting his assassination. Another inscription (in Latin) records the Christmas Mass celebrated here by the French Mar-quis de Nointel in 1673, for an audience of 500.

In summer, buses and boats run to the cave from Andíparos Town, or else it's a two-hour walk. Then you descend more than 70 metres (230ft) from the cave entrance to the vaulted main chamber. There are concrete steps now, and electric lighting, making the descent easier, but the effect is still breathtaking. The entire cave is actually twice as deep as the part to which you are allowed access, but the rest has been closed because it would be too dangerous.

Andíparos

Once, more than 5,000 years ago, this small, pretty island was joined to Páros. A narrow channel now separates the two, plied by frequent car ferries and excursion boats bringing visitors to its famous cave, **Spílio Stalaktitón** ❷❸ (Cave of the Stalactites). Most day-trippers bypass characterful **Andíparos Town**, so it is relatively easy to find rooms here outside the month of August. Beyond a husk of modern hotels and Athenian second homes is the 1440s-vintage *kástro*, one of the finest such in the Cyclades, here a square compound with just a single arched entrance and a cistern/well complex inside (still in use). Tourism – with many patrons styling themselves refugees from the tumult of Páros – has helped Andíparos defy the depopulation trends of other small islets, retaining nearly 1,000 inhabitants.

Andíparos measures only 11km by 5km (7 miles by 3 miles), so there are no daunting distances. The approaching ferry passes two islets; on one, **Saliangós**, British excavators in 1964 revealed a Neolithic (pre-4000 BC) set-tlement, including a fat female figurine now in the Parikiá museum. The other islet belongs to the Goulandrís family, who established the eponymous museum in Athens.

Beaches are surprisingly numerous, the better ones on the east and south coasts. **Glýfa** is the closest to the town **Agios Geórgios** faces the goat-grazed island of Despotikó, while **Kalógeros** is the exception to the west-coast rule. **Faneroméni** chapel stands alone on a southeastern cape.

Páros

Parikiá ❷❹ (also called Páros) is the attractive capital of this heavily visited island. In August, make sure you book ahead or get off the ferry quickly, as the cheaper rooms go fast – although in the evening they are empty as tenants take in the famous nightlife. Parikiá is as pretty as Mýkonos Town, but not so labyrinthine. The beautiful 6th-century **Ekatondapylianí Church** (Our Lady of a Hundred Doors) retains its Byzantine form, and includes a side chapel adapted from a 4th-century BC building. By the church is a **Byzantine**

Museum (daily 10am–2pm, 6–9pm; charge) full of icons, while the prize exhibit at the nearby **Archaeological Museum** (Tue–Sun 8.30am–3pm) is a chunk of the Parian Chronicle, embossed on a marble slab. The ancient **cemetery** is on the seafront, while the 13th-century Venetian *kástro* southwest along the water incorporates a classical watchtower and is otherwise largely built of masonry pillaged from a 6th-century temple that stood here.

In beautiful **Náousa** ㉕, on the north coast, the little harbour's colourful fishing boats seem to nudge right up against the quayside houses. Though the village has become notably fashionable, with upmarket boutiques, accommodation and restaurants, the harbour still retains its traditional charm. There are half a dozen fine **beaches** around the bay and on the far side of the peninsula, accessible on foot or by taxi-boat. **Monastíri** on the west side of the bay is part gay/nudist; protected **Langéri** on the east shore has heaped dunes; while windsurfers repair to **Sánta María**, facing the straits with Náxos. Páros has plenty of other decent beaches, especially on the southeast coast at **Hrysí Aktí** (Golden Beach), just north of **Dryós**, with its attractive cove.

Lévkes ㉖, the Ottoman-era capital, is the largest inland village, beautifully set, intrinsically attractive and indifferent to tourism, although there is now a residential literary retreat centre for translators. From Lévkes, **walkers** can follow a surviving portion of the old marble-paved *kalderími* that used to cross the entire island. Go east to Pródromos and Mármara, with views en route to looming **Náxos** ㉗ across the straits *(see pages 182–3)*, or north to Kóstos, then west to **Maráthi**, whose ancient tunnel quarries – still active until the early 20th century – supplied the world with some of the finest marble.

Southwest of Parikiá lies the much-visited **Valley of the Butterflies** (Petaloúdes), a walled garden with huge trees. The black-and-yellow butterflies – actually Jersey tiger moths – are colourful and countless in summer (June–Sept daily 9am–1pm and 4–8pm; charge). En route, stop in at **Hristoú stou Dássous**, a picturesque 18th-century

The summer visitors to Petaloúdes, south of Parikiá, are not butterflies but Jersey tiger moths.

BELOW: exploring the tunnel quarries at Maráthi.

convent whose church, unusually, is off-limits to men (in Greece it's usually the other way around). Downhill from Petaloúdes is **Poúnda**, from where the small ferry sails every half-hour to Andíparos, 10 minutes away.

Mílos

Mílos is a geologist's paradise. The colours and shapes of rock formations, caves, cliffs and hot springs make it eerily beautiful. Snaking streams of lava formed much of the island's coastline. The lava dripped into caves and solidified as it hit the sea, thrusting up weird rock formations that take on animal shapes, shadowed purple in the rays of the setting sun. Offshore clusters like the Glaronísia are popular boat excursions. On the map, Mílos resembles a bat in flight; almost all the island's population of just over 4,500 inhabits the northeastern wing; the southwestern wing is ruggedly beautiful.

Modern Miliots are possessed of a quiet sophistication and worldliness. They have graciously adapted to the thin stream of tourism the island receives, concentrated in **Adámas** ㉘

(Adámanda), the main port, and Pollónia, a smaller anchorage in the north east. The closest of several open-ai hot springs is at Kánava beach, 3km (2 miles) east; the water wells up at 50°C (120°F) in the shallows, mixing to a comfortable temperature. Inside **Agía Triáda** church in Adámas, Cretan-styl icons dominate. Links have always beer strong between Mílos and the "Grea Island": Cretan refugees founded Adá mas in 1841 (though ancient tomb have been found on the town site), and the island was colonised by Minoan who came to Mílos to trade obsidian.

Pláka ㉙ (Mílos), the island's attrac tive capital, 4km (2½ miles) northwest has both an **Archaeological Museun** (Tue–Sun 8.30am–3pm; charge), whic contains a cast of the famous Venu de Milo, and a **Folklore Museum** (Tue–Sat 10am–2pm and 6–9pm, Su 10am–2pm; charge). The latter, set i an old house, is packed with divers exhibits from rock specimens and goa horns to samples of local weaving. A climb up the old *kástro*, with its vas rain-collection system and churche of **Panagía Thalássitra** and **Kímisi**

Minerals and Mining

Mílos is, in reality, a far older, cooled-down version of Santoríni – at some point in the distant past a volcano collapsed, leaving a caldera, which became today's huge central bay. Its volcanic mineral wealth has always been extensively mined: in prehistory for obsidian, nowadays for bentonite, perlite, barite, gypsum, sulphur, kaolin and china clay. Gaping quarries disfigure the landscape, especially in the east, and the local mining companies still provide employment for a quarter of the islanders. Kímolos has quarries from which Fuller's earth and, to a lesser extent, bentonite, are extracted. The latter has a number of uses (it even turns up as an ingredient in Nivea cream). Ironically, the chalk which gave the island its name (*kimoliá* in Greek) is no longer extracted locally.

tis Panagías, provides splendid views of the well-protected bay and, weather permitting, over many other islands. The escutcheon on **Panagía Thalássitra** is of the Crispi family, who wrested Mílos from the Sanudi in 1363.

Southwest of Pláka about 1km (½ mile) lies the verdant **Vale of Klíma**, where the ancient Meliots – their "dialogue" immortalised by Thucydides prior to their annihiliation by the Athenians in 416 BC – built their city. Excavations undertaken by the British School in Athens in the late 1800s uncovered a Dionysian altar, remains of an ancient gymnasium with a mosaic, and a well-preserved Roman-era theatre. Nearby, a marble plaque marks the spot where a farmer unearthed the Aphrodite of Mílos (Venus de Milo) in 1820. In a feat of robbery approaching that of the appropriation of the Parthenon friezes (though the French were the villains rather than the British this time) she was whisked off to Paris, never to return. The statue was probably carved in the 1st century BC – of Parian marble, since Mílos lacks suitable stone.

Below ancient Melos lurk the **Christian catacombs** (closed for works for safety reasons). Carved into the hillside, they are the earliest evidence of Christian worship in the country. Hundreds of tombs arranged along three subterranean corridors held as many as 5,000 bodies, all now vanished. Though cheerily lit by tiny electric lanterns, the frescoes and religious graffiti are hard to discern, and only the initial 50 metres (164ft) were open to the public prior to the current works. Steps from the catacomb area lead down to the shore and one of the island's most picturesque villages, **Klíma**, with brightly painted boathouses at sea level, carved into the volcanic cliff.

Mílos's best beaches are in the southwest "bat wing", starting with **Paleo-óri** – its far end part-naturist, with steam vents in the sand near which eggs can be fried, and hot water bubbling up in the sea – and ending with isolated **Triádes**, facing the sunset.

Others hereabouts are easiest (or only) accessible by boat.

Ten km (6 miles) northeast from Adámas lies the rubble of the ancient city of **Phylakope** (Fylakopí; closed for ongoing excavation), whose script and art resembled that of the Minoans. It flourished for 1,000 years after 2600 BC. The famous flying-fish fresco from here is now in Athens, but many objects are in the Pláka museum. All around Phylakope are strewn flakes of obsidian, used for sharp tools before bronze became common; visitors came to Mílos for it from 7000 BC. Mílos's polychrome geology is especially impressive here. Next to the site glitters the **Papafrángas ravine**, where precipitous stone steps take you down for an atmospheric swim in a pool connected to the sea by an inlet running under a rock bridge. **Sarakíniko**, futher west, is another inlet framed by wind-sculpted white rock formations.

Pollónia ③⓪, 12km (7½ miles) northeast of Adámas, is a wind-buffeted resort popular with boardsurfers and scuba-divers. Decent beaches are limited to **Voúdia** (Tría Pigádia), with the

The Venus de Milo was entrusted to the French Consul in Istanbul (she probably lost her arms in transit), to keep her safe from local lime-kiln operators. The Consul promptly shipped her off to France, where Louis XVIII put her on display in the Louvre. She has been there ever since.

BELOW: poppies and daisies carpet this field on Mílos.

An ice-cold frappé *hits the spot.*

island's best hot springs erupting, to an ideal temperature, in a rock formation just offshore, at the far right as you face the sea. Pollónia is also the point of departure for several small daily ferries across to Kímolos.

Kímolos

This tiny island – 41 sq km (16 sq miles), with a population of about 750 – is an alluring temptation when seen from Pollónia on Mílos, about a nautical mile across a strait. The boat takes only 20 minutes to cross to **Psathí**, Kímolos's little port. Some ferries to and from Adámas also stop here. **Kímolos** or **Hóra**, the one, hilltop town, is a 15-minute walk up from the quay; at its core is a two-gated, 16th-century *kástro*, which, unlike the ones on Sífnos and Andíparos, is mostly uninhabited and derelict. Just outside the *kástro* precinct stands un-whitewashed, well-preserved **Agios Ioánnis Hrysóstomos** church, of the same era.

Kímolos, once a pirates' hideout, today provides a limited refuge from the more crowded islands – there are fewer than 200 tourist beds. Although

BELOW: the steep, terraced slopes of Folégandros.

blessedly undeveloped (the mining and lack of water sees to that), it has half a dozen beaches – going anticlockwise along the south and east shores – **Elliniká**, **Bonátsa**, **Kalamítsi**, **Alykí**, **Skála** and **Prássa**, all within easy walking distance, some with tavernas and a few rooms to let. The northern half of the island is abandoned and inaccessible except on foot; on the eastern shore between Klíma and Prássa, **thermal springs** of varying utility pour into the sea.

Folégandros

The sheer palisades of Folégandros's coast have deterred outside invasion over the centuries and so lent the islanders security. Despite its tiny size – 32 sq km (12 sq miles) populated by barely 700 people – its role in recent history has not been insignificant: many Greeks were exiled here during both the 1930s Metaxás dictatorship and the 1967–74 junta. Its ancient and early Christian ties with Crete were strong, and many paintings of the Cretan School can be found in its churches today.

For such a small island, Folégandros as a fair number of beaches, especially in the less sheer eastern and southern coastlines. The easiest to reach are ivádi (with an organised campsite); ardiá, by the port; **Angáli**, at the narow waist of the island on the west nore; naturist **Agios Nikólaos** just eyond; and **Livadáki** in the far southest. From Livádi hamlet it is possle to walk (strenuously) south to the emote, scenic beach at **Katergó**.

A paved road (and bus service) nks **Karavostási**, the port, to the apital, **Folégandros** or **Hóra** , a nagnificently sited medieval town ith an inner *kástro* perched above sheer drop to the the sea. The dazling, wedding-cake church of Kímisis s Theotókou presides over the town nd marks the general direction of the **Irysospiliá**, the "Golden Cave" in the liff beyond, now accessible only to echnical climbers. Folégandros is now ecidedly trendy with both Greeks and oreigners, something reflected in the ariety, prices and mixed clientele of he numerous bars, tavernas and lodgngs in and around Hóra.

The island's second settlement, **Ano Meriá**, is actually a series of straggly hamlets strung out along the ridge road, comprising stone houses, a few shops and cafés, farms and knoll-top chapels; the bus continues out here regularly to drop walkers at the start of trails to most of the beaches noted previously. Threshing cirques, for processing the barley that is still grown here, are conspicuous as well.

Síkinos

Rocky Síkinos, despite the usual variety of harbour-side lodgings, couldn't be less like its larger neighbour, Ios. Although connected to Piraeus and other Cyclades regularly by ferry, and by caique to Ios and Folégandros in summer, Síkinos (with just over 200 permanent inhabitants) so far seems to have shrugged off tourism. It also escapes mention in the history books for long periods, but there are antiquities and churches to be seen.

The main beaches, **Aloprónia** (also the port), Dialiskári and **Agios Geórgios** to the northeast, and **Agios Pandelímonas** to the southwest, face Ios.

Detail of a ruined kástro doorway on Síkinos.

BELOW: one of the numerous tavernas in Hóra, Folégandros.

From Aloprónia harbour there's a regular bus or an hour's hike to **Síkinos Town** ㉜, consisting of conjoined **Hóra** and **Kástro**, with yet another such Venetian defensive complex at its heart. There are few places to stay but several tavernas and *kafenía*, some serving limited-production local wine – Síkinos's former name, Oenoe, alludes to a long history of producing wine (*oinos* in ancient Greek). The half-ruined convent of **Zoödóhou Pigís** (church open in the evening) dominates Kástro to the northeast.

Síkinos has few obvious diversions other than walking. One destination of note, the **Iroön** ㉝ at **Episkopí**, is an elaborate Roman family temple-tomb, incorporated into a 7th-century church. Hikers can continue down to the coast at Agios Pandelímonas and thence back to Aloprónia.

Ios

A small island with few historic attractions, Ios has drawn the young and footloose since the 1960s. The contemporary influx, who flock here to party by night and hit the beach by day, are a faint echo of their hippie forbears; "family" tourism is now actively promoted, holiday villas are sprouting north of the harbour, and rough camping is a thing of the past.

The centre of Ios's nightlife shifts constantly among dozens of bars and dance clubs in the tiny capital town, **Hóra** ㉞ (also called **Ios**). By 11pm, the last beach stragglers (a bus runs regularly between the beach and Gialós harbour, via Hóra, to bring them back) have arrived for the night-time revels; once ensconced inside a bar, they could be anywhere in the Mediterranean. Veteran Hellenophile travel writer Michael Haag less charitably deemed them "a plague of locusts who pack snack bars, boutiques and discotheques, appreciating nothing, giving nothing, taking everything."

The results of high-testosterone tourism have been twofold: Ios is no longer poor, and traditional life has disappeared, since there are no small remote villages where people keep up the old traditions. Weddings were once week-long feasts for all comers, now, unless they are held in winter

Walking on Amorgós

The best part of the well-marked and well-mapped Amorgian trail system links Egiáli in a triangular route with both Tholária and **Langáda**, handsome villages with excellent tavernas and seaward views. Hardy hikers can strike out beyond Langáda, first past the ancient **Theológos Monastery** with its frescoes of John the Evangelist, and then on a spectacular corniche trail to **Stavrós** church, at the base of **Mount Kríkelos**, the island's highest point, rising to 822 metres (2,696ft). In the week after Easter, the icon of Hozoviótissa goes walkabout *(periforá)*; devout pilgrims, some walking barefoot as a penance, follow it back from Egiáli to the monastery for five hours along the ancient trail that was the island's lifeline before the dawn of the age of the car.

ney last an evening, as everyone is so busy tending tourist-related enterprises. However, with all the action concentrated in and around Hóra, it is still possible to find quiet corners and relatively empty beaches.

Ios is not devoid of natural beauty or charm; even the bleary-eyed can see it. Gialós harbour is one of the Aegean's prettiest. The hilltop Hóra, capped by a windmill and blue church domes, reached by a long marble stairway from the port, appears vaguely Levantine with its tufts of palm trees and kasbah-like layout.

The most famous Ios beach is **Mylopótas 🕒** (Mylopótamos), with organised water sports and youth-oriented campsites. Alternatives include posher **Manganári Bay** in the south, served by both bus and caique; superior **Agía Theodóti** in the northeast; and Psathí in the east. Between them stand the remains of **Paleókstro 🕒**, a Venetian fortress containing the marble-clad ruins of what was the medieval capital. At a lonely spot towards the island's northern tip, beyond Plakotó Cove, is a series of **prehistoric graves**, one of

which the islanders believe, and fiercely contest, is **Homer's**.

Amorgós

Narrow, rugged and mountainous, Amorgós is a haven for walkers, bohemians and connoisseurs of still vibrant island culture, rather than for beachcombers. Before a road was opened between them in the late 1970s, the two port-resorts of Katápola and Egiáli were gateways to two effectively separate islands; ferry schedules still alternate in calling at them. **Katápola 🕒** is bigger and more commercialised and with fewer beaches, but more convenient to the uphill **Hóra 🕒** (or Amorgós Town), accessible by a regular bus service or a well-preserved *kalderími*. Its whitewashed houses and numerous domed and belfried churches cluster around a 13th-century Venetian castle.

Half an hour east of Hóra, clinging limpet-like to a 180-metre (590ft) cliff – French explorer and botanist Joseph Pitton de Tournefort likened it to a "chest of drawers" – the spectacular 11th-century Byzantine **Panagía Hozoviótissa Monastery 🕒** (daily

In the village of Langáda, Amorgós, a boy in local costume performs a traditional dance.

BELOW: Amorgós, a magnet for walkers.

There are more than 40 churches and chapels in Amorgós Town (Hóra), including Agios Fanoúrios, the smallest church in Greece, which can accommodate a congregation of two.

8am–1pm and 5–7pm) is home to a revered icon of the Virgin from Palestine, as well as to three hospitable monks who treat visitors to a shot of *rakómelo* (spiced spirit) with *loukoúmi*, and a ground-floor treasury-museum. The 20–21 November festival, despite being subject to dodgy weather, is attended by pilgrims from Athens and across the Cyclades. Below the monastery, **Agía Anna** beach is the most famous of several protected south-coast coves.

In the opposite direction out of Hóra, **Agios Geórgios Valsamítis**, 4km (2 miles) southwest, is built atop a sacred spring that had served as an oracle since pagan times, and was only cemented over in the 1950s (though the flow still irrigates lush gardens). Vivid frescoes adorn a sort of gazebo over the *ayíasma* inside the church where the water is still audible, and (briefly) accessible for collection.

Because there were reasonable anchorages, three ancient cities thrived here. **Minoa** (just above Katápola) is still being excavated; **Arkesíni**, in the far southwest, comprises a burial site and dwellings on Cape Kastrí, plu the well-preserved Hellenistic fortre at **Agía Triáda**, near modern Arkesí village. Of ancient **Aigiale** (abov modern **Egiáli** and its beaches), ve little remains, but the nearby village **Tholária** (Vaults) takes its name fro Roman tombs in the vicinity.

Anáfi

In legend, Apollo conjured up Anáfi t shelter Jason and the Argonauts whe the seas grew rough and they riske losing the Golden Fleece; an Apoll shrine was built here in thanksgivin Divine intervention has never agai been reliable. Earthquakes originatin on its volatile neighbour **Santoríni (** *(see page 185)* usually affected Ana with tidal waves and a rain of volcan detritus. Anáfi's appearance has prol ably not altered much since then: it sti looks like a rough boulder heaved u out of the sea and kept in place only b the benevolence of a tenacious god.

However, a different god is involve now: **Zoödóhou Pigís Monastery (** was erected over the old Apollo ten ple in the island's southeast corner, an incorporates plenty of marble mason fragments from its predecessor. Abov the monastery, with festivities 11 da after Easter and on 7–8 Septembe perches the smaller **Monastery (** **Kalamiótissa**, on a 450-metre (1,480f high limestone pinnacle that is Anáfi most distinctive feature. A swoopin but well-engineered path takes yc there; some people stay overnight the top to catch the sunrise.

Fewer than 300 people live on tl island today, surviving mainly by fis ing and subsistence farming. In rece years, though, the economy has bee boosted slightly by summer tourist mostly Austrian and Greek, attracte by Anáfi's peace and quiet, and super south-facing beaches. Connectio are improving slowly – besides a ma caique to Santoríni, there are mai line ferries from Piraeus, which i 2009 actually continued on to certai Dodecanese – a useful link if it lasts.

BELOW:
Hozoviótissa
Monastery clings to
an Amorgós
cliffside.

The south-facing harbour, **Agios Nikólaos**, has some facilities, but the main town, **Hóra** ❷ (or Anáfi Town), a short bus ride or half-hour walk up, offers a wider choice and finer setting. It's a windy place, sharing anti-earthquake vaulted roofs with Santoríni.

The closest of the beaches is **Klisídi**, walkable east from Agios Nikólaos, with reliable food and lodging. From near there, the old path (and a newer road, inland) heads further east to superb **Roúkounas** beach, with dunes, the **Katelímatsa** coves, and **Monastíri** beach – all clothing-optional except the last, owing to its proximity to Zoödóhou Pigís. Inland from Roúkounas looms **Kastélli**, site of both ancient Anaphe and a Venetian castle.

The Back Islands or Minor Cyclades

The so-called "**Back Islands**" between Náxos and Amorgós were far more inhabited in antiquity. Now Donoússa, Iráklia, Skhinoússa and Ano Koufonísi have populations of 100 to 200 each, and appreciable summer tourism, especially Athenians, although only Ano Koufonísi could be said to be overtly commercialised (eg it has the only ATM – bring plenty of cash with you to the others). Mains power only arrived during the mid-1980s, and fresh water scarce on all these islets. Getting to them is fairly easy: the somewhat bucky, splashy but reliable small caique *Express Skopelitis* (nicknamed the *Cylopníktis* or "dog-drowner" by the unkind) plies an almost daily schedule between them, leaving Amorgós at dawn and returning from Náxos around 3pm. Several times a week faster, more comfortable Blue Star ferries call from Piraeus as well.

Hilly **Donoússa**, remote from the others due east of Náxos, has good south-facing beaches near **Stavrós** port at **Kéndros** and **Livádi**, the latter below **Mersíni**, the only inland hamlet. Ill-advised bulldozing has ruined what was until recently a comprehensive network of cobbled paths. Flattish

Ano Koufonísi has perhaps the best, southeast-facing beaches of the group, stretching in a line from the appreciably developed seaside Hóra: **Fínikas**, **Harakópou**, **Fanó** and **Porí**, all linked by a road or path. **Káto Koufonísi** has a seasonal taverna and more beaches, served by a regular excursion caique; big **Kéros** island opposite has a significant 3rd-millennium BC archaeological site, which yielded many museum treasures – but chartering a boat to go there is expensive. **Skhinoússa** is far quieter, with most facilities in the hilltop Hóra; there are 16 beaches scattered around the island, of which only **Tsigoúri** has amenities. Solitude-seekers prefer nearby **Alygariá** and **Almyrós** in the south.

Iráklia (or Iraklía) is the largest of the "Back Islands", and has two proper settlements: the northerly port of **Agios Geórgios**, with all tourist facilities; and smaller **Hóra** (aka Panagía after its main festival date). Compared to its neighbours, Iráklia's beaches are disappointing, but it does have an undeniable attraction in the huge **Cave of Agios Ioánnis** in the far south. ❑

By ferry or by caique, an excursion out to the Back Islands could include a quiet day on the beach.

BELOW: a sunny backstreet.

NÁXOS

**Rugged Náxos is the largest of the Cyclades.
It offers lush green valleys, even in the height
of summer, and sweeping sandy beaches**

BELOW: the Portára
gateway of the
unfinished temple
of Delian Apollo.

Náxos is the largest, most populous and fertile of the Cyclades. High mountains, long beaches, hidden villages, fortification towers, medieval churches, and fascinating history make any visit here too short.

Hóra ❶ (Náxos Town) is a labyrinth of mansions, castle walls, towers, post-Byzantine churches and ancient to medieval ruins. The **Orthodox Cathedral** to the northeast marks the Fontána district; the adjacent residential Boúrgo quarter is full of arched passageways and narrow lanes. Higher up,

within the gated *kástro*, live Catholic descendants of the Venetian overlords: look for their coats of arms over doorways. The former French Commercial School, built into the ramparts, briefly educated Níkos Kazantzákis until his outraged father came to rescue him from the Jesuits. Today it houses the **Archaeological Museum** (Tue–Sun 8.30am–3pm; charge), with a huge and excellent collection (including Cycladic figurines). Just north of Fontána, the Grotta area has the remains of a Cycladic settlement (*c.*2500 BC).

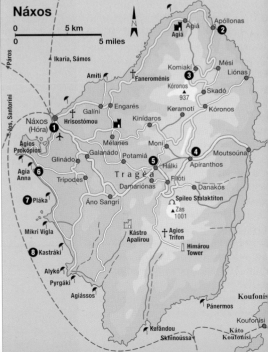

On **Palátia** islet (connected by a causeway) to the north of Hóra's ferry dock, a colossal free-standing marble door frame, the **Portára**, marks the entrance to the **Temple of Delian Apollo** of 540–530 BC. It was never completed, despite the efforts of Lygdamis, Náxos's tyrant. Had it been, it would have been Archaic Greece's largest temple.

The rest of the island rewards exploration by hired car, bus or on foot. Hemmed in by the Cyclades' highest ridges, the interior recalls the wilder parts of the Peloponnese. **Mount Zas** (a corruption of Zeus) is 1,001 metres (3,284ft) high, but not hard to climb for superb views. Náxos villages are numerous, and reception of foreigners varies from one to another. In the central **Tragéa** region, olive and fruit trees conceal Byzantine churches and crumbling fortified manors.

On the northern shore of Náxos, at the end of a bus line, is the little resort of **Apóllonas ❷**. A huge *kouros* (Archaic statue of an idealised youth) lies on the hillside above it, abandoned around 600 BC when the marble cracked. (Two other flawed *kouroi*, smaller but more elaborately worked, repose at Flério, 10km/6 miles east of Náxos, respectively in a walled garden at Melanés, and up a nearby hillside.)

On the road from Apóllonas to Hóra, handsome **Komiakí ❸** (Koronída), the island's highest village, looks over terraced vineyards, and is home of the local *kítron* liqueur – and of emery miners until nearby deposits became unprofitable. Un-whitewashed **Apíranthos ❹** (Aperáthou), 20km (12 miles) south, was settled by Cretan refugees in the 17th and 18th centuries, and is the natal village of Manólis Glézos, the leftist activist, later politician, who tore down the Nazi flag from the Partheon on 30 May 1941. The town is the start of a spectacular trail over Stavrós pass to Moní village.

Filóti, 8km (5 miles) further at the foot of Mount Zas, is the second-largest settlement; a paved road leads south to the 20-metre (65ft) Hellenistic

Himárou Tower. The Tragéa extends west from Filóti to **Hálki ❺**, with several fine churches, the best being 11th-century **Panagía Protóthronis**, with important frescoes, including a 12th-century *Annunciation*. Next door is the 17th-century **Grazia-Barozzi Tower**, one of many such defensive towers scattered across Náxos.

From Halkí a good road heads north to **Moní**, known for its handicrafts and restaurants with mountain views. Just before the village is the turning for **Panagía Drosianí** (Church of the Dewy Virgin), possibly dating from the 6th century and with several layers of frescoes nearly as old.

Some of the best beaches in the Cyclades line the southwest coast. The merged resorts of **Agios Prokópios** and **Agía Anna ❻** at the north end are the main bases for holidaymakers; the long white sands of **Pláka ❼** just southeast have fewer facilities, and more scantily clad beachcombers, the further you go. **Kastráki ❽**, beyond Mikrí Vígla headland, offers more of the same, but there are emptier beaches beyond at **Pyrgáki** and **Agiássos**. ❑

The gigantic kouros at Apóllonas, left unfinished in around 600 BC, weighs 30 tonnes and is 10.5 metres (34ft) long. Naxian marble has always been prized and was used for the famous lions of Delos (see page 168).

BELOW: laid-back sightseeing on the ferry to Náxos.

SANTORÍNI

Santoríni's whitewashed villages cling to volcanic cliffs above beaches of black sand. It is an island shaped by geological turmoil, and one of the most dramatic in all Greece

ailing into the bay of Santoríni is one of Greece's great experiences. Broken pieces of a volcano's rim Santoríni and its attendant islets – ace a multicoloured circle around a ep submerged caldera that, before e cataclysmic volcanic eruption in out 1500 BC, formed the island's gh centre. The resulting earthquakes, dal waves and rains of pumice that llowed the eruption devastated much the Aegean, and contributed to the d of Minoan civilisation. The island's ng crescent, formed of solidified lava, ems at sunset still to reflect fire from e dormant volcano.

The sensual lines of Cycladic archi-cture, augmented here with anti-rthquake barrel-vaulting cemented ith local pozzolana (sandy volcanic h), are doubly disarming on San-ríni, set against the smoky purple or sty orange striations of weathered va in the background. Thera is the and's ancient name, and Thíra the ficial one in modern times. Greeks, owever, prefer the medieval Santoríni, ter Saint Irene of Thessaloníki, mar-red by Diocletian in AD 304.

Only excursion boats or small local rries put in at **Skála Firás**, 580 steps elow Firá (*skála* means both landing age and staircase in Greek); most acraft dock at ugly **Athiniós**, 10km miles) further south. **Firá ❶** (Hóra), e capital, sits high on the rim, its hite houses mostly rebuilt in con-ete after a devasting 1956 earthquake.

The town is largely pedestrianised, its winding cobbled streets terraced into the volcanic cliffs.

Firá has an **Archaeological Museum** (Tue–Sun 8.30am–3pm; charge) and an even better **Museum of Prehistoric Thera** (Tue–Sun 8.30am–7.30pm; joint charge with above) featuring Cycladic art and artefacts from the Akrotiri site. The **Mégaro Gýzi Museum** (Mon–Sat 10.30am–1.30pm and 5–8pm, Sun 10.30am–4.30pm; charge) occupies a beautiful 17th-century Catholic man-sion spared by the 1956 earthquake,

Main attractions
FIRÁ
ANCIENT THERA
AKROTÍRI
IA
KAMÁRI
PÉRISSA
PÝRGOS

LEFT: church in Firá.
BELOW: view towards the volcano cone of Néa Kaméni.

You don't need to walk up the 580 steps from Skála Firás to Firá, or charter a donkey: there is also a cable car.

BELOW: remains at Thera, on the Mésa Vounó headland.

stuffed with antiquarian engravings, documents and maps as well as pre-earthquake photographs. The **Lignós Folklore Museum** (daily 10am–2pm; charge) near the northeast edge of town has a mock-up of a traditional house, complete with wine cellar.

Although packed with more jewellers and chichi boutiques than strictly necessary, Firá can still enchant, especially over a drink at sunset while contemplating the midnight-blue caldera waters with their half-protruding volcanic islets at the centre. Traditionally, Santoríni was said to be the main Greek home of vampires – possibly because corpses failed to decompose completely in the lava soil – and at this witching hour the undead do seem a distinct possibility.

Ancient Thera and Akrotiri

East of Firá, the landscape slumps into fertile, level, pumice-rich fields, though in the southeast some hills shrug themselves up. On one of them, the non-volcanic Mésa Vounó headland, sits ancient **Thera ❷** (Tue–Sun 8.30am–3pm), founded in around

915 BC beside the only freshwat spring on the island, still flowing, a remained inhabited (with a Hellenis zenith) until medieval times. The b approaches are the fine, if twistir cobbled paths up from either Kam or Períssa (*see opposite*).

In the south, ancient **Akrotiri** (closed indefinitely for safety reason a Minoan town preserved in volcan ash like Pompeii, had comfortab two-storey houses, good plumbing a attractive little squares, only about percent excavated thus far; no bor have been found, which suggests th the inhabitants had some warning the pending eruption, and fled wi their valuables (though leaving oth artefacts behind). The beautiful fr coes, pots and furniture found he are in the National Archaeologic Museum in Athens (*see page 116*).

Ia and the caldera

Santoríni's population swells fivefo in summer from about 12,000; wh Firá is the most developed touri centre, many other places offer acco modation and places to eat, althoug bus services are hopelessly ove crowded. **Ia ❹** (Oía), on the island northernmost peninsula, is amor Greece's most photographed villag carefully restored since the 1956 eart quake buried most of its famous cav houses with landslide lava. Today, the same cave-houses converted into excl sive accommodation are an Ia speci ity. A steep walk down twisting sto steps from the western end of tow leads to the tiny twin ports of **Armé** and **Ammoúdi**. The gentle trail-hi along the caldera's edge from Ia **Imerovígli** (3km/2 miles north of Fir allows you to experience the island tempestuous geology from close up.

The volcano is only dormant, n extinct; besides regular earthquake it has produced the two cinder-con of **Néa** and **Paleá Kaméni** (the Bur Islets) out in the caldera. Regul boat tours from both Skála Firás ar Ammoúdi take you to them, where y

can swim to sulphurous hot springs off Paleá, and hike up to a crater on Néa which still emits gas and steam; the last actual eruption was in 1950. Tours and regular small ferries from Ammoúdi continue to **Thirassía**, the only one of Santoríni's satellite islets which is inhabited, with a pace of life still stuck in pre-tourism once the day-trippers have gone – there are tavernas, and rooms to rent, though not many beaches.

Coastal resorts and the central plain

After Firá and Ia, the next major resorts are **Kamári ❺** and **Périssa ❻** on the east coast. Both have roasting hot, black-sand beaches (the one at Périssa is 8km/5 miles long); Kamári is pitched at families, Périssa at the youth market. From ancient Thera (*see opposite*), between the two, another good path heads west to Santoríni's summit, **Profítis Ilías** (566 metres/1,860ft), home to multiple antennae and an eponymous 18th-century monastery (now home to just one monk) that is the focus of the island's major 19–20 July festival.

From here, a steep road descends to conical **Pýrgos ❼** village on the central plain, its houses arrayed around a Venetian citadel with several bulbous churches. It contrasts with **Mesariá ❽** further north, which seems to consist only of more church domes, until the approach reveals a warren of dwellings and alleys sunk below ground level. The farmland around and between features yellow grain sheaves, vines twisted into wreaths to protect grapes against the wind, and tiny thick-skinned tomatoes, grown without water for concentrated flavour, then dried. Small caves, natural or dug out, are used as toolsheds, barns and sometimes even as homes.

Most of the island's half-dozen or so **wineries** are between Pýrgos and Megalohóri village; all offer tastings, and many lay on interesting tours of their *canáves* (cellars). Santoríni is famous for its crisp, dry whites, especially the Sigála label, and amber, high-alcohol dessert wine *visánto* (imitating the Italian *vinsanto*). Cánava Roússos, towards Kamári, has a full-on **wine museum** (daily noon–8pm; charge), installed in a 300-metre (1,000ft) long gallery. ❏

Volcanic Santoríni is believed by many to be the origin of the lost kingdom of Atlantis, which was swallowed up by the sea.

BELOW:
nestled in the volcanic cliffs, the streets above Ammoúdi port, Ia.

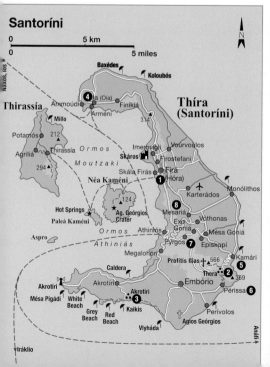

Santoríni

0 ___ 5 km
0 ___ 5 miles

Thirassía

Baxédes
Koloubós
Ammoúdi ❹ Ia (Oía) Finikiá
Arméni
Millo
Potamós 212
Agriliá Thirassía *Ormos* Imerovígli Vourvoúlos
Skáros
Moutzaki Firostefáni
294 Skála Firás Firá ❶ (Hóra)
Néa Kaméni
Karterádos Monólithos
Hot Springs Ag. Geórgios ❽ Mesariá
Paleá Kaméni Crater Exo Vóthonas
Gonia
Aspro *Ormos* Athiniós Mésa Goniá
Athiniás Pýrgos ❼ Episkopí
Megalohóri Kamári
Profítis Ilías 566 ❺
Caldera Thera ❷ 369
Akrotíri Embório
Akrotíri Akrotíri Périssa ❻
Mésa Pigádi White ❸ Perívolos
Beach Grey Kaikis
Beach Red Agios Geórgios
Beach Vlyháda

*Thíra
(Santoríni)*

314

Iráklio

Naxos, Ios
Anáfi

THE SPORADES AND EVVIA

Skiáthos, Skópelos, Alónnisos, Skýros and Evvia

The Sporades – meaning "sporadic" or "scattered" – is a group of four islands in the northwest Aegean. Evvia, extending along the Greek mainland south of the Sporades, is Greece's second-largest island, after Crete.

Mainlanders have long appreciated Skiáthos's beaches and made annual pilgrimages, though they are now outnumbered by foreigners. In spite of a rich history, Alónnisos is the least developed of the Sporades in terms of tourism, while Skópelos is also compromised in terms of beaches and level of development. Skýros, the largest and in many ways the most interesting of the group, is remote from the others, with an independent spirit and a deeply entrenched local culture. Evvia, despite easy access from the mainland, has been mostly unspoilt by tourism. Its diverse landscape and rich history make it almost a microcosm of the whole country.

Hopping between Skiáthos, Skópelos and Alónnisos is very easy, but reaching Skýros involves a longer trip via Evvia, with only fitful summer connections with its three northern neighbours. Skiáthos alone of the Sporades has an international airport with regular charter arrivals, mainly from Britain, Italy and Scandinavia, and flights to Athens. Skýros Airport receives planes from Athens to Thessaloníki, scheduled to allow long weekends away. Conventional ferries, catamarans and hydrofoils run to the three northerly Sporades from Vólos and Agios Konstandínos on the mainland.

The islands are what remains of a mountain range that detached from the mainland in a geological convulsion and "sank". Prevailing winds and other factors produce reliable winter rainfall and lush vegetation, notably pine forests. Summers can be humid, especially on south-facing shores, but the *meltémi* helps keep a lid on temperatures.

The traditional trade route between the Mediterranean and the Black Sea passes the Sporades. This strategic position has often brought unwanted callers, including invasion fleets and pirates, so ancient remains and major archaeological sites are few. ❏

PRECEDING PAGES: Orthodox priests; Lalária beach, Skiáthos. **LEFT:** Karababa Turkish castle, Evvia. **FROM TOP:** Skiáthos town bathers; tasty *magirevtá*; a Skópelos miss.

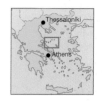

THE SPORADES

Once exclusive resorts for the rich and famous, the Sporades now attract Greek and foreign holidaymakers alike, whether for the nightlife of Skiáthos or the quieter charm of Alónnisos

Main attractions
KOUKOUNARIÉS BEACH
KÁSTRO OF SKIÁTHOS
SKÓPELOS TOWN
PALEÁ ALÓNNISOS
WALKING ON ALÓNNISOS
NATIONAL MARINE PARK
SKÝROS CARNIVAL
SKÝROS TOWN

he Sporades islands are popular destinations, known more for their lush vegetation and equable climate than their archaeological sites.

Skiáthos

The 1,200-metre (3,940ft) sandy scythe of **Koukounariés ❶** is used as evidence on thousands of local postcards that the Aegean can produce the kind of beach normally associated with the Caribbean. Propriety would prevent as many postcards from featuring **Mikrí Krassás** (Small Banana Beach) because it caters for nudists. That, and the thumping all-day bars at many south-coast beaches, exemplifies the relaxed nature of tourism on Skiáthos, long nicknamed "the straight Mýkonos".

The island has beaches for all occasions, not least because some among the alleged 50 (plus more on surrounding islets) will always be sheltered, whatever the wind direction. Koukounariés and "Small Banana" are near neighbours at the west end of the twisting, busy 13km (8½-mile) coast road from the town; there are half a dozen others along it and many better ones on Skiáthos's northwest coast. The best of these are adjacent **Mandráki** and **Eliá**; most have a taverna or at least a *kantína* selling drinks and snacks. A path leading down from a track's end usually indicates a beach below; with luck it won't be as crowded as Koukounariés.

Anticlockwise round the island boat trips pass the rocky and largely inac-cessible northern shoreline, where the only construction is **Kástro ❷**, the abandoned 16th-century capital once connected to the rest of Skiáthos by a drawbridge. For 300 years the inhabitants huddled on this windy crag, hoping the pirates would pass them by. During World War II Allied stragglers and commandos hid out here, waiting for evacuation to Turkey by a friendly submarine. Nowadays it is an obligatory stop for the excursion caiques, after they have dipped into three technicolour grottoes and dropped

LEFT: restored doorway, Skiáthos Town. **BELOW:** Cape Kástro in the north.

Skópelos's traditional stone farmhouses (kalývia) all have distinctive outdoor ovens where the island's famous plums were once dried to become prunes.

anchor at **Lalária**, a cove famous for its smooth, round stones, and before proceeding to a beach taverna (usually at Megálos Asélinos) for lunch.

A scooter or hired car is necessary to follow mostly unpaved roads looping through the mountains towards the north shore. They provide stunning views as well as the chance to pop into monasteries which, with the Kástro, are more or less the only buildings of historic interest. Of these, the grandest and closest to town is **Evangelistrías** (daily 10.30am–2.30pm and 5–8pm), with frescoed **Panagía Kehreás** further west, set above a stream valley and **Lygariés** beach.

Fires started by the Nazis in August 1944 destroyed most of the pretty pre-war town; only the bluff-top old quarter in the southwest escaped. But **Skiáthos Port ❸** makes up in liveliness what it lacks in architectural merit. In fact, its nightlife is probably the most important consideration, after the beaches, for the visitors – mostly young Italian and Greek fashionistas, plus a few Central Europeans – that Skiáthos attracts in large numbers in August. Their pref-

erences change annually, but it's no difficult to spot which places are in vogue this season, whether one's taste is for beer and blues, wine and Vivaldi tsípouro and trance, or caipirinhas and 1950s rock and roll. The two classies and trendiest foci are the quay of the Old Port and a shoreline strip at the star of the airport road, just past the yacht marina. Skiáthos is a major sailing and chandlery centre, elaborating on a tradi tion of caique-building.

The one nod to culture in the tow is the **Aléxandros Papadiamándi Museum** (Tue–Sun 9.30am–1.30pm and 5–8pm; charge) on Mitropolítou Ananíou, lodged in the 19th-centur home of one of Greece's pioneering short-story writers, who also officiate as a priest. **Galerí Varsákis** above the Old Port stands in for a formal ethno graphic museum, but prices for the admittedly rare antiques are double what they would be elsewhere.

Skópelos

If Kefaloniá has become, somewha reluctantly, "Captain Corelli's Island lushly wooded Skópelos has enthusias

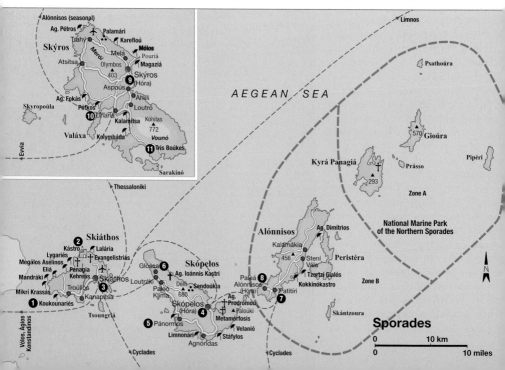

tically embraced the sobriquet of "The Island of *Mamma Mia*", partly shot here in 2007, with boat tours on offer to filmic locales. Not that the island was any less photogenic or alluring before then; its beaches are consistently underrated, and unlike Skiáthos, it has not suffered too many forest fires.

Visitors waiting in **Vólos** rather than Agios Konstandínos for passage to Skópelos (the alternative is to fly to Skiáthos and catch a hydrofoil, catamaran or ferry) may enjoy the excellent **Archaeological Museum** (Tue–Sun 8.30am–3pm; charge). On display, among lots else, are the contents of a grave discovered in 1936; the gold crown and ornate weapons almost certainly belonged to Staphylos, a semi-legendary Minoan who colonised Skópelos.

The island's distinguished past is demonstrated not so much by prominent sites – except for the three intriguing Hellenistic **Sendoúkia** tombs on Mount Délfi – as by the exceptionally fine vernacular houses in **Skópelos Town ④** (Hóra), arrayed around a harbour lined with cafés and tavernas under mulberry trees. The town was only lightly damaged in the 1965 earthquake, and escaped Nazi vindictiveness thanks to Alphonse, the philhellenic Austrian local commander, and is therefore the most "authentic" and traditional capital of the three northern Sporades (Skýros being in a class by itself). Slate roofs, wooden balconies, idiosyncratic local shops and flagstone streets give Hóra a serenity and dignity rarely found in Skiáthos in season.

On the slopes of **Mount Paloúki**, east of the bay, perch three medieval **monasteries**, all inhabited to some degree; the most architecturally distinguished, its church dome supported by coral-rock columns, is **Metamórfosis**. These are just some of the reputed 40 monasteries on the island, plus 360 churches, 123 of them tucked among the houses of Hóra, crowned by a Venetian castle set on ancient foundations.

Mixed sand-and-pebble beaches speckle the south and west coasts. Closest to town are cramped **Stáfylos**, site of the Minoan tomb, and the far superior, long **Velanió** just beyond, with views to Évvia and a nudist zone. **Agnóndas** is the island's

Skópelos Town can lay claim to some distinguished houses, which its inhabitants are proud to adorn.

BELOW: whiling away the afternoon in Skópelos Town.

St Rigínos the Boring

A legend tells of a rampaging dragon on Skópelos that proved itself to be resistant to all conventional attempts to get rid of it. The local priest (and later patron saint of the island), one Rigínos, was implored to direct a sermon at the beast, the islanders having heard enough of his homilies to think that it might do the trick. Finding itself as bored as any human, the dragon reared up and fled until it could go no further. The pious Rigínos, determined to save his flock, followed doggedly and, on cornering his quarry on a clifftop, prepared to deliver another lengthy homily. Despairing at the prospect, the dragon chose to dive to its death. The impact it made on landing created a deep ravine on the south coast that is today known as the *Drakondóskhisma* (Dragon's Rift).

*Last port of call...
Alónissos.*

second port, with popular waterside tavernas; **Limnonári** nearby has a better, white-sand beach. **Pánormos ❺**, about halfway along the coast road, is a major resort and yacht anchorage, although beaches at nearby **Miliá** and **Kastáni** are far better and sandier than the coarse-pebble shore.

The road continues past three hamlets: **Paleó Klíma**, declared uninhabitable after the 1965 quake, but its houses since mostly acquired and restored by outsiders, **Agii Anárgyri** (which suffered the same fate) and **Athéato** (Mahalás), the most architecturally distinguished of the three, still inhabited by a few local people. Just beyond sprawls hillside **Glóssa ❻**, Skópelos's second town, apparently settled by Thessalian mainlanders. It, too, is currently in the grip of a minor real-estate boom, thanks not least to its sweeping views. At the end of the paved road, down some steep curves, lies the second, somewhat dozy port of **Loutráki**. There are a few more beaches beyond Glóssa, notably beside **Agios Ioánnis Kastrí**, a church perched in postcard-perfect style on a rock monolith.

Alónnisos

This rugged island is full of ghosts whispering what might have been. On a hill west of **Patitíri ❼**, the last port on ferry, catamaran or hydrofoil routes, is **Paleá Alónnisos ❽** (Hóra), the former capital shattered by an earthquake in March 1965. This compounded the blow the islanders had already suffered when all their grapevines withered and died from phylloxera during the 1950s. Alónnisos seems to have been always jinxed: the ancient capital, Ikos, literally disappeared when the ground on which it stood slumped into the sea.

In 1970, Palaeolithic-era evidence was found that could mean that Alónnisos was inhabited before any other Aegean island, and it was considered a prize worth fighting over by Philip of Macedon and the Athenians. Its famous **wines** were once shipped all over ancient Greece in amphorae stamped "IKION"; today there is a modest revival of the industry based on phylloxera-resistant vines, though you're more likely to be offered the luscious local **apricots** or pickled *tsitsíravla* (terebinth) shoots.

A marked, cobbled path links Patitíri and Paleá Alónnisos (45 minutes' walk); there is also a bus. By 1977, coercive government policies had forced the abandonment of Hóra by locals; as at Paleó Klíma on Skópelos, it was left to Athenians and foreigners to buy up the old ruins and restore them in variable taste. The effect is somewhat twee, and most food and drink is predictably overpriced (though nightlife is Greek-flavoured), but the views west to Skópelos and north as far as Mount Athos are undeniably spectacular.

The way the island has adjusted to its unrealised potential and bad luck is something for which many visitors are grateful. Alónnisos remains the least developed of the Sporades, with second-home ownership on a par with short-term tourism, which tends to be low-key and trendy, with art exhibitions and a homeopathy academy – although there are two Italian all-inclusive resorts. Walkers are admirably catered for with an accurate topographic map, numbered and maintained paths, and a walking guide written by resident expat guide Chris Browne.

Usable, accessible beaches are concentrated on the more protected south and southeast coasts. Several are a short distance by path or track from Hóra, but superior ones lie northeast of functional Patitíri, Roussoúm Gialós and Vótsi ports at **Kokkinókastro** (site of ancient Ikos), **Tzortzí Gialós** and **Leftó Gialós**. Improved roads make wheeled access easy (and safer than on Skiáthos or Skópelos), though in peak season there are still morning taxi-boats from Patitíri up the coast as far as **Agios Dimítrios**. **Kalamákia** is an authentic fishing port – nearby waters are rich in marine life – while yachts like to put in at **Stení Vála**.

National Marine Park

Alónnisos, as well as half a dozen islets scattered to the east and north, fall within the **National Marine Park of the Northern Sporades**, established in 1992 to conserve declining fish stocks and provide sanctuary to seabirds and marine mammals, in particular the severely endangered Mediterranean monk seal, of which fewer than 400 survive worldwide. Two of the islets

Skyrians have got used to land appropriations by the air force, but are currently up in arms about a plan for 111 wind turbines, to be installed on Vounó by the Athonite monastery that owns the mountain.

LEFT: a goatman at Skýros Carnival.
BELOW: a flock of sheep on Skýros.

TIP

The Mános Faltáïts Museum on Skýros (daily, summer 10am– noon and 6–9pm; winter 10am–noon and 5.30–8pm; charge), in a mansion north of the town, is a private collection presenting the life of the island through local art and crafts, rare documents, costumes and photographs.

– **Pipéri** and **Gioúra** – are off-limits to all but licensed scientists for conservation reasons. **Skántzoura**, with its empty monastery, is rather out of the way, but seasonal **caique excursions** from Patitíri visit others. The first stop is **Kyrá Panagiá**, which belongs to Megístis Lávras monastery on Mount Athos and itself has a 10th-century monastery, slowly being restored, and inhabited by one farmer-monk. With enough passengers to defray fuel costs, peak-season tours extend to northerly **Psathoúra**, with the tallest (26 metres/81ft) lighthouse in the Aegean (built in 1895, now solar-powered) and a lovely white-sand beach to swim off. Olive-covered, only seasonally inhabited **Peristéra**, cradling Alónnisos to the east, is the usual final afternoon swim-stop in low season. Passengers are most unlikely to spot seals, but will probably encounter dolphins.

Skýros

The main character in the "goat dance" of **Skýros Carnival**, staged in the four weekends before Lent and with its roots in a pre-Christian pagan festival, is the *géros* (old man) who wears a goat

BELOW: sunset over the Aegean.

pelt and kid skin mask, plus tens of kilograms of sheep bells, which he shakes noisily with waist movements. The *géri* are accompanied by their "brides" the *korélles* (maidens), young men in drag. Foreign visitors enjoying the spectacle ought perhaps to know that the third type of figure (the *frángos*), a buffoon dressed in ridiculous clothes and blowing on a *bouroú* or conch shell, represents, well, a foreigner.

Visitors should not take the mockery to heart. Only recently has Skýros shed its near-complete economic dependence on the Greek navy and air force and courted foreign tourism, mostly Italian, French, Dutch and British, although the island has been well known to Greeks for years. The effects of the summer season have not yet eclipsed a vigorous and idiosyncratic local culture, even if the older generation, which faithfully wore the vaguely Cretan island costume, has pretty much died off. Cubist white houses often contain amazing collections of copperware, embroidery and painted ceramics, the last acquired by trade or piracy and serving as a spur to the development of a local pottery industry based at several kiln-workshops at Magaziá beach. Carved wooden furniture passed down though the generations is often too small to be practical, so may be hung on the wall.

Skýros Town ❾ (Hóra) is on the northern half of the island, fanning out on the lee side of a rock plug overlooking the east coast. Life in the town is played out all along the meandering main street or *agorá*, which begins near the downhill edge of what is a remarkably workaday place, albeit with picturesque archways and churches. A left fork in this thoroughfare leads down towards a plaza at the northern edge of town, where a nude bronze male statue representing *Immortal Poetry* (in memory of Rupert Brooke, *see opposite*) commands the view. Just below this is a worthwhile **Archaeological Museum** (Tue–Sun 8.30am–3pm; charge), with fine Geometric-era pottery, and the

Mános Faltáïts Museum (*see opposite*). The right-hand option wanders up to the *kástro*, the old Byzantine/Venetian castle built atop the ancient acropolis where, in legend, King Lykomedes raised Achilles and later threw Theseus to his death. Sadly, since a 2001 earthquake the *kástro* and the monastery inside are permanently closed for safety reasons.

Long, sandy **Magaziá** beach below Hóra merges seamlessly with one at **Mólos**, which terminates at **Pouriá** point with sea-weathered, squared-off rocks quarried by the Romans. There are better, if sometimes exposed, beaches in the north at **Karefloú** and **Agios Pétros**, bracketing the airport-air force base, and the site of Bronze Age **Palamári** (Mon–Fri 7.30am–2.30pm; free). The paved loop road continues through pines past other coves with mediocre beaches like Atsítsa, until reaching longer, sandier **Péfkos**. **Linariá** ⓾, the ferry port, also has accommodation and tavernas, but most visitors will continue on the circuit back towards Hóra, perhaps pausing at **Aspoús**, with a good beach.

At one time Skýros may have been two islands. Today's halves – **Merói** and **Vounó** – join in a noticeably flat valley connecting Kalamítsa Bay with Ahílli fishing port. In contrast to northerly Merói, Vounó (dominated by Mount Kóhilas) is relatively barren, though strong springs emerge on the northwest flank facing the "divide", and there is enough pasture on the heights for the island's wild ponies, which have been bred here since ancient times. Beaches, except for **Kolymbáda**, are few and compare poorly with those in the north. Most visitors are bound for **Trís Boúkes** ⓫ and the **grave of Rupert Brooke**. Serving as a naval officer in the fleet bound for Gallipoli, the poet died of blood poisoning on a French hospital ship on 23 April 1915 and was buried in the olive grove here.

Roads beyond this point are minimal, and accordingly **boat excursions** from Linariá are popular. They visit **Sarakinó islet** with its sandy inlet and sea-caves in the sheer coastal cliffs extending all the way up to Ahílli, home to seemingly innumerable Eleonora's falcons. ❏

Fishing boats bobbing in Skýros harbour.

BELOW:
the Mános Faltáïts Museum above Skýros Town.

EVVIA

Greece's second-largest island is largely unspoilt by tourism, and little-known to foreigners. Although barely separated from the mainland, Evvia has a distinctive character

BELOW: the new bridge to Halkída.

Halkída, the capital of Evvia (Euboea) is close enough to the mainland for a drawbridge and a new suspension bridge to arc over. Aristotle is supposed to have been so frustrated by trying to understand the rapid, fluctuating tides in the **Évripos** channel here that he killed himself by jumping into the roiling waters.

In antiquity Evvia's most prominent cities were Chalcis (modern Halkída) and nearby Eretria (Erétria), which both established colonies across the Mediterranean. Evvia then came under the control, over subsequent centuries, of the Athenians, Macedonians, Romans, Byzantines and Ottomans, and became part of Greece in 1830, after the War of Independence.

Halkída ❶ (Hálkis) is now an industrial town, but the **Kástro** district, with a 15th-century **mosque** and ornate **fountain**, plus the Crusader-modified **Church of Agía Paraskeví**, are worth visiting. In the newer district, lodged in the old prison, are an **Archaeological Museum** (Tue–Sun 8.30am–3pm charge) and a **Folklore Museum** (Wed–Sun 10am–1pm, Wed also 6–8pm charge), as well as a 19th-century **synagogue** still used by the remaining Jewish Romaniote community. **Erétria ❷** to the south is a crowded, grid-plan summer resort where ro-ro ferries land from Skála Oropoú on the mainland. The small **Archaeological Museum** (Tue–Sun 8.30am–3pm) and adjacent archaeological site are very good.

The road south hugs the coast past the attractive resort of **Amárynthos** until just before **Alivéri**, where it turns inland to a junction at **Lépoura**. The northerly option here goes through **Háni Avlonaríou**, with a large and unusual 13th-century **Basilica of Agios Dimitríos**, before continuing to **Stómio** beach. Next the road threads through **Platána** resort to the nondescript harbour at **Paralía Kýmis** and ferry to **Skýros. Kými** proper, up the hill, is a sizeable town, and start of a dramatic mountain road back to Halkída.

Southern Evvia, reached by the ther option at Lépoura, is drier and ss green. From the main road beyond Imyropótamos, along the slimmest art of the island, there are views down the sea on either side. Near **Stýra ❸** re the ruins of three mysterious stone uildings, known locally as "Dragon ouses" (*drakóspita*). The most conincing theory is that they are temples uilt by slaves or immigrants working earby quarries in the classical era.

The main town in the south is árystos ❹, stuck in a 1970s timearp, with a long beach, scattered oman ruins and a Venetian tower. On **Mount Ohi** (1,399 metres/4,617ft) st inland there's the medieval **Casello Rosso**, another *drakóspito* and e start of the traverse through the uperb **Dimosári Gorge**.

Northeast of Halkída, **Stení ❺** on e slopes of **Mount Dírfys** (1,743 etres/5,718ft), is a favourite goal for thenians seeking clean air and grill estaurants. **Prokópi ❻**, on the main ad north, sits on a broad upland purhased by Englishman Edward Noel the 1830s. On Mount Kandíli to the west, the family estate of his descendants is now available for holiday lets and hosts special-interest courses. Prokópi was settled after 1923 by refugees from Cappadocia who brought with them the relics of 18th-century Saint John the Russian (actually Ukrainian). They are revered in the 1960s church.

North of Prokópi lie some of Evvia's finest beaches; most renowned (and developed) is **Angáli**. Just uphill is **Agía Anna ❼**, with an excellent **Folklore Museum** (Wed–Sun 10am–1pm, 5–7pm; charge). Continuing along this coast, you pass the beaches of **Paralía Kotsikiás**, **Psaropoúli** and **Ellinphiká**, the last the smallest and prettiest.

Límni ❽ on the southwest coast is Evvia's beauty spot, a 19th-century port with an interesting **Ethnographic/ Archaeological Museum** (Mon–Sat 9am–1pm, Sun 10.30am–1pm; charge), and **Agíou Nikoláou Galatáki Convent** in the hills behind, its narthex vividly frescoed. The closest beaches are at **Spiáda** and **Hrónia**, on the way to **Loutrá Edipsoú ❾**, a spa town and ferry port with some imposing Belle Epoque and Art Deco hotels. ❑

The famous bronze statue of Poseidon poised to throw a trident, in Athens's Archaeological Museum (see page 116), was found in 1928 in the sea off Cape Artemision (Akti Artemísio) in the north.

THE NORTHEAST AEGEAN

Thásos, Samothráki, Límnos, Agios Efstrátios,
Lésvos, Psará, Híos, Ikaría, Sámos

The northeast Aegean islands have little in common other than a history of medieval Genoese rule. Northerly Thásos, Samothráki, Agios Efstrátios and Límnos in the north have few connections with the south Aegean; indeed, Thásos belongs to the Macedonian province of Kavála, and Samothráki to Thracian Évros. Greeks' affection for these islands, so convenient for the mainland, exceeds that of foreign tourists. Except for marble-cored Thásos, these isles, as well as Lésvos, are volcanic, their gentle slopes home to lava-tolerant oaks.

Lésvos, Híos and Sámos to the southeast were once prominent in antiquity, colonising across the Mediterranean and promoting the arts and sciences, though little evidence of ancient glory remains. All three served as bridges between Asia Minor and peninsular Greece and were joined to Asia Minor until Ice Age cataclysms isolated them. Turkey is still omnipresent on the horizon, just 2km (1 mile) away across the Mykale Straits at Sámos. Híos, Sámos and Ikaría are rugged limestone and schist (with a bit of granite, too, on Ikaría), forested with pine, olive and cypress. Delicate wild flowers, especially on Sámos, heighten their appeal, and numerous small mammals and birds thrive, having (like Lésvos's red squirrel) migrated over from Anatolia before the rising sea marooned them. Beaches vary from long shores of fist-sized pebbles to sheltered, sandy crescents.

As ever, transport to, between and on these islands varies with population and level of tourism. Samothráki has a skeletal bus service and overpriced ferries from Alexandroúpoli; Thásos has frequent buses and regular car ferries from Kavála and Keramotí. Límnos and Lésvos have regular flights and sailings from Piraeus, Lávrio and Thessaloníki, plus from each other; Híos is linked daily with Athens and Lésvos, less regularly with Sámos and Ikaría. Ikaría is connected to certain Cycladic islands. Sámos is best connected, with hydrofoil links with all the isles from Pátmos to Kós, plus ferries to Rhodes, and receives more international charters than the runner-up, Lésvos. ❑

PRECEDING PAGES: the Roman aqueduct on Lésvos; off Metállia beach, Thásos. **LEFT:** view from Pétra, Lésvos. **FROM TOP:** a beach on Sámos; lazy feline; Lésvos pottery.

THÁSOS, SAMOTHRÁKI AND LÍMNOS

Greece's most northerly islands see relatively few foreigners, but they offer more than enough by way of ancient ruins, empty beaches and picturesque villages

Whether you want to wander through olive groves, laze on sandy beaches or take in some major archaeological sites, you will be happy on these northerly islands.

Thásos

Just 7 nautical miles (12km) from mainland Macedonia, Thásos – always a favourite retreat of northern Greeks – has, since the 1980s, welcomed a cosmopolitan assortment of foreigners. Yet the island seems relatively unspoilt, with package tourism well quarantined. Almost circular, mountainous Thásos is essentially a giant lump of marble, mixed with granite and schist, crumbling into white sand at the island's margins. Lower elevations, covered in olive plantations, remain attractive, but the "Diamond of the North" (*Diamándis tou Vorrá*) had its lustre severely dulled in 1981, 1985, 1989 and 1993 by forest fires, deliberately set by developers wanting cheap building land. Thásos is now three-quarters denuded of its original pine forest, which survives only in the northeast. Elsewhere, only the inland villages and a thin fringe of surrounding vegetation were saved. The bus service around the coastal ring road is quite adequate, although most visitors hire motorbikes or cars (Thásos is small enough for a long day tour). The east and south coasts have better beaches; the west coast has access to most inland villages.

Thásos's past glory, fuelled by local gold deposits, is evident at the harbour capital of **Liménas ❶** (Limín, also just Thásos), where substantial remnants of the town have been excavated; choice bits of the ruined acropolis are illuminated by night. The biggest area of the Old City, behind the picturesque fishing harbour that traces the confines of the old commercial port, is the **agora**. In the nearby **Archaeological Museum** (Tue–Sun 9am–3pm; charge), the prize exhibit is a 4-metre (13ft) high Archaic *kouros* carrying a ram.

Main attractions
ANCIENT THÁSOS
ALYKÍ
SAMOTHRÁKI (HÓRA)
SANCTUARY OF THE GREAT GODS
MÝRINA KÁSTRO
EVGÁTIS BEACH
ALLIED WORLD WAR I CEMETERIES

LEFT: view over Mýrina, Límnos.
BELOW: old agora, Liménas, Thásos.

Locally made honey, candied walnuts and tsípouro, the fire-water of northern Greece, are favourite souvenirs of Thásos.

Beginning at the **Temple of Dionysos**, a path permits a rewarding walking tour of the ancient walls and acropolis. First stop is the Hellenistic **theatre** (open only for summer festival performances). Continue to the **medieval fortress**, built by a succession of occupiers from the masonry of a Temple of Apollo. Tracing the course of massive 5th-century BC walls brings you to the foundations of a **Temple of Athena**, beyond which a **Shrine of Pan** is visible in badly eroded relief on a rock. From here a vertiginous "secret" stairway plunges to the **Gate of Parmenon**, the only ancient entry still intact, at the southern edge of town.

The first village clockwise fro Liménas, slate-roofed **Panagía ❷**, a large, busy place where life revolv around the *platía*, with its plane tre and four-spouted fountain. **Potami** further down the valley, is less arc tecturally distinguished: visitors com mainly for the sake of the **Polýgnot Vagís Museum** (summer Tue–S 9.30am–12.30pm, 6–9pm, Sun 10an 1pm, winter mornings only; fre featuring the work of the eponymo locally born sculptor. Beyond, the ro drops to Potamiá Bay.

Skála Potamiás, at its south end, all lodging and tavernas, with more that to the north at **Hrysí Ammoud**

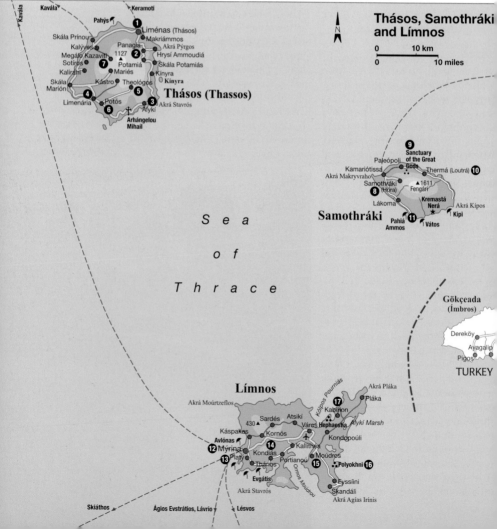

In between stretches a fine, blond-sand beach. There are even better strands at **Kínyra**, 24km (15 miles) from Liménas, but most tourists schedule a lunch stop at one of the several tavernas of **Alykí ❸** hamlet, architecturally preserved thanks to adjacent ruins: an ancient temple and two atmospheric Byzantine basilicas. The local topography of a low spit, sandy to the west, nearly pinching off a headland, is strikingly photogenic. So too is the **Convent of Arhángelou Mihaíl** 5km (3 miles) to the west, high above a barren coast – but mainly from a distance; it has been renovated hideously.

At **Limenária ❹**, now the island's second town, mansions of departed German mining executives survive. More intriguingly, it's the starting point for a safari to hilltop **Kástro**, the most naturally pirate-proof of the inland villages. Beyond Limenária, there's little to encourage a stop.

Theológos ❺, actually reached from the overdeveloped resort of **Potós ❻**, was the island's Ottoman capital, a linear place where most houses have walled gardens. **Mariés** sits piled up at the top of a wooded valley, just glimpsing the sea. By contrast, **Sotíros** enjoys phenomenal sunsets, best enjoyed from its central taverna under enormous plane trees. Of all the inland settlements, **Megálo Kazavíti ❼** (Megálo Prínos) has the grandest *platía* and the best-preserved traditional houses, snapped up and restored by outsiders. Ground-floor windows still retain iron bars, reminders of pirate days.

Samothráki

Samothráki (Samothrace) raises forbidding granite heights above stony shores and storm-lashed waters, both offering poor natural anchorage. Homer described Poseidon perching atop 1,611-metre (5,285ft) **Mount Fengári**, the Aegean's highest summit, to watch the action of the Trojan War just east. Fengári and its foothills occupy much of the island, with little level terrain except in the far west. Its southwest

flank features scattered villages lost amid olive groves varied by the occasional poplar. North-facing slopes are damper, with chestnuts and oaks, plus plane trees along the numerous watercourses. Springs are abundant, and waterfalls even plunge directly to the sea at **Kremastá Nerá** in the south.

Only the northwest of the island has a rudimentary bus service. Tourism is barely developed, and the remaining islanders prefer it that way. In its absence the population has dipped below 3,000, as farming can only support so many. Boats and occasional hydrofoils dock at **Kamariótissa**, the functional port where rental vehicles are in short supply.

Hóra or **Samothráki ❽**, the official capital 5km (3 miles) east of Kamariótissa, is more rewarding, nestling almost invisibly in a circular hollow. A cobbled commercial street serpentines past sturdy, basalt-built houses, many now unused. From outdoor seating at the two tavernas on Hóra's large *platía*, you glimpse the sea beyond a crumbled Byzantine-Genoese fort at the edge of town.

Unlike the elitist Eleusinian Mysteries, the Samothracian cult of the Kabiroi was open to all comers, including women and slaves. But, as at Eleusis, the details of the rites are unknown, for adherents took a vow of silence.

BELOW:
the tumbling waters of Foniás Canyon on spring-abundant Samothráki.

The 4th-century BC statue of Victory (Athena Nike) was discovered in 1863 by a French diplomat named Charles Champoiseau, who immediately sent it to Paris. The Greek government has long demanded its return, but so far has had to settle for a plaster copy.

Samothráki's other great sight lies 6km (4 miles) from Kamariótissa along the north coast road. From the late Bronze Age until the advent of Christianity, the **Sanctuary of the Great Gods ❾** was the major religious centre of the Aegean. Local deities of the original Thracian settlers were syncretised with the Olympian gods of later Aeolian colonists, in particular the *Kabiroi*, or divine twins Castor and Pollux, patrons of seafarers (who needed all the help they could get in the habitually rough seas hereabouts).

The sanctuary ruins (daily, summer 8am–7.30pm, winter until 3pm; charge) visible today are mostly late Hellenistic, and eerily impressive, if overgrown. Obvious monuments include a partly re-erected Doric temple of the second initiation; the peculiar round Arsinoeion, used for sacrifices; a round theatre area; and the fountain niche where the celebrated Winged Victory of Samothrace, now in the Louvre, was discovered. The site **museum** contains finds from the Archaic to Byzantine eras.

Some 6km (4 miles) further east, hot springs, cool cascades and a dense canopy of plane trees make the spa hamlet of **Thermá ❿** (Loutrá) the most popular base on the island, patronised by an uneasy mix of the elderly infirm and young bohemian types. Hot baths come in three temperatures and styles – including outdoor pools under a wooden shelter – while cold-plunge fanatics make for **Gría Váthra** canyon to the east. Thermá is also the base camp for the climb up Mount Fengári, a six-hour round trip.

The villages south of Hóra see few visitors, though they lie astride the route to **Pahiá Ammos ⓫**, the island's only sandy beach. From **Lákoma** village, it's about 8km (5 miles) by road to the beach, where a single seasonal taverna operates. Beyond Pahiá Ammos you can walk to smaller **Vátos** nudist beach, but you'll need a boat – or to drive clockwise completely around Samothráki – to reach the pebble beach of **Kípi** in the far southeast.

Límnos and Agios Evstrátios

Dominating the approaches to the Dardanelles, Límnos has been occupied since Neolithic times, and always prospered as a trading station and military outpost. The Greek military still controls much of the island's area, including half the airport, belying an otherwise peaceful atmosphere. The volcanic terrain dwindles to excellent beaches, or produces excellent wine and other products. The surrounding sea yield plenty of fish, thanks to periodic migrations through the Dardanelles.

Most things of interest are found in the port-capital, **Mýrina ⓬**, or a short distance to either side – luckily since the bus service is appalling and rental vehicles in short supply at peak season. Volcanic stone has been put to good use in the older houses and street cobbles of Mýrina, while sumptuous Ottoman mansions face the northern town beach of **Romeïkós Gialós**, with its popular cafés. The southerly beach of **Néa Máditos** abuts the fishing port with its seafood tavernas.

Mýrina's admirable **Archaeological Museum** (Tue–Sun 8.30am–3pm; large) holds finds from the island's several ancient sites. Public evidence of the town's Ottoman period is limited to an inscribed fountain and a dilapidated, circular dervish hall behind a supermarket, both near the harbour end of the long market street. Festooned over the headland above town, the ruined local *kástro* is worth climbing for sunset views.

The road north from Mýrina passes popular **Rihá Nerá** beach en route to an even better one at **Avlónas**. In the opposite direction lie decent beaches at **Platý** ⑬ and **Thános**, with terraced namesake villages on the hillsides just above. Continuing southeast from Thános brings you to **Evgátis**, acknowledged as the island's best beach. **Kondiás** ⑭ village just beyond is home to the **Balkan Art Gallery** (Sat–Thur 10am–2pm, 7.30–9.30pm), the result of a 2005 residential seminar organised by the Bulgarian painter Svetlin Russev.

Two **Allied cemeteries** maintained by the Commonwealth War Graves Commission flank the drab port town of **Moúdros** ⑮. During World War I, Moúdros was the principal base for the disastrous Gallipoli campaign. Of roughly 36,000 casualties, 887 are interred outside Moúdros on the way to **Roussopoúli**, while 348 more lie behind the village church at **Portianoú**, across the bay.

Límnos's major archaeological sites are all in the far east of the island. **Polyokhni** ⑯ (Polyóhni), southwest of Roussopoúli, was a fortified town even older than Troy, but was destroyed by an earthquake in 2100 BC and never rebuilt. **Hephaestia** (Ifestía) on the north coast was the island's ancient capital until the Byzantine period. The foundations of a temple of Hephaestos and a Roman theatre are visible. Across the bay at **Kabirion** ⑰ (Kavírio) was a sanctuary to the *Kabiroi*. Not much remains except the stumps and bases of columns.

A tiny wedge of land south of Límnos, **Agios Evstrátios** (Aï Strátis) is without doubt the most desolate spot in the northeast Aegean, especially since a 1967 earthquake devastated the single village. Owing to junta-era corruption, reparable dwellings were bulldozed and the surviving inhabitants (22 were killed) provided with ugly, prefabricated replacement housing on a grid plan. This, plus two dozen surviving old buildings on the left, is what you see when disembarking the mainline ferries stopping here on the Lávrio–Límnos–Kavála route, or (in summer) the small ferry based in Límnos – together these constitute Aï Strátis's lifeline, as all supplies must be imported.

Fish are the only thing in local abundance. There is little arable land aside from the valley partly clogged by the prefabs. This inevitably sad settlement can muster just 200 permanent residents. There are a couple of taverna-cafés and three *pensions* for tourists, most of whom are Greek. Beaches 90 minutes' walk north or south are unlikely to contain another soul. ❏

In the Polyokhni ruins, Italian archaeologists discovered a hoard of gold jewellery from the 3rd millennium BC. It is now on display in Athens.

BELOW:
bronze statue of the emperor Augustus found in the sea off Agios Evstrátios.

LÉSVOS, HÍOS, IKARÍA, FOÚRNI AND SÁMOS

These were some of ancient Greece's wealthiest islands, although today there are more reminders of their dramatic, more recent history

These volcanic islands, with their gentle wooded slopes, have long been popular with Greek visitors, who appreciate the ease with which they can be reached from Athens, as well as their other natural advantages.

Lésvos

Greece's third-largest island, measuring 70 by 40km (43 by 25 miles) at its widest, Lésvos is the antithesis of the *nisáki* (cute little islet). Between far-flung villages lie 11 million olive trees producing 45,000 tonnes of oil every year. Shipbuilding, fish-curing, *oúzo*-distilling and livestock-rearing remain important, but none rivals the olive, especially since it complements the second industry – tourism. Nets to catch this "black gold" are laid out in autumn, as soon as the tourists leave.

Lésvos was a preferred Roman holiday spot, what with its thick southern forests, idyllic orchards and hot springs known for their healing properties – the island's thermal baths and spa facilities are still a considerable draw. The Byzantines considered it a humane exile for deposed nobility, while the Genoese Gattilusi clan held court here from 1355 until 1462. To the Ottomans it was the "Garden of the Aegean", their most productive, strictly governed and heavily colonised Aegean island.

Following 18th-century reforms within the empire, a Christian land-owning aristocracy developed, served by a large population of labouring peasants. This quasi-feudal system made Lésvos fertile ground for post-1912 leftist movements, and its habit of returning Communist MPs since the junta fell has earned it the epithet "Red Island" among fellow Greeks. The years after 1912 also saw a vibrant local intelligentsia emerge, but since World War II Lésvos's socio-economic fabric has shrunk considerably with emigration to Athens, Australia and America. However, the founding here in 1987 of the University of the Aegean has helped arrest decline.

Main attractions
THEÓPHILOS & THÉRIADE MUSEUMS
MÓLYVOS
HÍOS TOWN BAZAAR
MASTIC VILLAGES
SYKIÁS OLÝMBON CAVE
NÉA MONÍ
ARMENISTÍS BEACHES
SÁMOS ARCHAEOLOGICAL MUSEUM
EVPALÍNIO ORYGMA
KÍMISIS TIS THEOTÓKOU CHURCH
CLIMBING MOUNT KÉRKIS

LEFT: a mosaic from Néa Moní, Híos.
BELOW: taking the shade in Plomári.

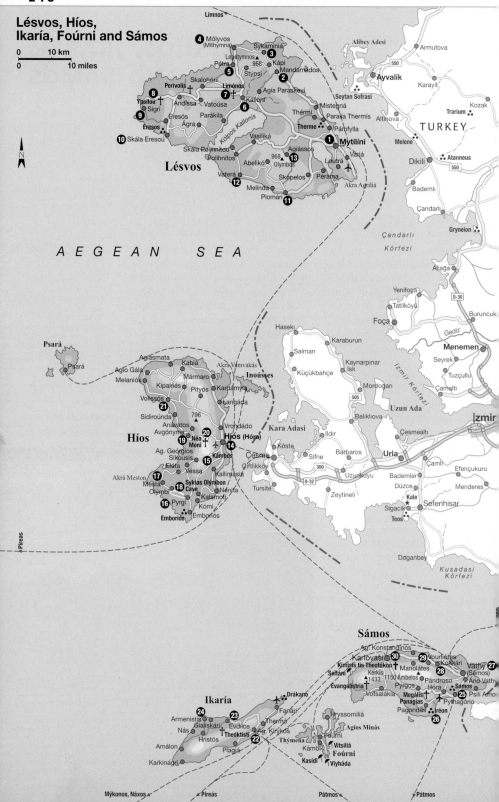

**Lésvos, Híos,
Ikaría, Foúrni and Sámos**

0   10 km
0   10 miles

TURKEY

A E G E A N   S E A

Límnos

Mólyvos
(Mithymna)
Sykaminiá
Lepétymnos
Pétra
Kápi
Stýpsi
Mandamádos
Skalohóri
Limónos
Agía Paraskeví
Perivolís
Kalloní
Andíssa
Vatoúsa
Ypsiloú
Sigri
Eresós
Parákila
Ágra
Thérmi
Mistegná
Paralía Thermís
Therme
Pámfylla
Ágra
Vasiliká
Skála Eresoú
Skála Polihnítou
Polihnítos
Agiássos
Olýmbos
Abelikó
Vaterá
Melínda
Plomári
Skópelos
Pérama
Akra Agriliá
Mytilíni
Varjá
Leutrá

Lésvos

Psará
Psará

Agiásmata
Agío Gála
Melaniós
Kabiá
Mármaro
Kipiariés
Pityós
Kardámyla
Volissós
Langáda
Sidiroúnda
Anávatos
Avgónyma
Néa
Moní
Híos (Hóra)
Ag. Geórgios
Síkousis
Eláta
Véssa
Kámbos
Kallimásiá
Akrá Meston
Mestá
Sykiás Olýmbon
Cave
Nénita
Olýmbi
Kalamotí
Pyrgí
Kómi
Emborios
Emborios

Híos

Inoússes
Akrá Vamvakás

Haseki
Karaburun
Salman
Küçükbahçe
Kaynarpınar
Isk
Mordoğan
Balıklıova
Kara Adası
Çeşme
Çiftlikköy
Tursite
Zeytineli
Köste
Sifne
Barbaros
Uzunkuyu
Ildır
Çeşmealtı
Urla
Bademler
Düzce
Menderes
Seferihisar
Sığacık
Teos
Doğanbey
Izmir
Uzun Ada

*Kuşadası
Körfezi*

Sámos
Ag. Konstandínos
Karlóvasi
Vourliótes
Kokkári
Kérkis
Kímisis tis Theotókou
Seïtáni
Manolátes
Vathy
(Sámos)
Áno Vathy
Évangelístria
Ámbelos
Pýrgos
Pándroso
Sámos
Vótsalákia
Hóra
Megális
Panagías
Pythagório
Psilí Ámo
Iréon
Pagóndas

Ikaría
Drákano
Fanári
Armenistís
Gialiskári
Évdilos
Thermá
Ag. Kírykos
Nás
Theóktisti
Hristós
Amálon
Plagiá
Karkinágri
Hryssomiliá
Agios Minás
Foúrni
Thýmena
Kámbi
Vitsiliá
Kasidi
Foúrni
Vlyháda

Mýkonos, Náxos
Pireás
Pátmos
Pátmos
Pireas

Mytilíni ❶, the capital (its name a popular alias for the entire island), has a revved-up, slightly gritty atmosphere, as befits a port town of almost 30,000. Behind the waterfront, assorted church domes and spires enliven the skyline, while Odós Ermoú one street inland contains an entire bazaar, from the fish market to a clutch of pricey antique shops. On the headland to the northeast sits the medieval *kástro* (Tue–Sun 8.30am–2.30pm; charge), with ruins from various eras.

Behind the ferry dock is the two-wing **Archaeological Museum** (Tue–Sun 8.30am–3pm; charge), the new gallery featuring Hellenistic mosaics depicting scenes from Menander's comedies, and engaging terracotta figurines in the old wing.

Even more noteworthy are two museums at **Variá**, 4km (2½ miles) south of town. The **Theóphilos Museum** (daily 10am–4pm; charge) contains more than 60 paintings by locally born Theóphilos Hatzimihaíl, Greece's most celebrated Naïve painter. The adjacent **Thériade Museum** (Tue–Sun 9am–2pm, 5–8pm; charge) was founded by another native

son who, while an avant-garde art publisher in Paris, assembled this astonishing collection, with works by Chagall, Miró, Picasso, Léger and others.

The road running northwest from Mytilíni follows the coast facing Turkey. **Mandamádos** ❷, 37km (23 miles) from Mytilíni, has a surviving pottery industry and, on the outskirts, the enormous **Monastery of the Taxiárhis**, with its much-revered black icon of the Archangel Michael. At **Kápi** the road divides; the northerly fork is wider, better-paved and more scenic as it curls across the flanks of **Mount Lepétymnos**, passing by the handsome village of **Sykaminiá** ❸, the birthplace of novelist Strátis Myrivílis.

You go back down to sea level at **Mólyvos** ❹ (officially Míthymna), the linchpin of Lésvos tourism, and understandably so: the ranks of sturdy tiled houses climbing to the medieval castle are an appealing sight, as is the stone-paved fishing harbour. But its days as a retreat for bohemian artists and alternative activities are over, with package tourism dominant since the late 1980s. **Pétra** ❺, 5km (3 miles) south, accommodates

The Theóphilos Museum in Variá contains the largest collection of works by Greece's most famous Naïve painter.

BELOW:
Mólyvos surmounted by its medieval castle.

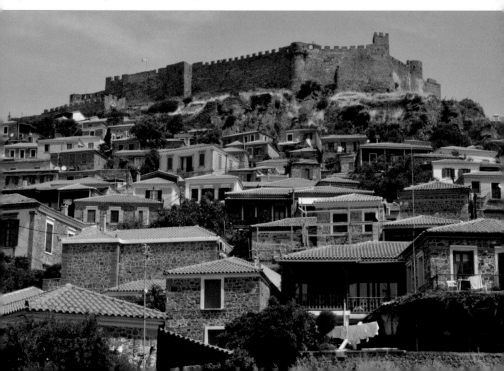

Lésvos claims to produce the finest olive oil in all Greece. The olives are harvested in November and December, and pressed within 24 hours of being picked.

BELOW: a monastery on Híos.

the overflow behind its long beach; inland looms a rock plug crowned with the **Panagía Glykofiloússa** church. At its foot the 18th-century **Vareltzídena Mansion** (Tue–Sun 8.30am–2.30pm; free) with its extensive murals is well worth a look, as is the frescoed, 16th-century church of **Agios Nikólaos**.

From Pétra, head 17km (11 miles) south to **Kalloní ⑥** market town and the turning east for **Agía Paraskeví** with the excellent **Museum of the Olive-Pressing Industry** (Wed–Mon 10am–6pm; charge), in the old communal olive mill.

Alternatively, head west past **Limónos Monastery ⑦**, which is home to a small ecclesiastical museum, before continuing towards more rugged western Lésvos, with its lunar volcanic terrain. Stream valleys foster little oases, such as the one around **Perivolís Monastery** (daily 10am–1pm and 5–6pm), 30km (19 miles) from Limónos, decorated with wonderful frescoes. After 10km (6 miles), the **Monastery of Ypsiloú ⑧**, on top of an extinct volcano, contemplates the abomination of desolation – complete

with scattered trunks of the "Petrified Forest", prehistoric sequoias mineralised by volcanic ash.

There are more fossilised trees in and around **Sígri ⑨**, 90km (56 miles) from Mytilíni, a sleepy place flanked by good beaches, and very much the end of the line, though most years it's an alternative ferry port. Many people prefer livelier **Skála Eresoú ⑩**, 14km (9 miles) south of Ypsiloú, for a beach experience on its 3km (2 miles) of sand. In particular, numerous lesbians come to honour Sappho, who was born here.

Southern Lésvos, between the two gulfs, is carpeted with olive groves and chestnut forests, rolling up to 968-metre (3,176ft) **Mount Olymbos**. Back on the coast is **Plomári ⑪**, Lésvos's second town, famous for its *oúzo* industry; the Varvagiánni distillery lays on tours. Most tourists choose to stay at pebble-beach **Agios Isídoros** 3km (2 miles) east, although **Melínda** 6km (4 miles) west is more scenic. **Vaterá ⑫**, with its 7km (4½-mile) sand beach, reckoned the best on the island, lies still further west, reached by a different road. En route, you can stop for a soak at the restored **medieval spa** – one of four on the island – outside **Polihnítos**, 45km (28 miles) from Mytilíni. Inland from Plomári, the remarkable hill village of **Agiássos ⑬** nestles in a wooded valley under Ólymbos. Its heart is the major pilgrimage church of **Panagía Vrefokratoússa**, centre of the 15 August festival, Lésvos's biggest. Local musicians are considered among the island's best.

Híos, Inoússes, Psará

Although Híos (alias Chíos) has been important and prosperous since antiquity, the Middle Ages made the Híos of today. After the Genoese seized control here in 1346, the Giustiniani clan established a cartel, the *maona*, which controlled the highly profitable trade in gum mastic. During their rule, which also saw the introduction of silk and citrus production, Híos became one of the wealthiest and most cultured islands in the Mediterranean.

In 1566 the Ottomans expelled the Genoese, but granted the islanders numerous privileges, so that Híos continued to flourish until March 1822, when poorly armed agitators from Sámos convinced the reluctant Hiots to participate in the independence uprising. Sultan Mahmut II, enraged at this ingratitude, exacted a terrible revenge. A two-month rampage, commanded by Admiral Kara Ali, killed 30,000 islanders, enslaved 45,000 more, and saw all the island's settlements razed, except the mastic-producing villages. Híos had only partly recovered from this outrage when a March 1881 earthquake destroyed much of what remained and killed 4,000 people.

Today Híos and its satellite islet Psoússes are home to some of Greece's wealthiest shipping families. The catastrophic 19th century ensured that **Híos Town** or **Hóra** ⑭ (population 25,000) seems off-puttingly modern at first glance. But scratch the ferroconcrete surface and you will find traces of the Genoese and Ottoman years. The most obvious medieval feature is the *kástro*; moated on the landward side, it lacks a seaward rampart, destroyed after the 1881 earthquake.

Just inside the *kástro*'s impressive **Porta Maggiore** stands the **Giustiniani Museum** (Tue–Sun 8.30am–3pm; charge), housing a regularly changing collection of frescoes and icons rescued from rural churches. On a small nearby square is the Turkish cemetery, with the tomb of Kara Ali – the admiral responsible for the 19th-century massacre, blown up along with his flagship by one of Admiral Kanáris's fire-boats in June 1822. Still further inside lies the old Muslim and Jewish quarter, with a derelict mosque, hamams (one restored) and overhanging houses.

The lively **bazaar** extends south of central **Platía Vounakíou**, with Aplotariás as its backbone – fascinating alleys between this street and Venizélou culminate in a wonderful Belle Epoque meat-and-produce gazebo. Also on Platía Vounakíou, the **Mecidiye Mosque** is now a locked warehouse for lapidary fragments; the **Archaeological Museum** (Tue–Sun 8.30am–3pm), in the south of town, well lit and well laid out, is more rewarding.

The sailors of Híos were such skilled navigators that, it is claimed, Christopher Columbus came to study with Hiot captains before his voyages.

BELOW: on the road to Pityoús, in the north-central part of Híos.

Most of the houses in the mastic village of Pyrgí are incised with black-and-white geometric patterns, known as xistá.

BELOW RIGHT: Agii Apóstoli, Pyrgí.

South of Hóra lies **Kámbos** , a broad plain of high-walled citrus groves dotted with the imposing sandstone mansions of the medieval aristocracy, set back from narrow, unmarked lanes. Many were destroyed by the earthquake, while a few have been restored as accommodation or restaurants. Irrigation water was originally drawn up by *manganós* or waterwheels; a few survive in the centre of ornately paved courtyards.

The onward road heads southwest towards mastic-producing southern Híos, with the 20 villages collectively known as the *mastihohoriá*, built as pirate-proof strongholds by the Genoese during the 14th and 15th centuries. Each village is laid out on a dense, rectangular plan, with narrow passages over-arched by earthquake buttresses, and the backs of the outer houses doubling as the perimeter wall.

Pyrgí, 21km (13 miles) from Hóra, is one of the best-preserved *mastihohoriá*. A passageway off its central square leads to Byzantine **Agii Apóstoli** Church, decorated with later frescoes. In Pyrgí's back alleys, tomatoes are laboriously strung for drying in September by teams of local women. Some 11km (7 miles) west, **Mestá** seems a more sombre, monochrome labyrinth, which retains defensive towers at its corners. Several houses have been restored as accommodation. Such quarters are typically claustrophobic, though, and guests will appreciate the nearby resorts of **Kómi** (with a sand beach) and **Emboriós** (with beach of volcanic pebbles).

Southeast of Mestá is the mastic-producing village of **Olýmbi**, after which the road south to the coast leads to th **Sykiás Olýmbon Cave** (Tue–Su 10am–8pm; charge). Stumbled acro as recently as 1985, this 150-million year-old cavern, a riot of stunning roc formations, is fantastically floodlit.

From Mestá, if you have your ow transport the beautiful, deserted we coast, with its many coves, is accessib via atmospheric **Véssa**, more open an less *kástro*-like than the other *mastih horiá*. Between the bays of **Kastélla** an **Elínda**, a good road snakes uphill t **Avgónyma**, a densely clustered vi lage well restored by returned Gree

Up a Gum Tree

The mastic bushes (*Pistacia lentiscus, skhiniá* in Greek) of southern Híos are the unique source of gum mastic. In the past, it was used as a chewing gum used to freshen the breath of the sultan's concubines; the Romans had toothpicks made from mastic because they found it kept their teeth white and prevented tooth decay; the "father of medicine", Hippocrates, praised its therapeutic value for coughs and colds; and lately some alternative medicine practitioners have made even more ambitious claims on its behalf.

The first stage of the mastic production process has remained unchanged since ancient times. In late summer, villagers make incisions in the bark of the trees, which weep resin "tears"; these are carefully scraped off and cleaned of leaves or twigs. Next, the raw "tears" are washed, then baked or sun-dried and re-formed at a processing plant. Some 150 tonnes of mastic are produced annually, most of it exported to Middle Eastern countries where it is a commonly used cooking spice; it also appears in Greek *mastíha* liqueur, *tsouréki* bread and the chrism oil *(myron)* used in the Chrismation (confirmation) ritual of the Orthodox Church. Mastiha Shop (www.mastihashop.gr) is a Greek chain of outlets retailing a diverse range of products using the substance, from shower gel and soap to chocolate and nougat.

mericans. Just 4km (2½ miles) north
erches the almost deserted, crumbling
návatos, well camouflaged against its
iff. In 1822, 400 Hiots leapt from it to
eir deaths rather than be captured.

Some 5km (3 miles) to the east, **Néa
Ioní** ⓴ (daily, summer 8am–1pm,
–8pm, winter 8am–1pm, 4–6pm)
onstitutes one of the finest surviv-
g examples of mid-Byzantine archi-
ecture, founded in 1049 by Emperor
Constantine Monomahos IX. It suf-
ered heavily in 1822 and 1881, first
ith the murder of its monks, plus the
illage of its treasures, and then with
e collapse of its dome. Despite the
amage, its mosaics of scenes from
e life of Christ, which emerged in
009 from a five-year restoration, are
utstanding. The outbuildings have
in in ruins since the events of the
9th century. By the gate, an ossuary
isplays the bones of the 1822 martyrs,
ogether with generations of monks.
he onward road eventually takes you
castle-crowned **Volissós** ㉑ in the
orthwest. To either side of this half-
mpty village are the island's finest
eaches – and visible scars from several
fires since 1981, which have burnt two-
thirds of Híos's forests.

Despite provincial appearances,
the peaceful, green islet of **Inoússes**
(Oinoússes), some 16km (10 miles)
north of Híos harbour by regular caique,
is actually among the wealthiest territories in Greece, home to the Lívanos,
Lemós and Patéras shipping families.
Appropriately, a marine academy that
trains seamen for Greece's merchant
fleet stands at the west end of the quay,
with a small private maritime museum
in the centre of the single town. Small
but decent beaches lie to either side.

The tiny islet of **Psará**, about 30km
(19 miles) offshore from Volissós,
derives its name from the ancient
Greek adjective *psarós* (grey) – and a
grey place it is, especially since 1824,
when 14,000 Ottoman troops landed
here to avenge continued harassment
of their shipping by Psaran Admiral
Kanáris, who commanded the third-
largest Greek fleet after those of Hydra
and Spétses. Some 27,000 islanders
died – many blowing themselves up
in a ridge-top powder magazine rather
than surrender – and only about 3,000

The Massacre of
Chios, *an 1824
painting by Delacroix
depicting the
slaughter of 1822,
caused controversy in
Europe and won
much sympathy for
the Greek cause.*

BELOW: the Turkish
cemetery on Híos.

escaped. The Ottomans burnt any remaining buildings and vegetation.

Today about 350 inhabitants remain on melancholy Psará, its bleakness relieved only by occasional fig trees. Besides the lone port village, there's just a monastery in the far north, frequented once a year at its 5 August festival. Six beaches lie northeast of the port, each better than the one before. Just a few tourists trickle over from Híos on the local ferry from Híos town; long-haul ferries call rarely from Sígri on Lésvos, Límnos and Kavála.

Ikaría and Foúrni

Narrow, wing-shaped Ikaría is named after the mythical Ikaros (Icarus), who supposedly fell into the sea nearby when his wax wings melted. One of the least developed large islands in the Aegean, Ikaría has little to offer anyone intent on ticking off four-star sights, but it appeals to those disposed to an eccentric, slightly Ruritanian environment. During both the 1930s Metaxás dictatorship and the 1946–9 Civil War, the island served as a place of exile, first for opponents of Metaxás

BELOW:
Ikaría butterfly.

and then hundreds of Communist Local people thought the latter wei the most noble, humanitarian fol they had ever met, and still vote Cor munist in droves.

Although little more than a fishin village, **Agios Kírykos** ㉒ is the cap tal and main southerly port. Its tou ist facilities are geared to the cliente at the neighbouring spa of **Therm** Beyond that, there is a long beach **Fanári** and a Hellenistic tower at **Cap Drákano**.

Taxis are far more reliable than th bus for the spectacular 41km (25-mil drive over the 1,000-metre (3,300f Atherás ridge to **Evdilos** ㉓, the nortl facing second port and would-be reso Another 16km (10 miles) takes yo past **Kámbos**, with its sandy beach an ruined Byzantine palace, to **Armei istís** ㉔. Only here do foreign touris congregate, for the sake of excelle beaches – **Livádi** and **Mesaktí**, just ea – though the surf can be deadly.

Nás, 4km (2½ miles) west, is name for the *náos* or temple of Artem Tavropolio, on the banks of the rive which drains to a popular pebble cov

Gialiskári, a fishing port 4km (2½ miles) east of Armenistís, is distinguished by its photogenic jetty chapel.

There are few bona fide inland villages, as the proud Ikarians hate to live on top of each other, and like to keep plenty of room for orchards between their houses. Above Armenistís are four hamlets lost in pine forest, and collectively known as **Ráhes**. At **Hristós**, the largest of these, people cram the café-bars all night long, sleep until noon, and carry their belongings (or store potent local wine) in hairy goatskin bags. The surrounding countryside completes the hobbit-like image, with vertical natural monoliths and troglodytic cottages for livestock made entirely of gigantic granite or slate slabs. One of these formations, inland from Kámbos, shelters the **chapel of Theoskepastí**, just above frescoed **Theóktisti monastery**.

Foúrni, one of several islets southeast of Ikaría, makes a living from its thriving fishing fleet and boatyards. Seafood dinners figure high on the agendas of arriving tourists, who mostly stay in the main – and surprisingly large – port town. A partly paved road links this with

Agios Ioánnis Hrysóstomos in the south – superior beaches like **Vlyháda**, **Kasídi** and **Vitsiliá** nearby – and Hryssomiliá in the far north, the only other habitations. Good beaches within walking distance south of the port include **Kámbi**, just over the ridge, with lively tavernas, or the naturist beach of **Aspa** beyond.

Sámos

Sámos, an almost subtropical island with vine terraces, cypress and olive groves, surviving forests of black and Calabrian pine, hillside villages, and beaches of every size and kind, appeals to numerous tourists. Half a dozen wildfires since 1986 – the worst in July 2000 – and commercialisation have blighted the eastern half of the island, but impassable gorges, the Aegean's second-highest mountain, and beaches accessible only on foot hold sway in the far west.

Natural endowments usually take precedence over man-made ones, and Sámos has an identity problem owing to a 15th-century depopulation and later recolonisation. First settled in the 13th century BC, by the 7th century AD Sámos was a major maritime power

On 17 July 1912, a certain Dr Ioánnis Malahías declared Ikaría liberated from the Turks, and until 5 November (and unification with Greece) it was an independent republic.

BELOW: the remote chapel at Gialiskári port, Ikaría.

One column is all that remains of Polykrates' great temple to Hera. He planned it to be the largest temple in Greece, but it was never completed.

BELOW: giant *kouros* in the Archaeological Museum, Vathý.

thanks to its innovative triremes (warships), still shown on local wine labels. The island's zenith came under the rule (538–522 BC) of **Polykrates**, a brilliant but unscrupulous tyrant who doubled as a pirate. Wealth, however it was accumulated, supported a luxurious capital of 60,000, and a court attended by the likes of philosopher-mathematician Pythagoras, the astronomer Aristarhos and the bard Aesop. Decline ensued with Polykrates' death at the hands of the Persians, and the rise of Athens.

Heavily developed **Pythagório ㉕** occupies the site of Polykrates' capital, three of whose monuments earned Herodotus' highest praise: "I have spoken at greater length of the Samians because of all the Greeks they have achieved the three greatest constructions." From the immense harbour mole constructed by ancient slaves (the first great construction), you can watch Mount Mykale in Turkey majestically change colour at dusk.

The 1,040-metre (3,412ft) **Evpalínio Orygma** (Eupalinos' Tunnel), an aqueduct engineered by Eupalinos of Megara in the 6th century BC through the hill-

side northwest of town, is the secon marvel, and one of the technologic wonders of the ancient world. Surve ing was so good that two work crew beginning from either end, met wit no vertical error and a horizontal one c less than 1 percent. You can visit muc of it (Tue–Sun 8.45am–2.15pm; charge along the catwalk used to remove spo from the water channel far below.

The ruins of the third constructio the **Hera Temple ㉖** (Iréon), stan 8km (5 miles) west of Pythagório, pa coastal Roman baths and the airpor But Polykrates' grandiose commissio was never actually completed, and By antine builders later dismantled it fc cut stone.

Vathý or **Sámos Town ㉗**, built alon a deep inlet on the north coast, has bee the capital and main port since 183 The **Archaeological Museum** (Tue Sun 8.30am–3pm; charge) is one of th best in the provinces, with a rich trov of finds from the sanctuary of Her Given pride of place is a 5-metre (16f almost intact *kouros* (male votive statue the largest ever found. The small-objec collection in a separate wing confirm the Middle Eastern slant of worship an clientele at the temple, with orientalise ivories and locally cast griffin's heads.

Ano Vathý, the large village clin, ing to the hillside 2km (1 mile) soutl east, existed for almost two centuri before the harbour settlement. A plea ant stroll will take you through stee cobbled streets separating 300-yea old houses, their overhanging secon storeys in lath and plaster more aki to northern Greece and Anatolia tha the central Aegean.

The first stop of note on the nort coast road is **Kokkári ㉘** after 12k (7½ miles), a former fishing village no devoted to tourism. The original cent is cradled between twin headlands, ar windsurfers zip along off a long, wes erly pebble beach. Overhead loom th now much-denuded crags of **Mou** **Ambelos** (1,150 metres/ 3,773ft), fo merly a favourite of hikers. Paths still (up directly from behind Kokkári, whi

cars climb a road just past **Avlákia** to **Vourliótes** ㉙, a thriving village with several tavernas. A trail (and a separate road from the pleasant coastal town of Agios Konstandínos) carry up to more dramatically set **Manolátes**, where some of the tavernas stay open in winter.

The coastal highway continues west to **Karlóvasi** ㉚, 29km (18 miles) from Vathý; just before it is reached, a side road leads up through Kondakéïka to the **Church of Kímisis tis Theotókou** at Petaloúda, a bit beyond, the oldest (late 12th century) and most vividly frescoed of several on the island.

Karlóvasi is a somewhat dishevelled place, sprawling over several districts. **Néo**, the biggest, has ornate mansions, and cavernous, derelict warehouses down by the water at **Ríva**, vestiges of the leather-tanning trade that thrived here before 1970. **Meséo** is more villagey, as is **Ano** (or Paleó), lining a vegetated valley behind the sentinel church of Agia Triáda. **Limín**, just below Ano, has the most local tourist facilities, including the ferry port.

West of here beckon some of Sámos's best beaches, including **Potámi**, a sand-and-pebble stretch visited by most of Karlóvasi at weekends. Beyond Potámi, you have to walk to a pair of remote, scenic beaches at **Seïtáni**.

Karlóvasi lies roughly halfway round an anticlockwise loop of the island, threading an interior dotted with small villages of tiled, shuttered houses and churches with striped domes. At Agii Theodóri junction 5km (3 miles) south of Karlóvasi, the southwesterly turn takes you past **Ormos Marathókambos** port to **Votsalákia**, Sámos's largest beach resort. More secluded coves lie further west along the road curling around the base of **Mount Kérkis** (1,433 metres/ 4,700ft), which forms the west end of the island. The refuge of several hundred guerrillas, then Civil War fighters, from 1943 to 1948, it is usually climbed from **Evangelístria Convent** on the south slopes – a full day's outing.

The southeasterly choice of route at Agii Theodóri heads for Pythagório. You could schedule stops in **Pýrgos** for a can of local honey, and at the **Monastery of Megális Panagías**, just below Mavratzéï, which has smudged frescoes dating from after 1586.   ❑

Pythagório (formerly Tigáni) was renamed as recently as 1955, to honour the great Samian Pythagoras – an irony, since the mathematician exiled himself in disgust at the greed of the tyrant Polykrates.

BELOW: fishing boats in Pythagório harbour.

THE DODECANESE

Rhodes, Kárpathos, Kásos, Hálki, Kastellórizo, Tílos,
Sými, Nísyros, Kós, Psérimos, Astypálea, Kálymnos,
Télendos, Léros, Lipsí, Pátmos, Arkí, Agathonísi

The term "Dodecanese" is relatively new. While these far-flung islands were ruled by the Ottomans, they were known, incongruously, as the southern Sporades. In the early 1900s, in response to the withdrawal by the Young Turks of historic privileges granted by various sultans, 12 islands (*dódeka nisiá* in Greek) jointly protested. Their rebellion failed, but the name stuck – hence the Dodecanese (*Dodekánisos* in Greek). In fact, there have always been many more than 12 islands in this archipelago, depending on how you count: 14, 18 or (including every desert islet) even 27 islands.

The 18 islands in these chapters are divided into three sections. Rhodes, as the capital and main local transport hub, appears separately. The collective term "Southern Dodecanese" means the islands immediately around Rhodes, most easily reached by a domestic or international flight into the mother island, followed by a feeder flight or ferry.

"Northern Dodecanese" islands, on the other hand, use Kós as a touch-down point, though some, such as holy Pátmos, are also easily reached from Sámos in the northeast Aegean. Seasonal catamarans or hydrofoils fill in the gaps between aircraft and conventional boats.

The Dodecanese were Greece's final territorial acquisition in 1948. Before that they were ruled (briefly) by the British; before which there had been a 21-month occupation by the Germans; who had succeeded the Italians on their capitulation in late 1943. The Italians had ruled since 1912 with delusions of recreating the Roman Empire, leaving Art Deco follies to mark their passing. They had taken over from the Ottomans, who ousted the Knights of St John in 1523 and administered these islands (except for Rhodes and Kós) with benign neglect. To walk the streets of Kós or Rhodes is to witness a cultural patchwork: a minaret on one corner facing an Italian villa, across an expanse of excavated Hellenistic foundations, overshadowed by the fortifications of the crusading Knights. ❑

PRECEDING PAGES: the port of Gialós, Sými; church in Mandráki, capital of Nísyros.
LEFT: mosaic work on Nísyros. **FROM TOP:** view from Kritiniá castle, Rhodes; exhibit in the Kós Archaeological Museum; young island-hoppers.

RHODES

According to the ancient Greeks, Rhodes was "more beautiful than the sun". Even today's brash resorts cannot dim the appeal of its benign climate, entrancing countryside and fascinating history

Main attractions
MUSEUM OF MODERN GREEK ART
RODÍNI PARK
STREET OF THE KNIGHTS
PALACE OF THE GRAND MASTERS
ANCIENT KAMEIROS
MONÓLITHOS CASTLE
THÁRRI MONASTERY
LAHANIÁ SQUARE
PIGÉS KALLITHÉAS
KÁLATHOS BEACH
PANAGÍA CHURCH, LÍNDOS

LEFT: Líndos, on the east coast. **BELOW:** the temple on Monte Smith.

The capital of the Dodecanese and fourth-largest Greek island, Rhodes (Ródos) has been on the package-tour trail since the 1970s. It is one of the most cosmopolitan resorts in Greece, attracting every conceivable nationality in a seasonal repertory lasting from April to November: Italians and Spaniards in August (especially in the Old Town), Germans in spring and autumn out in the countryside, Scandinavians intent on sunshine and cheap booze in early summer, Israelis on special gambling sprees, Brits and Russians seemingly all the time.

But far from the madding crowds in Neohóri (Rhodes New Town) and the serried ranks of umbrellas and sun-loungers on the northern beaches, you can still find a more unspoilt island light years away from the laddish T-shirts and tawdry knick-knacks of the resorts. Frequent bus services run down both coasts from beside the "New Market", but it is worth hiring a car, jeep or powerful motorbike if you really want to explore deserted beaches, remote monasteries and castles perched above citrus groves.

Patchwork history

The legacy of ancient Greeks, crusading Knights of St John, besieging Ottomans and imperial Italians forms a fascinating palimpsest in Rhodes Town, from castle turrets to the late classical street plan. There are temple pillars and Byzantine churches, mosques with

minarets, plus the twin bronze deer guarding the waters of Mandráki harbour where, supposedly, the Colossus of Rhodes once stood.

This wondrous statue depicting Apollo Helios, the work of local sculptors Kharis and Lakhis, stood over 30 metres (100ft) tall. Impressive by any standards, legend made it even more so by describing it as standing astride the harbour entrance. But to do so it would have to have been more than 10 times its actual size, an impossible engineering feat. Wherever it actually

The bronze deer guarding the port recall the time when the island was plagued by snakes. The Delphic oracle suggested the introduction of stags, which did the trick by spearing the serpents with their antlers.

BELOW:
Mandráki quay.

was, the monument stood until it collapsed in an earthquake in 226 BC. The bronze was sold for scrap in the 7th century AD.

Late in the Byzantine era, Rhodes was governed by the Genoese – until the Knights of St John, who had fled Jerusalem via Cyprus, captured the city in 1309, beginning a rule that lasted 213 years, under 19 Grand Masters. They substantially refortified the city, and raided Ottoman shipping. Finally, in 1522, Sultan Süleyman the Magnificent took Rhodes after a six-month siege that pitted 200,000 warriors against 650 knights. The Grand Master and 180 surviving brethren surrendered and, with a number of civilians, were allowed safe conduct to Malta. The Ottomans held the island for 390 years. Churches were converted to mosques, and Christians were banned from living within the city walls.

In 1912, Italy occupied Rhodes while at war with Turkey, and embarked on a massive archaeological construction programme. During World War II, when Italy capitulated in 1943, the Germans took over. Rhodes was liberated by the Allies in 1945, and the Greek flag hoisted three years later when the Dodecanese became united with Greece.

These days, the island is still under siege – by tourists. Present-day **Rhodes Town ❶** (Ródos) divides neatly into the New Town (Neohóri), settled by Greeks in Ottoman times, and the Old City. The contrast is marked: fast food, designer clothes and beaches on two sides, versus cobbled streets and a village-like feel.

The New Town

Here, smart shops abound, peddling designer labels at Western European prices and above (except during the August and February sales). Inexpensive umbrellas are big business here, and you can have any logo you like embossed on them. Sit and watch the world go by from one of the expensive, touristy pavement cafés at **Mandráki** port. Marginally cheaper are the cafés inside the Italian-built **covered market ❹** (Néa Agorá), whose highlight is a whimsical raised gazebo where fish were once sold.

Excursion boats leave Mandráki quay by 9am for the island of Sými, usually calling first at Panormítis Monastery, or heading down the east coast to Líndos. But all scheduled services (except for hydrofoils) depart from **Kolóna** harbour, a 15-minute walk east.

Mandráki, guarded by the lighthouse bastion of **Agios Nikólaos** ❸ (St Nicholas's Fort), is also an established port of call on the international yachting circuit, with local charters, too. Along the west quay stands a cluster of Italian-built monuments (*see page 245*), in its time the Foro Italico: they include the provincial administration building with its Gothic arches, the **Church of the Annunciation** ❸ (Evangelismós) next door, with superb 1950s frescoes by neo-Byzantine artist Fótis Kóntoglou; and across the way the post office, town hall and municipal (originally the Puccini) theatre, all in quick succession.

Opposite the theatre, the **Mosque of Murad Reis** ❸ stands beside one of the island's larger Muslim graveyards. On the other side of this is the **Villa Cleobolus**, where Lawrence Durrell

lived from spring 1945 to spring 1947, while working as a British-occupation civil servant. A stroll along popular **Élli beach**, past the **casino** installed in the Italian-era Albergo delle Rose, brings you to Rhodes's northernmost point, with its Italian-built **Aquarium** (daily; summer 9am–8.30pm, winter 9am–4.30pm; charge). Immediately south, on Ekatón Hourmadiés (Hundred Palms) square (actually an oval), stands the **Museum of Modern Greek Art** ❸ (Tue–Sat 8am–2pm, Fri 5–8pm; charge). Housed in the Nestorídeio Mélathro, this is the most important collection of 20th-century Greek painting outside Athens.

Inland Neohóri was once the nightlife capital of the Dodecanese, but a change in tourism patterns combined with the 2008–9 economic slump has cut a huge swathe through the bars – perhaps 40 remain from a 1990s zenith of 200. Surviving establishments tend to line Orfanídou and its perpendicular streets, just in from westerly, wind-buffeted **Psaroupoúla** beach.

Some 2km (1 mile) southwest of Mandráki, **Monte Smith** – more correctly,

Monte Smith, the hill west of town, is named after the British admiral Sir Sidney Smith, who kept watch from here for the Napoleonic fleet in 1802.

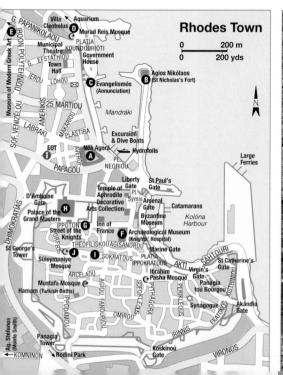

BELOW: the stone walls of Eleftherías, or Liberty, Gate.

The sublime Aphrodite Bathing wrings out her tresses in Rhodes' Archaeological Museum.

BELOW: Street of the Knights (Odós Ippotón) in Rhodes Old Town.

Agios Stéfanos hill – offers panoramic views over the town and sea on both sides. This was the site of Rhodes's Hellenistic acropolis, with a stadium, a heavily restored *odeion* and evocatively re-erected columns of a Temple of Apollo dating from the 3rd century BC. In the far south, en route to Líndos, **Rodíni Park**, set in a canyon, was the home of the ancient rhetoric school and is today a shady, cool streamside retreat with little dams, bridges and – on the clifftop to the south – a large fenced reserve for the miniature Rhodian deer, *Dama dama*.

The Old Town

The medieval walled town, a Unesco World Heritage Site, with its ramparts and 11 surviving gates, is so well preserved a visitor half expects to bump into a Knight of St John in one of the narrow cobbled streets. Many of the streets follow their right-angled ancient predecessors: in the maze-like Ottoman quarters, it's easier to get lost.

Step through the northernmost **Liberty Gate** (Pylí Eleftherías) into **Platía Sýmis** to view the founda-

tions of a Temple of Aphrodite, and an Ottoman wall-fountain. Contiguous **Platía Argyrokástrou** is flanked by the Inn of the Order of Auvergne and the **Decorative Arts Collection** (Tue–Sun 8.30am–2.45pm; charge), with costumes, ceramics and carved woodwork gathered from old houses across the archipelago. Just opposite stands the **Byzantine Museum** (Tue–Sun 8.30am–2.45pm; charge), situated in the former Knights' cathedral, now known as **Panagía Kástrou**. Much of its collection of icons and frescoes rescued from rural chapels has moved to the Palace of the Grand Masters.

Next stop is the 15th-century **Knights' Hospital ❻**, now the **Archaeological Museum** (Tue–Sun 8.30am–3pm). Among the exhibits in the Hellenistic statuary gallery is the eerily sea-eroded *Aphrodite Adioumene*, Durrell's "Marine Venus", and the more accessible *Aphrodite Bathing*, wringing out her tresses.

From the museum, the **Street of the Knights ❼** (Odós Ippotón) leads in medieval splendour uphill to the **Palace of the Grand Masters ❽** (*see*

Grand Masters' Palace

The **Palace of the Grand Masters** (summer Mon 12.30–7pm, Tue–Sun 8am–7pm, winter until 2.45pm; charge) was almost completely destroyed when a munitions store in the nearby church of St John exploded in 1856, killing 800 people. During 1937–9 it was rebuilt by the Italians as a summer residence for King Victor Emmanuel and Mussolini, neither of whom ever used it. Traipse up the grandiose staircase to view ostentatious upper-floor decorations, including Hellenistic mosaics brought here from Kós. Two adjacent ground-floor galleries are devoted to ancient Rhodes and medieval, pre-Ottoman Rhodes, which, with their coverage of daily life in the Hellenistic city and the role of the Knights' outpost as a trade entrepôt respectively, are jointly the best museums on Rhodes.

below). Italian-restored, and preserved from commercialisation, the thoroughfare houses more inns of the Knights, as their lodgings were divided by linguistic affinity. The **Inn of France**, emblazoned with the heraldry of several Grand Masters, is the most imposing.

The main commercial thoroughfare is **Sokrátous ❶**, a "Golden Mile" packed with fur and leather shops, jewellers, lace and embroidery stalls, and every other kind of tourist paraphernalia imaginable. Sokrátous links **Platía Ippokrátous** with its ornate fountain and Kastellanía (medieval "stock exchange") with the pink **Süleymaniye Mosque ❷** at the top of the hill, recently restored but not yet open to the public. The Old Town still has a sizeable Turkish minority, using the active Ibrahim Pasha Mosque on Plátonos, though since the Cyprus crises they deliberately keep a low profile.

Another still-functioning Ottoman monument, esteemed by Orthodox and Muslim alike, is the **hamam** (Turkish baths, signed as Dimotiká Loutrá; Mon–Fri 10am–5pm, Sat 8am–5pm; charge) on Platía Aríonos.

The other local minority that dwelt in the Old Town were the Jews, deported to Auschwitz by the Nazis in June 1944. Few returned, and their **synagogue** (Sun–Fri 10am–3pm) on Simíou is essentially maintained as a memorial, although it also has an excellent museum on the former life of the community and its far-flung diaspora. The **nightlife**, pitched at Greek rather than foreign tourists, comprises a score or so of high-decibel, annually changing bars on Miltiádou and its offshoots.

The west coast

Rhodes's west coast is the damper, windier, greener side of the island, with agriculture at least on a par with tourism. Scrappy shingle beaches failed to slow hotel construction at **Ixiá** and **Triánda**, busy resorts that blend into each other and Neohóri. A road leads inland 5km (3 miles) from Triánda to the site of **ancient Ialysos ❷** (summer Tue–Sat 8am–7pm, Sun 8.30am–2.45pm, winter until 2.45pm; charge), better known today as **Filérimos**, after the Byzantine monastery established here. Of the ancient city, only a Doric fountain and

The magnificent walls of the Old Town date from the 14th century and are up to 12 metres (40ft) thick in places. The only access is on Tuesday and Saturday from 8am to 11am, starting at the Palace of the Grand Masters and ending at the Koskinoú Gate.

BELOW: carved fragment in the Rhodes Archaeological Museum.

At Ialysos, a Via Crucis leads to a giant cross, re-erected in 1995 as a replica of a 1934-vintage Italian one destroyed during the war to prevent Allied airmen from using it as a landmark.

some Hellenistic temple foundations are evident. The restored Gothic **monastery**, with its vaulted chambers, early Christian mosaic floor and rampant bougainvillea is the main attraction.

Kremastí, back on the coast, is famous for its annual festival of the Virgin (15–23 August), but is otherwise undistinguished. The **airport** lies between here and **Paradísi** village, to whose cafés tourists often resort for solace when their homeward charter flights are delayed (a not uncommon occurrence).

Just past Paradísi, another inland turning leads to a famous Rhodian beauty spot, the **Petaloúdes** ❸ (Butterfly Val-

ley). The access road crosses the canyon about halfway along its length. Head upstream or downstream, along paths and over bridges, past the *Liquidambar orientalis* (sweetgum) trees on which Jersey tiger moths roost during summer. Black and yellow when at rest, they flash bright red wing-tops in flight. From the top of the valley, about 6km (4 miles) inland from **Soroní** on the coast road, a dirt track leads to the **Monastery of Agios Soúlas**, which has a major festival on 29–30 July featuring donkey races.

The other big tourist attraction on the west coast, 32km (20 miles) from Mandráki, is **ancient Kameiros** ❹ excavated after 1929. Though no single

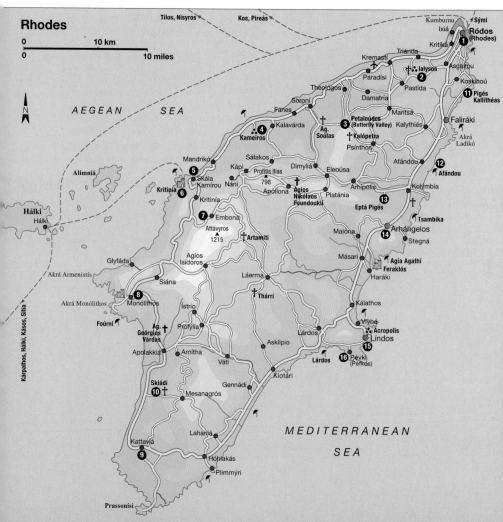

monument stands out, it's a remarkably complete Doric townscape, without the usual later accretions. Unusually, there were no fortifications, nor an acropolis on the gently sloping hillside.

Back on the coast again, **Skála Kamírou 5** (alias Kámiros Skála) is a small port with touristy fish tavernas, and afternoon ferries for the tiny island of **Hálki** opposite. **Kritinía 6** castle just overhead, one of the Knights' rural garrisons, is today a dilapidated shell but merits a visit for the views out to sea. The chapel has been consolidated in anticipation of a small museum opening here in 2011.

The interior and far south

Inland from Skála Kamírou, sitting at the base of 1,215-metre (3,986ft) Mount Attávyros, **Embona 7** is the centre of the Rhodian wine industry; products of the private Emery winery (daily 9.30am–3.30pm) are considered the best. Roads looping around the base of the mountain through conifer forests to east and west converge on the attractive village of **Siána**, famous for its honey and *soúma* – a strong

grape-distillate spirit that is deceptively smooth. Some 4km (2½ miles) further, flat-roofed **Monólithos 8** village gives access to the eponymous **castle** perched on a narrow pinnacle, with a 200-metre (656ft) sheer drop all around. The road then continues down to the secluded **Foúrni** beaches.

Inland Rhodes is the perfect antidote to the tourist extravagances of the coastal resorts, its rolling hills still partly wooded despite repeated fires started by arsonists since the late 1980s. Spared so far is densely shady **Mount Profítis Ilías** (798 metres/2,618ft), from where an old trail descends to the village of **Sálakos**, where "Nymph" brand spring water is bottled.

Alternatively, from **Apóllona** on the mountain's south side, a paved road leads through a burnt zone, the result of a 2008 fire, to **Láerma**, and thence to the Byzantine **Thárri Monastery**, which was reinhabited in 1990 by monks who oversaw the cleaning of its vivid 13th- to 15th-century frescoes. The road continues in roundabout fashion via Profýlia and Kiotári to **Asklipió** village, where slightly later frescoes in the

Aï-Geórgis Hostós, a tiny, subterranean chapel below Filérimos Monastery, an Italian restoration of the original, has 14th- to 15th-century wall-paintings.

BELOW LEFT: the modern Trianda Hotel.
BELOW: bringing in the grapes at Embona.

church of **Kímisis tís Theotókou** are in better condition, owing to the dry climate. Together these constitute the finest Byzantine art *in situ* on the island.

From Asklipió you return to the southeast coast at **Kiotári**, which has been developed for tourism, with a number of large hotels, and **Gennádi**, with vast stretches of open gravel beach. Further south, **Plimmýri** has a lovely medieval church and its beach is sandy and more sheltered; while **Prassonísi** (Leek Island) at Rhodes's southern tip is tethered by a broad, sandy causeway much favoured by windsurfers. The main island coast road loops back to Monólithos via the villages of **Kattaviá ❾** and **Apolakkiá**, 4km (2½ miles) north of which is the tiny Byzantine chapel of **Agios Geórgios Várdas**, with smudged but most engaging frescoes.

Most inland villages here are moribund, with house owners living in Rhodes Town or overseas. They've sold up en masse to Germans at **Lahaniá** near Plimmýri, though the wonderful square with its taverna and twin fountains beneath a plane tree remains traditional. From here head northwest to the

fine hilltop village of **Mesanagrós**, wit its 13th-century chapel hunched ami the larger foundations of a 5th-centur basilica. If you're overtaken by darknes and can't face the drive back to town, th kindly keepers at **Skiádi Monastery ❶** just to the west may invite you to use th (gender-segregated) guest quarters.

The east coast

The east coast, sandier and more she tered than the west, with a warmer se was only developed for tourism after th 1970s, and much of it remains unspoi **Koskinoú** is famous for its ornat doorways and intricate pebble-mosai courtyards. Immediately downhil **Pigés Kallithéas ❶** (daily 8am–8pm charge), a former spa, is a splendi orientalised Art Deco folly built b the Italians and complete with dome pavilions and palm trees. One rotund is home to a small exhibition space an a permanent gallery on the history c the spa, which had its heyday fror 1910 to 1940. Below the spa, variou rock-girt beaches with supplemente sandy patches are popular, as there ar no other swimming spots this close t

...hodes Town with any real character. Wall-to-wall, multi-storey hotels pitched mainly at families characterise the north end of **Faliráki Bay**. Faliráki proper, to the south, is now but a shadow of its former youthful, boozy self since a 2003 crime spree prompted a police crackdown, and the financial downturn of 2008–9 administered the *coup de grâce*.

Immediately south looms **Cape Ladikó**, where *The Guns of Navarone*, starring Anthony Quinn, was made in 1961. Beyond the cape stretches the long pebble-and-sand beach of **Afándou** ⑫, scarcely developed except for the 18-hole golf course just inland.

Heading inland from the Italians' model-farm scheme at **Kolýmbia**, you reach the leafy glades of **Eptá Pigés** ⑬ (Seven Springs), one of Rhodes's most popular beauty spots. These springs feed a small reservoir dammed by the Italians to irrigate their Kolýmbia colony. If you do not suffer from claustrophobia you can explore an aqueduct-tunnel leading to the little lake, or you can walk there overland, in the company of peacocks screaming in the trees.

Inland beauty spot

The Greek answer to fertility drugs, **Tsambíka Monastery**, teeters high on the headland behind Kolýmbia, overlooking a sandy namesake beach to the south. It is believed that the Virgin, to whom the monastery is dedicated, can make women fertile. The otherwise undistinguished church is therefore a magnet for childless women, who come as barefoot pilgrims to revere an 11th-century icon at the 8 September festival.

Arhángelos ⑭, 29km (18 miles) from Rhodes Town, is the island's largest village, although its former crafts tradition is now not in evidence other than in some pottery studios on the bypass road. Good beaches are found nearby at **Stegná** and at **Agía Agathí**, the latter reached via the little resort and fishing port of **Haráki**, overlooked by the crumbled Knights' castle of **Feraklós**. Better than any of these, however, is the long, undeveloped beach at **Kálathos**, beyond Haráki. Although quiet, the village has a number of bars and tavernas, some set right beside the 4km (2½-mile) beach.

If a childless woman conceives after praying at Tsambíka Monastery, the child is named Tsambíkos or Tsambíka, names unique to Rhodes.

BELOW LEFT: the 200-metre/yd long aqueduct-tunnel at Eptá Pigés.
BELOW: Haráki resort and bay.

BELOW: a popular
beach at Pévki.
BELOW RIGHT:
pebble mosaic in
Líndos.

Líndos

There are regular buses to cover the 56km (35 miles) from Rhodes Town to **Líndos** ⓯, but it's more relaxing to take a boat trip and enjoy the coastal scenery. Huddled beneath yet another Knights' castle, Líndos, with its tiered, flat-roofed houses, appears initially to be the dream Greek village. Medieval captains' mansions have ornate gateways and vast pebble-mosaic courtyards. Near the main square, the **Panagía Church** (Mon–Sat 9am–3pm, 6.30–8pm, Sun 9am–3pm) preserves 18th-century frescoes. The hottest spot on Rhodes, its narrow lanes teem with day-trippers and local overnighters in high season. Donkeys, the Lindian taxi service, haul tourists up the steep gradient to the ancient acropolis, with its Temple of Lindian Athena, Hellenistic stoa, and unbeatable views.

Late into the night the village throbs to the beat of numerous bars, while by day the sand lining the northerly former port is dense with sunbathers, packed together like sardines in a can. The southern harbour, with a quieter beach, is known as St Paul's Bay, in honour of the Apostle who lande< here in AD 58.

Ancient Lindos dates back to th Bronze Age, thanks to the only pro tected harbour on the island asid from Rhodes Town. With such ba< ren surroundings, it always lived fron the sea (though a spring provide ample water). In the 1960s, the 40km (25-mile) stretch of sunset coastal view attracted Italian, German and Britis< painters, writers and hippie drop-out< Past alumni include the newspape astrologer Patrick Walker (1931–95 academic and writer Germaine Gree American humorist S.J. Perelman an< various members of Pink Floyd. Bu now Líndos's days as an artistic colon are long over, superseded by the era o mass tourism.

Around the limestone headlan< **Pévki** ⓰ (Péfkos) is less frenetic tha< Líndos; it was originally an annexe o the latter but is now a package resor in its own right. Its beaches are sma< and hidden away. At **Lárdos**, 4km (2< miles) west, the long, gravelly beac< is obvious as you approach, and < encroached upon by large hotels. [

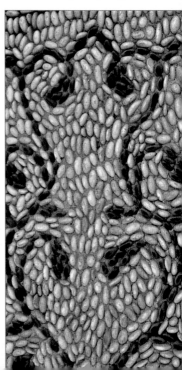

Italian Architecture in the Dodecanese

The Greeks understandably wanted to forget the Italians' wartime presence, but now recognise that their architecture had some merit.

Thirty-one years of Italian rule in the Dodecanese left a significant architectural heritage, which has only recently begun to be appreciated. Many structures were long neglected, apparently a deliberate policy by the Greeks, who would prefer to forget the entire Italian legacy, but since the late 1990s maintenance and repair work has been undertaken. In Lakkí, on Léros in the Northern Dodecanese, the grand boulevards and landscaped squares have undergone a thorough renovation in recent years (see page 267).

These buildings are often erroneously dubbed "Art Deco"; while some, like Rhodes Aquarium and the stadium, certainly contain elements of that style, most are properly classed as Rationalist, or (on Léros) Streamline Modern. They grew out of various post-World War I European architectural, artistic and political trends, particularly Art Deco's immediate predecessor, Novecento, which originated in a movement born in Milan in 1922. The collectivist ideologies of the time were also influential, as were the paintings of Giorgio di Chirico, the Greek-Italian painter born in Vólos in 1888.

From 1924 to 1936, Italy attempted to combine Rationalism and local vernacular elements, both real and semi-mythical, into a supposed generic "Mediterranean-ness". Every island got at least one

specimen in this "protectorate" style, usually the police station, the post office, covered market or governor's mansion, but only on the most populous or strategic Dodecanese islands like Rhodes, Kós, Kálymnos and Léros were plans drawn up for sweeping urban reordering.

On Rhodes, this meant the creation of a Foro Italico (administrative centre) at Mandráki. The evolving imperatives of Fascism also required a square (in Rhodes, the Piazza dell'Imperio in the Foro Italico) for large-scale assemblies. There were also structures in neo-Crusader style, such as the Cathedral of St John (now Evangelismós).

The period 1936–41 was marked by intensified Fascist ideology and increased reference to the islands' Latin heritage (the Romans and their purported successors, the Knights of St John). This entailed "purification", stripping many public buildings in Rhodes (although not in Kós, where a 1933 earthquake devastated much of the town) of orientalist ornamentation, and replacing it with Póros stone cladding to match medieval structures in the Old Town. Added to this was a monumental severity and rigid symmetry – as with the theatre in Rhodes – echoing institutional buildings (especially Fascist Party headquarters) in Italy. Many Old Town buildings from the Knights' era were restored or, in the case of the Palace of the Grand Masters (see page 238), entirely rebuilt. ❑

ABOVE: Evangelismós, Rhodes New Town. **RIGHT:** the rebuilt Palace of the Grand Masters, Rhodes Old Town.

THE SOUTHERN DODECANESE

These islands, the farthest from the mainland, which mostly lived in the past from seafaring, have developed a corresponding character, culture and architecture

he Southern Dodecanese are among the most tranquil and unspoilt of the islands. They still ing, in places, to traditional customs d and live by farming, boat-building d fishing as well as tourism.

ásos

ásos is the southernmost Dodeca-ese island, and the poorest. Remote id barren, its plight was accentuated a comprehensive Ottoman massacre 1824. Before and since Kasiots took the seas, distinguishing themselves pilots, and helping to dig the Suez anal. In six clustered villages on the orth flank, many houses lie aban-ned: summer sees a homecoming expatriated Greek-Americans, espe-lly for the major festivals, 17 July gía Marína) and 15 August (Dormi-on of the Virgin).

The capital, **Frý ❶** (pronounced "ree"), is a bit shabby in parts, but does have a couple of tavernas and attractively enclosed fishing port, e **Boúka,** with a narrow entrance. nboriós, down the coast, was the d commercial port, now silted up it still picturesque. The only con-ntional tourist attractions here are o caves, **Ellinokamára** and **Seläï,** yond **Agía Marína**, the most attrac-e inland village.

Except at peak season when a few ntal scooters or quad-bikes appear, u face long, shadeless hikes or expen-e taxi rides to get anywhere. The only

half-decent beach, for instance, is **Héla-tros,** almost 15km (9 miles) from Frý in the southwest, via **Agios Geórgios Hadión,** one of two rural monasteries. The indolent should take up offers of boat excursions to better beaches on the offshore islets of **Makrá** (one big beach) and **Armáthia,** which has five sandy beaches.

Frý has a tiny airstrip with puddle-jumper planes to Rhodes, Kárpathos and Sitía (Crete). Fares are affordable, and a flight may be your only option when arriving or leaving in heavy

Main attractions
BOÚKA PORT
APELLA BEACH
ÓLYMBOS VILLAGE
HIKING NORTHERN KÁRPATHOS
BLUE GROTTO OF PERASTÁ
EMBORIÓ WATERFRONT
AGÍOU PANDELÍMONA MONASTERY
GIALÓS HARBOUR
SÝMI FRESCOED CHURCHES

PRECEDING PAGES: windmills on Kárpathos. **LEFT:** all dressed up for the festival of St John. **BELOW:** Kásos.

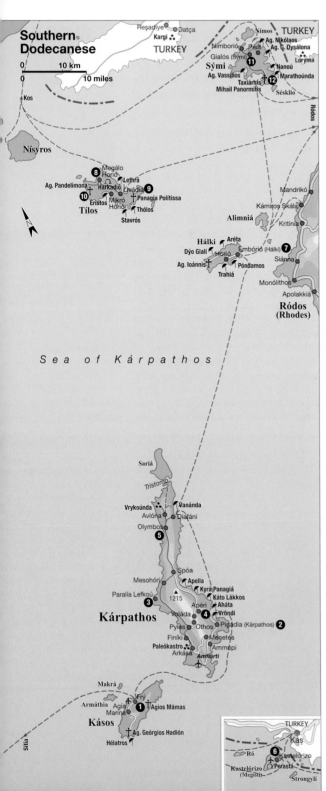

seas, when inter-island ferries skip th
exposed anchorage at Frý.

Kárpathos

Wild, rugged and sparsely populate
Kárpathos just edges out Kós as th
second-largest Dodecanese islan
marooned in crystalline sea rough
halfway between Rhodes and Cret
With vast expanses of white-san
beaches, usually underused, and cragg
cloud-topped mountains soaring t
1,215 metres (3,949ft), it makes u
in natural beauty for what it lacks i
compelling man-made sights.

Direct seasonal flights serve Ká
pathos from overseas; the alternativ
involves a domestic flight or ferry fro
Rhodes. The capital and southerly ha
bour of **Pigádia** ❷ (also known
Kárpathos) has undergone a touris
boom since the 1990s; in any case, th
town only dates from the mid-19
century, though photos from the 195
show an attractive profile before th
eyesore concrete blocks went up. Mar
families have returned wealthy fro
America, especially the East Coast, an
you're as likely to hear "Have a goo
one" as *"Kaliméra"*.

Just north of Pigádia, massive
sandy **Vróndi** beach, with windsu
boards and kayaks for rent, swee
past the 5th-century basilica of **Ag
Fotiní**. Some 7km (4½ miles) sou
of town is **Ammopí**, the island's lon
est established resort, with three cov
(two sand, one pebble). Many of Ká
pathos's better beaches are served
excursion boat. Among these, on t
east coast, are **Kyrá Panagiá** (with t
most facilities and turquoise water),
lonelier, more unspoilt **Aháta**, **Ká
Lákkos** and especially **Apella**. Seve
coves in the **Amfiárti** region near t
southerly airport are home to worl
class windsurfing schools. **Arkása**,
the western shore, is somewhat inexp
cably a resort, as the only convenie
beach is 1km (½ mile) south at **Agí
Nikólaos**; on the headland opposi
are remains of the **Paleókastro**, t
Mycenaean-classical acropolis, wi

e mosaic-floored Byzantine church
f **Agía Sofía** at the beginning of the
limb. Heading north, the next sub-
cantial settlement besides the little
ort of **Finíki** is **Paralía Lefkoú ❸**,
e main rival to Ammopí as a beach
ase. An outstanding topography of
eadlands shelters three horseshoe
ays of white sand; there are plenty of
laces in which to stay and to eat.

Despite the road network being
nostly paved now, exploring Kárpathos
an be challenging. The few filling sta-
ons are all near Pigádia, limiting the
nge of small scooters, and strong
inds can blow two-wheelers off the
oad. Booking a rental car or jeep in
dvance for pick-up at the airport
enlarged in 2008) is the best solu-
on. There are buses and pricey taxis
o the less remote mountain villages
ke **Apéri ❹**, the elegant medieval
apital, said to have the highest per
apita income in Greece; **Voláda**, with
tiny Venetian citadel; and **Othos**, the
ighest on the island at 400 metres
,300ft), famous for its sweet, amber
ine from vineyards on the often mist-
virled ridge above.

Although the road there is to be
paved in 2010, northern Kárpathos
is most easily visited via the port of
Diafáni, served both by local caiques
from Pigádia and most main-line ferries. It makes a peaceful and congenial
base, except in August, with coastal
walks to good beaches in either direction, but most use it as a stepping-stone
to reach **Olymbos ❺**, the island's most
distinctive village, clinging to a moun-
tainside 600 metres (1,968ft) up.

Older Olymbos houses consist of
one divided room built around a central wooden pole, the "pillar of the
house", to which are attached embroi-
deries and usually a wedding portrait
(and often wedding wreaths) of the
owners. On a raised wooden platform
behind a carved rail is rolled-up bedding, plus chests of dowry linens and
festival clothes. The rest of the room is
crammed with plates, lace, crochet and
other souvenirs – a kitsch explosion
of fairground colours – gathered by
seafaring relatives. Even modern villas
often have their front rooms decked
out in the same way, a shrine for family photos and icons.

Olymbos was virtually cut off from the rest of Kárpathos for centuries. The road from the south was only completed in 1979; before that one walked five hours to Spóa, the first village with a road.

BELOW:
unmistakable
Olymbos, on
Kárpathos.

On 1 May every year, wreaths made of wild flowers and garlic are hung outside homes to ward off evil. On some islands, the wreaths are burnt as part of the celebrations on St John's Eve (23–4 June).

BELOW: Olymbos's 18th-century windmills, perched on the hill crest.

Olymbos existed in a time-warp for a long time, but tourism by amateur anthropologists – and thousands of day-trippers annually – has dragged the place into the modern era, and the local people are now well used to visitors. It is best to stay the night, when you'll hear the Dorian-influenced local dialect in the tavernas and see the women clomp off in their high leather boots to the terraces below at dawn. Older women still wear traditional costumes (intricately embroidered jackets, scarves and pinafores) on a daily basis as well as for festivals, although lately a good deal of the embroidery is imported.

Bread and biscuits are baked in several communal ovens. The flour was formerly ground by the village's several 18th-century windmills, two of which were restored as working museum pieces in the mid-1980s.

Besides the hike between Olymbos and Diafáni, there's the half-day walk via **Avlóna** hamlet to **Vrykoúnda**, where a cave-shrine of St John the Baptist is the focus for a major festival on 29 August. More advanced treks from Avlóna go to Trístomo inlet or back down to Diafáni via **Vanánda** beach.

Kastelórizo

Kastelórizo's official name, Megísti, means "Biggest" – biggest, that is, of a local mini-archipelago, for this is actually one of the smallest inhabited Dodecanese islands. It's also the first point in Europe, coming from the east, and only a few nautical miles away from Kaş in Turkey, where locals go shopping. Before 1900, Kastellórizo had a thriving town of almost 10,000 supported by its schooner fleet. The sale of the fleet to the British, World War I bombardment of French positions here by the Ottomans, and an earthquake in 1926 sent the island into terminal decline, despite its role during the 1930s as a sea-plane halt.

The final nail in the coffin came in July 1944, when a fuel depot exploded, levelling more than half the port. The town had already been looted, and few chose to return after the war, when the population dropped to about 200. The US even tried to persuade Greece to cede Kastelórizo to Turkey in 196

exchange for limited hegemony in
yprus. Recovery from this nadir is
ue in part to the return of expatriate
assies" from Perth and Sydney to
ild retirement homes, and also to
e island's use as the location for the
91 Oscar-winning film *Mediterraneo*,
hich spurred a wave of tourists.

This limestone island is fringed by
eer cliffs, with no beaches at all.
hat remains of the red-roofed port
wn **Kastelórizo** ❻ is overseen by a
lf-ruined, red-stone Crusader castle,
hich is responsible for the island's
alianate name. The keep houses
small **Archaeological Museum**
ue–Sun 8.30am–3pm; free) of local
nds, while beyond in the cliff-face is
reece's only Lycian house-type tomb.
he quayside mosque, dating from
755, is now home to the **Historical
ollection** (Tue–Sun 8.30am–3pm;
ee), with a photo archive and ethno-
aphic section.

Also worth seeing, a 45-minute walk
om town, is the remote monastery
Agios Geórgios toú Vounoú with
ebble-mosaic flooring and the fres-
ped subterranean crypt-chapel of

Agios Harálambos. Boats will ferry
you to the satellite islet of **Ró**, topped
by a Hellenistic fortress, or to the
cathedral-like **Blue Grotto of Perastá**
on the southwest coast which, according to local people, rivals its namesake
in Capri. The cave is about 45 metres
(147ft) long and 28 metres (92ft) high,
and the rays of the morning sun create
spectacular effects inside. The journey
there involves a 90-minute round-trip,
plus some time to swim in the deep,
glowing waters.

Kastelórizo lies 70 nautical miles
(114km) from Rhodes, and ferries or
catamarans make the long trip only
two or three times a week. The tiny airstrip receives almost daily flights from
Rhodes, though seats can fill long in
advance. The island is now an official
port of entry to Greece, and ironically
it's more accessible from Kaş, Turkey,
which sends daily ferries.

Hálki

Ninety minutes by boat from Skála
Kamírou on Rhodes, Hálki (or
Chálki) is pretty, welcoming and very
popular, despite being barren, almost

*Hálki was more
productive before sea
water infiltrated its
water-table. Now
fresh water is
imported by tanker.*

LEFT: a fisherman
lays out his nets in
Livádia harbour,
Tílos. **BELOW:**
Emborió, Hálki.

The most famous ancient Tiliot was the poetess Irinna, whose verses – like Sappho's – have mostly not survived.

beachless and lacking a fresh water supply. **Emborió ❼** (Hálki), the harbour and only settlement, has numerous waterfront tavernas and abundant accommodation in its restored neo-classical mansions, though most of these are block-booked from April to October by tour companies. **Agios Nikólaos** has the highest belfry in the Dodecanese, nearly matched by a free-standing clock tower nearby.

The island's only sandy beach – artificially supplemented – is at **Póndamos Bay**, 400 metres/yds west; just overhead, **Horió** village has been deserted since the 1950s but offers spectacular views from its crumbled Knights' fortress. Tarpon Springs Boulevard, built with money from Hálki sponge fishermen who emigrated to Florida, ends at the Monastery of **Agios Ioánnis**, in the west of the island; an expensive bus goes there daily. The monastery has a huge courtyard tree and cells in which to stay the night. There are no other good roads, so pebble coves like **Aréta** and **Dýo Gialí**, on the north shore, or **Trahiá** under the castle, are reached only by boat trips.

Between Hálki and Rhodes, **Alimniá** (aka Alimiá) island has been mostly deserted since World War despite having good wells and excellent anchorage. The inhabitants aided the Allies under the very noses of German forces manning submarine pens here. When detected, the islanders were deported to Rhodes and Hálki punishment, and the few returnees left again in the 1960s. With only another Knights' castle, the derelict village and seasonally grazing sheep to be seen, the island is a very occasional excursion destination from Hálki.

Tílos

Tranquil Tílos has only seen significant tourism since the mid-1980s. is home to several thousand goats but only about 500 people (the population shrinks to 100 in the winter). Though the island is bare on its limestone heights, neighbouring Nísyros deposited rich lava soil in the lowlands which with ample groundwater allow the Tiliots to farm, rather than sail their neighbours do. Indeed, before the 1970s it was the granary of the Dodec

ese, with undulating fields of wheat sible from far out to sea.

The island capital, **Megálo Horió ❽**, is ghtly inland, topped by a Knights' cas- that incorporates a classical gateway nd stone from the ancient acropolis. looks south over an orchard-planted ain to red-sand **Eristos** beach, the ngest on Tílos. The harbour and main sort of **Livádia ❾** has a long shingle each, behind which development is eadily filling in all open space, with nple accommodation and eating pportunities. You can walk on a good th system or go by scooter to the ost remote beaches, and there's a bus rvice, so boat trips are only offered hen numbers justify. The closest coves e **Lethrá**, **Stavrós** and **Thólos**, with e Knights' castle of Agriosykiá (one f seven on Tílos) en route. Just west Livádia is the ghost village of **Mikró orió**, abandoned in the 1950s. There's other castle here, and a late-hours bar a restored house.

The trans-island road passes another rt and a cave at **Harkadió**, where iocene midget elephant bones were und in 1971; a museum to display

them has been built but is not yet open. Once past Megálo Horió, the road ends at the 15th-century **Monastery of Agíou Pandelímona ❿** (summer 10am–7pm, winter 10am–4pm), tucked into a spring-fed oasis-ravine. The church has a few frescoes and a fine marble floor. The big island knees-up is here, running for three days from 25 July and including the famous "Dance of the Cup". Almost as important is the 23 August festival at **Panagía Polítissa Monastery** near Livádia, for which special boats are laid on from Rhodes the previous day.

Sými

As you approach Sými on a day-trip boat from Rhodes, flotillas of boats flee the port of **Gialós ⓫** for remote beaches around the island. The foreign "residents" and overnighters are escaping the daily quota of trippers. Gialós is a stunning spectacle, with its tiers of pastel-coloured houses, and a legally protected architectural reserve. But when the tour boats hoot their arrival, it becomes a mini-Rhodes, with mediocre waterside tavernas touting for

During the 1890s, Sými was actually more populous than Rhodes Town; decline set in with Italian restrictions on the sponge trade.

LEFT: the ferry from Rhodes approaches Pédhi. **BELOW:** island woman.

The Symiots have been renowned for their boat-building since antiquity. In legend they built the Argo, in which Jason sailed off to find the Golden Fleece.

BELOW: local transport in Horió.
RIGHT: Gialós, Sými.

business, and stalls selling imported spices and sponges, plus other knick-knacks. As soon as the trippers leave in mid-afternoon, peace is restored: there is room to walk on the quay and you will get a stronger drink.

Symiots are famous as boat-builders, and you can still see boats taking shape at the Haráni yards. Until it was surpassed by Kálymnos after World War II, Sými was also the sponge-diving capital of the Aegean, a role assured by an Ottoman imperial grant of monopoly in the trade. The Nazi German surrender of the Dodecanese to the Allies, which effectively ended World War II, was signed in Les Katerinettes restaurant on 8 May 1945.

Built in a protected gulch and thus stiflingly hot in summer, Gialós is beautiful at night when the bay reflects the lights from the houses above. Popular with the yachting fraternity, and a discerning clientele who book the limited accommodation independently, the notably expensive "Hydra of the Dodecanese" has plenty of bars and tavernas scattered about. It is not, however, an island for the unfit, the elderly or the

very young, who would have to manage the 357 steps of the **Kalí Stráta**, the broad stair-street climbing to the upper town of **Horió**. Follow arrows to the worthwhile local **museum** (Tue–Sun 8.30am–2.30pm; charge), which highlights Byzantine and medieval Sými. Overhead is the Knights' castle, which was built on the site of – and using material from – the ancient acropolis.

The only other significant habitation is the valley of **Pédi** to the east, where flat land and a few wells allow vegetable cultivation. On the south side of the bay here, reached by a marked trail, lies the naturally sandy beach of **Agios Nikólaos**, the only one on Sými. A new yacht marina is being built on the north shore to accommodate overflow from Gialós. All Sými's other beaches are pebble; walk across the island, through the remaining juniper forest, to **Agios Vassílios** in the southwest (no facilities), or take a boat excursion to **Agios Geórgios Dysálona**, **Nanoú** or **Marathoúnda** on the east coast. Nanoú and Marathoúnda both have good tavernas if you want to make a full day of it.

Beyond Haráni, the coastal track heads north, then west to the bay of **Nimborió**, where a Byzantine floor mosaic and catacombs can be found just inland. Other notable sacred art is found at the remote frescoed churches of **Agios Prokópios, Kokkimídis, Agía Marína Nerás** and **Megálos Sotíros** all on or just off the main road south to the most important island monastery, **Taxiárhis Mihaíl Panormítis** ①.

The Archangel Michael is the patron saint of local sailors, and his feast day (8 November) brings pilgrims here from all over the Aegean. Even though the monastery was pillaged during World War II, the central church with its myriad oil lamps is still an atmospheric place, set in the middle of a giant pebble-mosaic courtyard. Things are tranquil once the tour boats have gone – it's usually the first stop coming from Rhodes.

THE NORTHERN DODECANESE

Closer to Turkey than to Greece, these islands have a discernible Eastern influence. As well as the Ottomans, the Italians and the Knights of St John have also left their mark

rom the windmills of Astypálea to the beaches and ancient ruins of Kós, the spirituality of Pátmos and the tranquillity of the tiny, sparsely inhabited isles, the Northern Dodecanese have something for everyone.

Astypálea

Bleak, butterfly-shaped Astypálea, with about 1,500 inhabitants, is geographically closer to the Cyclades than the Dodecanese; on a clear day both Amorgós and Anáfi appear distinctly on the horizon. It belongs administratively to the Dodecanese, yet is distinctly Cycladic in architecture and culture, which is hardly surprising since it was in fact settled from Mýkonos and Tínos in the 15th century.

Ferry connections are still biased towards the Cyclades and Piraeus rather than Rhodes, with which the most reliable link is by air. In high summer short-term accommodation fills up, while outsiders have renovated old houses in Hóra as summer residences. A single stretch of road linking the main resorts has been paved, taverna food has improved, and a bank ATM has been installed, but further momentous change is unlikely.

Many visitors stay in the principal, functional port of **Péra Gialós** or **Skála**, which dates from the Italian era. A long stair-street connects Skála with **Hóra ❶**, the capital, with a line of derelict windmills trailing off to the northwest. At the pinnacle of things

sits the tan-walled *kástro*, the finest example outside of the Cyclades proper, not a legacy of the Knights of St John, but a 13th-century effort of the Venetian Quirini clan. Until the late 1940s more than 300 islanders dwelt inside, but now it is abandoned, except for two fine churches: **Evangelístria**, supported by the vaulting of the northwest entrance, and **Agios Geórgios** overlooking the sea.

Just west of Hóra's ridge, **Livádia ❷** is the island's second resort, between citrus orchards and a sandy if somewhat

Main attractions
HÓRA, ASTYPÁLEA
MANDRÁKI, NÍSYROS
STÉFANOS VOLCANO, NÍSYROS
KÓS TOWN ANTIQUITIES
BRÓS THERMÁ HOT SPRINGS
CLIMBING MOUNT DÍKEOS
PÓTHIA ARCHITECTURE AND
    ARCHAEOLOGICAL MUSEUM
AGÍA KIOURÁ CHAPEL
AGÍOU IOÁNNOU TOÚ THEOLÓGOU
    MONASTERY, PÁTMOS

LEFT: windmills in Plátanos, Léros.
BELOW: the black volcanic shore of Nísyros.

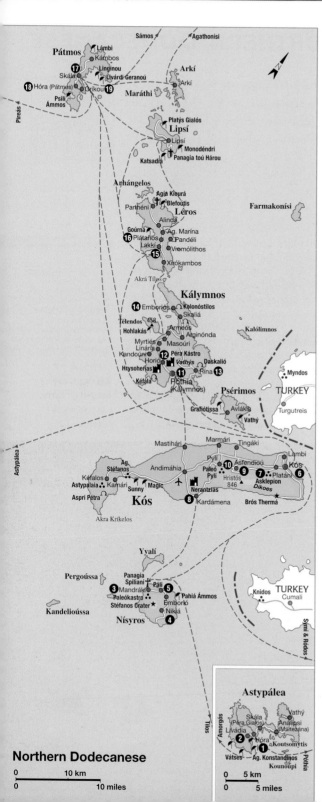

Northern Dodecanese

| 0 | 10 km |
| 0 | 10 miles |

| 0 | 5 km |
| 0 | 5 miles |

scruffy beach. Better beaches, like nud ist **Tzanáki**, and taverna-equippec **Agios Konstandínos**, lie further south east, out on the western "wing". **Kam inákia** and **Vátses** beaches beyond ca be reached by the rough onward track or on boat excursions.

The "body" of the butterfly is a long isthmus, just 100 metres/yards across at its narrowest point, by **Stenó** and **Mamoúni** beaches. **Maltezána** (offi cially Análipsi) to the east has become another resort, more through proxim ity to the airport than any intrinsic merit. Near Maltezána are the best o Astypálea's many Byzantine church floor **mosaics**. A single bus plies regu larly between Livádia and Maltezána otherwise it's a single elusive taxi, or a rented motorbike or car.

Nísyros

In legend Greek Poseidon, pursuing the Titan Polyvotis, tore a rock from nearby Kós and crushed his adversary beneath it. The rock became Nísyros The groaning of the Titan is still aud ible beneath the surface of the caldera in Nísyros's most impressive feature the volcano which forms the heart o the island. Currently dormant, it was last active in 1933, and vulcanism still dominates Nísyros, from black pebbles on the shore to a thermal spa.

Once you're away from its harbour **Mandráki ❸** proves an attractive capital. Wooden balconies hang cheer fully from tall, white houses ranged around a central communal orchard Overhead, a Knights' castle shelters the **Monastery of Panagía Spilianí** while to the south, the Doric citadel o **Paleókastro** is more impressive.

Mandráki by night is lively, with many tavernas and *kafenía* found, unu sually, inland. There are few hotels, as most folk come just for the day from Kós to tour the volcano. In some estab lishments, you can order *soumáda*, a non-alcoholic drink now made from imported almonds. The island's green interior – from which wild almonds have sadly disappeared – is best appre ciated by walking some of the remaining trail system.

The main **Stéfanos** crater, 260 metres (853ft) across, punctuates the nearly lifeless Lakkí plateau, 13km (8 miles) southeast of Mandráki. Tour buses make the trip every morning. With stout shoes, you can visit the caldera floor, braving a rotten-egg stench. Yellow crystals form around hissing steam vents while mud boils out of sight – the voice of Polyvotis. The adjacent Polyvotis crater is smaller but more dramatic and rarely visited. The Greek power corporation made exploratory geothermal soundings here until 1993, when it departed in the face of islander hostility – though not before ruining the 1,000-year-old *kalderími* back down to Mandráki.

Two scenic villages perch above Lakkí: **Emborió**, almost abandoned and being bought up for restoration by outsiders, and livelier **Nikiá** ❹, with a quirky round *platía*. The Emboriots moved down to the fishing port of **Páli** ❺. The biggest sandy beach is 6km (4 miles) around the northeast coast, at **Pahiá Ammos**. West of Páli, the old spa at **Loutrá** (daily, but erratic hours; bring a towel; charge) has been restored with EU funds.

Kós

The second-largest Dodecanese in population, Kós is (just) the third-largest in size after Rhodes and Kárpathos. It follows the lead of Rhodes in most things: a sea-transport hub for a gaggle of surrounding islands; a shared history, give or take a few years; a similar Knights' castle guarding the harbour, plus a skyline of palms and minarets; and an agricultural economy displaced by tourism.

However, Kós is much smaller than Rhodes, and much flatter, with only one mountain range, Díkeos, rising to 846 metres (2,775ft) in the southeast. The margin of the island is fringed by excellent beaches, which are most easily accessible by motorbike or even pedal-bike, for which cycle paths are helpfully laid out.

Kós is by no means unspoilt, and even early or late in the season you'll have plenty of company; visits in midsummer, especially without a reservation, are emphatically not recommended. Yet the overdevelopment has

Kós has been inhabited since Neolithic times. Between 1500 and 1100 BC it had a powerful naval fleet, which took part in the Trojan War.

BELOW: a hike along the caldera of Nísyros's semi-active volcano.

At the entrance to Kós harbour, the Nerantziás castle (or Castle of the Knights) occupies a site where, in antiquity, there once was an island, linked to the mainland by a bridge which you can still see today.

BELOW: in Kós's Archaeological Museum.
RIGHT: a Greek Orthodox priest takes to his wheels.

compensations: surprisingly good restaurants scattered across the island, ample water-sports opportunities and a good infrastructure.

Kós Town

Although the Minoans colonised the site of present-day **Kós Town** ❻ during the late Bronze Age and classical eras, the main island city-state was Astypalaia, on the far southwestern cape of Kéfalos, an ally of Rhodes in the Dorian Hexapolis. Spartan sacking during the Peloponnesian War and a subsequent earthquake (Kós is very susceptible to them) forced the population to relocate to the northern site, a process that had been completed by the mid-4th century BC. According to the geographer Strabo (*c.*64 BC–AD 24), the new town was a success: "She was not large but inhabited in the best way possible and to the people visiting by sea pleasant to behold."

Yet another earthquake in 1933 devastated most of Kós Town, except for the Ottoman bazaar of Haluvaziá, but gave Italian archaeologists a perfect excuse to excavate the ancient city comprehen-

sively. Hence much of the town centre is an archaeological park, with the ruins of the Roman *agora*, the eastern excavation, lapping up to the 18th-century Loggia Mosque and the "Plane Tree of Hippocrates", under which the father of medicine is said to have taught. It is not really 2,500 years old, although it probably is one of the oldest trees in Europe, and now dependent on a life-support system of metal scaffolding.

The western digs offer covered mosaics and the *Xystós*, the colonnade of an indoor running track. Just south stand an over-restored *odeion*, which is sometimes used for summer performances, and the **Casa Romana** (Tue–Sun 8.30am–2.30pm; charge), a restored Roman villa with floor mosaics and murals. The Italian-founded **Archaeological Museum** (Tue–Sun 8.30am–2-.30pm; charge) on Platía Elevtherías has a predictable Latin bias in its exhibits, although the star piece, a statue purportedly of the great healer Hippocrates, is in fact Hellenistic. Also on this square is the 18th-century Defterdar Mosque, still used by Kós Town's 50 or so Muslim families but not open to the public.

Around the island

Hippocrates himself (*c.*460–370 BC) was born and practised on Kós, but probably died shortly before the establishment of the **Asklepion ❼** (Tue–Sun, summer 8am–6pm, winter 8.30am–2.30pm; charge), the ancient medical school 4km (2½ miles) southwest of town. The site is more impressive for its position overlooking the straits towards Turkey than for any surviving structures.

The masonry was thoroughly pilfered by the Knights to build the massive **Nerantziás castle** (Tue–Sun, summer 8am–6pm, winter 8.30am–2.30pm; charge), which, unlike the one at Rhodes, was for strictly military purposes. It's a double fort, the smaller inner one dating from the mid-15th century, and the outer circuit completed in 1514.

Between the Asklepion and Kós Town, pause at **Platáni**, roughly halfway, to eat at one of four excellent Turkish-run tavernas. As on Rhodes, most local Muslims have chosen to emigrate to Turkey since the 1960s. There was a small Jewish community here too, wiped out with the Rhodian one in 1944, leaving behind only their marvellous Art Deco **synagogue** by the town *agora*.

The road east of town dead-ends at **Brós Thermá**, enjoyable hot springs that run directly into the sea. West of town, within easy cycling distance, are the package resorts of **Tingáki** and **Marmári**, with their long white beaches, and less frenetic **Mastihári**, with a commuter boat to Kálymnos.

All three of these take a back seat, tourism-wise, to **Kardámena ❽** on the south coast, 25km (15 miles) from Kós Town but just 7km (4½ miles) from the airport. It's the island's cheap-and-cheerful resort, with little to recommend it aside from suggestively named cocktail bars and a long, sandy and jam-packed beach. The only cultural diversion is the Knights' castle near **Andimáhia**, a two-hour walk inland for the energetic.

In the far southwest, facing Nísyros, are more scenic and sheltered **beaches**, with names like "**Sunny**" and "**Magic**", the latter arguably the best. At nearby **Agios Stéfanos**, twin 6th-century

The Asklepion, Kós's ancient medical school and hospital, has two underground chambers with a statue of Aphrodite, believed to be where venereal diseases were treated.

BELOW: the remains of the Asklepion.

The Asklepion

The Asklepion is named after Asklepios, who lived around 1200 BC and, according to legend, was the son of Apollo and Coronis. His cult developed in Kós, and he became revered as the Greek god of healing. Shrines were built to him all over Greece, usually on a spot where there was a natural spring, and people flocked to them from all over the ancient world, hoping for cures for their ailments. The most famous of the Asklepions is this one on Kós, which houses a spa fed by two natural springs. The complex was discovered in 1902 by two archaeologists, the German Dr Hertsok and the Greek Iákovos Zaráftis. It is popularly believed that Hippocrates, after whom the medical Hippocratic oath is named, worked and taught here, but this is unlikely to be true.

Although the sponge-diving industry has declined in Kálymnos (see page 266), there are still workshops in Póthia where you can see sponges being cleaned and trimmed.

BELOW: swapping news after a service in the church forecourt, Póthia.

basilicas are among several early Christian monuments. The Kéfalos headland beyond saw the earliest habitation of Kós: **Aspri Pétra** cave, home to Neolithic man, and classical **Astypalaia**, birthplace of Hippocrates, of which only the little theatre remains.

The appealing villages on the wooded northern slopes of **Mount Díkeos**, collectively known as **Asfendioú ❾**, have retained their traditional character, with whitewashed houses and attractive churches. At **Ziá**, tavernas seem more numerous than permanent inhabitants, and are especially busy at sunset and later. **Asómati's** vernacular houses are slowly being bought up and restored by foreigners. The surrounding forest provides welcome relief from summer heat; in cooler weather a path from Ziá allows the ascent of **Hristós** peak on Díkeos, with magnificent 360° views (allow three hours for the round trip).

On the western flank of Mount Díkeos, the Byzantines had their island capital at **Paleó Pylí ❿** (Old Pylí), today a jumble of ruins – except for the intact Arhángelos church, with fine 15th-century frescoes – below a castle at the head of a spring-fed canyon. Modern Pylí, 3km (2 miles) downhill, paradoxically offers something more ancient: the **Harmyleio**, a subterranean Hellenistic family tomb with 12 niches.

Kálymnos

First impressions of Kálymnos, north of Kós, are of an arid, mountainous landmass with a decidedly masculine energy in the main port town of Póthia. This is due to the former dominant industry, sponge-diving, only lately supplanted by tourism and commercial fishing. But the island's prior mainstay *(see page 266)* is in ample evidence in the home decor of huge sponges or shell-encrusted amphorae, and the souvenir shops overflowing with smaller sponges.

Póthia ⓫ itself (population 16,000), the second-largest town in the Dodecanese, is noisy, colourful and workaday Greek, its brightly painted houses rising in tiers up the sides of the valley flanks. Mansions and vernacular dwellings with ornate balconies and

wrought-iron ornamentation (an island speciality) are particularly evident in the Evangelístria district.

The most dazzling conventional attraction is the **Archaeological Museum** (Tue–Sun 8.30am–3pm; charge), which opened in 2009. Stars of the displays from all eras include a huge Hellenistic bronze of a clad woman and an unusual robed, child-sized *kouros* (most were naked).

To the northwest loom two castles: **Hrysoherías**, the Knights' stronghold, and the originally Byzantine fort of **Péra Kástro** with several frescoed churches, standing above the medieval capital of **Horió** ⑫, still the island's second town.

The east coast is harsh and uninhabited except for the green, citrus-planted **Vathýs Valley** extending inland from a deep fjord, which comes as a surprise amid all this greyness as you round a high curve in the approach road. **Plátanos** and **Metóhi** hamlets used to live from the sweet-smelling mandarin and orange orchards here, though many of these are now for sale. Yachts call at little **Rína** ⑬ port, from where

there are boat trips to the nearby cave of **Daskalió**, a place of ancient worship, and purportedly of refuge during the Italian era. The limestone strata are riddled with other, visitable stalactite caves. The best are **Kéfala** in the far southwest, and **Skaliá** and **Kolonóstilos** in the far north.

Most visitors stay at the beach resorts on the gentler west coast, locally referred to as **Brostá** (Forward). Local people and Greek holidaymakers tend to gravitate towards beaches at **Kandoúni** and **Linária**, although less developed **Platýs Gialós,** just north, is reckoned the island's best. Foreign package tourists used to patronise **Myrtiés**, **Masoúri** and **Armeós**. three contiguous, heavily developed resorts now fallen on hard times.

You could escape the crowds by heading north towards **Arginónda** and **Emboriós** ⑭, the end of the road 19km (12 miles) from Póthia, but at a price: most beaches are rough shingle rather than comfortable round gravel, and the bus service beyond Armeós is sparse. In any case, Kálymnos is just the right size to explore by scooter or on

Póthia has an orphanage where, until recently, Orthodox priests would come to choose a bride before they were ordained. A woman without a dowry was reckoned to have little chance of finding a husband outside the Church.

LEFT: anchors propped up for sale outside a Póthia chandlery. **BELOW:** a church spire pierces the sky in Kálymnos.

Sponge-Diving

Sponge-diving in Kálymnos is now dying out. It has a long history, but in the past it was hard and often dangerous work.

Kálymnos has been a sponge-fishing centre from ancient times, although a combination of fishing restrictions and marine blight have diminished the trade since the 1960s. Sponges come in various grades: the coarser ones for industry, the finer ones for cosmetic and artistic use. Although cheap artificial sponges now dominate the market, many people will still pay extra for the more resilient natural sponge.

Sponges were traditionally "cured" in two stages. First the divers trod them underfoot on the deck of the caique to "milk" them of unwanted organic matter; then they strung them together and dropped them back into the sea for a few more days of cleaning.

Sponge-curing can be observed at various Póthia factories, especially on the east side of the bay. Older operations have stone tubs of salt water, others bubbling vats of diluted acid which bleach the sponges. This is a concession to tourist tastes but it actually weakens the fibres. After this optional process, they are rinsed in salt water again and finally laid out to dry in the factory courtyard.

Over the years sponge-fishers developed various methods of gathering their quarry: spearing them in shallow water; dragging a heavy blade and net along the sea-bottom so that everything – stones and seaweed as well as the odd sponge – was pulled up together; and diving – the most difficult and dangerous method.

In the old days, naked divers used to sink themselves with the heavy, so-called *skandalópetra* or "scandal stone" tied to their waists. Holding their breath, they scraped off the sponges fixed to rocks that they had spied from the surface. They could usually get two or three sponges before they had to surface for air – the better divers could dive to 40 fathoms. This was before the "machine" was introduced late in the 19th century.

The "machine" is the local term for the first diving apparatus, which consisted of a rubber suit with a bronze helmet connected to a long rubber hose and a hand-powered air-pump. The diver was let out on a long cable and given enough air-hose for his final depth, where he could stay much longer, thanks to the constant air supply. Too long and too deep, as it turned out. Compressed air delivered to divers at these greater depths bubbled out of solution in their bloodstream as they rose, invariably too rapidly. The results of nitrogen embolism – known as decompression sickness or, more commonly, the "bends" – included deafness, incontinence, paralysis and, all too often, death.

By the 1950s the physiological mechanism was understood and the death and damage rate halted, but too late to help hundreds of Kalymnian crewmen. Although the "machine" now seems quaintly antiquated, it was innovative enough for its time to enrich the boat captains and sponge wholesalers, who benefited from the proceeds of the divers' dangerous work.

Ironically, the increased efficiency in sponge-harvesting helped to wind up the industry. The Greek seabed was stripped bare, and Kalymnian boats had to sail increasingly further afield. Over-exploitation of Mediterranean sponge beds was the rule even before a virus devastated them during the late 1980s. Today, sponge-divers are a rare breed, but two or three caiques still set out from Póthia in late April for six months of sponge-diving. ❏

LEFT: the first diving apparatus or "machine" – here on display outside a taverna – revolutionised the trade.

foot via the surviving path network, and boat excursions are also offered.

Psérimos and Télendos

The cheapest of these, by the daily shopping caique from Kálymnos, is to tiny **Psérimos** (population around 25). Massive crowds of day-trippers from Kós flopping on Avlákia port's sandy beach here can exceed the capacity of Avlákia's few tavernas; if you stay the night, you will find the islanders more receptive. After dark, the only sounds will be the wind rustling through cala-mus thickets, or the tinkle of goat bells. If you tire of the main harbour beach – which doubles as the main street – the best alternatives are **Vathý**, just half an hour's walk east, or secluded **Grafiótissa** a similar distance west, 300 metres/yds of fine sand at the base of cliffs.

Seen from Myrtiés or Masoúri at dusk, the bulky islet of **Télendos**, which was split off from Kálymnos by a mid-6th-century AD earthquake, resembles a snail; others claim to see the silhou-ette of a petrified princess staring out to sea, jilted here by her lover. The reg-ular **caique** from Myrtiés (daily 8am–midnight every half-hour in season) can be piled high with supplies as well as passengers.

The single waterside hamlet (perma-nent population 15), also named Télen-dos, huddles under mammoth **Mount Ráhi** (458 metres/1,502ft). Halfway up the north side of the mount, a long trek away, perches the fortified chapel of **Agios Konstandínos**. Less ener-getic souls content themselves with the ruined Byzantine monastery of **Agios Vassílios**, at the northern edge of the hamlet, or the Byzantine baths of **Agios Harálambos**. Télendos is more upmar-ket than Psérimos, and less oriented for day-trippers. Most tavernas are stylish and friendly, and accommodation designed with intent to lure custom over from the main island. Beaches are limited in number and size; the best is scenic **Hohlakás**, 10 minutes west, with coin-sized pebbles.

Léros

Léros, with its half-dozen deeply indented bays, looks like a jigsaw puzzle piece that has gone astray. The deepest inlet, that of **Lakkí** ⑮ (now the main ferry port), sheltered an important Italian naval base from 1935 onwards, and from here was launched the submarine that torpedoed the Greek battleship *Elli* in Tínos harbour on 15 August 1940.

Today Lakkí seems bizarre, a planned town built during 1935–8 to house the staff of the Italian naval base here, and far too grand for the present popula-tion. Its Rationalist-Streamline build-ings (a popular style in the 1930s, Art Deco-influenced, but more practical) have lately been restored, although the landscaped squares and wide boule-vards remain spookily empty. The local atmosphere is not cheered by the presence of three hospitals for children with disabilities and adults suffering from mental illness, though these insti-tutions have been almost completely phased out and the facilities turned over in part to the University of the Aegean's nursing faculty.

Télendos was joined to Kálymnos until AD 554, when an earthquake sundered the two. Buildings of a town that sank into the resulting channel are supposedly visible in exceptional circumstances.

BELOW:
view of Agía Marína from Plátanos, Léros.

The ancient worship of the goddess Artemis may be responsible for one custom peculiar to Léros: all property is inherited down the female family line.

The rest of the island is more inviting, particularly the fishing port of **Pandéli**, with its waterfront tavernas, just downhill from the capital of **Plátanos** , draped over a saddle, with a well-preserved Knights' castle and its Panagía toú Kástrou Church. South of both, **Vromólithos** has the best easily accessible and car-free beach on an island not known for good, sandy ones. In most places sharp rock reefs must be crossed when getting into the water. **Agia Marína**, beyond Plátanos, is the hydrofoil and catamaran harbour and, like Pandéli, offers good tavernas, plus more whimsical Italian architecture.

Alinda, 3km (2 miles) north around the same bay, is the oldest established resort, with a long beach right next to the road – and a poignant Allied War Graves cemetery containing casualties from the Battle of Léros in November 1943, when the Germans ousted an insufficiently supplied British commando force.

In ancient times Léros was sacred to Artemis, and on a hill next to the airport runway are knee-high remains of the goddess's "temple" – now thought to be an ancient fort. Artemis' reputed virginity lives on in the place name **Parthéni** (*parthenos* is the Greek for virgin), the other side of the airport: an infamous concentration camp during the junta, now a scarcely more cheerful army base, as it was in Italian times. Things perk up at the end of this, with one of the island's better beaches, **Blefoútis**, plus the unusual chapel of **Agía Kiourá**, decorated by junta-era prisoners with strikingly heterodox religious murals, which the Established Church has always loathed – they are legally protected from further desecration.

Other bays tend not to be worth the effort spent getting there. **Goúrna**, in the west, is long, sandy and gently shelving, but also windy. **Xirókambos** in the south refuses to face the facts of a poor beach as it struggles to be a resort; caiques from Myrtiés on Kálymnos call here in season.

Lipsí, Arkí, Maráthi, Agathonísi

The name **Lipsí** (aka Leipsoí) is supposed to derive from Kalypso, the nymph who held Odysseus in thrall

BELOW: view of Lipsí Town.

for years. The little island (population around 750) has been transformed by tourism, real-estate development and regular ferry/catamaran services since the 1980s. The single harbour town (also called Lipsí) has been spruced up, accommodation has multiplied, bulldozer tracks and paved roads creep across the landscape, and scooters are made available to explore them.

An extraordinarily long esplanade links the ferry quay with the village centre, marked by the three-domed cathedral of Agios Ioánnis. Behind this is the main square with tavernas and an **Ecclesiastical Museum** (daily, erratic hours; free) with some amusing exhibits. As befits a dependency of Pátmos, older houses have their windows outlined in bright colours that change periodically. Beaches are scattered across the island. The sandiest are the town beach of **Liendoú**, **Platýs Gialós** in the northwest, with a seasonal taverna, and **Katsadiá**, a double bay in the south, facing Léros, again with a taverna. The most secluded are naturist pebble coves at **Monodéndri** in the southeast, facing scenic islets.

Lipsí appears verdant, but farming is dependent on well water; there is only one spring in the west. Although tractors and pumps are audible by day, the nights are given over to the sea's lapping, the crowing of errant roosters, or perhaps a snatch of music from one of three bars.

Three more remote islets north of Lipsí are far less developed and can be more quickly reached from Pátmos. The permanent population of **Arkí** is just 45, and falling. There is no real village or fresh water, although a ferry dock has been built and an adjacent sandy beach created. Accommodation and tavernas are adequate in both quality, and quantity – except during mid-summer. **Maráthi**, across a channel, gets some day-trips from Pátmos and Lipsí, for the sake of its long sandy beach. It has just three permanent inhabitants, and an equal number of places to stay and eat.

Agathonísi, off towards Sámos (where shopping is done, children go to school and many islanders live in winter), is more of a going concern with its three hamlets and population

Lacemaking in the shade – a local lady keeps the old crafts alive.

BELOW: vivid colour outlines the steps to this house.

Our Lady of Death

Shortly before Hohlakoúra Bay on Lipsí stands the triple-apsed church of Panagía toú Hárou (Our Lady of Charon), focus of a miracle repeated annually since 1943. The church is so named for its icon (now a copy) of the Virgin cradling the crucified Christ, the only such in the Greek world (the original is now kept in the town cathedral). In thanks for a favour granted, a parishioner left a sprig of lilies by the icon; they duly withered, but mysteriously revived on 23 August, the Orthodox day of the Virgin's Assumption into heaven. Each year on that date the icon, with rejuvenating flowers, is processed with suitable ceremony to its old home and then back to the cathedral. Don't try travelling between the islands on this day (called *Asómatos* in Greek). It's a major holiday and all ferry tickets sell out early.

The Monastery of St John was built as a fortress to protect its treasures from pirates (there are even slits for pouring boiling oil over attackers). The massive walls were restored after an earthquake in 1956.

BELOW: mosaic adorning the monastery of St John the Theologian.

of about 100. Connections are better too, with hydrofoils and a catamaran dovetailing well with appearances of the small ferry *Nísos Kálymnos*. The islet is much in the news lately as a favourite landing point for illegal immigrants (*see page 56*), but has a cult following amongst many foreign tourists. Most of them stay at the little port of **Agios Geórgios**, with a convenient beach and reliable tavernas. More secluded beaches lie around the headland at **Spiliás** and **Gaïdourávlakos**, or in the far east of the island at **Póros** and **Thóli**, the latter with a Byzantine granary just inland.

Pátmos

Pátmos has been indelibly linked to the Bible's Book of Revelation (Apocalypse) ever since tradition placed its authorship here, in AD 95, by John the Evangelist. The volcanic landscape, with its strange rock formations and sweeping views, seems suitably apocalyptic. In 1088 the monk Hristodoulos Latrenos founded a monastery here in honour of St John the Theologian (as John the Evangelist is known in Greek), which soon became a focus of scholarship and pilgrimage. A Byzantine imperial charter gave the monks tax exemption and the right to engage in sea-trade, concessions respected by the island's later Venetian and Ottoman rulers.

Although Pátmos is no longer ruled by the monks, their presence tempers the rowdier elements found in most holiday resorts. While there is the usual quota of naturist beaches, nightlife is genteel, and the clientele upmarket (including the Aga Khan's family, plus various ruling or deposed royal families). Those who elect to stay here appreciate the unique, even spiritual, atmosphere that Pátmos exudes once the day-trippers and cruise-ship patrons have departed.

Skála ⑰ is the port and largest village, best appreciated late at night when crickets serenade and yacht-masts are illuminated against a dark sky. By day Skála loses its charm, but all island commerce, whether shops, banks or travel agencies, is based here. Buses leave regularly from the quay for the hilltop **Hóra** ⑱, but a 40-minute

cobbled path short-cutting the road is preferable in cool weather.

Hóra's core, protected by a massive, pirate-proof fortress and visible from a great distance, is the **Agíou Ioánnou toú Theológou Monastery** (Monastery of St John the Theologian; daily 8am–1.30pm, Tue, Thur, Sun also 4–6pm). A photogenic maze of interlinked courtyards, stairways, chapels and passageways, it occupies the site of an ancient Artemis temple. The Treasury (charge) houses the most impressive monastic collection in Greece outside Mount Athos. Among priceless icons and jewellery, the prize exhibit is the edict of Emperor Alexios Komnenos granting the island to Hristodoulos. The library (open only to ecclesiastical scholars) is depleted, but still contains 4,000 books and manuscripts.

Away from the tourist thoroughfares, Hóra is silent, its thick-walled mansions with their pebble courtyards and arcades the preserve of wealthy foreigners who snapped them up in the 1960s. Consequently, rooms for short-term lets are hard to come by. From Platía Lótza in the north there is one of the finest views in the Aegean, taking in at least half a dozen islands on all but the haziest day.

Just over halfway down the path from Hóra to Skála stands the small **Apokálypsis Monastery** (same hours as main monastery), built around the grotto where John had his Revelation. A silver band on the wall marks the spot where John lay his head, while in the ceiling is a great cleft in the rock through which the divine Voice spoke.

Pátmos's remote beaches are surprisingly good, with great seascapes offshore and (usually) excellent tavernas. Buses ply between **Gríkou** ⑲ resort and northerly **Kámbos**, where the beach is popular with Greek families. The biggest sandy bay is exposed **Psilí Ammos** in the far south, accessible by boat trip or a half-hour walk from the road's end, and favoured by naturists. Beaches north of Skála include (in order) **Melóï**, site of the island campsite; long **Agriolivádi**; **Lingínou**, with a double cove, and popular with nudists; isolated **Livádi Geranoú**, with an islet to swim to; and finally **Lámbi**, which has irresistible, multicoloured volcanic pebbles. ❏

Cats are everywhere on Pátmos.

BELOW:
the Agíou Ioánnou toú Theológou Monastery.

CRETE

Greece's southernmost island – and the largest – is characterised by soaring mountains, a proudly independent people, and unique remains of the first great European civilisation

C rete (Kríti), claimed by many Greeks to be the most authentic island, is by far the largest. It stretches 256km (159 miles) from east to west and varies between 11 and 56km (7 and 35 miles) in width. A massive mountainous backbone dominates, with peaks stretching skywards to over 2,450 metres (7,958ft) at two points. In the north the mountains slope more gently, producing fertile plains, while in the south they often plunge precipitously into the sea. *Megalónisos* (The Great Island) is what Cretans call their home, meaning great not just in size.

Great can certainly be applied to the Minoan civilisation, the first in Europe and one with which Crete is inexorably entwined. Visitors by the thousand tour through the ruins of Minoan palace complexes, before heading towards one of the scores of excellent beaches. With three major airports, Crete cannot be classified as undiscovered, but by its scale and variety it manages to contain the crowds and to please visitors with widely divergent tastes. While a car is essential for discovering the best of the island, car hire is, unfortunately, comparatively expensive.

Most of Crete's 500,000 population live along the north coast. The mountains, honeycombed with caves, nurture a proud and ruggedly independent people whose formidable mustachioed menfolk still sometimes dress in baggy breeches, black leather knee-boots and black crocheted headscarves. Crete also has a particular musical tradition, characterised by *mantinádes* (rhyming couplet songs) and dances such as the spectacular *pentozális*. These are almost invariably accompanied by the *lýra*, the ubiquitous lap-fiddle.

For more than half the year snow lies on the highest peaks, which provide a dramatic backdrop to verdant spring meadows ablaze with flowers. This, as botanists and ornithologists know well, is *the* time to visit. The former come to see more than 130 plant species unique to the island, while the latter are thrilled

Main attractions

IRÁKLIO ARCHAEOLOGICAL MUSEUM
KNOSSÓS
ZAKROS PALACE
PHAESTOS PALACE
PLAKIÁS BEACHES
ARKÁDI MONASTERY
RÉTHYMNO OLD QUARTER
HANIÁ OLD QUARTER
KASTÉLLI MUSEUM

PRECEDING PAGES:
Agios Nikólaos;
Knossós. **LEFT:**
Koulés fort. **BELOW:**
Morosíni fountain.

BELOW:
at the Iráklio
Archaeological
Museum.

by more than 250 types of birds heading north. These migrants briefly join such rare residents as Bonelli's eagle and Eleonora's falcon. And in spring the island is redolent with sage, savory, thyme, oregano and the endemic *díktamo* (dittany).

Crete, much more than other Greek islands, is a place both for sightseeing and for spending time on the beach. Minoan ruins are the major attractions: as well as the archaeological sites, the Archaeological Museum in the capital, **Iráklio ❶**, houses a unique collection of artefacts from Europe's oldest civilisation. But there are also Greek, Roman and Venetian remains, and literally hundreds of Byzantine churches, many with rare and precious frescoes, usually from the 13th to 16th centuries. These paintings often have a distinct Cretan style, recognisable by elongated figures and attention to detail. (Many of the churches are kept locked: enquire at the nearest café for the key.) Dozens of monasteries have fallen into disuse over the years, but others still function and have treasures as rich as their histories.

Homer's "island of 100 towns" can also be called an island of 100 beaches. Some are simply a place where a boat can be beached, but many are superb stretches of sand. On others, nudity though not officially sanctioned, is tolerated. The bathing season – especially on the south coast facing the Libyan Sea – is long, stretching from Easter until late autumn.

Iráklio (Heraklion)

The capital of Crete since 1971, greater Iráklio has a population of 138,000 and is the fourth-largest city in Greece. It vaunts the highest per capita income of any Greek city but, except in the Old Quarter, there is little evidence of this prosperity in either public infrastructure or architectural elegance.

Most tourists head for the Minoan ruins of Knossós, but this should be combined with a visit to the outstanding **Archaeological Museum ❷** in order fully to comprehend the site and its contents. While the main building is closed for ongoing renovations, an adjacent annexe (Mon noon–5pm, Tue–Sun 8am–3pm; charge) does di

play some of the most famous exhibits. The tourist office is almost next door, and both are moments from the cinemas and restaurants of **Platía Elevtherías B** (Freedom Square), popular with both locals and visitors.

Iráklio's other major attractions date from the Venetian era, testifying that this was Crete's most prosperous period in historical times. Head seawards to the old harbour and visit the Venetian **Arsenáli C** (covered boathouses) and the restored, nocturnally illuminated **Koúles fortress D** (Tue–Sun 8.30am–3pm; charge), whose three reliefs of the Lion of St Mark announce its provenance. **Mount Gioúhtas**, ever-present in the background, resembles a recumbent figure, which is said to be that of Zeus. A few minutes' walk to the west of the old harbour on Sofoklí Venizélou Street, the **Historical Museum E** (Mon–Sat 9am–5pm; charge) has collections from early Christian times onwards.

Head inland now towards the upmarket cafés of **Platía Venizélou** (Venizélou Square, also known as Lion or Fountain Square), which takes its popular names from the stylish 17th-century **Morosíni Fountain F** and guardian marble lions. Overlooking the square is the Venetian **Loggia G** (city hall) flanked by the churches of **Agios Márkos H** and, set in its own little square, **Agios Títos I**. All three of these buildings have been heavily restored to repair war damage. Since 1966, when it was returned from St Mark's Basilica in Venice, the skull of St Titus, St Paul's Apostle to Crete and the island's first bishop, has been housed in Agios Títos.

Walk south through the noisy "market street", redolent with tantalising smells and jammed with people, but very touristy (the true city markets take place in Iráklio's suburban streets) and then west to the cathedral of **Agios Minás J**. More interesting than the cathedral is the **Icon Museum** (summer Mon–Sat 9.30am–7.30pm, winter Mon–Fri 10am–4pm; charge) housed in the little church of **Agía Ekateríni K**, which contains some exquisite icons, six of them the work of the 16th-century master, Mihaíl Damaskinós, a peer of El Greco.

The soon to reopen Archaeological Museum in Iráklio is best visited in the afternoon, when it is quieter. You can take a break in the garden café – but remember to retain your museum ticket for readmission.

BELOW: the Venetian Koúles fort overlooking Iráklio harbour.

Iráklio's Morosíni Fountain, built by the Venetians in the 1620s, originally had a giant statue of Poseidon on top (matching the sea gods around the basin below the lions), but he disappeared during the Turkish occupation.

Challenging but rewarding is a circumambulation of the 15th-century city walls which, in their day, were the most formidable in the Mediterranean. The walls stretch for nearly 4km (2½ miles) and in parts are 29 metres (95ft) thick. En route, pause on the Martinengo bastion at the tomb of the great Irákliot author and excommunicated iconoclast Níkos Kazantzákis (1883–1957) to enjoy the views, and to consider his defiant epitaph – "I hope for nothing, I fear nothing, I am free" – reflecting his long fascination with Buddhism. Keen admirers will make for the **Kazantzákis Museum** (summer daily 9am–7pm, winter Sun 10am–3pm; charge) in his natal village of **Myrtiá** (Ottoman Varvári, 24km/15 miles) due south of Iráklio. Displays illustrate his turbulent personal, literary and political life both in Greece and abroad – he spent long years effectively exiled by the Church – with one room entirely devoted to Zorba.

The best beaches near Iráklio are at **Ammoudári** (Almyrós), just west of town, and at **Tobroúk** and **Amnisós** to the east. The latter, which was the port

for **Knossós**, has the best sands but lies under the airport flight path.

To Knossós and beyond

Excursions from Iráklio will not only delight Minoan aficionados, but provide opportunities to savour the attractive countryside. The most famous site, of course, is the palace of **Knossós ❷**, a mere 5km (3 miles) southwest of the city centre, and easily reached on a No. 2 bus from Iráklio *(For a full exploration of the remains at Knossós, see pages 298–9.)*

At **Arhánes ❸**, 12km (8 miles) south of Knossós, an **Archaeological Museum** (Wed–Mon 8.30am–3pm; free) has caused a stir with items, apparently of a human sacrifice, recovered from a Minoan temple at **Anemospiliá**, contradicting received notions of Minoan society as uniformly pacifist.

A steep climb from Arhánes leads to the summit of **Mount Gioúhtas** (811 metres/2,660ft), from where you can admire the panorama. At the top are Minoan peak sanctuary, a 14th-century chapel and caves in which notionally immortal Zeus is supposedly buried

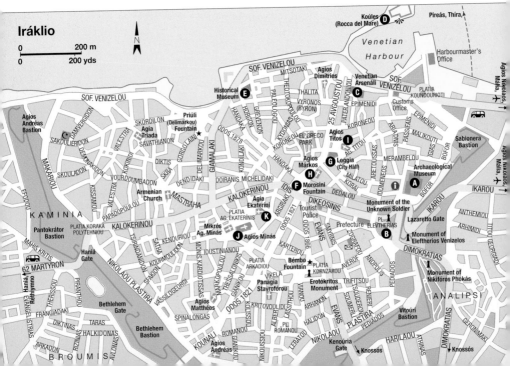

Iráklio

0 — 200 m
0 — 200 yds

N

Pireás, Thira,

Koúles (Rocca del Mare) ❶

Venetian Harbour

Harbourmaster's Office

SOF. VENIZELOU

Agios Dimitrios

Venetian Arsenáli

SOF. VENIZELOU

PLATIA KOUNDOURIOTI

Agios Nikolaos, Mália

MITSOTAKI

Historical Museum ❺

PALEOLOGOU

THALITA

VYRONOS (BYRON)

AΓ. ANDONIOU

EPIMENIDI

Customs Office

SOF. VENIZELOU

THEOTOKOPOULOU

25 AVGOUSTOU

PATER. ANDONIOU

KORONEOU

EPIMENIDI

Priúli (Delimárkou) Fountain

GREVENON

HORSON

HANDAKA

KORONEOU

EL GRECO PARK

Agios Titos ❶

ARIADNIS

PASSIFAIS

MALIKOUTI

GIGAS

Sabionera Bastion

Agios Andréas Bastion

SKORDILON

Agia Triada

SAVATHIANON

ODOS 1878

GIAMALAKI

DELIMARKOU

KONIDAKI

KORONEOU

HANDAKA

Agios Márkos ❼

AΓ. TITOU

Loggia (City Hall)

MERAMBELOU

ARETOUSSAS

Archaeological Museum ❶

SAKOULIERIDON

DAMVERGIDON

DEMOKRATIAS

VALESTRA

DIKTIS

GORGOLAIN

DENDIDAKI

DOIRANIS MICHELIDAKI

Morosini Fountain ❻

KORAI

IDOMENEOS

MILATOU

DEDALOU

IKAROU

Agios Nikolaos, Mália

MAKARIOU

SKOULADON

KISSAMOU

VALESTRA

YOURDOUMBADON

KOKKINI

Armenian Church

MASTRAHA

KALOKERINOU

Agia Ekaterini

DIKEOSINIS

Tourist Police

Monument of the Unknown Soldier

Lazaretto Gate

ANTHEMIOU

ARHIMIDI

KAMINIA

PAPADOPOULOU

PLATIA KORAKA

KALOKERINOU

PLATIA AG. EKATERINIS

ODOS 1821

Prefecture

ELEVTHERIAS

Monument of Eleftherios Venizelos

TITOU GEORGIADI

Pantokrátor Bastion

POLYTEHNIOU

TSIRANIDAON

SATHA

KENOURIOU

Mikrós Ag. Minás

Agios Minás ❿

KARTEROU

EVANS

SMIRNIS

EVANS

DIMOKRATIAS

MAHIS KRITIS

62 MARTYRON

Hanía Gate

NIKOLAOU PLASTIRA

KOUMMOULTON

IOUSTINIANOU

PLATIA ARKADIOU

Bémbo Fountain

PLATIA KORNZAROU

AVEROF

ANDOULI

PLASTIRA

THERISSOU

PIRANTHIOU

EVANGELISTRIAS

FRANGIADAKI

Bethlehem Gate

MARKOPOULOU

THESSALONIKIS

GIANIKOU

VIKELA

Panagia Stavroforóu

Erotokritos Monument

TRIFITSOU

RENIERI

SOLINERI

Monument of Nikifóros Phokás

ANALIPSI

DIKTINAS

TARAS

Agios Matthéos

SPINALONGAS

ODOS 1821

KRITOVOULIDIS

PL. PLATIRA

PEDIADOS

Vitoúri Bastion

DIMOKRATIAS

GERONIMAKI

ARKADON

RIZINIAS

HALKIDONAS

Bethlehem Bastion

KOUNALI

ROMANOU

GIANIKOU

ALBERT

PL. ROMANOU

LERATOU

NIKOLAOU

PLASTIRA

HARILAOU

ATHINAS

BROUMIS

Agios Andréas

Kenouria Gate

Knossós

Knossós

thus giving rise to the ancient axiom "All Cretans are Liars"). Some 6km (4 miles) south of here, **Houdétsi** village offers the **Museum of Musical Instruments of the World** (summer daily 8am–4pm, winter Sun 10am–3pm; charge), assembled by prominent musician Ross Daly, who lives and conducts workshops locally.

Týlissos ❹, 13km (8 miles) southwest of Iráklio, possesses three well-preserved small palaces, or large villas (daily 8.30am–3pm), and is one of the few modern villages to retain its original pre-Hellenic name. Twenty kilometres (13 miles) further west on the same road, the elongated village of **Anógia**, where wool is spun and where many homes have looms, is a weaving and embroidery centre. Many local people still wear traditional dress on a regular basis, the men in particular looking like rebels in search of a cause. This is no stage setting: Anógia has a long tradition of resistance and revolt. The village was razed by the Ottomans in 1821 and 1866, and in 1944 the entire male population of the village was killed by German troops.

From Anógia the paved road climbs to the magnificent **Nída plateau**, from where it is a 20-minute uphill stroll to the **Idéon Andron** (**Cave**); this was the nursery, if not the birthplace, of Zeus. Here the god was hidden and guarded by the *Kouretes*, who clashed their weapons to drown the sound of his cries, while the nymph Amalthea fed him goats' milk. Keen hikers might like to push on to the summit of **Mount Ida ❺** (Psilorítis), at 2,456 metres (7,958ft) the highest point on Crete. The trail, part of the European E4 route, is well marked with red-and-white blazes; allow about seven hours for the round trip.

East from Iráklio

Return to Iráklio and continue eastwards along the E75 highway for 24km (15 miles) to the notoriously tatty resorts of **Hersónisos ❻**, **Stalída** (Stális) and **Mália ❼**. However, their beaches at least have good, if heavily subscribed, sand. Hersónisos features scanty Greek and Roman remains, while close to the beach near Mália is a renowned Minoan site.

Human remains found at Anemospiliá suggest that when the temple was destroyed by an earthquake (around 1700 BC) a priest was in the act of ritually sacrificing a youth.

BELOW: replica detail of the procession fresco, South Propylon, Knossós.

Minoan Glory

The most renowned Minoan ruins – Knossós, Phaestos (Festós), Mália and Káto Zákros – date from the Neo-palatial period (1700–1450 BC). Great unfortified palaces, brilliantly decorated, were built; beautiful pottery and magnificent jewellery, used for both religious purposes and personal adornment, were produced.

The first palaces of the Proto-palatial period (2000–1700 BC), of which scant remains survive, were almost certainly destroyed by earthquakes, but it's still debatable what ended the Neo-palatial period. In the Post-palatial period (1450–1100 BC) mainland Mycenaeans had supplanted the Minoans and by the Iron Age (after 1100 BC) Dorian city-states had replaced the old palaces. Surviving Minoans (Eteo-Cretans) retired to the mountains and continued to maintain their old traditions.

The Islands in Film

The islands are proof that a great setting does not necessarily make a great film, although there have been a few memorable ones.

Postcard-perfect beaches, stage-set ports and eight months' sunny weather annually suggest ideal film locations. But luminous scenery and light have not guaranteed quality movies, with many island-shot films lacking coherent plot.

Boy on a Dolphin (1957) starred Alan Ladd, Sophia Loren – and Hydra, the first island on the big screen. But the most famous, thanks to Míkis Theodorákis's soundtrack, is Michael Cacoyánnis's Crete-set *Zorba the Greek* (1964), retelling Níkos Kazantazákis's novel *Alexis Zorbas*, shot at coastal Pláka and Kókkino Horió, between Réthymno and Haniá. Alan Bates and Anthony Quinn played the leads; Quinn had already starred in blockbuster *The Guns of Navarone* (1961), as the Greek member of an Allied commando team charged with destroying an impregnable German artillery emplacement. Its locations were Cape Ladikó on Rhodes (where a bay is named after Quinn), and the sheer cliffs at Agios Geórgios Dyssálonas on Sými.

There was then quite a gap – disregarding trashy, Santoríni-set *Summer Lovers* (1982) – until Greece returned to filmic fashion. Rhodes Old Town (and briefly, Sými) starred in *Pascali's Island* (1988), reworking Barry Unsworth's novel, with Ben Kingsley as an Ottoman spy and fixer. Luc Besson's *The Big Blue* (1988) was the top box-office French film of that decade and, while loosely based on the lives of two champion free-divers, had more atmosphere than narrative. The title translates nicely as *Tó Apérando Galázio* – the name of innumerable island bars – but the movie mostly put Amorgós on the tourism map. The sharp-eyed will spot Katápola in the divers' childhood scenes; a southwesterly bay hosted the deep-dive episodes.

The slight *Shirley Valentine* (1989) showcased Mýkonos beaches and a 40-something, unhappily married woman's (Pauline Collins) affair with a Greek *kamáki* (Tom Conti), the era's stereotypical (now extinct) Romeo. Its most enduring contribution was linguistic: "she's an ex-Shirley Valentine" became universal shorthand for British women staying in Greece after the romance that anchored them there ended.

The award for Worst Greek-Shot Film Ever goes to Paul Cox's *Island* (1989), set in Astypálea's Hóra, with Iréne Pappás not redeeming Indo-Euro-Greek nonsense. Things perked up with Italian-produced *Mediterraneo*, filmed on Kastellórizo and garnering 1991's Best Foreign Film Oscar; this warm-hearted portrayal of a World War II backwater did for this tiny island what *The Big Blue* had done for Amorgós.

Since then, the biggest splashes have been made by *Captain Corelli's Mandolin* (2001), shot on Kefaloniá (with pre-war-and-earthquake Agía Evfimía recreated using sets), *Lara Croft Tom Raider: The Cradle of Life* (2003), partly shot on Santoríni, and *Mamma Mia!* (2007), filmed on Skópelos (especially Kastáni beach). The virulently anti-resistance politics of Louis de Bernières's eponymous novel incensed many Kefalonians, and filming (with Nicholas Cage and Penélope Cruz) was conditional on controversial material being omitted; the vapid result sank without trace. *Mamma Mia!*, starring Meryl Streep and Pierce Brosnan, has been a smash hit, despite being no more intellectual than the musical. *Fugitive Pieces* (2007), a version of Anne Michaels's best-selling Holocaust novel partly set on Zákynthos (Lésvos, Hydra and Kefaloniá in the film) came announced as an important work, but proved to be middlebrow in the telling. ❏

SCIROCCO

LEFT: photogenic Santoríni, made for celluloid stardom.

The **Palace** at Mália (Tue–Sun
30am–3pm), traditionally associated
ith King Sarpedon, brother of Minos,
contemporary with that at Knossós.
ne ruins are not as extensive as those
Knossós or Phaestos but, even with-
t reconstruction, are more readily
derstood. The remarkable number
store rooms and workrooms, as well
the simpler style of architecture,
ggests a country villa more than
palace. Excavations unearthed the
rysólakkos (Golden Pit) from the
oto-palatial period (1900–1700 BC).
ne name is derived from the numer-
s gold artefacts found in this enor-
ous necropolis.

From either Mália or Hersónisos,
visting mountain roads lead up to
e **Lasíthi Plateau ⓼**, around 840
etres (2,756ft) above sea level and
km (36 miles) from Iráklio. This
rtile and impeccably cultivated
nd supports potatoes, cereal crops,
ples and pears. The visitor can well
lieve that Crete was the granary of
ome, and may recall Pliny's statement
at whatever is produced in Crete is
comparably better than that pro-

duced in other parts. **Psyhró** in the plateau's southwest corner is home to the
giant **Díkteo Andron** (Diktean Cave;
daily, summer 8.30am–7pm, winter
8.30am–3pm; charge), supposedly the
birthplace of Zeus.

Before leaving the plain, try to visit
Tzermiádo and its Neolithically inhabited **Trápeza Cave**, the mythical home
of Kronos and Rhea, the parents of
Zeus. **Agios Geórgios** offers the **Cretan Folklore Museum** (summer daily
9am–4pm) with household, craft and
agricultural exhibits.

Agios Nikólaos and around

Descend via Neápoli to **Agios Nikólaos
⓽**, 69km (43 miles) from Iráklio, invariably abbreviated by tourists to "Ag
Nik" and once the Saint-Tropez of Crete
before the current slump. This tourist
paradise, overlooked by the eastern
mountains, is magnificently situated
on the Gulf of Mirabéllo. Here, and
at neighbouring **Eloúnda ⓾** (10km/6
miles away), are some of the island's
best and most expensive hotels. Unfortunately Agios Nikólaos does lack a
decent beach, having built a football

*Black knitted
headscarves (saríkia),
pleated, baggy trousers
(vrákes) and custom-
made, high boots
(stivánia) are the
traditional dress still
worn in many parts of
Crete.*

BELOW: woven
goods in Anógia.

There are thousands of windmills across the Lasíthi Plateau, but only a few unfurl sails in June to pump up water for irrigation.

pitch over its best one, although there are some passable sands a little way to the east. Restaurants and hotels, bars and cafés cluster around Agios Nikólaos's Mandráki harbour and the small so-called bottomless lake, connected to the harbour by a canal. Although it is not what most visitors come here for, the town does have a pleasant **Archaeological Museum** (Tue–Sun 8.30am–5pm; charge) and a **Folk Museum** (Tue–Sun 10am–2pm; charge).

The nearby island of **Spinalónga** with its ruined Venetian fortress is readily reached from Eloúnda by boat. (In 1589 the Venetians made the peninsula of Spinalónga an island by cutting a canal.) Aristotle Onassis considered building a casino here, but fortunately did not; in recent years the place has come into the public spotlight following the publication of Victoria Hislop's novel *The Island*.

Clinging to the hillside 11km (7 miles) from Agios Nikólaos is **Kritsá ⓫**, which claims to be "the largest village in Crete". Here, lovely if damaged 14th-century frescoes adorn the church of **Agios Geórgios Kavoúsiotis** just

uphill. Immediately below Kritsá the church of **Panagía Kyrá**, whic is Crete's greatest Byzantine treasu (daily 8.30am–5.30pm; charge). Th whole of the interior is a picture-boo Bible, the story told in beautiful 13th 15th-century frescoes.

Some 3km (2 miles) beyond th church lie the ruins of **ancient La** (Lató; Tue–Sun 8.30am–2.30pn charge). The pleasure here lies not s much in the fairly extensive remains o a Graeco-Roman city (although the are worth seeing) but the superb view From the northern acropolis, loo across plains covered with an infini of olive and almond trees to the coa and to Agios Nikólaos (once the po for Lato) and beyond, to the Gulf o Mirabéllo and the Sitía mountains.

East of Agios Nikólaos, a motorwa is currently being extended, to bypa some of the sites below en route t Sitía. After 19km (12 miles) on the o road, **Gourniá ⓬** (Tue–Sun 8.30an 3pm; charge) is reached. Spread over ridge, overlooking the sea, are remair not of another palace, but of stree and houses of a Minoan town, the be

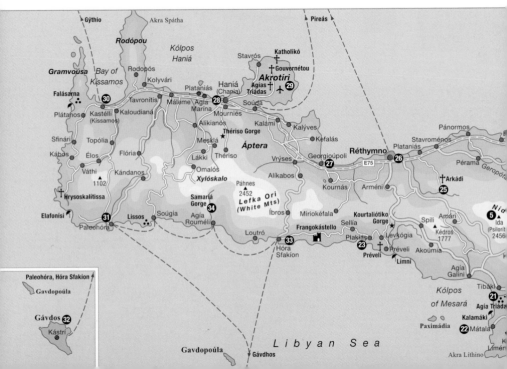

reserved on the island. Especially in
▸ring, when the site is covered with
riot of flowers and their perfume
lls the air, even those bored with old
ones will be delighted to be here.
From highways new and old, a side
▸ad drops to the unspoilt fishing
llage of **Móhlos**, with the cleanest
vimming on a coast generally beset by
de- and wind-borne debris. The tiny
land opposite, which can be readily
ached by strong swimmers, bears the
me name as the village and has scanty
linoan ruins. Some way beyond is the
rger island of **Psíra** where a Minoan
▸wn and port are being excavated.
3oth islands can be reached by hired
oat from Móhlos.)

itía and eastern Crete

tía **⑬**, 70km (43 miles) from Agios
ikólaos, is a laid-back town which, to
e delight of (mostly French and Ital-
n) visitors and the chagrin of locals,
as not yet hit the big time, though
is will undoubtedly change with the
)10 enlargement of the local airport
▸ receive overseas flights. Here are the
most obligatory Venetian fort, **Archae-**

ological Museum (Tue–Sun 8.30am–
3pm; charge), **Folklore Museum**
(Mon–Sat 10am–1pm; charge) and a
reasonable, in-town beach.

Still-active **Toploú Monastery** (daily
9am–1pm and 2–6pm, winter until
4pm), its tall 16th-century Italianate
bell tower beckoning like the minaret
of a mosque, stands in splendid isolation in the middle of nowhere, beyond
Sitía. Its greatest treasure is a minutely
detailed 18th-century icon painted
by Ioánnis Kornáros. The monastery
derived its name from a renowned
artillery piece (*top* is Turkish for can-
non) which formerly protected it. The
monks also had other methods of protecting themselves: observe the hole
above the monastery gate, known as
a machiolation, through which they
poured hot oil over their assailants –
a particularly unpleasant practice in
medieval times.

The Orthodox Church is currently
courting controversy by leasing some
of Toploú's vast landholdings for a
7,000-bed tourist complex just north
on Cape (Akrá) Síderos, complete with
golf course, outraging environmental-

*Lake Voulisméni at
Agios Nikólaos was
once said to be
bottomless, and the
home of spirits.
Unromantic modern
surveyors have found
that it is about 70
metres (230ft) deep
and fed by an
underground river.*

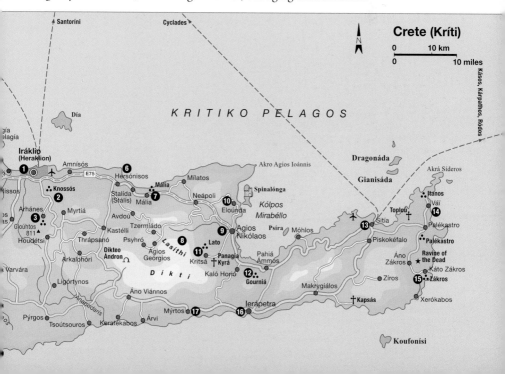

The 16th-century Venetian fortress on Spinalónga, near Agios Nikólaos, was used as a leper colony until 1957 – the last in Europe.

BELOW: Sitía harbour.

ists who point out that there is very little water left for such a development in eastern Crete.

After a further 9km (6 miles), **Váï** is renowned for its myriad palm trees and the large, sandy beach that suggests faraway tropical regions. The inedible-date palm trees (*Phoenix theophrasti*) are not the species associated with desert islands, but are actually native to Crete and southwestern coastal Turkey. The beach here is usually crowded: for a more relaxed time, make for the quieter, palm-free **Ítanos**, 1km (½ mile) farther north.

Southwards from Váï is **Palékastro**, which hit the headlines in the 1990s because of the discovery of what may be the largest Minoan town yet – sadly, funds are lacking to uncover it. Nearby beaches, especially at the southern end of the bay, are well worth visiting.

Zákros

Some 20km (12 miles) further on you come to inland **Ano Zákros** and beachside **Káto Zákros**, the latter adjacent to the fourth great Minoan **palace of Zakros** (daily, summer 8.30am–

5pm, winter 8.30am–3pm). Hikers wi prefer to make their way from upper t lower Zákros by walking through th spectacular **Ravine of the Dead**, wher caves were used for Minoan burials.

The ruins at Zákros, 43km (27 miles from Sitía, from the Neo-palatia period, are often waterlogged, partl because Crete is tipping over long tudinally, with its eastern end sinkin below and its western end rising abov sea level and coastal water-tables (ther is also a still-active spring muddyin things even further). The main site ha its customary central courtyard an royal, religious and domestic building and workshops radiating outward Close by are the remains of a Minoa town and a sheltered Minoan harbou which were ideally situated for trad with the Levant and Egypt.

Unusually, the Zákros dig was orig nally privately funded. In 1961, prom nent Greek archaeologist Nikólao Pláton was asked by the Pomerance a New York business couple, if an Minoan sites had still to be excavate Yes, he told them. So what, they aske was the problem? Money, was the repl

'ith that, the Pomerances underwrote ̶e dig with no strings attached. Pláton ̶ed in 1992 at the age of 83, but exca- ̶tions continue.

Back at Gourniá, a flat road crosses ̶e island's isthmus to **Ierápetra** ⓰ ̶5km/22 miles from Agios Nikólaos), ̶e largest town on the south coast. ̶espite a small Venetian fort and ̶gns of hopeful gentrification, it's an ̶n-atmospheric supply point for the ̶gion's farmers, who have carpeted the ̶astal plain 10km (6 miles) either side ̶ town with plastic vegetable green- ̶ouses and pretty well put a damper ̶ in-town tourist development.

Eighteen km (11 miles) to the west ̶es the pretty little village resort of **Mýrtos** ⓱, with whitewashed houses ̶d a small museum of finds from two ̶arby Minoan villas. Eastwards 24km ̶5 miles) from Ierápetra is the more ̶nventional "strip" resort, and gently ̶elving beach, of **Makrygiálos**. From ̶ere a minor coastal road leads to the ̶iginally 14th-century **Kapsás Mon- ̶tery**, built snugly into the cliffs at the ̶trance to a gorge. Encased in a silver ̶sket is the skull of Gerondoyánnis, a 19th-century faith healer who, despite not being canonised, is a cult figure.

South from Iráklio

The main road south-southwest from Iráklio, over a lower point in the island's spine, goes via **Agía Varvára**, near which is the **Ómfalos** or "navel stone" supposedly marking the centre of Crete. Just beyond it you will have a breathtaking view of the **Mesará Plain**. Rich soil and a benign climate make this a cornucopia, producing a high percentage of the island's crops.

At the edge of the plain, 40km (25 miles) from Iráklio, is the almost sacred village of **Agii Déka** (Holy Ten), with its heavily restored medieval church, into which are incorporated fragments from the nearby site of Gortyn. Agii Déka is renowned because in AD 250, during the persecution of the Christians under Emperor Decius, 10 men were executed here. They are not only among the most revered of Cretan saints, but are also glorified as the first in a long line of Cretans willing to sacrifice themselves to oppose the tyrannical occupiers of their beloved island.

The plantation of palm trees at Váï, which has existed since classical times, is not unique – this native palm also grows near Préveli and Plakiás near Réthymno. The Váï trees are now fenced in to protect them.

BELOW: Váï's palm-fringed beach.

Ierápetra is proud of its position as the most southerly town in all Europe.

After another 1km (½ mile), you reach **Gortyn** (modern Górtys; daily 8am–7.30pm, winter until 3pm; charge). This was the capital of the Romans who first came to Crete in the 2nd century BC but weren't in firm possession of the island until 67 BC, after a three-year campaign. Outstanding and upstanding are the Roman *odeion*, the theatre and a triple-naved basilica, although Italian excavations continue. The last is by far the best-preserved early church in Crete, built to house the tomb of St Titus, Crete's first bishop, who died in AD 105. However, the most renowned artefacts are some stone blocks incorporated into the *odeion*. About 2,500 years ago more than 17,000 characters were incised on these blocks to produce the Law Code of Gortyn, which starkly differentiates the rights of free men and slaves.

Those in search of more ruins, or of health and good swimming, may wish to head south to **Léndas** (72km/ 45 miles from Iráklio). Nearby ancient **Lebena** was the port for Gortyn, and its therapeutic springs made it a renowned healing sanctuary with an **Asklepion** (temple to Asklepios, the god of healing). Traces of this sanctuary, with mosaic floors and large baths can be seen. In an attempt to equal, if not emulate, the ancients, nude bathing has beccome popular at **Dytikós** Léndas's best beach, 15 minutes' walk beyond the headland at the western end of the village.

Phaestos (Festós), Crete's second great Minoan site, occupies a magnificent location 16km (10 miles) west of Gortyn (daily summer 8am–7 .30pm, winter 8am–5pm). Most of the remains date from the Neo-palatial period, although part of the floor plan of the Proto-palatial palace is discernible. State rooms, religious quarters workshops, store rooms and functional plumbing can all be identified. An outstanding sight is the Grand Stairway on the west side. Nearby, again on a glorious site with views of the Libyan Sea, are the attractive Minoan ruins of **Agía Triáda** (winter 8.30am–3pm summer 10am–4pm), which was probably a summer villa.

Next, on to **Mátala** , 70km (4 miles) from Iráklio. This seaside vi

BELOW: large pots *(píthi)* are still made as in Minoan times.

ge first gained renown when the andstone caves in the cliffs around he small, sandy beach – actually ncient tombs – became home to ubstantial colonies of 1960s and 970s hippies; Joni Mitchell stopped y too, and her song *Carey Get Out our Cane* refers explicitly to the lace. Today Mátala is a mainstream esort, expensive and often crowded ut in season, the cave-dwellers long nce evicted and the cliff become an rchaeological site. The main beach s still excellent, but for more seclu- on walk half an hour south to "**Red each**", although **Kalamáki** beach the north is much larger and has Minoan site, Kommos (closed for xcavations).

The even larger south-coast resort f **Agía Galíni** also lies on the Gulf f Mesará, though a little further est, 70km (43 miles) from Iráklio. Mátala proved too boisterous, then gía Galíni, whose nightlife goes on to the small hours, will be far more . The harbour, with a short quay and pedestrianised main street jammed ith tavernas and bars, is enclosed within steep hills covered with modest hotels.

West to Réthymno

You are now in western Crete, and Réthymno province; **Plakiás ㉓**, flanked by half a dozen beaches and a spectacular mountain backdrop, lies some 40km (25 miles) from the provincial capital, and nearly as far from Agía Galíni. The main cultural excursion from Plakiás is to **Préveli Monastery** (13km/8 miles), passing en route the evocative but fenced-off ruins of **Agios Ioánnis Monastery** (also known as Káto Préveli), and a much-photographed arched **bridge**. Préveli itself (seasonally variable hours between 8am–7.30pm; charge) has a superb position, and a courtyard fountain with the inscription "Wash your sins, not just your face."

A double bronze statue of a gun-toting monk and a Commonwealth soldier commemorates Préveli's crucial role in sheltering defeated stragglers from the 1941 Battle of Crete; they were evacuated to Egypt by submarine from **Límni** beach below at the mouth

The text of the Law Code of Gortyn is written in "ox-plough" fashion, reading left to right along one line, then right to left along the next.

BELOW:
the Fortétsa, Réthimno's ancient stronghold.

The remains of two palaces can be seen at Phaestos: the first was built around 1900 BC and destroyed by an earthquake 200 years later; the other was seriously damaged around 1450 BC, in the undetermined calamity that affected all the Minoan palaces.

BELOW: navigating the waters off the coast near Réthymno.

of the **Kourtaliótiko Gorge**, which has a local palm forest nearly as large as that at Váï.

West of Plakiás along the coast, the next resort of consequence huddles around the the Venetian **castle of Frangokástello**, overlooking a good sandy beach. On 17 May 1828, 385 freedom fighters from Sfakiá, commanded by mainlander Hatziyiánni Daliani, were killed here by the Turks; it is said that the mysterious *drossoulítes* (dewy ones), an atmospheric mirage particular to late May, are their ghosts.

Back in Iráklio, the oleander-lined E75 highway runs west towards Réthymno. Some, however, might prefer more leisurely travel along the picturesque but winding old road. Alternatively, leave the new road 25km (16 miles) along to arrive in **Fódele**, a small village rich in orange trees and locally made embroidery. A restored house here is claimed as the birthplace in 1545 of Doménikos Theotokópoulos, better known as El Greco. Back on the expressway, turn seawards after a further 18km (11 miles) to reach the popular resort of

Balí ㉔, clustered around three small bays at the foot of a hill.

At **Stavroménos** or **Plataniás**, just before Réthymno, turn southeast for the beautifully situated **Arkádi Monastery** ㉕ (9am–8pm), 80km (50 miles) from Iráklio or 25km (16 miles) from Réthymno, Crete's most sacred shrine. In 1866, the monastery, sheltering hundreds of rebel fighters and their families, was attacked by the Turks. Rather than surrender, the abbot ordered that gunpowder stored in the now roofless room in the northwest corner of the courtyard be ignited, thus killing both enemy (supposedly 1,500 Ottoman soldiers died in the blast) and Cretans. This act of defiance brought the plight of the island to the public eye and garnered much European sympathy for the cause of independence.

Réthymno

Réthymno ㉖, 77km (48 miles) from Iráklio, prides itself on being Crete's intellectual capital – it is the seat of the University of Crete, founded in 1973, which now has some 6,000 students. Réthymno still possesses an intact Old

Town with a small and extremely picturesque Venetian harbour guarded by an elegant lighthouse, although most of the medieval walls disappeared early in the 20th century. The only surviving remnant is the Porta Guora, or Great Gate, leading into Four Martyrs Square. The martyrs in question were four men who, during the period of Turkish occupation, refused to accept (or pay lip service to) the Muslim faith, as demanded by their occupiers, and were beheaded on this spot for their insistence that they would prefer to die as Christians.

West of the harbour looms the immense **Fortétsa** (daily 8am–8pm, winter until 6pm; charge), said to be the largest Venetian castle ever built. The most intact, and most interesting, structure inside is the **Sultan Ibrahim Mosque** dating from 1646, with one of the largest domes in Greece. Réthymno's other monumental attractions – the ornate, still-flowing **Rimóndi Fountain**, the Venetian **loggia** and the **Nerandzés Mosque** – incorporating a Venetian church – all lie between the harbour and the fortress.

Venetian houses with unexpected architectural delights can be found in the narrow streets linking these sights, while Ottoman features in the shape of fountains with calligraphic inscriptions and overhanging enclosed wooden balconies – the famous local *kióskia* – are evidence that the population of Réthymno was almost one-third Muslim before 1923.

Sun-worshippers will make for Réthymno's wide beach, beginning immediately east of the harbour; backed by a palm-shaded promenade stretching for several kilometres past the new town. The water gets cleaner and the beach less crowded as you go.

Réthymno and Haniá to the west are joined by the E75 and a less used old road. Leave the highway after 23km (14 miles) for **Georgioúpoli ㉗** at the mouth of the River Almyrós, a pleasant resort with a long beach; 4km (2½ miles) inland is Crete's only natural lake, **Kournás**.

Haniá

Haniá ㉘ (Chania), 59km (37 miles) from Réthymno, is Crete's second city

When Arkádi Monastery exploded, one infant was blown into a tree and survived. She grew up to become a nun.

BELOW:
Arkádi Monastery can lay claim to a significant past.

Akrotíri Monasteries

The Akrotíri peninsula has a cluster of historic **monasteries**. The first encountered, 16km (10 miles) from Haniá, is 17th-century **Agías Triádas** (aka Zangarólon; daily 7.30am–2pm and 5–7pm; charge), built in Venetian Rococo style, splendid but somewhat commercialised. A further 4km (2½ miles) away stands **Gouvernétou** (Mon–Tue, Thur and Sat–Sun 9am–noon and 5–8pm, 4–7pm in winter) – older, plainer and austerely religious, though with fine frescoes in its church. From Gouvernétou a rough 40-minute downhill scramble leads to the abandoned, enchanting and possibly enchanted **Katholikó Monastery**, concealed in a goat-patrolled ravine. Dating from about 1200, this is, if not the oldest, certainly one of the first monastic settlements on Crete.

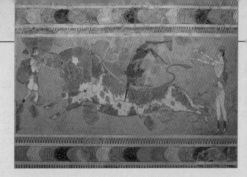

A Cretan Myth

The story of the Minotaur is a complicated one that has survived through the centuries and is known all over the Western world.

K ing Minos, mythical king of Knossós, was the son of Zeus and the Phoenician princess Europa. Zeus, in the form of a bull, had seduced Europa and taken her off to Crete, where Minos and his brothers, Rhadamanthys and Sarpedon, were born. Minos spent nine years in the Diktean Cave with his father learning the arts of kingship, after which he banished his brothers and became sole ruler of Crete.

Wishing to consolidate his power, Minos asked Poseidon for a sign of approval and the god provided a white bull from the sea to be sacrificed. However, the animal was so beautiful that Minos could not bring himself to kill it, so he sacrificed another in its place. This lack of gratitude enraged Poseidon, who made Pasiphaë, the wife of Minos, fall in love with the bull.

Daedalos, an ingenious member of the court, built a model of a cow for Pasiphaë in which she could hide while the bull mounted her. The result of this union was a curious child, the half-man, half-bull Minotaur. Minos was, understandably, furious when he found out about Pasiphaë's son and, after taking advice from the Oracle at Delphi, ordered Daedalos to build a huge labyrinth under the court where the Minotaur was to live.

In the meantime the white bull had been taken to the Peloponnese by Herakles as one of his 12 tasks. There it did great damage and Minos' son, Androgeus, set out to hunt it. While out hunting, Androgeus was killled by a jealous Athenian rival. In response, Minos immediately sent his fleet to Athens and after a long war, defeated the Athenians. The Cretan king then demanded a tribute; the sacrifice of seven young men and seven maidens of Athens every year, who were to be delivered to the labyrinth to be killed by the Minotaur.

One year Theseus, son of the Athenian king Aegeus, volunteered for the sacrifice. While on Crete he met and fell in love with Ariadne, the daughter of Minos, who helped Theseus find his way through the labyrinth by providing a ball of thread that he could unravel to mark his way and prevent him getting lost. He entered the maze, killed the Minotaur with his father's sword, and released the surviving captives.

Triumphant, he and Ariadne fled by sea, but the story does not have a happy ending. Theseus turned out to be a fickle lover. He soon abandoned Ariadne on Náxos, where she became the consort of the god Dionysos. Theseus was forgetful as well as fickle. He promised his father that if he survived his battle with the Minotaur he would show a white sail on his ship as he returned home. Unfortunately, this slipped his mind, and when his father saw the ship approaching harbour with no white sail visible he assumed his beloved son was dead. Overcome with grief he threw himself into the sea and drowned. ❏

ABOVE: the *Bull-Leaping Fresco* from Knossós, now at the Iráklio Archaeological Museum. **LEFT:** *Theseus Slaying the Minotaur*, a bronze by Antoine-Louis Barye.

and was its capital until 1971. It claims to be one of the oldest continuously inhabited cities in the world. Its jewel is the boat-free outer Venetian harbour. The quayside is wide and backed by characterful, colourful old buildings, whose reflections shimmer in the water. The ambience is of the Levant and this is the place for the *vólta*, the evening stroll.

The restored 1645-vintage **Mosque of Küçük Hasan** (Yali Tzami), by one year the oldest mosque in Crete, stands at one end of the quay and now hosts art exhibitions; the **Fírkas Bastion** occupies the other end, next to the **Naval Museum** (daily, summer 9am–4pm, winter 9am–2pm; charge), with good displays on the Battle of Crete and subsequent occupation. On the bastion, in December 1913 the King of Greece officially raised the national flag for the first time on Crete. Behind the Naval Museum, at the top of Theotokopoúlou, the the **Byzantine Museum** (summer Tue–Sun 8.30am–7.30pm; charge) has a small but fine display of mosaics, icons and jewellery. Both Theotokopoúlou and its perpendicular Angélou have splendid examples of domestic Venetian architecture.

Full of relics from ancient Kydonia, Haniá's predecessor, the **Archaeological Museum** (Tue–Sun 8am–7.30pm, Mon 1–7.30pm) occupies the church of the Franciscan Friary, one of the best preserved and largest of a dozen Venetian churches scattered across the Old Town. Two blocks west, on Kondyláki, is the **Etz Hayyim Synagogue** (Mon–Fri 9am–12.30pm and 6–8pm), the sole reminder of Haniá's pre-World War II Jewish community of about 350; it has been lovingly restored from its wrecked state, including the subterranean *mikveh* or ritual bath, which taps a natural spring.

In the New Town, visit the lofty glass-roofed cruciform **market**, which was opened by Elefthérios Venizélos in 1913 and is still overflowing with vegetables, fruit, fish, meat, herbs and spices, cheese and wine.

Akrotíri

Akrotíri ㉙ (*see box page 291*), a limestone peninsula stretching northeastwards from Haniá to enclose enormous, strategic **Soúda Bay**, is full of interest. First visit the hill of **Profítis Ilías**, where revolutionary Cretans gathered in 1897 to demand union with Greece. Here are the simple graves of Elefthérios Venizélos, born outside Haniá at Mourniés, and his son Sofóklis.

Other graves, 1,527 of them, are found at the immaculately maintained **Commonwealth Cemetery** near the Soúda shore, where British and Commonwealth troops killed during the 1941 Battle of Crete are buried. Equal honour is given to three times that number of Germans buried in the well-tended cemetery at **Máleme**, 16km (10 miles) west of Haniá.

Southwest from Haniá

Return to Haniá and take the road west, which hugs the coast, passing several busy small resorts like **Agía Marína** and **Plataniás** that merge imperceptibly with each other, before winding through low hills to emerge

> The appearance of the town [Haniá] was striking, as its irregular wooden buildings rose up the hill sides from the sea, interspersed with palm trees, mosques and minarets. There was no mistaking we were in Turkey.
>
> Henry Fanshaw Tozer, 1890

BELOW:
church and shrine
on the road to
Kastélli.

The lighthouse at Haniá, designed like a minaret, dates from the period 1830–40, when Crete was handed over to Egypt as a reward for helping the Turks crush the rebellious Greeks.

BELOW: Haniá harbour in the early morning light.

at a viewpoint over the broad **bay of Kíssamos**, cradled by the **Gramvoúsa peninsula** and the **Rodópou promontory**, together resembling rabbit's ears on the map.

A descent to the broad coastal plain brings you to pleasant but characterless **Kastélli** ㉚ (Kíssamos; 42km/26 miles from Haniá), mostly visited for its ferry connection to the Peloponnese but also endowed with a superb **Archaeological Museum** (Tue–Sun 8.30am–2.30pm; free), opened in 2006, and particularly strong on the Hellenistic and Roman town here – the highlight is the mosaic of the four seasons on the villa floor upstairs. The closest memorable beach lies 17km (11 miles) west, via Plátanos village at **Falásarna**, with a small ancient city thrown into the bargain.

From Kaloudianá 4km (2½ miles) east of Kastélli, a good road leads south through unusually well-watered countryside. There are chestnut orchards at **Élos** – where the harvest is celebrated with a Chestnut Festival on 15 October – and villages like **Topólia**, **Kefáli** and **Váthi** have lovely old chapels with

14th-century frescoes. Beyond Váthi the route forges straight through a gorge to the **Hrysoskalítissa** (Golden Stairway) **Convent** (8am–sunset; charge), 39km (25 miles) from Kastélli. The name refers to the legend that one of the 90 steps descending from the terrace was made of solid gold; only the extremely pure at heart can see it as such. Some 5km (3 miles) beyond the road ends at **Elafonísi**, a small isle sheltering a shallow lagoon and a pale sand beach of near-tropical beauty; it is a protected zone and thus pretty undeveloped, but it gets hopelessly crowded in season.

A busier road from Tavronítis on the north coast leads via **Kándanos**, with more frescoed late Byzantine chapels to **Paleohóra** ㉛ (76km/47 miles from Haniá), a friendly resort with a ruined Venetian castle plus protected pebble beaches and long sandy beaches, the latter a favourite with windsurfers. Boats leave twice weekly for the isle of **Gávdos** ㉜, Europe's southernmost point, which is finally being developed touristically but still remains blissfully calm outside August.

Hóra Sfakíon ㉝, 75km (47 miles) via an entirely different road from Haniá, is the "capital" of rugged Sfakiá, celebrated as the one corner of Crete that never fully submitted to Venetian, Ottoman or Nazi rule. Like Préveli, it was a major evacuation point for fleeing Allied soldiers after the Battle of Crete. The current major role of this small, cliff-hanging port is as the local small-ferry terminus, with more services to Gávdos and a daily line west along the roadless coast as far as Paleohóra, stopping en route at tiny resort-settlements like Loutró, Agía Roúmeli and Soúgia.

But you needn't rely on the boats – west of Hóra Sfakíon is some of the best shoreline trekking in the islands. The path threads "**Sweetwater Beach**" – the closest good one to the town – en route to **Loutró**, pleasant, although again beachless, before traversing **Agios Pávlos beach** with its Byzantine chapel on the way to Agía Rouméli (*see page 296*) – a long day's hike. Only the most experienced and fit hill-walkers should tackle the next tricky section to enjoyable **Soúgia**, which does have a beach, before the easy final-day section via **ancient Lissos** to Paleohóra. Lissos was known in antiquity for its Temple of Asklepios, where people suffering from various ailments came from all over the island, hoping for a cure. The temple is long gone, but its mosaic floor can still be seen.

Gorge of Samariá

For most active, first-time visitors, however, the one walk that must be done is the spectacular, five- to six-hour traverse of the **Gorge of Samariá** ㉞, at 16km (10 miles) one of the longest in Europe. The hike starts with a sharp stairway descent from **Xylóskalo**, 1,200 metres (3,937ft) above the sea, at the southern end of the vast **Omalós** plain, itself a 45km (28-mile) tortuous drive from Haniá. Within an hour or so of walking, the path is 600 metres (1,968ft) lower in altitude; some 10km (6½ miles) below the start point, the village of **Samariá**, abandoned in 1962, and its frescoed church of **Agios Nikólaos** come into view.

The going now gets tougher underfoot, even though there is less of a

St John the Hermit is thought to have lived and died in a cave near the Katholikó Monastery.

BELOW:
octopus hanging out to dry.

The cliffs around the Samariá Gorge are the home of the rare and elusive Cretan wild goat, the agrími *or* krí-krí.

gradient, and involves criss-crossing the river-bed, which usually has water in it. Flash floods can occur in spring and autumn, and patrolling wardens' warnings should be heeded. The gorge progressively narrows and the walls soar straight upwards for 300 to 600 metres (1,000–2,000ft). Soon after passing Aféndis Hristós Chapel, the **Siderespórtes** (Iron Gates) are reached and the gorge, scarcely penetrated by sunlight here, is little more than 3.5 metres (11ft) wide. Only a giant could stretch out and touch each side of the gorge simultaneously (something brochures promise for everyone).

The gorge is completely enclosed in a national park strictly administered by the Haniá Forest Service, which specifically forbids a long list of activities including camping, and making fires or loud noises (including singing). Since its creation in 1962, the park has functioned well as a wildlife refuge. You are most unlikely to spot any *krí-krí* (wild goat), but botanists will be delighted, and ornithologists may glimpse vultures overhead.

You are well and truly out of the narrows when you reach old **Agía Rouméli**, abandoned after World War II, but you still face another kilometre (½ mile) of hot-afternoon tramping to reach its modern successor on the coast. A cold beer and refreshing swim off the long sand-and-pebble beach are in order, but be aware of the time (and the seat quota) of the last boat out in either direction, or you may find yourself making an unplanned overnight stop here. If you forget the time, or if you decide you would like to stay the night anyway, try the Tara Rooms or Calypso Hotel. These two establishments are run by two brothers: the hotel is pleasant and comfortable, the Tara Rooms more basic, but cheaper – and there is a taverna downstairs (*see Accommodation, page 324*).

The gorge is open 1 May–31 October from dawn to about 4pm (charge), subject to amendments for bad weather. After 4pm you will only be allowed into the first 2km (1 mile) from either end, and the wardens ensure that nobody camps in the gorge. ❏

BELOW: the "Iron Gates", Samariá Gorge. **RIGHT:** wild blooms. **OPPOSITE:** maintaining the boat at Agía Galíni.

CENTRE OF EUROPE'S FIRST CIVILISATION

Until 1894, the Minoan civilisation was little more than a myth. Now its capital is one of the largest and best-restored sites in all Greece

Knossós is a place of questions, many of them unanswered. Some visitors to the site find the concrete reconstructions and repainted frescoes (often extrapolated from very small existing fragments) aid comprehension. But for many, used to other, more recent, ruins that are clearly defensive or overtly religious, the site is mysterious. Can we hope to look back at fragments of a culture from 3,500 years ago and understand its imperatives and subtleties?

In legend, Knossós was the labyrinth of King Minos, where he imprisoned the Minotaur, the human-taurine child of his wife Pasiphaë. In reality, the place was probably not a palace in the modern sense, but perhaps an administrative and economic centre, unified by spiritual leaders.

Among the 1,300 rooms of the main palace were both the sacred and the commercial: lustral baths for holy ceremonies; store rooms for agricultural produce; workshops for metallurgy and stone-cutting. Nearby are the Royal Villa and the Little Palace.

Try to visit early or late in the day (better still, visit out of season), to avoid the worst of the substantial crowds, and to avoid being swept along by the flow. Look for the subtle architectural delights – light wells to illuminate the larger rooms; hydraulic controls providing water for drinking, bathing and flushing away sewage; drains with parabolic curves at the bends to prevent overflow.

The site is open 8am–7.30pm daily in summer, and 8.30am–3pm in winter (charge).

ABOVE: a (replica) fresco depicting the capture of a wild bull decorates the ramparts of the north entrance, leading to the road Knossós's harbour at Amnisos.

RIGHT: wandering around Knossós – but the scale of the site is n apparent from the air: nearly 2 hectares (5 acres) of palaces rule population of perhaps 100,000.

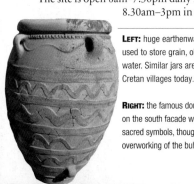

LEFT: huge earthenware jars, *píthoi*, were used to store grain, olive oil, wine or water. Similar jars are still made in a few Cretan villages today.

RIGHT: the famous double horns now sitting on the south facade were once regarded as sacred symbols, though perhaps this is an overworking of the bull motif of the site.

CONTROVERSIAL RESTORATIONS

In 1878 a local merchant, Minos Kalokairinos, uncovered part of Knossós, but the Turkish owners of the land prevented further excavation and even wealthy Heinrich Schliemann got entangled in unproductive negotiations for purchase.

However, once Crete gained autonomy in 1898, the way was open for archaeologist Arthur Evans (pictured above with a 1600 BC steatite bull's head) to purchase the site and begin excavating. He worked here from 1900 until 1931, though by 1903 most of Knossós had been uncovered.

Evans's use of reinforced concrete to reconstruct long-gone timber columns, and his completely speculative upper-storey reconstructions, have received considerable criticism. Moreover, the Minoan frescoes are not only arbitrarily placed, but almost completely modern, painted from scratch by assistants Piet de Jong and Emile Gilliéron. Others have charged that Evans, a fairly typical Victorian chauvinist, manipulated evidence to fit his theory of the thalassocratic Minoans as prehistoric proto-British imperialists. It's also clear that both the restoration and fresco-retouching was heavily influenced by the Art Nouveau and Art Deco styles prevalent at the time.

ABOVE: the Cup Bearers fresco.

RIGHT: Sir Arthur Evans, the English archaeologist whose reconstruction of Knossós, a significant quantity of it based on conjecture, was to prove controversial.

VE: Evans's use of reinforced concrete to strengthen and
ort crumbling structures is here apparent.

☆ INSIGHT GUIDES ─ TRAVEL TIPS
GREEK ISLANDS

TRANSPORT · ACCOMMODATION · EATING OUT · ACTIVITIES · A – Z · LANGUAGE

TRANSPORT

GETTING THERE
AND GETTING AROUND

GETTING THERE

By Air

Greece has good air connections with the rest of the world and is served by numerous international airlines. Charter flights to the islands generally operate from mid-April to the end of October, even into November to Rhodes and Crete. Unless you are on a multi-stop or round-the-world ticket, tickets are generally bought online. The airlines' own websites can often be a good source of discount tickets, matching prices offered by general travel sites.

The majority of schedule airline passengers travelling to Greece make Athens's Elefthérios Venizélos Airport (www.aia.gr) their point of entry, though a number of flights (from the rest of Europe only) arrive at Thessaloníki's Makedonía Airport, which gives easier access to certain north Aegean islands. Scheduled flights (easyJet and a few others) also go most of the year to Rhodes, Crete (Iráklio), Mýkonos and Corfu.

Between Venizélos Airport, central Athens and Piraeus there are various connecting services. Line 3 of the metro (closed for works until late 2010) takes you – surprisingly slowly, every half-hour – into town for €6. Alternatively, take the X95 express bus all the way to central Sýndagma Square (Platía Syndagmátos), the X94 to Ethnikí Amyna metro station or the X96 express bus to Piraeus port. All express buses depart from outside arrivals, with the same frequency (every 15 minutes) and the same fare (currently €3.20). Unless the metro

overhaul improves speed, express buses are scarcely slower than the metro.

A taxi from Venizélos Airport to the centre of Athens will cost about €28–40 depending on time of day or night and your final destination, but including airport supplement and per-bag fee. Traffic congestion has improved since the opening of the Attikí Odós (ring road) round northern Athens, but the journey time can still amount to over an hour.

By Sea

Most visitors entering Greece by sea do so from Italy. You can catch a boat to Greece from Venice, Ancona and Bari, but the most regular service is from Brindisi.

Daily ferry lines (less frequent in low season) connect Brindisi with the three main western ports: Corfu, Igoumenítsa and Pátra. Corfu is a 6½-hour trip; Igoumenítsa 8 hours; and Pátra 11 to 14 hours, depending on whether you take a direct boat or one that makes stops in Corfu and Igoumenítsa. The "Superfast" ferries between Ancona and Pátra offer an efficient 22-hour crossing.

Igoumenítsa is the ideal port of call for southern Corfu, Paxí and Levkáda, while Pátra is best if you want to head directly to Athens or the southern Ionian islands. Regular buses and trains connect Pátra and Athens (4 hours by bus, 5 hours by train). If you plan to take your car on the boat, you should definitely make reservations well in advance. Otherwise, arriving a few hours before the departure time should suffice, except during peak seasons when booking in advance is essential for seats or berths.

By Land

From Europe

The most direct overland route from northwestern Europe to Greece is a long one: 3,000km (1,900 miles) from London to Athens – a rather arduous and impractical travel option if you are just trying to get to Greece for a brief holiday.

One or two remaining reputable **bus** lines connect Athens and Thessaloníki with many European cities (the journey, though, is very long and uncomfortable, taking 3½ days from London for example, and is little cheaper than the flight).

The various **trains** you can take from northwest Europe will take about as long as the bus, and cost considerably more, but fares include the Italy–Greece ferry crossing, and may get you to Greece feeling somewhat more intact.

From Asia via Turkey

If you are travelling strictly overland to Greece from Asia you will pass through Istanbul and cross into Greece at the Évros River. Roads are good, and the journey from Istanbul to Thessaloníki takes approximately 15 hours; several bus companies serve the route.

The train has the appeal of partially following the route of the old Orient Express, with better scenery than the road. But, unless you're a great rail fan, the journey time can be off-putting: 17 hours Istanbul–Thessaloníki by the timetable, up to 19 hours in practice, including long halts at the border.

Another popular option is to take one of the small boats between western Turkish ports and select

Greek islands just opposite. Fares are overpriced for the distance involved, but it is undeniably convenient. The most reliable links are from Çesme to Híos (all year), Marmaris to Rhodes and Kuşadası to Sámos.

GETTING AROUND

Public Transport

By Air

Flying during the season is considerably more expensive than travelling by boat, bus or train (up to three times more than a ferry seat, just under double the price of a boat berth). Fares vary wildly with demand, but as an example the 45–55-minute flight between Athens and Sámos costs anywhere between €50 and €140 one way in economy class.

All four of the domestically operating airlines are now largely web-based, with few walk-in offices outside airports and heavy surcharges for tickets bought through agencies. Olympic Air (www.olympicairlines.com) is the privatised successor to troubled Olympic Airways, which was notorious for delays and cancellations in its prior incarnation. Aegean (tel: 80111 20000; www.aegeanair.com) and newcomer Athens Airways (tel: 80180 14000; www.athensairways.com) provide competition on major island routes, while Iráklio-based Sky Express (tel: 28102 23500; www.skyexpress.gr) makes useful peripheral flights from Crete to other islands. Always leave plenty of leeway in your domestic flight arrangements if you have to be back in Athens for an international flight. Island flights are often full for weeks at a time in summer; it is prudent to buy August seats in June at the latest.

By Bus

The KTEL is a syndicate of nationwide bus companies, including the islands, whose buses are affordable and generally punctual, although on the larger islands like Crete and Lésvos frequencies can be sparse because of village depopulation. Buses on the more idiosyncratic rural routes may have a distinctly personal touch, their drivers decorating and treating the coach with great care.

Generally there is only one KTEL station per town; exceptions include Athens, with two terminals, and Iráklio (Crete), with three. On smaller islands, tickets are still sold on the bus, but on large islands like Rhodes or Crete you should buy them in advance from ticket booths.

Island buses

On the islands buses may be converted school buses, ultramodern coaches, or even (as on Lipsí) small mini-vans. Some drivers ricochet through mountain roads at death-defying speeds; accidents, however, are rare. Stow your luggage carefully to be on the safe side.

A bus of some description will usually meet arriving ferries (even if a boat is delayed) to transport passengers up the hill to the island's hóra, or capital. Bus stops are usually in main squares or by the waterfront in harbours, and vehicles may or may not run to schedule. A conductor dispenses tickets on the bus itself; often the fare required and the ticket will not show the same price, with the lower old price over-stamped. This isn't a con, but merely a practice – bus companies use pre-printed tickets until the supply is finished, which may take several years.

Athens city buses and trams

With a new, post-Olympics generation of modern, air-conditioned vehicles, travelling by Athens's blue-and-white city buses is much less of an ordeal than it used to be. They are still usually overcrowded, and routes can be a mystery (placards at the stops list only the sequence of subsequent stops). But they are eminently reasonable, at €1 per ticket (valid for 1½ hours, including transfers) or €3 for an all-day pass, both valid on all means of transport, including the tram from Sýndagma down to the coastal suburbs. Single tickets are sold individually or in books of 10, from some street-corner kiosks and special booths at bus and metro

stations. Most bus and tram services run until midnight, or slightly after.

Trolley buses, with an overhead pantograph, are marginally faster, and serve points of tourist interest; No. 1 links the centre of Athens with the railway stations, No. 5 passes the Archaeological Museum, and No. 7 does a circuit of the central districts.

The most useful suburban services for tourists are the orange-and-white KTEL Attica buses going from Mavromatéon 14, by Pédio toú Areos Park, to Rafina and Lávrio (alternative ferry ports for the Cyclades) and Soúnio (for the famous Temple of Poseidon there).

Athens Metro

The Athens metro system opened in January 2000, halving travel times around the city and making a visible reduction in surface traffic. The stations themselves are palatial and squeaky-clean, with advertising placards kept to a minimum. However, 2008–9 saw a huge rise in pickpocketing and bag-snatching at the central stations – beware. The old ISAP electric line, in existence since the early 1900s, has been refurbished and designated Line 1 (green on maps); it links Piraeus with Kifissiá via the city centre. Line 2 (red) links Agios Dimítrios in the south with Agios Andónios in the northwest of town, with extensions planned all the way down to Glyfáda and up to Thivón. Line 3 (blue) joins Egáleo and the airport, via Monastiráki. The main junction stations of the various lines are Omónia, Sýndagma and Monastiráki. Athens now has a unified fare structure for all means of public transport, so that tickets are completely interchangeable. Note that the express bus ticket into town from the airport is void the minute you

BELOW: doing the donkey work on pedestrianised Hydra island.

ABOVE: island-hopping boats wait in Nísyros harbour.

Gamma class – also known as *touristikí*, deck, or third – is the classic, cheap way to travel the Greek seas. Sadly, open-air deck seating is becoming a thing of the past as older boats are retired, and you may well be forced inside to take up "pullman" seats or occupy the "low class" snack bar.

Catamarans/"high speeds"
Fleets of sleek new "high speed" *(tahyplöö)* ferries or true catamarans, made in France or Scandanavia, are steadily supplanting conventional *(symvatikó)* craft (as a stroll around the quays at Piraeus will confirm). They have some advantages over hydrofoils *(see below)* – they can be even faster, most of them carry lots of cars, and they are permitted to sail in wind conditions of up to Force 8, whereas "dolphins" are confined to port above Force 6.5 or so. The bad news: there may be no cabins (because they mostly finish their runs before midnight), food service is even worse than on the old ferries and there are no exterior decks. The aeroplane-seating salons are ruthlessly air-conditioned and subject to a steady, unavoidable barrage of banal Greek TV on overhead monitors (even in *diakikriméni* or "distinguished" class). Cars cost roughly the same to convey as on the old-style boats, but seats are priced at hydrofoil levels.

Catamarans come in all shapes and sizes, from the 300-car-carrying behemoths of NEL Lines and Hellenic Seaways in the northeast Aegean, Cyclades and central Dodecanese, to the mid-sized ones plying the Argo-Saronic, to the tiny *Sea Star* in the Dodecanese. The useful *Dodekánisos Express* and *Dodekánisos Pride* serve more of the Dodecanese islands, and can take cars each.

Hydrofoils
Catamarans have proved expensive to operate, so a network of scheduled hydrofoil services to many islands still survives. Like catamarans, hydrofoils are more than twice as fast as the ferries and about twice as expensive, but as ex-Polish or ex-Russian river craft, are not really designed for Aegean conditions – the small rear sundecks will be swamped with spray in anything over Force 5.

Hydrofoils (nicknamed *delfínia* or "dolphins" in Greek) connect Piraeus with the Argo-Saronic archipelago (Égina, Angístri, Póros, Hydra, Spétses), although, frustratingly, the Égina–Angístri lines tend to be

leave that bus. If you're caught by the ubiquitous plain-clothes inspectors with an old ticket, or no ticket, you get a spot fine of 60 times the standard €1 fare (this is true of Athens public transport overall).

By Train
The Greek rail service, known as OSE, is quite limited, both in the areas it reaches and frequency of departures, although it is somewhat cheaper than the bus. The only line island travellers are likely to use is the run from Athens to Pátra (where the station is virtually opposite the docks). Be sure you specify an Intercity express departure rather than a stopping train. Return tickets have a 20 percent reduction, while students and people under 26 are usually eligible for certain discounts. All the common rail passes are honoured in Greece, although you may still have to pay certain supplements and queue for seat reservations.

By Sea
Ferries
Piraeus is the nerve centre of the Greek ferry network, and the chances are you will pass through it at least once during your stay. In diminishing order of importance, Rafina, Lávrio, Vólos, Thessaloníki, Kavála and Pátra are also useful. In high season, especially to the Cyclades and Dodecanese, routes vary from "milk runs" on antiquated boats stopping at five islands en route to your destination, to semi-direct ones on newer craft. There is often little or no price difference, so it is well worth comparison-shopping before buying. It is also advisable not to purchase your ticket too far in advance: only in August to early September and around election times do all classes

of tickets actually sell out, but there are frequent changes to schedules which may leave you trying to get a refund if you booked early.

Personalised, computerised, advance ticketing for all boats is mandatory, so it is no longer possible to purchase tickets on board – or even on the gangway – as in the past. The only exceptions seem to be a few of the ro-ro short-haul ferries (eg Igoumenítsa–Lefkímmi).

When you buy a ticket at Piraeus, get detailed instructions on how to find its berth – the quays are long and convoluted; the staff who take your ticket should also make sure you are on the right boat. *(See Coping with Piraeus, page 117 for some guidance.)*

Above all, be flexible when travelling the Greek seas. Apart from schedule changes, a bad stretch of weather can keep you island-bound for as long as the wind blows above Force 7. Strikes, too, are often called during the summer, and usually last for a few days. Out on the islands in particular, the best way to secure accurate, up-to-the-minute information on the erratic ways of ferries is to contact the Port Authority *(limenarhío)*, which monitors the movements of individual boats. Port Authority offices are usually located on the waterfront of each island's principal harbour, away from the cafés.

If you are travelling by car, especially during the high season, you will have to plan much further ahead because during the peak season car space is sometimes booked many weeks in advance. The same applies to booking a cabin for an overnight trip during summer – and, from early August to early September, often for just a simple seat.

Athens's Rush Hours

Driving through Athens during its multiple rush hours (8–10am, 2–3pm, 4.30–5.30pm, 8–10pm) is not for the faint at heart. The twin perils of traffic jams and pollution reached such heights in the capital that a law was introduced during the 1980s: on even days of the month only cars with even-numbered licence plates are allowed in the centre; on odd days only those with odd-numbered plates. However, this has done little to improve the congestion, noise and smog in Athens, as many families have two cars (one of each type of number plate) and alternate them according to the day of the week. Fortunately for foreign visitors (if not for the environment), the law does not seem to be enforced against hired or foreign-number-plate cars.

entirely separate from the other three lines. From Vólos there is service to the three northerly Sporades (Alónissos, Skiáthos, Skópelos), while in the northeast Aegean there are local, peak-season services between Thásos or Samothráki and the mainland. In the Dodecanese all the islands between Sámos and Kós, inclusive, are well served.

Phone numbers for the few surviving hydrofoil companies are constantly engaged, or else spew out only pre-recorded information in rapid-fire Greek, so are of little use to non-Greek-speaking visitors. The best strategy is to approach the embarkation booths in person. In Piraeus these are on Aktí Miaoúli quay (for Aegean Flying Dolphins and Hellenic Seaways). At Vólos, apply to the gatehouse for the harbour precinct; elsewhere, tickets are best obtained from travel agents in the various towns.

Port Authority numbers
The Ionian Islands
Corfu, tel: 26610 32655
Itháki, tel: 26740 32909
Kefaloniá (Argostóli), tel: 26710 22224
Levkáda, tel: 26450 92509
Paxí, tel: 26620 32259
Zákynthos, tel: 26950 28117

The Saronic Gulf Islands
Aegina, tel: 22970 22328
Hydra, tel: 22980 52279
Póros, tel: 22980 22274

Salamína, tel: 467 7277
Spétses, tel: 22980 72245

The Cyclades
Andros, tel: 22820 71213
Íos, tel: 22860 91264
Kéa, tel: 22870 21344
Kýthnos, tel: 22810 21290
Mílos, tel: 22870 22968
Mýkonos, tel: 22890 22218
Náxos, tel: 22850 22300
Páros, tel: 22840 21240
Santoríni, tel: 22860 22239
Sérifos, tel: 22810 51470
Sífnos, tel: 22840 33617
Sýros, tel: 22810 82690
Tínos, tel: 22830 22348

The Sporades
Alónnisos, tel: 24240 65595
Skiáthos, tel: 24270 22017
Skópelos, tel: 24240 22180
Skýros, tel: 22220 93475

The NE Aegean Islands
Foúrni, tel: 22750 51207
Híos, tel: 22710 44433
Ikaría (Agios Kírykos), tel: 22750 22207
Ikaría (Évdilos), tel: 22750 31007
Lésvos (Mytilíni), tel: 22510 24515
Lésvos (Sígri), tel: 22530 54433
Límnos, tel: 22540 22225
Psará, tel: 22720 61252
Sámos (Vathý), tel: 22730 27318
Sámos (Karlóvassi), tel: 22730 30888
Sámos (Pythagório), tel: 22730 61225
Samothráki, tel: 25510 41305
Thásos (Liménas), tel: 25930 22106
Thásos (Prínos), tel: 25930 71290

The Dodecanese Islands
Astypálea, tel: 22420 61208
Hálki, tel: 22460 45220
Kálymnos, tel: 22430 29304
Kárpathos (Pigádia), tel: 22450 22227

Kásos, tel: 22450 41288
Kastellórizo, tel: 22460 49270
Kós, tel: 22420 26594
Léros (Lakkí), tel: 22470 22334
Nísyros, tel: 22420 31222
Pátmos, tel: 22470 31231
Rhodes, tel: 22410 22220
Sými, tel: 22460 71205
Tílos, tel: 22460 44350

Crete
Agios Nikólaos, tel: 28400 22312
Haniá, tel: 28210 98888
Iráklio, tel: 2810 244956
Kastélli, tel: 28220 22024
Réthymno, tel: 28310 22276
Sitía, tel: 28430 27117

● Piraeus Port Authority, tel: 21045 11311 or 21041 47800 (recorded outgoing message in Greek only – this is also true of most busy island ports).
● For more on island-hopping by ferry, see the features on Island-Hopping (page 83), and Coping with Piraeus (page 117).

Kaïkia and Taxi-Boats

Apart from conventional ferries, catamarans and hydrofoils, swarms of small kaïkia (caiques) offer seasonal excursions, pitched mostly at day-trippers. Since they are chartered by travel agencies, they are exempt from Ministry of Transport fare controls – as well as from the 30-year-old scrap-the-boat rule that is increasingly enforced in Greece for scheduled services – and they can be very expensive if used as a one-way ticket from, say, Sámos to Pátmos.

On many islands where there are remote beaches with difficult overland access – most notably Hydra, Itháki, Sými, Hálki, Alónnisos and Pátmos – local "taxi-boats" provide a fairly pricey shutttle service. They are useful, but be aware that they usually run at set hours rather than on

Car Hire (Rental)

Hiring a car in Greece is not always as cheap as you might hope, owing to demand, high insurance premiums and import duties. Prices – from €18 to €35 per day – vary according to the type of car, season and length of rental and should include CDW (collision damage waiver) and VAT at 18 percent (13 percent in the Dodecanese and northeast Aegean). Payment can, and often must, be made with a major credit card. A full home-country driving licence (for EU/EEA residents) or an International Driving

Permit (for all others) is required and you must be at least 21 years old.

You can book a car in advance through major international chains such as Hertz, Avis, Budget or Sixt – their websites have all-inclusive quotes and booking/payment facilities. But there are many reputable, smaller chains, some particular to Greece, that offer a comparable service at lower rates. These include Kosmos (www.kosmos-carrental.com), Reliable (www.reliable-rentacar.com), AutoUnion (www.autounion.gr) and Autorent (www.autorent.gr).

Breakdowns

The Greek Automobile Association (ELPA) offers a breakdown service for motorists, which is free to AA/RAC members (on production of their membership cards).

Phone 10400 for assistance nationwide. Some car-hire companies have agreements instead with competitors Hellas Service (dial 1057), Interamerican (dial 1168) or Express Service (dial 1154), but these call centres can be slow to dispatch aid. Preferably, ring a local garage number, especially if this is what the hire company instructs you to do.

demand – check on the return times before you set out.

Private Transport

Yacht Charter

Chartering a yacht is one of the more exotic ways of island-hopping in Greece. It is by no means cheap, although hiring a boat with a group of friends may not far exceed the price of renting rooms every night for the same number of people.

Depending on your nautical qualifications and your taste for autonomy, you can either take the helm yourself or let a hired crew do so for you. There are thousands of yachts available for charter in Greece, all registered and inspected by the Ministry of the Merchant Marine. For more information, see our feature on sailing on page 80. You may also find the following organisations worth consulting before chartering:

The Hellenic Professional Yacht Owners' Association
Freattýdos 43, Zéa Marína,
185 36 Piraeus; tel: 21045 26335,
www.hpyoa.gr
The Hellenic Yacht Brokers' Association
Zéa Marína, 185 36 Piraeus;
tel: 21045 33134, www.hyba.gr

Taxis

Taxis in Greece, especially in Athens, merit a guidebook to themselves. There are three stages to the experience.

First: getting a taxi. It is almost impossible at certain times of the day in Athens, and probably hardest before the early afternoon meal. When you hail a taxi, try to get in before stating your destination. The drivers are very picky and often won't let you in unless you're going

in their direction. If you see an empty taxi, run for it and be aggressive – otherwise you will find that some quick Athenian has beaten you to it.

Second: the ride. Make sure the taxi meter is on "1" when you start out, and not on "2" – that's the double fare, which is only permitted from midnight to 5am, or outside designated city limits. Once inside, you may find yourself with company. Don't be alarmed. It is traditional practice for drivers to pick up two, three, even four individual passengers, provided they're going roughly in the same direction. In these cases, make a note of the meter count when you get in. In fact, because taxis are so cheap, they can end up functioning as minibus services.

Third: navigating. You need to know exactly where you are headed. There is no equivalent requirement of London's "The Knowledge" for Athens drivers, and many will not even have a street atlas in the cab.

Fourth: paying up. If you have travelled with other passengers, make sure you aren't paying for the part of the trip that took place before you got in. You should pay the difference in meter reading between embarking and alighting, plus the minimum fare (currently €2.85). Otherwise, the meter will tell you the straight price, which may be adjusted according to the tariff that should be on a laminated placard clipped to the dashboard. There are extra charges for each piece of luggage in the boot, for leaving or entering an airport or seaport, plus bonuses around Christmas and Easter.

Some drivers will quote you the correct price, but many others will try to rip you off, especially if it seems that you're a novice. If the fare you are charged is clearly above the correct price, don't hesitate to argue, in whichever language, until you get it back down to a normal and fair price.

BELOW: hiring a boat can be an option.

These rules apply more to Athens than to the islands, although it is still necessary to be pretty assertive on Crete and Rhodes. Shared taxis, Athens-style, are not the norm in the islands, except (oddly) on Kálymnos, where they wait for passengers and only depart when full.

In recent years various radio taxi services have started up in Athens and most larger island towns. They can pick you up within a short time of your call to a central booking number, although there is a small surcharge of under €2 for this.

Cars

Having a car in the rural areas of the Greek islands enables you to reach a lot of otherwise inaccessible corners; however, driving a car in Athens (or any sizeable island town like Iráklio or Rhodes) is usually a liability. Tempers soon run short as signage, especially warnings of mandatory turning lanes, is practically non-existent.

EU-registered cars are no longer stamped into your passport on entry to the country. They can circulate freely for up to six months, and are exempt from road tax as long as this has been paid in the home country – however, you are not allowed to sell the vehicle. Non-EU/EEA nationals will find that a bizarre litany of rules apply to importing cars, chief among them that you must re-export the car when you depart, or have it sealed by Customs in an off-road facility of your choosing.

Driving in Greece

All EU/EEA licences, and licences held by returning diaspora Greeks irrespective of issuing country, are honoured in Greece. Conversely, all other licences – this includes North American and Australian ones – are not valid, as many tourists from those nations attempting to hire cars have discovered to their cost. These motorists must obtain an International Driving Permit before departure (issued by the AAA or CAA in North America on the spot for a nominal cost); the Greek Automobile and Touring Club (ELPA) no longer issues them to foreign nationals in Greece. With the advent of the single European market (EU), insurance Green Cards are no longer required, although you should check with your home insurer about the need for any supplementary premiums – many policies now include pan-European cover anyway.

Greek traffic control and signals are basically the same as in the rest of Continental Europe, although roundabouts are handled bizarrely by French or English standards – in most cases the traffic entering from the slip road, not that already in the circle, has the right of way – watch for "stop" or "yield" signs or pavement markings.

Motorway speeds are routinely in excess of the nominal 100–120kph (62–75mph) limits, and drivers overtake with abandon. On other island roads, posted limits are typically 70–90kph (40–55mph). A red light is often considered not so much an obligation as a suggestion, and oncoming drivers flashing lights at you on one-lane roads means the opposite of what it does in the UK. Here, it means: "I'm coming through" (although often it can mean "Watch out, police control ahead"). Greece has the highest accident rate in Western/Mediterranean Europe after Portugal, so drive defensively – particularly in August, when Athenians return to their natal islands and apply urban driving habits to backcountry roads.

Greece has a mandatory seatbelt law (€175 fine for non-observance), and children under 10 are not allowed to sit in the front seat. It is an offence to drive without your licence on your person (another draconian €175 fine). Every car must also carry a first-aid kit, reflective warning triangle and 3-litre fire extinguisher (although hire companies tend to skimp on this). Police checkpoints at major (and minor) junctions are frequent, and in addition to the above offences you can be penalised for not having evidence of insurance, paid road tax or registration papers in/on the vehicle.

Super and normal unleaded petrol, as well as lead-substitute super, are readily available throughout Greece, although filling up after dark can be tricky. Most garages close around 8pm and, although a rota system operates in larger towns, it is often difficult to ascertain which station is open. Petrol stations operated by multinational companies usually take credit cards, but Greek ones like Eko and Jetoil often don't unless they are on heavily travelled routes.

Parking in the larger island towns is uniformly a nightmare; even assuming you find a convenient space, residents-only schemes and pay-and-display systems are the norm. Sometimes tickets are sold from kiosks, sometimes from a machine. When in doubt about a

spot, don't park there – fines are typically €60 and upwards.

Road maps
Gone are the days when visitors had to suffer with mendacious or comical maps that seemed based more on wishful thinking (especially projected but unbuilt roads) than the facts on the ground. There are now three commercial Greek companies producing largely accurate maps of the country: Road Editions, Emvelia and Anavasis. They can be found countrywide, in tourist-shop racks and better bookshop chains like NewsStand or Papasotiriou. Anavasi is generally the best for individual islands, especially for hiking routes, although Road Editions' overview maps of Crete and the Ionian islands are very useful.

Motorcycles and Bicycles
On most Greek islands you will find agencies that hire small motorcycles, various types of scooters, 50cc and under, and even mountain bikes. These give you the freedom to wander where you will, and weekly rates are reasonable.

For any bike of over 50cc, both helmets and a motorcycle driving licence are theoretically required, and increasingly these rules are enforced (although note that a typical UK car driving licence also covers bikes up to 125cc). The ill-fitting helmets offered are a bit of a joke, but if you refuse them you may have to sign a waiver absolving the dealer of criminal/civil liability – and police checkpoints (see above) can be zealous, levying €175 fines on local people and visitors alike for non-usage of helmets.

Before you set off, make sure the bike – of whichever sort – works by taking it for a test spin down the street. Brakes in particular are often mis-set, lights may need new fuses or bulbs, and spark-plugs get fouled. Otherwise, you may get stuck with a

ABOVE: it's preferable to wear a helmet.

lemon, and be held responsible for its malfunctioning when you return it. Reputable agencies now often furnish you with a phone number for a breakdown pick-up service.

Above all, don't take unnecessary chances, like riding two on a bike designed for one. More than one holiday in Greece has been ruined by a serious scooter accident. It is strongly suggested that where possible you stick with traditional scooters of 50–100cc displacement, with skinny, large-radius, well-treaded tyres. The new generation of automatic, button-start *mihanákia/ papákia* (as they're called in Greek slang), with their sexy fairings and tiny, fat, no-tread tyres, may look the business but they are unstable and unsafe once off level asphalt. In particular, if you hit a gravel-strewn curve on one of these you will go for a spill, and at the very least lose most of the skin on your hands and knees. In any case, consider buying a pair of biker's gloves – they can be had for around €20. You may feel stupid wearing them in summer, but you'll feel even more stupid with your hands wrapped in gauze for the balance of your holiday.

Ferry/Catamaran/Hydrofoil Timetables

The best schedule resource is the website of the GTP (Greek Travel Pages), www.gtp.gr, which is fairly accurate, with updates at least every few weeks.

Alternatively, major tourist information offices (Rhodes, Iráklio, etc) supply a weekly schedule, and most offices hang a timetable in a conspicuous place so that you can look up times even if the branch is closed. This should, however, not

be relied on implicitly – last-minute changes are common. In general, for the most complete, impartial and up-to-date information on each port's sailings the best source is the Port Police (in Piraeus and most other ports), known as the *limenarhío*.

Be aware that when you enquire about ferries at a travel agent, they will sometimes inform you only of the lines with which they are affiliated.

TRANSPORT

ACCOMMODATION

EATING OUT

ACTIVITIES

A – Z

LANGUAGE

A CCOMMODATION

HOTELS, INNS, RENTED ROOMS AND CAMPSITES

How to Choose

There is a broad range of accommodation in Greece, from de luxe hotels to campsites. Many hotels, especially in or close to Athens, underwent much-needed upgrading in the run-up to the 2004 Olympic Games, hosted by Greece. Listed are a sample of different categories across the country.

On the islands the main type of affordable lodging is private rented rooms (enikiazómena domátia), which these days are increasingly self-catering studios (if only just a mini-kitchen in the corner) or full-on apartments (diamerísmata). These are classified separately from hotels, but also subject to official regulation.

In general, when looking for any kind of accommodation, local public or private tourist offices can be of help if you are in a fix – most obviously if no rooms are on offer when you disembark at the dock. The best system, though, increasingly used even by backpackers equipped with mobile phones or visiting an internet café, is booking a room yourself a few days (or, in summer, weeks) in advance.

Hotel and Rented-Room Categories

The Greek authorities have six categories for hotels, currently expressed as letters but being gradually replaced by a star system (no-star = E, five-star = de luxe), although this is being resisted by some hoteliers. Although letters/stars are supposed to be an accurate reflection of the hotel's amenities, a swimming pool or tennis court could

place an establishment in the A/4-star or B/3-star bracket even though in every other respect it has indifferent facilities. Also, the number of rooms can limit a hotel's maximum rating, so you commonly encounter 14-room C-class hotels that are superior in every respect to a nearby 50-room B-class.

The following general principles apply, however: Luxury, A-, B- and C-class hotels all have private bathrooms. Most D-class hotels have en suite bathrooms, while the almost extinct E-class hotels don't.

Luxury and A-class hotels must have a bar and at least one restaurant and offer a full choice of breakfasts. B- and C-class should provide a buffet breakfast – "enhanced continental" in substance – at a separate dining room, but classes below that will often offer little better than a bread roll, jam and coffee, if even that.

Luxury and A-class hotels will have some or all of these auxiliary facilities: a swimming pool, fitness centre, sauna and/or health spa, "private" beach, conference hall and other businessperson's amenities, internet access from the rooms or wi-fi signal in the lobby (usually for an extra charge), entertainment programmes for children, 24-hour desk attendance, and "tamed" taxi service. To remain competitive, many B- and C- class hotels offer some kind of internet access, often free.

Traditional Settlements and Restoration Inns

Traditional settlements (paradosiakí ikismí) are villages that have been recognised by the Greek government as forming an important part of the

national heritage, and as such are protected from modern intrusions and constructions by law. Buildings in these villages were variably restored as inns under Tourism Ministry initiative back in the 1970s and 1980s. All of these inns have long since been privatised, although still protected by law. Such houses and villages are, in their different ways, strikingly beautiful, and highly recommended for a long retreat in rural Greece.

Since then, private renovators have brought other, generally higher-quality, inns into service, again rescuing older buildings at risk on a wide range of islands. Restoration inns are known to exist in the following locations, and more are appearing all the time:
Hydra Town (several sponge-captains' mansions, done up as hotels)
Ía, Santoríni (interlinked village houses)
Ermoúpoli, Sýros (many fine Belle Epoque mansions converted to hotels)
Mestá, Híos (several restored houses, as room-only or entire apartments, plus an inn)
Avgónyma and **Volissós**, Híos (entire restored houses for rent)
Kámbos region, Híos (a few restored mansions, usually with restaurant on-site)
Mytilíni, Lésvos (several restored-house inns, from basic to luxurious)
Psará island (basic accommodation in a restored prison)
Rhodes Old Town (several high-quality, and expensive, restoration inns)
Haniá, Crete (many fine restoration inns around the Old Harbour)

Réthymno, Crete (many restored inns in old-town Venetian buildings)
Gialós and **Horió**, Sými (many old houses restored and divided into apartments)
Emborió, Hálki (houses restored and divided into apartments)
Corfu (three restored olive mills or manor houses in remote locations)
For a selection of the above, see the appropriate region under *Accommodation Listings* following.

Booking Direct and Internet Resources

Most of our listings below provide a contact website, which usually also enables direct booking, increasingly common in an era where the clout of package operators is diminishing. Often significant discounts for online booking are offered, and the high-season price category given generally only applies from mid-July to early September, if that; rates usually include breakfast. Although all web bookings require a credit card deposit, the hotel may not accept credit cards for final payment – ask in advance. Hotel evaluation websites like TripAdvisor should be approached with caution – there have been many instances of rival hotels employing

shills (usually identified as "A Reader") to "diss" each other's establishements.

Mountain Refuges, Monasteries, Hostels

Mountain refuges are run by the various Greek mountaineering clubs. The only one in the Greek islands is the popular, well-run Kallérgi hut in Crete's White Mountains, near the Gorge of Samariá (elevation 1,680 metres/5,111ft; tel: 28210 33199).
The *xenónes* (guest lodges) of monasteries or convents are intended primarily for Orthodox pilgrims. About the only ones in the islands routinely used to hosting the heterodox are Kastrianís on Kéa, Skiádi in southern Rhodes, Agíou Ioánni Prodrómou on Hálki, and possibly Goniá on Crete's Rodópou peninsula. You will have to dress appropriately and behave accordingly. Doors may close as early as sunset and some kind of donation may be expected.
Greece has a limited (and steadily dwindling) number of official, YHA-affiliated youth hostels. Surviving hostels are found only in Athens and on Crete at Iráklio, Réthymno and Plakiás. For these you theoretically need a YHA card; however, you can

often buy a card on the spot or just pay an additional charge for the night. There is also private, unaffiliated hostel-type accommodation of varying quality and repute in Athens and on Corfu.

Camping

Numbers of visitors to Greece still rough it in one form or another, whether by sleeping on the deck of overnight ferries or setting up camp by a secluded beach. Organised, privately managed campsites in the islands are limited, however, to Santoríni, Sífnos, Sýros, Páros, Náxos, Íos, Lésvos and Corfu.
The most beautiful campsites in Greece, however, are usually the ones you find on your own. While in most places it is officially illegal just to pitch a tent or park a camper van, if you are discreet you will rarely be bothered, especially in peak season when there are often no rooms to be had. That always means asking permission from the owners of the land if you seem to be on private property, avoiding unofficial campsites set up in popular tourist areas (which can get pretty squalid), and always leaving the place looking better than it did when you arrived.

ATHENS

Acropolis View
Webster 10 and Robértou Gáli, Makrygiánni
Tel: 21092 17303
www.acropolisview.gr
The implied view of the Acropolis is available from only a few of the 32 rooms, but also from the roof terrace. The rooms themselves are small but clean and well cared for, and the hotel has had the inevitable pre-Olympic makeover. The quiet but metro-handy location is excellent. €€
Airotel Alexandros
Timoléondos Vássou 8, Ambelókipi
Tel: 21064 30464
www.airotel.gr
Located on a private crescent behind a chapel which helps shield it from

busy Vassilísis Sofías, this comfortable accommodation belies a slightly forbidding exterior. The high-ceiling lounge is flanked by the brick-and-pastel-panelled breakfast salon, doubling later in the day as the Don Giovanni restaurant. Most fair-sized rooms have notably firm beds, and deep balconies which ensure privacy; baths are small but marble-clad. Free off-street parking; wi-fi signal. €€
Athens Backpackers
Makrí 12, Makrygiánni
Tel: 21092 24044
www.backpackers.gr
Newest established (2005) of several hostels in the city, this Australian/Greek-run outfit is certainly the best

located (near Akrópoli metro) and liveliest, with popular roof bar, free wi-fi throughout and a few apartments as well as rather plain but clean multi-bed dorms. €
Cecil
Athinás 39, Centre
Tel: 21032 17079
www.cecil.gr
A well-restored 1850s vintage mansion has become a characterful small hotel, right down to its iron-cage, inter-war lift. For preservation reasons, varied-decor rooms only have ornamental balconies, but they offer parquet floors, iron bedsteads, double glazing, pastel colours on a blue base, and re-tiled baths. Common areas

include a first-floor breakfast room with original wooden floor and painted ceiling, a roof garden and a street-level café. €€

PRICE CATEGORIES

Price categories are for a double room for one night in high season:
€ = under $70
€€ = $70–140
€€€ = over $140

Grande Bretagne
Sýndagma Square
Tel: 21033 30000
www.grandebretagne.gr
Perhaps the most famous hotel in Athens, oozing history and class, the Grande Bretagne is an neoclassical building dating originally from 1846. A 2002–3 renovation restored every period detail to its Belle Epoque glory. Highlights of the common areas include the seventh-floor pool-garden, the basement spa (best in town) and the bar with its 18th-century tapestry of Alexander the Great. Rooms are large, typically 35–40 sq metres (375–430 sq ft). Ultra-expensive, of course: never much less than €350 per night. €€€€

Hera
Falírou 9, Makrygiánni
Tel: 21092 36682
www.herahotel.gr
Yet another result of the wave of pre-Olympic upgradings, the Hera has perhaps the best roof-garden in this neighbourhood, with (unusually) a heated bar-restaurant for all-year operation up top. Rooms themselves are on the small side but have everything you'd expect in this (A) class; fifth-floor suites have bigger balconies (though bathrooms are much the

same throughout). The dome-lit atrium-breakfast room, and friendly staff, are further assets. €€€

Hermes
Apóllonos 19
Tel: 21032 35514
www.hermeshotel.gr
The Hermes has all-marble baths (variable in size) in the oak-effect floored rooms, which also vary; front-facing ones are smaller but face a communal terrace. The rear ones don't but are larger, some with sofas. The mezzanine breakfast room is decorated with group manager Dorína Stathopoúlou's professional photographs of the 2004 Olympics. The relaxing street-level lounge-bar is naturally lit by a light well. If they're full, you'll be offered space in one of their three affiliated hotels nearby. €€

Marble House
A. Zínni 35, Koukáki
Tel: 21092 28294
www.marblehouse.gr
This inexpensive, clean and friendly hotel near Pláka is one of the best deals in Athens. Close to the Syngroú-Fix metro. Some rooms now have air-conditioning (the others have powerful ceiling fans), most have balconies, and breakfast is available for an extra charge. It was renovated in 2003–4 and,

given its low rates, advance booking is mandatory. After-hours arrivals must make special entry arrangements. €

Museum
Bouboulínas 16, Exárhia
Tel: 21052 38038
www.museum-hotel.gr
Since acquisition by the Best Western chain, the Museum has had its original rooms redone and a new wing of larger units added. The standard rooms are on the small side, inevitably with the feel of an American hotel, but the junior suites are spacious, and their bathrooms are a notable improvement on the standards. The executive suites will suit most tastes, with completely marble-clad bathrooms. No restaurant; breakfast given in the bar, which is slightly below ground level. Free wi-fi. €€

Orion/Dryades
Emmanouíl Benáki 105/Dryádon 4, Exárhia
Tel: 21033 02387
www.orion-dryades.com
Two co-managed, almost adjacent hotels (joint reception in the Orion) serve a younger crowd who have outgrown hostels but still like to take advantage of this inexpensive accommodation, with self-catering kitchens in each well-maintained building. Some bathrooms are down

the hall in the Orion, but the pricier Dryades is fully en suite, though wood panelling makes rooms a tad on the gloomy side. Some have balconies with views. €

Phaedra
Herofóndos 16
Tel: 21032 38461
www.hotelphaedra.com
At the junction of two usually quiet pedestrian streets, the Phaedra offers the best-value budget accommodation in Pláka. While not all the cheerfully tile-floored roooms are en suite, each has an allocated bathroom, while some have balconies overlooking a square with a Byzantine church. Breakfast (optional) served in pleasant ground-floor salon. €

St George Lycabettus
Kleoménous 2, Kolonáki
Tel: 21072 90711
www.sglycabettus.gr
Since its pre-Olympics refit, the St George has styled itself as a boutique hotel, oriented towards business-people. The cool, comfortable rooms and suites are elegant but subdued, while the rooftop pool is a big selling point. Southwest-facing rooms and suites (more expensive) have one of the best views in the city. Basement sauna and gym, two restaurants on-site and free off-street parking. €€€

CORFU

There are almost 500 licensed hotels on the island, although many remain in the firm grip of tour operators from May to October, closing in winter. The following are open off-season and/or to independent travellers. Additionally, if you have a car, you can usually find apartments on a walk-in basis at the less packaged resorts of Astrakerí, Kalamáki, Afiónas and Aríllas in the north, plus Paramónas and Boúkari in the southwest.

Kérkyra Town and around

Bella Venezia
Napoleóndos Zambéli 4
Tel: 26610 46500
www.bellaveneziahotel.com
A neoclassical mansion renovated in 2006, well adapted as a B-class hotel set in a central yet quiet location on the south edge of town. The rooms are quite plush, but there is no swimming pool or any extra amenities except a large patio garden with a bar. Open all year. €€

Corfu Palace
Dhimokratías 2, north end of Garítsa Bay
Tel: 26610 39485
www.corfupalace.com
This is the town's only "lux" class establishment, and it enjoys a high level of repeat clientele, including VIPs and foreign dignitaries, especially in May and September, when advanced bookings should be made. They come for the huge rooms with marble bathtubs, the big breakfasts and the assiduous level of service. Open all year. €€€

Grecotel Corfu Imperial
Komméno
Tel: 26610 88400
www.grecotel.com
Perhaps the best and most contemporarily decorated hotel on the island, and

ABOVE: elegant luxury at the Grande Bretagne, Athens.

stratospherically expensive. Three grades of accommodation: standard rooms, bungalows, and a few super-luxe villas with their own pools. All the facilities you would expect for the price. €€€

Konstantinoupolis
Zavitsiánou 11, Old Port
Tel: 26610 48716
www.konstantinoupolis.gr
An 1862 building, once a backpackers' dosshouse, now lovingly restored as a well-priced two-star hotel with sea and mountain views. Comfortable rooms done in pastel colours with light-wood furniture, cosy common areas, lift, free wi-fi; open all year. €€

Kontokali Bay Resort and Spa
Kontókali
Tel: 26610 99000
www.kontokalibay.com
Slightly more affordable and larger than the Corfu Palace, consisting of a hotel wing and bungalows in a leafy environment with two "private" beaches and three pools. The 2007-built spa is one of the most sumptuous on the island. Lots of facilities for kids, including one of the pools. €€€

Siorra Vittoria
Sofías Pandová 36, Kérkyra Town

Tel: 26610 36300
www.siorravittoria.com
Opened in 2005, this boutique hotel in an 1823-vintage mansion is still in the hands of the same family. Just nine stylish rooms and suites, some interconnecting for families, have beamed ceilings, flat-screen TVs and tasteful Belle Epoque furnishings. The best unit, with a view of the Néo Froúrio, is the top-floor suite. Open all year. €€€

Centre-west of Corfu

Casa Lucia
Sgómbou hamlet, at Km 12 of Kérkyra–Paleokastrítsa road
Tel: 26610 91419
Fax: 26610 91732
www.casa-lucia-corfu.com
Peaceful setting at the very centre of the island, which usually hosts special-interest holidays (yoga, t'ai chi, alternative therapies). This restored olive-mill complex is set among lovingly tended gardens and comprises 11 units ranging from studios to family cottages. Most have kitchens, all share a large pool; furnishings are resolutely 1980s. Open

Apr–Oct; winter lets also available. €€

Fundana Villas
Accessed by side road from Km 17 of Kérkyra–Paleokastrítsa road
Tel: 26630 22532
www.fundanavillas.com
Another 1980s restoration inn, this time converted from a 17th-century manor, with a commanding ridge-top position in the middle of a gorgeous nowhere. Units from double studios to family apartments; most have brick-and-flagstone floors; several adjoin the pool. The old olive-press works have become an informal museum. Open Apr–Oct. €€

Levant Hotel
Above Pélekas, right beside "Kaiser's Throne"
Tel: 26610 94230
www.levanthotel.com
A 1990s hotel in traditional style, with superb views both east and west over the island. Rooms are wood-floored, baths marble-trimmed, ground-floor common areas faux-rustic. There's a small pool, and some of the island's best beaches a few kilometres away; an overnight stop to plan on if hiking the Corfu Trail. Open Apr–Oct. €€

Liapades Beach Hotel
Liapádes
Tel: 06630 41370
www.liapadesbeachhotel.gr
Two smallish wings of studios and larger apartments make up this amiable C-class hotel at one of the quieter beach resorts on this coast. Should you not wish to self-cater, there is an affiliated taverna. Open Apr–Oct. €€

Pelekas Country Club
Km 8 of Kérkyra–Pélekas road
Tel: 22610 52239
www.country-club.gr
Corfu's most exclusive rural hotel since 1992, just 26 units occupying an 18th-century mansion in over 25 hectares (60 acres) of landscaped grounds. The outbuildings are self-catering studios and suites, all different and antique-furnished. Stylish breakfasts in the central refectory;

pool, tennis, helipad. Open Jan–Nov. €€€

The north of the island

Kalami Tourist Services
Tel: 26630 91062
www.kalamibay.com
An offshoot of the celebrated Nikolas taverna at Agní Cove, with the same family arranging quality accommodation (studios, apartments, free-standing cottages) on the surrounding hillsides. €€

Villa de Loulia
Perouládes, 500 metres/yds from beach
Tel: 26630 95394
Email: villadeloulia@yahoo.com
The third of Corfu's rural restoration inns, this 1803 mansion has been refurbished with high-standard furnishings and fittings in the four grades of rooms/suites. The bar, restaurant, lounge and breakfast area are in a separate structure flanking the large pool. Heating but only fans, no air-con. You pay for the exclusivity. Open Mar–Oct. €€–€€€

The south of the island

Boukari Beach
Boúkari, 4km (2½ miles) beyond Messongí
Tel: 26620 51791
Fax: 26620 51792
www.boukaribeach.gr
Two sets of sea-view A-class apartments sleeping up to four, with all amenities including coffee machines, just a few paces from the excellent co-managed restaurant. The same family also has a larger, co-managed hotel, renovated in 2004 in somewhat IKEA style but with sea views from all rooms. Open Apr–Oct. €€

PRICE CATEGORIES

Price categories are for a double room for one night in high season:
€ = under $70
€€ = $70–140
€€€ = over $140

THE IONIAN ISLANDS

Itháki

For rooms or villas across the island, contact one of these two travel agencies:

Delas
Tel: 26740 32104
www.ithaca.com.gr

Polyctor
Tel: 26740 33120
www.ithakiholidays.com

Captain Yiannis
East quay, Vathý
Tel: 26740 33311
www.captainyiannis.com
The closest thing to an exclusive "resort" on the island, with just 11 self-catering units (and 12 standard rooms, with white-tile-and-pine decor) set in ample walled grounds with a pool and tennis court. €€

Captain's Apartments
Kióni
Tel: 26740 31481
www.captains-apartments.gr
Set up on the hillside towards Ráhi hamlet, with commanding views of the bay, each spacious, air-conditioned studio has a good-sized full kitchen, cable TV, heating for winter use and a veranda; there is also a communal garden to relax in. €€

Nostos
About 200 metres/yds inland from the quay, Fríkes
Tel: 26740 31644
www.hotelnostos-ithaki.gr
Smallish but upmarket C-class hotel with a large pool, where most rooms look over a field towards the sunrise; renovated in 2007, although the rooms' appointments still don't quite match the setting and common areas. €€

Perantzada 1811 Art Hotel
Odysséa Androútsou, Vathý
Tel: 26740 33496
www.arthotel.gr
Chic and fairly expensive but by far the loveliest hotel in Vathý, in a renovated 19th-century mansion that survived the 1953 quake. The 19 understated and tasteful rooms (six in a new wing, added in 2007) have been individually designed and are very comfortable.

Not on the harbour front itself (and so quieter than some other places), the rooms look out over pretty rooftops to the sea. Breakfasts are excellent. €€€

Kefaloniá

Agnantia Apartments
28084 Tselendáta, Fiskárdo
Tel: 26740 51801–2
www.agnantia.com
Very well maintained and beautifully located (although a little way out of Fiskárdo), this apart-hotel stacked up on a hillside makes a lovely place to stay. As well as friendly and efficient service, the units are tasteful and comfortable with a small kitchen area, and most have a balcony with wonderful views over to Itháki. A good, and generous, breakfast is included. €€€

The Architect's House
Asos
Book through: Simply Ionian
Tel: 00 44 020 8451 2202
www.simplytravel.co.uk
This lovely traditional building, one of the few places to stay in Asos itself, has three double bedrooms to rent and is down by the harbour. There is plenty of space – a separate living room and kitchen – and the beach and good places to eat are close by. €€

Emelisse Art Hotel
Émblisi, near Fiskárdo
Tel/fax: 26740 41200
www.arthotel.gr
Expensive and chic, this boutique hotel (one of the small Tsímaras chain that has several properties in this part of Greece, including the Perantzada on Itháki) is set in a traditional building. The well-designed rooms and suites (in six grades) have luxurious bathrooms, and the infinity pool – one of six on site – has a lovely view. For this sort of money you expect to be pampered, and the service lives up to expectations. €€€

Ionian Plaza
Platía Vallianoú, Argostóli
Tel: 26710 25581
www.ionianplaza.gr
Excellent-value C-class designer hotel, the better of two similar ones on this square, with modern bathrooms and balconies overlooking the palm-studded square; the rooms are on the small side, but the bathrooms are well appointed and the staff friendly. Open all year. €€

La Cité
Lixoúri
Tel: 26710 92701
Fax: 26710 92702
This compact hotel four blocks in from the seafront has been completely renovated with stylish furnishings to add a touch of the French ambience its name suggests. Large swimming pool, well-kept gardens and a quiet but convenient location make it about the best option in town. €€

Moustakis Hotel
Agía Evfimía
Tel: 26740 61060/61030
www.moustakishotel.com
Smallish and tucked away behind the harbour front, this is the only bona fide hotel in town and one of the more pleasant, if bland, accommodation options. All rooms have air-con and balconies. Discounts are available for long stays. €€

Panas Hotel
Kilmatsiá Beach, Spartiá
Tel: 26710 69941
www.panas-kefalonia.com
A largish but very pleasant B-class hotel southeast of Argostóli on Lourdáta Bay, close to a decent beach, accessed through well-kept gardens. The rooms, all with balconies, are fine if a little plain. There are good facilities for children, including their own pool and play area. There are also a couple of restaurants and a poolside bar. €€

Regina's
Fiskárdo
Tel/fax: 26740 41125
Most of the smallish but

well-maintained rooms in this family-run guesthouse at the back of the village have balconies looking towards the harbour or across the pleasant courtyard. Better value and less snooty than many establishments here. €

Tara Beach
Skála
Tel: 26710 83341
www.tarabeach.gr
A large but unobstrusive hotel right on the excellent beach. The rooms are furnished to a slightly higher standard than usual (eg faux-antique beds), and if you feel too lazy to walk the few metres to the sea, there is a good pool in the lush gardens, beside which is a handy bar. €€–€€€

Trapezaki Bay Hotel
Trapezáki
Tel: 26710 31501
www.trapezakibayhotel.gr
Perched on the hillside just five minutes' walk from the eponymous beach, this 33-unit hotel run by a returned Greek-American couple, the heart and soul of the place, is only 1999-vintage but has already been renovated once. All the standard amenities, including restaurant and pool. Better value in high summer because prices are fixed for the entire season. €€ rooms, €€€ suites

White Rocks Hotel and Bungalows
Platýs Gialós, Argostóli
Tel: 26710 28332–5
Fax: 26710 28755
www.whiterocks.gr
Large, A-class resort hotel and bungalow complex, 1970s-vintage but well updated, behind the closest of three good local beaches

– there's a pool but you won't need it. Obliging staff and decent restaurants complete the picture. €€€

Kýthira

Kýthira has a short season, with most accommodation only open from May to October; advance booking is recommended. In case of difficulty, consult the following booking agent:
Porfyra Travel
Livádhi, Kýthira
Tel: 27360 31888
www.kythira.info
Porto Delfino
Kapsáli
Tel: 27360 31940–1
www.portodelfino.gr
A pleasant bungalow complex with views over the bay, Avgó islet and Hóra. Large infinity pool and spacious common areas; the rooms are plainly furnished but fairly large. €€–€€€
Xenonas Keiti
Hóra
Tel: 27360 31318
Lovely accommodation in – for a change – non-smoking rooms, set in a rambling 18th-century mansion. The hotel has a remarkably distinguished guest list, including a few Greek premiers. €€
Xenonas Porfyra
Potamós
Tel: 27360 33329
Fax: 27360 33924
Just eight studios, arranged around a pretty, walled courtyard in characterful Potamós. Unusually, it is open most of the year. €€

Levkáda

Nefeli
Agios Nikítas
Tel: 26450 97400
www.nefelihotel.gr
An attractive small hotel, with just 20 rooms, of which four are studios with kitchenettes. Rooms have small verandas with sea views. €€
Ostria
North approach road, Agios Nikítas
Tel: 26450 97483
Fax: 26450 97300

The 1970s-built rooms of this *pension* can be cell-like, but are enlivened by terracotta floor tiles, dried flowers and wall art. It's the unobstructed balcony views of the Ionian (save from four rooms) and the cool, trendy common areas (including a terrace bar open to all) that make the place a delight. The breakfast isn't always up to scratch. €€
Panorama
Atháni
Tel: 26450 33291
Fax: 26450 33476
One of the island's true hideouts: simple, clean rooms above an excellent grill-restaurant. There are superb views, and this is as close as you can stay to the stunning beaches of Gialós, Egremní and Pórto Katsíki – although you will still need your own transport to reach them. €
Porto Lygia
Lygiá
Tel: 26450 72000
www.portoligia.gr
Perched on a promontory away from traffic, with a lawn leading down to its own pebble beach, this B-class resort is a good choice for a seaside stay near (but not in) Levkáda Town. Rooms have blue-and-white livery and modern furnishings, although not all of them face the sea. €€
Santa Maura/Ayia Mavra
Spyrídonos Viánda 2, Levkáda Town
Tel: 26450 21308
Fax: 26450 26253
A pagoda-like period piece: it has a pre-earthquake ground floor, wood and corrugated tin upstairs. Rooms have air-con, double glazing, traditional shutters, balconies; lovely breakfast salon and garden patio. €€

Paxí

Paxos Beach Hotel
Gáïos
Tel: 26620 31211
www.paxosbeachhotel.gr
A hillside bungalow complex from where there is a path leading down through trees to its own small pebble beach about 2km (1 mile)

east of town. It's worth getting the higher three of five grades of unit. Closes early October. €€ standard room, €€€ suites
Planos Holidays
Lákka
Tel: 26620 31744
Tel: (UK) 01373 814200
www.planos.co.uk
One of two booking agencies in this little port, efficiently handling everything from basic studios to luxury villas.

Zákynthos

Ionian Star Hotel
Alykés
Tel: 26950 83416/83658
www.ionian-star.gr
A smallish and very well-kept hotel, with just 25 rooms. They are plain but spotless, refurbished in 2006, and offer excellent value. There is also a restaurant that concentrates on Greek food. €€
Levantino Studio Apartments
Nine km (5 miles) from Vasilikós
Tel: 26950 35366
www.levantino.gr
Ten quiet and attractive apartments set right behind a beach at the far end of the Vasilikós peninsula. All are equipped with a kitchen and some of them look out over the garden (which has a bar) and the sea. €€, low season internet offers €
Nobelos Apartments
Agios Nikólaos
Tel: 26950 27632/31400
www.nobelos.gr
These luxury apartments in the north of the island are eye-wateringly expensive but quite lovely. The four tastefully decorated suites are in a traditional stone-built house, each with an individual character. Along with excellent service, a good breakfast is provided and there is a secluded bay close by. €€€
Palatino
Kolokotróni 10 and Kolyvá
Zákynthos Town
Tel: 26950 27780
www.palatinohotel.gr
The Palatino is one of

Zákynthos Town's best-value options, stylish and well run. The rooms, designed principally for business travellers, are decent with all the trimmings, and the hotel as a whole has been well cared for. A buffet breakfast is provided, and there is also a restaurant. €€
Pansion Limni
Límni Kerioú
Tel: 26950 48716
www.pansionlimni.com
A friendly place in the far southwest, where guests are presented with bottles of home-made wine and olive oil. There is a new, higher-standard annexe, Porto tis Ostrias, with some large family apartments, 150 metres/yds along the beach from the original pension. € Limni, €€ Porto tis Ostrias
Porto Koukla Beach Hotel
Lithakiá
Tel: 26950 52393
www.pavlos.gr
A decent, large hotel at the far southwestern end of Laganás Bay. Popular with German and Austrian tour-group visitors, it is well away from the tawdriness further east. The gardens back onto a narrow beach, which is overlooked by the hotel's excellent, and cheap, taverna. €€
Sirocco Hotel
Kalamáki
Tel: 26950 26083
www.siroccohotel.gr
This is a very acceptable and peaceful option for Kalamáki, and the renovated and stylish standard rooms are reasonably priced, especially out of season; there are also superior rooms and four-person apartments. A large pool is set in an attractive garden, although the beach is not too far away. €€

PRICE CATEGORIES

Price categories are for a double room for one night in high season:
€ = under $70
€€ = $70–140
€€€ = over $140

Villa Katerina
Pórto Róma, Vasilikós
Tel: 26950 35456 (summer)
Tel: 26950 27230 (winter)
www.villakaterina.com
These two buildings, set in pretty gardens, offer studios both large and small, as well as two-bedroom apartments. It's within walking distance from Gérakas as well as Pórto Róma beach, the units are

very quiet, and the surrounding area is lovely, making it an excellent and fairly inexpensive choice. Studios €, apartments €€
Windmill/Anemomilos
Korithí, Cape Skinári
Tel: 26950 31132
www.potamitisbros.gr
Two converted windmills sleeping two to four people, along with four spacious rooms in a stone house

located at the far north end of the island, and close to the Blue Caves (to which the hotel management offers boat trips). This is a great get-away-from-it-all option.
€€
Zante Palace
Tsiliví
Tel: 26950 490490
www.zantepalace.com
This huge hotel, which opened in 2001, is on the

bluff overlooking Tsiliví Bay, giving great views across to Kefaloniá. The studios and one- or two-bedroom apartments (which look out over the bay) are good value, and there is an optional breakfast available. If you can't be bothered to walk down to the pleasant beach you can swim in the nicely sited pool. €€

THE SARONIC GULF

Aegina

Aeginitiko Archontiko
Égina Town, Junction Thomaïdou and Agíou Nikoláou
Tel: 22970 24968
www.aeginitikoarchontiko.gr
Converted neoclassical mansion-inn that preserves most period details, including a painted ceiling in the suite. The building, however, has been here since the 1700s, and early last century hosted such luminaries as local saint Nektários and poet Kóstas Várnalis. The old conservatory is now the breakfast hall. €€
Antzi Studios
Pérdika
Tel: 22970 61233
www.antzistudios.gr
A hillside complex spread over three wings (two stone-built), around a pool. The individual units in light pastel colours are done up to a very high standard, especially the bathrooms, without being pretentious. You can choose between more basic studios and proper apartments accommodating four people. All have sea views, and heating, making them options for winter use. €€ studio, €€€ apartment
Brown Hotel
Égina Town
Tel: 22970 22271
www.hotelbrown.gr
Right opposite the southerly town beach, a five-minute walk from the ferry quay, is this converted sponge

factory, now a hotel still owned by the original family, whose ancestry was partly English (hence the name). The common areas, rather than the adequate but unexceptional rooms, garner the B-class/3-star rating; the garden bungalows are quieter and desirable. €€

Angístri

Rosy's Little Village
South end of Skála, at clifftop
Tel: 22970 91610
www.rosyslittlevillage.com
There is a 1980s feel to this family-friendly resort with basic but adequate rooms, decorated in pastel shades, private pebble-strewn lido below, and decent on-site restaurant with a Greek menu despite a largely British clientele. € room, €€ house

Hydra

Bratsera
200 metres/yds in from centre quay Hydra Town
Tel: 22980 53971
www.bratserahotel.com
The top comfort and room size available on the island are at this A-class/4-star hotel occupying a former sponge factory. Vast common areas (bar, restaurant, conference room and medium-sized pool) serve as a de facto museum of the industry, with photos and artefacts. There are six grades of rooms and suites to choose

from. Open late Mar–end Oct. €€€
Miranda
Hydra Town
Tel: 22980 52230
www.mirandahotel.gr
Set in a mansion built in 1810, Miranda is a restoration hotel, with 14 differently decorated rooms: some traditional, others Art Deco. The classy atmosphere is enhanced by the in-house art gallery. Breakfast is served in the courtyard garden. Open Mar–Oct. €€€
Pityoussa
Hydra Town, southeast edge
Tel: 22980 52810
www.piteoussa.com
The best of the mid-range options, Pityoussa's designer units have CD/DVD players, mock-antique furnishings and modernised bathrooms, and most have balconies (or a private courtyard in the case of the "superior"-grade rooms). No breakfast is provided, however. €€

Póros

Manessi
Póros Town
Tel: 22980 22273
www.manessi.com
A neoclassical conversion hotel refurbished in 2008 to a high standard – soundproofing (necessary as you are opposite the main ferry dock), swag curtains, plush bedspreads, butler sinks and flat-screen televisions. Front rooms have balconies looking over the port. €€

Pavlou
Megálo Neório, Kalávria
Tel: 22980 22734
www.pavlouhotel.gr
Family-friendly hotel with a tennis court and pool, overlooking one of Kalávria's better beaches; both the very acceptable on-site restaurant and the comfortable rooms, most with unobstructed sea views, were renovated in 2007 to offer what is probably the best standard on the island. €€
Sto Roloï
Hatzopoúlou and Karrá 13
Póros Town
Tel: 22980 25808
Fax: 210 963 3705
www.storoloi-poros.gr
Póros's only traditional house restoration complex is located near the prominent hilltop clock tower (rolói), in a 200-year-old dwelling converted into three apartments. There are two more next door at Anemone House and the Little Tower, plus the more remote Limeri House and Studio, set around a pool. All retain period features such as Belle Epoque tiling, but are furnished with

reproduction traditional furnishings. Studios €€, houses €€€

Spétses

Armata Boutique Hotel
Inland from Dápia on pedestrian lane
Tel: 22980 72683
www.armatahotel.gr
A converted mansion hotel,

opened in 2004, with 20 very plush rooms, copious breakfast and (unusually for the island) a pool. €€€
Economou Mansion
Kounoupítsa shore
Tel: 22980 73400
www.spetsesyc.gr/economoumansion.htm
This is another restoration inn, occupying part of an

1851-vintage property. The ground floor of the main house has six well-converted rooms retaining ample period features; an outbuilding hosts two luxury sea-view suites. Breakfast is served by the fair-sized pool. €€€ but frequent internet/low season specials

Yachting Club Inn
Kounoupítsa. Under the same management as the Economou (phones identical; www.spetsesyc.gr/yachtingclubinn.htm), offers relatively modest accommodation in bland modern style but does have good views from the top floor and (unusually) is open all year. €€

THE CYCLADES

Amorgós

Aigialis
Órmos Egiális
Tel: 22850 73393
www.amorgos-aegialis.com
Modern, comfortable hotel built in tiers on the north hillside beyond the bay, with stunning views. Most rooms (in two grades) have been refurbished since 2006; there is a large outdoor pool and a decent restaurant, plus a stunning indoor spa and pool used year-round by local people – a telling accolade. €€€
Pagali Hotel
Langáda
Tel: 22850 73310
www.pagalihotel-amorgos.com
Assorted, large, white-decor rooms and studios in one of the more attractive villages of the island, often booked by special-interest groups. A main advantage is an excellent affiliated restaurant next door. €€
Panorama Studios & Pension
Hóra
Tel: 22850 74016
http://panorama-studios.amorgos.net
A mix of ordinary double rooms and self-catering studios in a commanding position, of a standard one notch up from the normal island decor of cheap pine furniture and white tiles. €€–€€€

Anáfi

Ta Plagia
Hóra
Tel: 22860 61308
www.taplagia.gr
The best accommodation

on the island (admittedly, there is not a huge amount of competition for this title), in a mix of rooms, studios and cottages with stunning views. Breakfast with local ingredients, and evening drinks and *mezédes*, offered in the on-site café. €

Andíparos

Mantalena
Kástro
Tel: 22840 61206
www.hotelmantalena.gr
High-standard rooms on the waterfront, with good views of the harbour and across to Páros; the same management also has studios, apartments and a small house in the village centre. €€

Andros

Andros Holiday Hotel
Gávrio
Tel: 22820 71384/71443
www.androsholidayhotel.com
Close to the sea, with panoramic views of the Aegean from all rooms, which were refurbished in 2007, with parquet floors and upgraded furniture. Common areas include a swimming pool, tennis courts, conference facilities and restaurant. €€
Eleni Mansion
Hóra
Tel: 22820 22270
www.elenimansion.gr
One of several boutique hotels in the town converted from 19th-century neoclassical mansions, this eight-room outfit has period furnishings and is located

on a quieter pedestrian street. €€
Paradise Lifestyle Hotel
Hóra outskirts, 800 metres/yds from the centre
Tel: 22820 22187
www.paradiseandros.gr
Partly occupying another old mansion, this 4-star outfit – twinned with the St George Lycabettus in Athens – is arguably the island's top lodging. The "Lifestyle" of the name refers to the swimming pool, tennis courts and airy balconied rooms, most of which have sea views. €€€

Folégandros

Anemomylos
Hóra
Tel: 22860 41309
www.anemomilosapartments.com
A fully equipped apartment complex built in traditional Cycladic style around a courtyard. Sweeping views from the balconies overhanging the cliff edge.€€€
Fani-Vevis
Hóra
Tel/fax: 22860 41282
Comfortable hotel in a neoclassical mansion house with 11 rooms, some overlooking the sea. €€
Castro
Hóra
Tel: 22860 41230
www.hotel-castro.com
A 500-year-old traditional house that is actually part of the ancient *kástro* walls. Quaint rooms have pebble-mosaic floors, barrel ceilings and spectacular views down sheer cliffs to the sea. €€

Ios

Acropolis
Mylopótas
Tel: 22860 91303
www.hotelacropolis.gr
Tiled rooms with 1980s decor and balconies or flagstoned terraces, in a blue-shuttered building overlooking the beach below, which is five minutes' walk away. €€
Ios Palace
Mylopótas
Tel: 22860 91269
www.iospalacehotel.com
Four-star hillside complex renovated in 2005, with comfortable, minimalist rooms in three grades, marble-lined bathrooms and balconies overlooking the sea. €€€

Kéa

Kea Beach
Koúndouros Bay
Tel: 22880 31230
Fax: 22880 31234
Luxury bungalow complex

PRICE CATEGORIES

Price categories are for a double room for one night in high season:
€ = under $70
€€ = $70–140
€€€ = over $140

5km (3 miles) south of Písses, the largest of several here, with all facilities from a nightclub to water sports. €€€

Porto Kea Suites
Livádi district, Korissía
Tel: 22880 22870
www.portokea-suites.com
Well-designed bungalow hotel, arrayed around a pool, mimicking local architectural elements with its stone cladding. The top standard on the island. €€€

Kýthnos

Porto Klaras
Loutrá
Tel: 22810 31276
www.porto-klaras.gr
State-of-the-art mod cons combined with tasteful real and reproduction antique furnishings in these newish studios and apartments, set in lovely tiered grounds overlooking the bay. €€

Mílos

Kapetan Tassos
Apollónia
Tel: 22870 41287
www.kapetantassos.gr
Designer apartments in traditional blue-and-white island architecture, with good sea views; 11km (7 miles) from Adamás, so you need transport. €€

Panorama
Klíma
Tel: 22870 21623
www.panorama-milos.com
Small seafront hotel, with simple, 1980s-style rooms. The main advantages are friendly family management and an on-site taverna. €

Windmills
Trypití
www.milos-island.gr/windmill/windmills.html
Six converted medieval windmills with beautiful views towards Adamás port. Most accommodate four people. €€€

Mýkonos

Cavo Tagoo
Hóra
Tel: 22890 23692

www.cavotagoo.gr
Jet-set luxury on a hillside 500 metres/yds north of Hóra. Beautiful furnishings, prize-winning Cycladic architecture, impeccable service, friendly atmosphere, good views, pool, and one of Mýkonos's best restaurants. €€€

Deliades
Ornós Beach
Tel: 22890 79430
www.hoteldeliadesmykonos.com
Built in 2001 with quiet good taste, a short walk up the hill from Ornós beach. Every room has a big terrace with sea view. Relaxed atmosphere, pool, on-site restaurant. €€€

Myconian Inn
Hóra
Tel: 22890 23420
www.myconianinn.com
On the upper edge of town, this hotel is convenient, quiet, unpretentious and tasteful. Balconies overlook the port. €€

Villa Konstantin
Agios Vasílios
Tel: 22890 26204
www.villakonstantin.com
700 metres/yds from town, in authentic island style but with all the luxuries. All units have terraces, most with sea views; some have kitchens, and many are suitable for groups or families. €€

Náxos

Apollon
Hóra
Tel: 22850 22468
www.naxostownhotels.com
An efficient, convenient place to stay in town with parking, on the picturesque pedestrianised museum square by the cathedral in Fondána district. Open all year. €€

Chateau Zevgoli
Hóra
Tel: 22850 26123
www.naxostownhotels.com
Quiet, plush and exclusive, high up in the kástro. A Venetian mansion with only 10 rooms, each lovingly decorated. One has a four-poster bed, most have great views. Open Mar–Nov. €€€

Iria Beach Art Hotel
Agía Anna
Tel: 22850 42600
www.iriabeach-naxos.com
The "art" tag is a clue to the designer suites (there are very few "standard" rooms here) that emerged from the 2008 refurbishment. Decor is warm rather than minimalist, however, and clearly pitched at the honeymoon market. €€€

Páros

Astir of Paros
Náoussa, Kolymbíthres beach
Tel: 22840 51986
www.astirofparos.com
One of Greece's finest de luxe hotels, right on the beach, across the bay from the town. Spacious rooms with balconies, and bathrooms lined with Parian marble. There is a large pool, golf course and extensive gardens. €€€

Dina
Parikía
Tel: 22840 21325
www.hoteldina.com
The Dina is a friendly hotel in the heart of the Old Town. Spotlessly clean rooms set around a lovely flowered courtyard. Only eight rooms, so book early. €

Pandrossos Hotel
Parikía
Tel: 22840 22903
www.pandrossoshotel.gr
On a pretty hill at Parikía's edge, yet in town. Beautiful views of the bay, pool, good restaurant, eclectic pastel rooms. €€

Santoríni

Aigialos Houses
Firá
Tel: 22860 25191
www.aigialos.gr
Every house is different in this complex, but all are tastefully luxurious, quiet and convenient, and have spectacular views, with balconies or terraces overlooking the caldera. €€€

Atlantis Villas
Ia
Tel: 22860 71214
www.atlantisvillas-santorini.com

These traditionally furnished cave-apartments are situated many white steps down the Ía cliffside. Very friendly, with all services, and caldera views from terrace and pool. €€€

Fanari Villas
Ia
Tel: 22860 71007–8
www.fanarivillas.com
Traditional skaftá (dug-out) cave houses converted into luxury accommodation. Pool, breakfast terrace, bar and 240 steps down to Ammoúdi Bay. Attentive, friendly service. €€€

Katikies
Ia
Tel: 22860 71401
Fax: 22860 71129
www.katikies.com
One of the best places to stay on the island. Lovely new apartments built on a clifftop in traditional style, spectacular views and a wonderful pool. Excellent service. €€€

Rose Bay
Kamári
Tel: 22860 33650
www.rosebay.gr
Four-star complex with large freshwater pool, chequerboard-tiled rooms and galleried maisonettes set just back from the beach. This is the best of several comfortable options here. €€€

Theoxenia Hotel
Firá, Ypapandí district
Tel: 22860 22740
www.theoxenia.net
Right on the main cliffside street, this attractive boutique hotel is friendly and efficient, and has all amenities you could wish for, including a spa tub. Upstairs rooms have caldera views. €€€

Sérifos

Areti
Livádi
Tel: 22810 51479
Fax: 22810 51547
The Areti is a family-run hotel built on a hill with superb views, 400 metres/yds from beach and 200 metres/yds from the port. Rooms, studios and

apartments available; peaceful terraced garden overlooking the sea. €€

Sífnos

Artemon Hotel
Artemónas
Tel: 22840 31303
www.hotel-artemon.com
Simple, attractive family hotel, redone in 2004, with rooms (some with balconies and/or iron beds) that overlook fields rolling towards the sea. €€

Elies Resort
Vathý Bay
Tel: 22840 34000
www.eliesresorts.com
Ultra-luxurious suite-and-villa resort with minimalist ethic; there are some "superior rooms" at the bottom of the scale that are almost affordable. Spa, pool, tennis court and "private" beach complete the profile of a self-contained resort. Open May–Oct. €€€

Myrto Bungalows
Artemónas
Tel: 22840 31490
www.bungalows-myrto.gr

This bungalow complex at the edge of town is newly built but in traditional style, with arches and wood shutters; the landscaped grounds are lovely and the studios take three people at a pinch. €€

Síkinos

Kamares
Aloprónia
Tel: 22860 51234
Traditional-style, affordable hotel with comfortable rooms, in a slightly better position than Porto Sikinos in terms of the view. €€

Porto Sikinos
Aloprónia
Tel: 22860 51220
www.portosikinos.gr
The best accommodation on the island: a complex of 19 Cycladic-style buildings right on the beach. Bar and breakfast area, but no restaurant. €€

Sýros

Dolphin Bay Hotel
Galissás
Tel: 22810 42924

www.dolphin-bay.gr
The largest, most modern resort-hotel on the island, with conference facilities, large swimming pool, restaurant and beautiful views over the bay. €€€

Faros Village
Azólimnos
Tel: 22810 61661
www.faros-hotel.com
This large beachside hotel is five minutes' drive away from the capital, with all the usual facilities, including two pools and restaurant. All rooms in the hotel and the bungalows have verandas with either sea or garden views. €€€

Omiros
Ermoúpoli
Tel: 22810 24910
Fax: 22810 86266
Email: omirosho@otenet.gr
The Omiros is a mid-19th-century neoclassical mansion restored to a high standard. Rooms are furnished in traditional style, and have views of the lively harbour. €€

Sea Colours
Ermoúpoli, Vapória district
Book through Teamwork Travel
Tel: 22810 83400

www.teamwork.gr
High-standard, veneer-floored apartments in various sizes (mostly studios), with internet access and their own swimming lidos, in one of the quietest, most scenic neighbourhoods. €€€

Tínos

Cavos Studios
Pórto beach
Tel: 22830 24224
www.cavos-tinos.com
Good beachside base in an island short on them; studio bungalows set in vast field-stoned grounds with rustic touches (niches, beamed balconies) and fully equipped kitchens. Some are semi-detached at ground level, some are in wings. €€€

Tinion
Hóra
Tel: 22830 22261
www.tinionhotel.gr
Charming old-world hotel in the centre of town, with tiled floors, lace curtains and a large veranda café. Open Apr–Oct. €€

THE SPORADES AND EVVIA

Alónnisos

Konstantina's Studios
Hóra (Paleá Alónnisos)
Tel: 24240 66165
www.konstantinastudios.gr
High up in the old renovated village, this small, traditionally renovated building houses eight studios and one apartment. All have exceptional sea views, flagstone floors and balconies with canvas deckchairs and marble-top tables. €€

Liadromia
Patitíri
Tel: 24240 65160
Email: liadromia@alonnissos.com
One of the first hotels to open in Alónnisos, it has an old-world charm with a dash of modernity. Rooms have stucco walls, stone floors and tasteful decor. Overlooking the harbour at

the north side of Patitíri Bay, and handy for all island facilities. €€

Milia Bay
Miliá
Tel: 24240 66032
www.milia-bay.gr
Tucked away overlooking the sandy Miliá Bay, this quiet retreat consists of 12 ecologically constructed self-catering apartments, all spacious and tastefully decorated; in-house restaurant. If you don't fancy the short walk to the beach there is a pool. €€€

Évvia

Island of Dreams
Erétria
Tel: 22290 61224
Fax: 22290 61268
An unusual resort on an island connected to the mainland by a short

causeway. Accommodation is in individual bungalows set among olive trees and all a short walk from a private beach. €€€

Karystion
Kriezótou 2, Kárystos
Tel: 22240 22391
www.karystion.gr
A busy foreigner-friendly hotel in the far south of Évvia, close to the fortress on Kárstos's coastal promenade. Neat, air-conditioned rooms were redone in 2005, and the common areas overlook (and to some extent occupy) part of the shoreline park. There's a good bathing beach immediately to the east. Open Mar–Oct. €€

Thermae Sylla Spa Wellness Hotel
Loutrá Edipsoú
Tel: 22260 60100
www.thermaesylla.gr

Perhaps Greece's only official anti-stress hotel, this magnificent edifice at the northern end of the promenade – the most renowned of several such hotels in this resort – is a turn-of-the-century

PRICE CATEGORIES

Price categories are for a double room for one night in high season:

€ = under $70
€€ = $70–140
€€€ = over $140

TRANSPORT

ACCOMMODATION

EATING OUT

ACTIVITIES

A – Z

LANGUAGE

experience brought up to date around the millennium, offering beauty and therapy treatments based on the waters of the ancient spa. €€€

Skiáthos

Aegean Suites
Megáli Ammos, 1.5km (1 mile) west of town
Tel: 24270 24069
www.santikoshotels.com
Refurbished in 2007, this suite hotel is the adults-only sister to its chain-mate the Skiathos Princess. Not a beachfront position, but high enough to avoid road noise and has its own parking. There being just 21 units adds to the exclusive feeling. They are all big (55–60 sq metres/592–646 sq ft), with bug screens, wi-fi and sound systems; "de luxe" ones differ only in having an unobstructed sea view. There is a large pool, small but pleasant gym, a stone-clad breakfast gazebo and a "live cooking" poolside restaurant. €€€
Atrium
Plataniás, 9km (5 miles) from town
Tel: 24270 49345
www.atriumhotel.gr
This four-star resort is tastefully modern without being over the top, with wood tones and white

surfaces predominating in the five grades of rooms or suites (including family-sized maisonettes). There are two pools, extensive lounges, a restaurant and, of course, wi-fi signal, as well as sweeping sea views south. €€€
Mandraki Village
Koukounariés, behind Strofyliá Lake
Tel: 24270 49670
www.mandraki-skiathos.gr
If you're not insistent on staying by the sea, this inland hotel, built in 2007 in broad landscaped grounds, may appeal to you. The junior suites are worth the small price difference over standards for their bigger bathrooms, and there are also family units, all in tasteful pastel colours – although the on-site restaurant is rather luridly hued. €€€

Skópelos

Adrina Beach
Pánormos
Tel: 24240 23371/23373
www.adrina.gr
This well-designed, 1990s-vintage hotel complex (42 standard rooms and 10 vine-draped bungalows) occupies a large tract of hillside between Pánormos and Miliá, overlooking a wood-decked saltwater pool

and private pebble beach. It is very popular – especially with Greek wedding parties – and often full, so booking well in advance is mandatory. €€€
Kyr Sotos
Hóra, just in from mid-quay
Tel: 24240 22549
wwww.skopelos.net/sotos
A rambling *pension* in a traditional old house, with wood-floored rooms, all en suite. This is a justifiably a favourite budget option on what can be an expensive island for accommodation. The rear units (which all have air-conditioning) facing the courtyard are quieter. If you can choose, the best is No. 4, which has a fireplace. Open all year. €
Skopelos Village
Hóra, far east side bay
Tel: 24240 22517
www.skopelosvillage.gr
This is the top accommodation in town, renovated in 2007 – when some of the *Mamma Mia!* film-cast parties took place here. Units range from studios up to family units that can sleep six people; all have nice touches like Victorian-style taps. There are two outdoor pools, wi-fi throughout the complex, a superior restaurant terrace, and a lovely clean white breakfast buffet salon. €€€

Skýros

Nefeli – Skyriana Spitia
Hóra
Tel: 22220 91964
www.skyros-nefeli.gr
A mix of standard hotel rooms and a stand-alone group of "traditional Skyrian houses" (actually cosy, two- to three-person studios), this is a well-run complex at the village entrance. Good low season deals take it out of this price bracket. €€€
Perigiali
Magaziá
Tel: 22220 92075
www.perigiali.com
Very welcoming and secluded mix of studios and well-furnished rooms with phones, overlooking a large garden where breakfast is offered. Open all year, with heating. €€
Skyros Palace
Gyrísmata, Péra Kámbou
Tel: 22220 91994
www.skiros-palace.gr
Tucked away at the northeastern end of the Magaziá–Mólos strip, down on the beach, the Skyros Palace is a fairly sumptuous place to stay, although its location may be a little inconvenient (and mosquito-ridden) for some. Free shuttle bus plies between the hotel and Hóra. Open summer only. €€€

THE NORTHEAST AEGEAN

Foúrni

Patra's Apartments
Foúrni port
Tel: 22750 51268
www.fourni-patrasrooms.gr
Fourteen tiered hillside apartments, renovated in 2003, are still one of the best choices here, with privacy guaranteed by the layout, but some of the best views in town. If you don't want to self-cater for breakfast, you can take it in the family sweet shop on the quay beneath the trees; upstairs from here there are cheaper but adequate and spotless rooms. €€

Híos

Volissos Travel in Volissós is a little booking office that handles 16 old village houses restored in the early 1990s by sculptor Stélla Tsakíri. Units, all with their period features preserved, usually accommodate two people, prices €–€€ (May–Oct). Tel: 22740 21413, www.volissostravel.gr.
Argentikon Luxury Suites
Kámbos
Tel: 22710 33111
www.argentikon.gr
Much the most opulent of the various Kámbos estates restored as holiday

accommodation, the Argentikon reopened in 2005 after a long closure, and is now one of the most exclusive lodgings in the Mediterranean. The suites are distributed over five buildings (two dating from the 16th century) and are furnished with valuable antiques. It's a self-contained resort, with full-service restaurant (breakfast typically delivered to one's suite), pool, spa, meeting room and extensive gardens. The estate is deliberately unmarked and unsigned – get directions on booking. €€€€

Chios Rooms
Egéou 110, Híos Town
Tel: 22710 20198
www.chiosrooms.gr
Upstairs rooms with high ceilings and tile-and-wood floors, some en suite, in a lovingly restored building managed by a New

Zealand/Greek couple. Best is the penthouse, with a private terrace. €

Kyma
East end of Evgenías Handrí
Tel: 22710 44500
Email: kyma@chi.forthnet.gr
A hotel in a converted neoclassical mansion (plus less attractive modern extension); the best old-wing rooms have large sea-view terraces, although fittings are due for a refurbishment. Pluses are the extremely helpful management and good breakfasts served in the original salon with a painted ceiling. €€

Markos' Place
South hillside, Karfás beach
Tel: 22710 31990 or 69732 39706
www.marcos-place.gr
Inside a disused medieval monastery, Márkos Kostálas has created a uniquely peaceful, leafy environment. Guests are lodged in the former pilgrims' cells; individuals are welcome at several single "cells", as are families (two "tower" rooms sleep four). Minimum stay four days; open Apr–Nov. €

Mavrokordatiko
Kámbos district, 1.5km (1 mile) south of the airport on Mitaráki lane
Tel: 22710 32900
www.mavrokordatiko.com
One of the more affordable restoration projects in the Kámbos, with heated wood-panelled rooms and breakfast (included) served in the courtyard with its *mánganos* (waterwheel). €€

Spitakia
Avgónyma
Tel: 22710 20513–4
www.spitakia.gr
A cluster of small but well-restored houses taking up to five people, near the edge of this stunningly set west-coast village. €€

Ikaría

Akti
On a knoll east of the hydrofoil and Caique quay, Agios Kírykos
Tel: 22750 22694
www.pensionakti.gr
Family-run pension that received a thorough

overhaul in 2006–7, upgrading all rooms and baths. Most have a balcony or terrace with stunning views; wi-fi signal through-out. Proprietress Marcia, raised in Ohio, is a mine of local information. An excellent choice if you have an early boat to catch. €

Daidalos
Aremenistís
Tel: 22750 71390
www.daidaloshotel.gr
One of the less "packaged"-feeling hotels in this resort, with decent breakfasts on a shady terrace, rooms appointed with quirky artistic touches and, like the Erofili (*see below*), an eyrie-pool above the sea. €€

Erofili Beach
Armenistís
Tel: 22750 71058
www.erofili.gr
Considered the best hotel on the island, though the ample common areas are more impressive than the sea-view rooms. Breakast is served inside, or just outside on a veranda. A small saltwater pool perches dramatically over Livádi beach. €€€

Lésvos

Clara
Avláki, 2km (1 mile) south of Pétra
Tel: 22530 41532
www.clarahotel.gr
The large, designer-furnished rooms (in grades up to one- and two-bedroom suites) of this pastel-coloured bungalow complex look north to Pétra and Mólyvos. Particularly renowned for its ample buffet breakfasts relying on local products. There are tennis courts and a pool. €€–€€€

Delfinia
1km (½ mile) south of Mólyvos
Tel: 22530 71315
www.hoteldelfinia.com
One of the first resort-type hotels erected around Mólyvos, and still one the best: a mix of standard rooms and bungalows set in 35 hectares (87 acres) of orchard and garden. The rooms could do with a

makeover, but the staff are friendly and willing, and the breakfast (served on an outdoor terrace) is substantial. There is also a castle-view pool and direct access to the best part of Psiriára beach. Open all year. €€–€€€

Pyrgos
Eleftheríou Venizélou 49, Mytilíni
Tel: 22510 25069
www.pyrgoshotel.gr
The town's premier restoration accommodation, with over-the-top kitsch decor in the common areas. Rooms, most with balconies, are perfectly acceptable, and there are three round units in the tower. "American" breakfast; secure off-street parking. €€€

Sandy Bay
Agios Isídoros
Tel: 22520 32825
www.sandybay.gr
While geared for package tours, this is still much the best hotel in this resort or neighbouring Plomári, set inland and uphill. Well-appointed rooms (although balcony partitions are lacking) set in a pleasant garden laid to lawn around the pool. €€

Vatera Beach
Vaterá
Tel: 22520 61212
www.vaterabeach.gr
A rambling, Greek/American-run hotel set behind the best beach on the island. Rooms with air-conditioning and minibar, free sunbeds, an in-house restaurant relying on own-grown produce; and free advice from proprietress Barbara. €€

Votsala
Paralía Thermís, 12km (7½ miles) from Mytilíni
Tel: 22510 71231
www.votsalahotel.com
Especially if you have transport, this makes an attractive alternative to staying in Mytilíni Town proper. This is a sophisticated beachfront hotel set in gardens, where the erudite owner makes a point of not having TVs in the rooms, or "Greek

nights", or a pool, or air-conditioning, or a spa – yet claims to have 60 percent repeat clientele. €€

Límnos

Afrodite Villa
Platý beach
Tel: 22540 23141
Email: contact@afroditivillas.gr
Run by returned South African Greeks who are continually overhauling the various wings and annexes of this complex, this comfortable small hotel has a large pool, sumptuous buffet breakfasts, and hosts occasional barbecue nights. €€

Evgatis Hotel
Evgátis beach
Tel: 22540 51700
Expanded in 2008, this small, modern hotel overlooks the best beach on the island (100 metres/yds across the road), with a decent attached taverna. You will need a car though, as Límnos bus service is almost non-existent. €€

Ifestos
Andróni district, Mýrina
Tel: 22540 24960
Fax: 22540 23623
An attractive small hotel whose rooms have a mix of seaward and hillside views, balconies, fridges and air-conditioning. €€

Porto Myrina Palace
Avlonas beach, 2km (1 mile) north of Mýrina
Tel: 22540 24805
Fax: 22540 24858
Considered the best – well, in truth, one of the very few – luxury resorts on the island, with grounds incorporating a small Artemis temple. There are tennis courts and a huge saltwater pool, and water sports off the beach are offered. That said, the assigned five stars is probably one too many. €€€

PRICE CATEGORIES

Price categories are for a double room for one night in high season:
€ = under $70
€€ = $70–140
€€€ = over $140

ABOVE: one of the private terraces at the Melenos, Rhodes.

Sámos

Amfilisos
Bállos beach, near Órmos
Marathókambos
Tel: 22730 31669
Fax: 22730 31668
The hotel itself is nothing extraordinary, but Bállos is a deliciously sleepy place for doing very little except exploring the coast to the southeast and sampling some excellent local tavernas. €€

Arion
1km (½ mile) west of Kokkári
Tel: 22370 92020
www.arion-hotel.gr
The best accommodation on Sámos's north coast, a family-friendly, well-designed hotel-wing and bungalow complex on a hillside. Famously good breakfasts. €€€

Doryssa Seaside Resort
Pythagorion, near airport
Tel: 22730 88300
Fax: 22730 61463
www.doryssa-bay.gr
One of the few actual beachfront resorts on Sámos, with a saltwater pool just in from the sand if the sea is too cold. Choose between the designer-refitted hotel wing or the meticulously constructed fake "village", no two houses being alike, and incorporating all the various vernacular styles of Greece. €€€

Ino Village
Kalámi district, 1km (½ mile) out of Vathý
Tel: 22730 23241
www.inovillagehotel.com

Well-run 3-star hotel with adequate parking, views, a big pool and (unexpectedly) a decent restaurant. The best-value choice for staying in or near the capital. €€

Kerveli Village
Approach to Kérveli beach
Tel: 22730 23631
www.kerveli-village.gr
This is a well-executed, smallish bungalow hotel set among olive trees and cypresses, with superb views across to Turkey and over Kérveli Bay. A good selection of beaches (including the private lido) and tavernas are within walking distance; or take advantage of in-house car rental. €€

Samothráki

Aeolos
Kamariótissa
Tel: 25510 41595
Fax: 25510 41810
Samothráki's port and capital is home to a few hotels, including this decent mid-range choice. The rooms are simple but spacious. Some have views overlooking the hills, others look towards the sea. There's a large swimming pool on site. €€

Mariva Bungalows
Loutrá (Thermá)
Tel: 25510 98258
Situated in the island's resort centre, these lovely flower-shrouded bungalows are built on a gentle hillside near the route to the Gría Váthra waterfalls. All units

are self-contained, comfortable and reasonably spacious. €€

Thásos

Alkyon
West waterfront, Liménas
Tel: 25930 22148
Fax: 25930 23662
Spacious rooms, all with harbour or garden views, plus gregarious Anglo-Greek management – and afternoon tea – make this a firm favourite with English-speaking travellers. Open most of the year. €

Thassos Inn
Panagía village
Tel: 25930 61612
Fax: 25930 61027
Quiet except for the sound of water in runnels all around, this modern building in traditional style has most of its rooms – all with balconies – facing the sea. €€

Thessaloníki

Capsis Bristol
Oplopioú 2, cnr Katoúni
Tel: 23105 06500
www.capsisbristol.gr
One of the city's first boutique hotels, with 16 rooms and four superior suites in an 1870s building near the trendy Ladádika district. On-site restaurant and separate bistro also shoehorned into the premises. €€€

Davitel Tobacco Hotel
Agíou Dimitríou 25
Tel: 23105 15002
www.davitel.gr
A tobacco warehouse (as the name would suggest) built in 1922, and renovated in 2004 as a thoroughly modern A-class hotel with 57 rooms furnished in minimalist style in smoky brown tones. There is a lobby bar and a breakfast lounge, but no restaurant. €€€

Orestias Kastorias
Agnóstou Stratiótou 14
Tel: 23102 76517
www.okhotel.gr
Much the most salubrious and most quietly located budget hotel in town, just a

few steps from Agios Dimítrios Basilica. Rooms in this 1920s building, the front-facing ones with balconies, were renovated in 2003 with simple solid-wood furniture and veneer floors; bathrooms are bit like retro-fitted ones in a French country inn. €

Le Palace
Tsimiskí 12
Tel: 257 400
www.lepalace.gr
Central hotel in a 1929-vintage building, thoroughly renovated in 2005 in vaguely Parisian style, Le Palace features spacious rooms double-glazed against the street noise. The buffet breakfast is notably generous; by contrast you have to book and order in advance for the on-site restaurant. €€€

Pella Hotel
Íonos Dragoúmi 61
Tel: 23105 24222
Fax: 23105 24224
The Pella is an understated, modern two-star establishment on a fairly quiet street. The rooms are blandly furnished but spotlessly clean and represent incredibly good value for the location, which is close to many Ottoman monuments and almost walkable to the port. €

Tourist
Mitropóleos 21
Tel: 23102 70501
www.touristhotel.gr
A rambling, Art Deco 3-star hotel dating from 1925 with parquet-floored common areas (including a cheerful breakfast room), a 1920s lift, and en suite rooms that were thoroughly renovated in 2003 while preserving period details. Very centrally located. It is understandably popular, so advance booking is required at all times. €€

RHODES

Andreas
Omírou 28D, Rhodes Old Town
Tel: 22410 34156
www.hotelandreas.com
An old favourite under friendly and dynamic new management, this *pension* in an old Turkish mansion was thoroughly refurbished in 2006. En suite rooms are in a variety of formats (including family-size, and a spectacular tower unit for two). A terrace bar serves evening drinks and excellent breakfasts. Two-night minimum stay. Open late Mar–Dec. €€

Elafos
Profítis Ilías
Tel: 22460 22402
www.elafoshotel.gr
After languishing neglected for decades, this Italian-built period piece from 1929 reopened in 2006 as a boutique hotel. The high-ceilinged units (the three suites are worth the extra charge) have considerable retro charm, and there are great views of sky and forest from the balconies. The ground-floor restaurant makes a good halt if touring. Open all year (there's a sauna for winter). €€

Lindian Village
Near Glýstra Cove, east coast
Tel: 22440 35900,
www.lindianvillage.gr
Formerly indifferent bungalow village thoroughly restored in 2005 to become one of the prime island properties, with a little artificial stream bubbling through it and golf-carts delivering guests and their bags to the units. The better suites have private pool-patios. Common amenities include two gourmet restaurants, spa/gym and private beach. €€€

Marco Polo Mansion
Agíou Fanouríou 42, Rhodes Old Town
Tel/fax: 22410 25562
www.marcopolomansion.gr
Superb conversion of an old Turkish mansion; all rooms en suite and furnished with antiques from the nearby eponymous gallery. There is also a one-storey wing of less opulent garden rooms. Large buffet breakfasts included. One-week minimum stay; advance booking always required. €€€

Melenos
Líndos, second lane above the north beach, by the school

Tel: 22440 32222
www.melenoslindos.com
No expense has been spared in these 12 exclusive suites with semi-private, pebble-mosaic terraces, from Kütahya tiles in the vast bathrooms to antiques and wood bed-platforms. There's an expensive bar-restaurant sheltering under a fabric marquee with stunning views. €€€

Miramare Wonderland
Ixiá
Tel: 22410 96251
Fax: 22410 95954
Fake-vernacular bungalows painted in traditional colours, in a landscaped setting just behind the beach, popular with package-tour patrons. Tasteful mock-antique furnishings and Jacuzzis in some baths. Common facilities include pools for both children and adults, two restaurants, three bars, a fitness centre, water sports and a children's club. A private mini-railway salvaged from a Welsh mine shuttles guests around the huge grounds. €€€

Niki's
Sofokléous 39, Rhodes Old Town
Tel: 22410 25115
www.nikishotel.gr
An excellent budget hotel, most rooms (redone in 2006) with balconies and air-conditioning. Helpful management and credit-card acceptance. €

Paraktio Apartments
Kiotári
Tel: 22440 47278
www.paraktio.com
Exceptionally well-appointed studios for couples, and galleried four-person apartments with huge seaview terraces, perched on a bluff just above a nice stretch of beach; the units are fully self-catering, but there is a small snack-and-breakfast bar on site. Friendly family management; no package bookings. €€

THE SOUTHERN DODECANESE

Hálki
Most accommodation is block-booked by package companies from April to October; here are two exceptions.
Captain's House
North of the church and inland
Tel: 22460 45201
Five-room, en suite *pension* in a converted mansion with garden bar and helpful management. €
Hiona Art Hotel
Emborió quay
Tel: 22460 45244
www.hionaart.gr
Occupying the old sponge factory on the south side of the bay, with its own lido, this historic building was gutted and completely

rebuilt in 2007–8 and should offer quality accommodation free of the damp and the staffing problems of the past. €€€

Kárpathos

Akrogiali Studios
Potáli Bay, Paralía Lefkoú
Tel/fax: 22450 71178
www.lefkos-akrogiali.de
Just eight spacious units, all with raised bed platforms in traditional Karpathian style and views towards the pebble beach; friendly management and mini-market downstairs for restocking. €
Astro
Ólymbos
Tel: 22450 51421

A good, relatively comfortable en suite guesthouse in this traditional village, kept by the two sisters who manage the Café Restaurant Zefiros, where breakfast is served. €
Atlantis
Pighádia (by the Italian "palace")
Tel: 22450 22777
www.atlantishotelkarpathos.gr
Well-appointed hotel with helpful staff in a quiet setting; easy parking and small pool. Space is held back for non-package travellers. €€
Glaros
Diafáni
Tel: 22450 51501
www.hotel-glaros.gr
The most comfortable lodgings here (although the term

is only relative in northern Kárpathos), 16 tiered studio units on the south hillside, some with four beds and all with great views north. €
Vardes Studios
Amopí beach
Tel/fax: 22450 811111 or 697 21 52 901
www.hotelvardes.gr
The best standard here among outfits accepting

Sidebar labels: TRANSPORT, ACCOMMODATION, EATING OUT, ACTIVITIES, A–Z, LANGUAGE walk-in trade, with huge studio units overlooking well-tended gardens some way inland. Family environment, good breakfasts available. €

Kásos

Angelica's Traditional Apartments
Frý
Tel: 22450 41268
www.angelicas.gr
A restored family mansion overlooking Boúka port has been converted into four, stone- or tile-floored apartments of varying sizes, from studio to family suite. Preference given to one-week stays. €€
Evita Village
Emboriós
Tel: 22450 41731
www.evita-village.gr
Built in 2007, this impeccable complex sits on a slight rise overlooking the sea, and represents the highest standard on the island with its large, open-plan studios. €€

Kastelórizo

Karnayo
Platía at west end of the south quay
Tel: 22460 49225
Email: karnayo@otenet.gr
The best restoration accommodation on the island, designed by a trained architect. Rooms, studios and a four-bed apartment occupy two separate buildings, with wood-and-stone interiors. €
Kastelorizo Hotel Apartments
West quay

Tel: 22460 49044
www.kastellorizohotel.gr
These air-conditioned, quality-fitted studios or galleried maisonettes, some with sea view, offer the best facilities on the island. Tiny plunge pool, and its own lido in the bay. €€€
Mediterraneo Pension
North end of the west quay
Tel: 22460 49007
www.mediterraneo-kastellorizo.com
Another architect-executed refurbishment, this offers simple but well-appointed rooms with mosquito nets and wall art, half with sea views, plus an arcaded ground-floor, waterside suite. Optional breakfast includes proprietor Marie's home-made marmalade. Unusually, open all year. €€ rooms, €€€ suite

Sými

Symi Visitor Accommodation, just in from Gialós's west quay, is an agency run by Wendy Wilcox and Adriana Shum, offering a variety of accommodation in all price ranges, from double studios to entire houses; tel: 22460 71785, www.symivisitor.com.
Albatros
Gialós marketplace
Tel: 22460 71707
www.albatrosymi.gr
Partial sea views from this exquisite small hotel with French co-management; pleasant second-floor breakfast salon. Families should also ask about their more expensive Villa Symeria. €
Aliki
Haráni quay, Gialós

Tel: 22460 71665
www.hotelaliki.gr
This 1895 mansion right on the quay was tastefully converted into one of Sými's most exclusive hotels during the 1990s. The tasteful rooms all have wooden floors and antique furnishings, though be aware that only some (at a premium price) have sea views and/or balconies. April–Nov. €€€
Les Catherinettes
North quay, Gialós
Tel: 22460 71671
Email: Marina-epe@rho-forthnet.gr
Creaky but spotless en suite *pension* above a restaurant of the same name, in a historic building with painted ceilings and sea-view balconies in most rooms. The management also offers three studios in Haráni, plus a family apartment. € rooms, €€ studios
Iapetos Village
Gialós, inland from square
Tel: 22460 72777
www.iapetos-village.gr
The best of several fair-sized bungalow complexes in Gialós, inaugurated in 2007. It comprises maisonettes sleeping up to six, and self-catering studios, arrayed (rather extravagantly for dry Sými) around a pool. The room decor is simple – exposed roof beams and pale tiles – but adequate. €€€

Tílos

Blue Sky Apartments
Ferry dock, above Blue Sky taverna
Tel: 22460 44294
www.tilostravel.co.uk

Nine well-appointed, galleried apartments above a popular taverna, with great views of Livádia Bay. €€
Eden Villas
Outside Megálo Horió, road to Skáfi beach
Tel: 22460 44094
www.eden-villas.com
Two superbly located three-bedroom villas sharing a pool; free wi-fi signal. Bookings by the week only, and it's often full; open all year, economical winter lets. Otherwise €1,300/week.
Eleni Beach
Livádia, about halfway around the bay
Tel: 22460 44062
www.elenihoteltilos.gr
Obliging management for large, airy, white-decor hotel rooms right on the beach, with insect screens and wi-fi signal. A new wing was added inland in 2007. €€
Irini
Livádia, 200metres/yds inland from mid-beach
Tel: 22460 44293
www.tilosholidays.gr
Long the top hotel on Tílos, Irini still wins points for its beautiful grounds and common areas, including a large pool, and only five minutes' walk from the beach. Package patronage is heaviest in May and September; otherwise individual travellers can usually find a vacancy. The same management keeps the hillside, 2007-revamped **Ilidi Rock Aparthotel**, which has outstripped its stable mate with a conference hall, gym (but no spa), private beach and one wing with disabled access. €€ Irini, €€€ Ilidi Rock.

THE NORTHERN DODECANESE

Astypálea

Astypálea Options
Restored studios or entire houses up in Hóra are beginning to show their 1980s vintage – despite 2003–5 upgrading – but still make for an atmospheric stay. Prices from €–€€ for

two people, according to season. Enquire at Kóstas Vaïkousis's antique shop on Gialós quay, or to reserve tel: 22430 61430 or 697 74 77 800.

Australia
Skála
Tel: 22430 61067

Fax: 22430 59812
Rooms and studios upgraded in 2002, with phones, fans and air-conditioning; there's an excellent affiliated restaurant below. €€
Kalderimi
East hillside, Livádia
Tel: 22430 59843

TRANSPORT

www.kalderimi.gr
Eleven variable cottages built in island style, impeccably equipped with air-conditioning, CD players, internet access and satellite TV, as well as embroidered curtains and some vaulted ceilings. Some units accommodate families. Open Apr–Oct. €€€

Kilindra Studios
Southwest slope of Hóra
Tel/fax: 22430 61131
www.astipalea.com.gr
Mock-traditional units (capacity three) built in 2000 in the shadow of the castle, offering all luxury amenities, including a swimming pool; open Apr–Dec. €€€

Maltezana Beach
Análipsi (Maltezána)
Tel: 22430 61558 (summer); 210 5624823 (winter)
www.maltezanabeach.gr
A state-of-the-art bungalow hotel built in 2003, the island's largest, with spacious, well-appointed standard rooms and even bigger suites arrayed around gardens and a pool. On-site restaurant; open Easter–mid-Sept. €€ standard room, €€€ suites

Kálymnos

Akroyali
Massoúri, lower road
Tel: 22430 47521 or 693 89 13 210
Email: acroyali@klm.forthnet.gr
Exceptionally tastefully appointed beachside apartments set quietly below the road, each sleeping two adults and two children; unsurprisingly they require booking months in advance. €€

Mousellis Studios
Final approach, Platý-Gialós Cove
Tel: 22430 48307
www.mousellis.gr
Hillside bungalow complex with sweeping views and on-site restaurant; units accommodate two to six, and while no stranger to package tours, is happy to take walk-in visitors. €€

Villa Melina
Evangelístria district, Póthia
Tel: 22430 22682

www.villa-melina.com
The town's top, and top-value, choice: en suite rooms, refurbished in 2006, in a late 19th-century sponge magnate's mansion, plus an annexe of modern studios behind the pool and gardens. Very good breakfasts served on the patio; open all year. €

Kós

Afendoulis
Evrypýlou 1, Kós Town
Tel: 22420 25321
www.afendoulishotel.com
Welcoming, family-run C-class hotel: cheerful en suite rooms with air-conditioning and fridges, most with balconies, plus some cooler basement "caves", much sought after in summer. Wi-fi in common areas; excellent breakfasts on request, served on front patio. Open Apr–late Oct. €

Alexis
Irodótou 9, Kós Town
Tel: 22420 25594
A backpackers' home-from-home in an inter-war villa overlooking the Hellenistic baths. Rooms large, though most not en suite. Self-catering kitchen and terrace. Open late Mar–early Nov. €

Fenareti
Mastihári
Tel: 22420 59028
Fax: 22420 59129
Hillside hotel in the least packaged of Kós's coastal settlements, overlooking the widest part of the beach; rooms and studios in a peaceful garden environment. €

Kos Imperial Thalasso
Psalídi
Tel: 22420 58000
www.grecotel.gr
One of the premier members of the Grecotel chain, this standard-wing and bungalow hotel with stunning common areas abuts a good beach in landscaped tiers. Individual units are spacious and well-appointed, though not cutting-edge. The thalasso-spa is of course the heart of the establishment.

Unfortunately when the wind is wrong there are whiffs from the nearby sewage plant. €€€

Léros

Alinda
Alinda beach road
Tel: 22470 23266
Fax: 22470 23383
The first hotel established here, this has well-kept 1970s-vintage rooms with a mix of sea and mountain views, plus a respected restaurant with garden seating. €

Archontiko Angelou
Alinda, signposted well inland
Tel: 22470 22749
www.hotel-angelou-leros.com
Marvellously atmospheric converted Belle Epoque mansion hiding amid orchards, with the feel of a French country hotel. Victorian bath taps, beamed ceilings, old tile or wood floors and antique furnishings. €€

Crithoni's Paradise
Krithóni, inland
Tel: 22470 25120
www.crithonisparadisehotel.com
Léros's top-rated accommodation, a low-rise complex with a smallish pool, disabled access and large, well-appointed rooms renovated in 2006. Buffet breakfast; open all year. €€€

Tony's Beach Studios
Vromólithos beach
Tel: 22470 24742
www.tonysbeachstudios.gr
Spacious but simply appointed units set in extensive grounds behind the best beach on the island; access for people with disabilities; ample parking, very quiet. Open May–Sept only. €€

Lipsí

Aphrodite
Behind Liendoú beach
Tel: 22470 4100
Built in 1997, this is an attractive studio-bungalow-hotel complex, with large units. It has a small bar near the sandy beach. Open all year in theory. €€

Galini Apartments
By the ferry jetty
Tel: 22470 41212
Fax: 22470 41012
Well-appointed rooms with balconies and fridges, and a welcoming family who might take you fishing or at least share their catch with you one night. €

Nefeli
Overlooking Kámbos beach, 700 metres/yds from the port
Tel: 22470 41120
www.nefelihotels.com
This 2008-built bungalow-hotel complex is Lipsí's most luxurious. Studios and one- and two-bedroom apartments share the same pastel decor; upstairs units are better ventilated. €€ studio, €€€ apartment

Nísyros

Porfyris
Mandráki centre
Tel/fax: 22420 31376
By default, the best conventional hotel on the island, though bathrooms and phone system are antiquated – only partly compensated for by fridges and air-conditioning. Rooms overlook either orchards and the sea, or the large saltwater pool. €€

Ta Liotridia
On the shore lane near the windmill, Mandráki
Tel: 22420 31580
Email: liotridia@nisyrosnet.gr
Two comfortable suites in a restored house – one of few such projects on Nísyros – for up to four people; worth the premium price for sea views and volcanic-stone-and-wood decor. Lively bar downstairs, but noise is not a problem. €€€

Pátmos

Asteri
Skála, Netiá district
Tel: 22470 32465

PRICE CATEGORIES

Price categories are for a double room for one night in high season:
€ = under $70
€€ = $70–140
€€€ = over $140

www.asteripatmos.gr
Great setting on a knoll overlooking the sea to the west, of which the lounge and breakfast salon takes full advantage. Rooms are variably sized; some have air-conditioning or disabled access. Own-grown produce at breakfast, easy parking, wi-fi signal. €€
Blue Bay
Skála, Konsoláto district
Tel: 22470 31165
www.bluebay.50g.com
This is the last building on the way out of town towards Gríkou, and spared the late-night ferry noise that plagues most hotels here. Rooms have fridges, balconies and air-

conditioning. Friendly Australian-Greek management; on-site internet café. €€
Galini
Skála
Tel: 22470 31240
Fax: 22740 31705
In a quiet cul-de-sac near the ferry quay, this C-class hotel offers B-class standards in furnishings and bathrooms, and excellent value. €€
Porto Scoutari
Hillside above Melóï beach
Tel: 22470 33124
www.portoscoutari.com
The island's top accommodation: enormous suites, arrayed around the pool, have sea views and

air-con, plus antique furnishings and original wall art, all refreshed in 2007. Elína the proprietor is a font of island knowledge. On-site spa, wedding packages available. Open Apr–Oct. €€€
Studios Mathios
Sápsila Cove
Tel: 22470 32583
www.mathiosapartments.gr
If you have a car or bike, these bucolically set superior self-catering units make an idyllic base, with their creative furnishing and decor, extensive gardens and a welcoming managing family. The coarse-pebble cove, however, is not very swimmable. €€

Télendos

On the Rocks
Tel: 2243 48260
www.otr.telendos.com
Just three smartly appointed rooms and a remote studio with double glazing, mosquito nets, etc. The rooms are set above an amiable Greek-Australian-run bar of the same name. €
Porto Potha
Tel: 22430 47321
www.telendoshotel.gr
At the very edge of things, but this hotel, a mix of standard doubles and studios, has a large pool and friendly managing family. €

CRETE

Agía Galíni

Neos Ikaros
Tel: 28320 91447
www.neosikaros.com
A bit out of the centre, at the foot of a hillside, but still handy for the seafront, this amphitheatrically arrayed, 29-unit hotel has large rooms with pine furniture, blue soft furnishings, air-con and fridge and, best of all, an inviting pool garden. €€

Agía Rouméli

Tara Rooms/Hotel Calypso
Tel: 28250 91231
Having hiked the Gorge of Samariá, reward yourself with a beach-side stay rather than pelting off immediately to Hóra Sfakíon. Two brothers offer either basic rooms, with a taverna downstairs, or a more comfortable nearby hotel. Closed when the gorge is (typically Nov–Easter). €–€€

Agios Nikólaos

Minos Beach Art Hotel
Ammoúdi district
Tel: 28410 22345
www.bluegr.com
De luxe coastal resort,

mostly bungalows plus a few suites amid mature gardens, set on a small peninsula studded with specially commissioned contemporary sculpture. A five-star outfit – rack rates for sea-view bungalows run from €400–600 double – with half a dozen on-site restaurants (there's a dress code at supper). €€€
Ormos/Crystal
Órmos district, 1.5km (1 mile) from centre
Tel: 28410 24407 or 28410 24094
www.ormos-crystal.gr
Two medium-sized sister hotels, set on a quiet bay looking towards town, each with a pool. The buildings – 1980s concrete blocks – aren't wildly exciting, but the rooms are fine and the price is right, often with seasonal offers online. €–€€
Sgouros Hotel
Kitroplatía Cove
Tel: 28410 28931
www.sgourosgrouphotels.com
This is a small sea-view hotel with just 22 rooms, all with veneer floors. The units (especially the bathrooms) are stylishly designed, and common areas are also tasteful and pitched at the business trade as much as the holiday visitor. Open all year. €€

Agios Geórgios Lasithioú

Rea
Tel: 28440 31209
Studio rooms rented upstairs from one of the village's best, meat-oriented tavernas – proprietor Maria's husband is the local butcher.

Eloúnda

Akti Olous
Skhísma district
Tel: 28410 41270
www.eloundaaktiolous.gr
The 70 well-maintained rooms at this efficient, family-run seafront hotel were renovated in 2006; the place gets a broad mix of nationalities. There's a roof pool, a tiny patch of beach and two restaurants (one at the beach). €€
Elounda Beach Hotel
Tel: 28410 41812
www.eloundabeach.gr
One of the most luxurious resorts in Greece, overlooking Mirabello Bay; many of the villas have a private pool and gym, and main-wing rooms are a generous 45 sq metres (485 sq ft). Private beach, spa, a number of on-site bars/restaurants, and a high repeat-visit rate among

the jet-set clientele. €€€
Elounda Mare Hotel
Tel: 28410 41102
www.eloundamare.gr
Rival to the Elounda Beach, its tone and emphasis is cosier and warmer – especially in the bungalows with their fireplaces, wood floors and private pools; the "Minoan Royalty Suites" have more contemporary design, the main building standard rooms fall somewhere in between. The bungalows and suites are stratospherically expensive – which doesn't deter a Russian nouveau riche clientele. On-site 9-hole golf course, spa, and water sports including scuba. "Only" three restaurants on site. €€€

Georgioúpoli

Anna's House
300 metres/yards across the

river bridge
Tel: 28250 61556
www.annashouse.gr
More accurately Anna's houses, or rather studios/ apartments, these 2006-built, flawless units are in a peaceful rural garden setting around a large pool, and one of the few local establishments not (yet) in complete thrall to the package trade. €€

Haniá

All listings are near the Old Harbour and open all year.
Casa Delfino
Theofánous 7
Tel: 28210 93098
www.casadelfino.com
The most luxurious – and expensive – of the various restored Venetian-mansion boutique hotels in the Old Town. The 22 units, all different and ranging from one-bedroom to penthouse, are all suite-format. A copious buffet breakfast is served in the pebble-mosaic courtyard; there is also a roof terrace. €€€
Nostos Hotel
Zambelíou 42–46
Tel: 28210 94740
www.nostos-hotel.com
Superbly renovated 15th-century church on a pedestrianised lane, with 12 mostly galleried, balconied units (some with harbour views), and a roof terrace looking to the White Mountains. All units have mini-kitchen, phone, TV. €€
Porto del Columbo
Corner Theofánous and Moskhón
Tel: 28210 70945
www.portodelcolombo.com
This restored Venetian mansion has previously served – in the following order – as the Ottoman military commmand, the French Consulate and Elefthérios Venizélos's offices before becoming a 10-unit boutique hotel. All rooms have dark-wood floors and ceilings plus antique furnishings; two of them are two-room suites. €€
Theresa
Angélou 8, west side of Old Port near Naval Museum

Tel: 28210 92798
www.pensiontheresa.gr
Just seven idiosyncratic rooms (sleeping up to three with their loft beds) with tasteful decor at this cosy pension – one of several on this lane – plus a great view terrace and communal kitchen. Loyal repeat clientele and new word-of-mouth introductions mean advance booking is essential from June to September. €€
Vranas Studios
Agíon Déka, corner Kalliníkou Sarpáki, near cathedral
Tel: 28210 58618
www.vranas.gr
Set back a bit from the water, so quieter, and more "modern" than most Old Town restoration projects, but none the worse for it. Tile-floored, wood-ceilinged rooms are spacious and furnished in contemporary manner; although self-catering, breakfast is available in the lounge. €€

Ierápetra

Cretan Villa Hotel
Lakerdá 16
Tel: 28420 28522
www.cretan-villa.com
An 18th-century mansion restored as a hotel; rooms are simple but with nice touches like exposed stone pointing, and are arrayed around a pleasant courtyard. Free wi-fi zone; friendly owner full of helpful local advice. €

Iráklio

Atrion
Hronáki 9
Tel: 2810 229225
www.atrion.gr
Suprisingly quiet but central B-class hotel, with 2003-renovated balconied rooms, free ADSL, cheerful restaurant and a conference centre for the business trade. €€
Kronos
Sofoklí Venizélou 2, corner Agaráthou
Tel: 2810 282240
www.kronoshotel.gr
Closest to the sea of all the city hotels, this C-class

establishment represents excellent value, with half the balconied rooms having harbour views, though decor is decidedly 1980s. €€
Lato
Epimenídou 15
Tel: 2810 228103
www.lato.gr
The city's first self-styled boutique hotel, this features slightly clinically appointed standard rooms and suites (the latter worth the extra money), two restaurants (one on the roof), conference/function roooms, a sauna and "mini-gym", plus unbeatable views over the old Venetian harbour. €€€
Lena
Lahaná 10
Tel: 2810 223280
www.lena-hotel.gr
Small hotel renovated in 2003 – much of the effort went into the common areas, so rooms are still in two grades: bathless with fan or en suite with air conditioning. Free wi-fi access. €–€€
Mirabello
Theotokopoúlou 20
Tel: 2810 285052
www.mirabello-hotel.gr
Excellent location makes up in part for the datedness of some of the rooms (the non-en suite ones being budget territory) and internet access (ISDN only). Balconies in all rooms, communal fridge, satellite TV lounge. €–€€
Rea
Kalimeráki 1, corner Hándakos
Tel: 2810 223638
www.hotelrea.gr
One of the best, central budget options, with a mix of en suite and sink-only rooms, all with fans and some with balconies. Other perks include left-luggage service, book swap, on-site car hire and long breakfast hours. €

Kastélli (Kíssamos)

Galini Beach
East end of seafront near sports stadium
Tel: 28220 23288
www.galinibeach.com

Modern but well-executed hotel with Art Deco touches, right behind pebbly Telonío beach. Air-conditioned, spotless rooms, full (not continental) breakfast served at sea-level terrace. €

Kolymbári

Selini Suites
Rapanianá district
Tel: 28240 83033
www.selinisuites.com
A mix of large studios and one-bed apartments in this beachfront holiday complex pitched at families, with plenty of children's amenities. €€

Loutró

Blue House
Tel: 28250 91337
A mix of seafront, en suite rooms and slightly more expensive upstairs units at this informal pension, as well as a very creditable on-site taverna. €
Porto Loutro
Tel: 28250 91433
www.hotelportoloutro.com
The largest hotel in this roadless, beachless settlement, spread over two premises (one five steps from the water). Rooms have beam ceilings, slate floors, marble-trimmed baths. Hospitable Anglo-Greek management. €€

Makrýgialos

White River Cottages
Aspropótamos district
Tel: 28430 51694
www.asprospotamos.com
The abandoned hamlet of Péfki, comprising a score of traditional stone cottages complete with original fireplaces, has been architect-restored since the 1980s as studio, one-bedroom and two-bedroom apartments around a

TRANSPORT
ACCOMMODATION
EATING OUT
ACTIVITIES
A – Z
LANGUAGE

swimming pool. Excellent local gorge-walking and flora-spotting opportunities, especially in spring or autumn, and you are just inland from some of the most protected beaches of southeastern Crete. €€

Mátala

Eva Marina
Tel: 28290 45125
www.evamarina.com
Blonde-pine furniture and white-tile decor in a small 1980s-vintage hotel, set in lush gardens just 100 metres/yds back from the sea. €
Matala Bay
Tel: 28920 45100
www.matalabay.gr
Good-value hotel just back from pebbly Kómos Bay (not Mátala's main beach), with a more recent annexe of family-oriented apartments. Welcoming staff, but the in-house restaurant gets very mixed reports. €€

Mýrtos

Myrtos Hotel
Mid-village
Tel: 28420 51227
www.myrtoshotel.com
Almost all-white decor in the rooms of this 1980s vintage, well kept and friendly hotel just five minutes' walk from the usually windless beach. Competent ground-floor restaurant, so half-board is available. €

Omalós

Exari
Tel: 28210 67180
www.exari.gr
One of the best of a cluster of hotels in this hamlet, aimed at walkers wanting an early start down the Gorge of Samariá; the in-house restaurant relies in part on products of the managing family's cheese factory. The name comes from a famous six-man (*exári* in Greek) local raiding party during one of the 19th-century rebellions against the Ottomans. €

Paleohóra

Plakiás
Just about every rented room, studio or apartment establishment near the beach or in the surrounding hamlets – some 150 of them in total – can be found, complete with photos and contact details, on the community website www.plakias-filoxenia.gr.
Rea
Tel: 28230 41307
Email: apap@cha.forthnet.gr
This small (14-room) family-run hotel in the backstreets of town has tile-floored, pastel-hued rooms and a garden bar where drinks and breakfast are provided. Just opposite is an annexe of more recently built apartments suitable for families. €
Sandy Beach
Tel: 28230 42138
Fax: 28230 42139
A cosy little hotel with just 12 rooms sited, as the name suggests, behind the town's main westerly beach, and close to the castle, with balconied sea-view rooms. Overflow guests will be sent to the same family's simpler Castello Rooms (tel: 28230 41143). €

Plataniás

Minoa Palace
West edge of "town"
Tel: 28210 36500
Fax: 28210 36555
www.minoapalace.gr
The Minoa Palace is well located outside the tatty main strip just before the river, although the beach is a short walk away across the road. The rooms and suites are up to five-star standard, although few of them have views. There are good pools, a centrepiece basement spa and half a dozen on-site restaurants and bars, the main one with a reputation for serving one of the best hotel buffet breakfasts to be had in the country. It is family-friendly, so it seems that the rack rates are not always levied. €€€

Réthymno

Fortezza
Melissinoú 16
Tel: 28310 55551
www.fortezza.gr
Recently (but tastefully) built hotel, inland under the shadow of the Venetian fortress (thus the name). Medium-sized pool in the back (although the beach is 10-minute walk away), terracotta-tiled floors and simple but quality furnishings. Good value for the comfort offered. €€
Olga's Pension
Souliou 57
Tel: 28310 54896
Fax: 28310 29851
A warren of eclectically decorated rooms and studios on different levels, some en suite and/or with sea views, connected by flower-filled terraces and passageways; a good central budget option. Discounted breakfasts offered at the family-run ground-floor café. €
Palazzo Vecchio
Melissinoú, corner Iróön Polytehníou
Tel: 28310 35351
www.palazzovecchio.gr
A 15th-century Venetian building converted into a complex of studios and apartments with warm-toned soft furnishings. Small patio pool with adjoining bar, but no restaurant. €€€
Sea Front
Arkadíou 159
Tel: 28310 51981
www.rethymnoatcrete.com
If you want to be on the beach, this – an old mansion converted into a *pension* with 10 well-equipped, wood-floored, en suite rooms – is the closest spot, while still convenient to the centre. The same owners manage the modern Sea View Apartments nearby, comprising four studios and two family units (which don't, however, have the sea views). €€
Veneto
Epimenídou 4
Tel: 28310 56634
www.veneto.gr

Another Venetian-mansion conversion in the centre of the Old Town, cosier than most of its rivals, with an arcaded courtyard, working wells and antique-furnished units, which all vary (bathrooms are state-of-the-art). Ten studios and suites are complemented by an on-site restaurant with a well-stocked wine-cellar. This is a favourite honeymoon venue. €€€

Sitía

Arhontiko
Kondyláki 16
Tel: 28430 28172
An old neoclassical mansion converted into a basic but atmospheric *pension* (most rooms are not en suite). There is an orchard-garden out front. €
Itanos
Platía Iróön Polytehníou
Tel: 28430 22900
www.itanoshotel.com
Waterfront B-class hotel, with a roof garden, restaurant and some disabled-friendly units. Common areas have been refurbished, but the rooms, while airy and bright, still have slightly dated furnishings. €€

Spíli

Heracles
Tel: 28320 22111
Fax: 28320 22411
Email: heraclespapadakis@hotmail.com
A superior establishment just off the main road, offering rooms with air-conditioned, insect-screened, balconied, white-walled units, some with good hillside views. The geologist proprietor acts as a sort of unofficial tourist information bureau, especially for local walks, and rents out mountain bikes. €

PRICE CATEGORIES

Price categories are for a double room for one night in high season:
€ = under $70
€€ = $70–140
€€€ = over $140

TRANSPORT

E ATING OUT

ACCOMMODATION

RECOMMENDED RESTAURANTS, CAFÉS AND BARS

EATING OUT

What to Eat

There is considerable regional variety in Greek cuisine, and you should keep an eye out for specialities you haven't seen before. It's also worthwhile shopping around for your taverna (especially in heavily visited areas), asking the locals what they suggest. For experienced travellers, the term "tourist *mousakás*" is shorthand for an exploitative version of this standard dish, slathered with potatoes and poorly executed béchamel sauce, with nary a slice of aubergine or a crumb of mince.

Some tavernas, especially in rural areas or on non-touristy islands, may not have menus out (though they're required to keep one somewhere for consultation), in which case it's essential to establish the price of at least the most expensive main courses.

Vegetarians are not well catered for in Greek restaurants; many dishes will include fish, meat or meat stock. Your best bet is mixing and matching from a selection of *mezédes* (little plates of food and dips, hot or cold), many of which are vegetarian or dairy-based.

Many Greek specialities are cooked in the morning and left to stand so food can be served lukewarm (occasionally stone-cold), but Greeks believe this is better for digestion and the steeping of flavours. For vegetarian dishes, they're right; for dishes containing meat, this is a downright dodgy practice, especially in summer.

Where to Eat

The more casual eating establishments have much the same style and set-up throughout the islands, and menus are similar in design and sequence (indeed, often pre-printed by drinks companies in return for including their logo).

However, the classical taverna is by no means the only kind of establishment. You will also find the *estiatório*, the traditional urban restaurant, which ranges from an *(ino) magirío* or tradesman's lunch-hour hangout, with ready-cooked *(magirevtá)* food and bulk wine, up to pricey linen-tablecloth places with bow-tied staff.

How Much to Pay

Greece is not as cheap as it used to be. A two-platter meal with bulk wine or local beer will cost at least €13 per person; €16–19 is a more realistic figure, especially adding another *mezés*. If you sample fish or bottled wine, budget €25–35 minimum per head. Fancy eateries run to €35–45 per person without wine. Our listings are mid-priced unless otherwise stated.

The ritual of families and friends patronising tavernas twice a week is much less observed now thanks to hard times. Most Greeks, not just students nursing one coffee all evening, have had to learn to be careful with money. It is still considered an honour to snaffle the bill and pay for everyone, but long gone are the days when diners would order more starters towards the end of the meal, destined never to be touched, just to impress.

The *psistariá* is a barbecue-style restaurant specialising in lamb, pork or chicken on a spit; a *psarotavérna* specialises in fish and shellfish; while the *gyrádhiko* and *souvlatzídiko* stalls purvey *gýros* and *souvláki* respectively, sometimes to a sit-down trade, garnished with salads.

Popular among the intelligentsia are *koultouriárika* restaurants, Greek nouvelle cuisine based on updated traditional recipes; and *ouzerí* (or *mezedopolío*, or *tsipourádika* in the northern islands), where the local tipple accompanies *mezédes* or small plates of speciality dishes.

When to Eat

For Greeks the main meal of the day is taken between 2pm and 3.30pm and, even in the cities, is usually followed by a siesta break lasting until 5.30 or 6pm.

The evening meal can either be another full meal, or an assortment of *mezédes*. This is usually eaten between 9pm and 11pm.

Breakfast in Greece is traditionally small, usually a pastry and coffee. There are, however, wonderful *pítta* and turnover options available from bakeries, for snacking on the hoof.

The Wines of Greece

While Greek wines have yet to obtain the status of French, Italian or antipodean rivals, there are many high-quality vineyards. Consult Kóstas Lazarákis's *The Wines of Greece* for a guide to drinking and buying. A bottle of decent wine costs €7–20 in a shop, double that in a taverna.

ACTIVITIES

A – Z

LANGUAGE

ABOVE: Lésvos is famous for its *oúzos*, such as the Kefi brand.

Drinking Water

Carrying a large plastic bottle of mineral water is common in Greece, but rather deplorable, as sunlight releases toxic chemicals from the plastic into the water, and the spent bottles contribute enormously to Greece's litter problem. Buy a sturdy, porcelain-lined canteen and fill it from the cool-water supply of bars and restaurants you've patronised; nobody will begrudge you this. Although unfiltered tap water is generally safe to drink, it may be brackish, and having a private water supply is much handier. On the larger islands, certain springs are particularly esteemed by the locals – queues of cars, and people with jerry-cans, tip you off. If you insist, bottled water (including sparkling) can be bought almost anywhere.

Some of the better, common mainland labels, available country-wide, include:
Boutari Nemea, a reliable, full bodied, mid-range red. There are other, premium versions of Nemea such as **Ktima Papaïoannou**;
Tsantali Rapsani, a reliable red from a tiny area on the border between Thessaly and Makedonía;
Spryopoulou Orino Mantinea, a smokily dry white made from *moskhofílero* grapes in the central Peloponnese;
Averof Katoï, a smooth red from Métsovo, though quality isn't up to its 1990s prime;
Athanasiadi, premium red and white from central Greece;
Lazaridi, two rival wineries run by cousins, in eastern Makedonía – their Merlots in particular are excellent.

Island Wines, Oúzo and Tsípouro

Many islands produce excellent vintages that they can't or won't export and which are only sold locally. Although barrelled/bulk (*me to kiló, hýma*) wines can be rough and ready, they're cheap (€4–12 per litre) and certainly authentic.

In Corfu, **Theotoki** is the local wine (red or white); the speciality of the island is a sweet liqueur called **Kumquat**, based on the tiny eponymous citrus fruit. In Kefalloniá **Robola** is a delicate, expensive white for which **Gentilini** is reckoned the best label. The grapes of Andípaxi are made into bulk wine.

On Rhodes, the private Émbonas winery Emery is esteemed for its

Villaré and **Vounoplagies** whites. The otherwise undistinguished CAIR cooperative makes a cheap and acceptable fake "champagne", while the **Triandafyllou** microwinery generally has a dozen products in any year.

Sámos in the northeastern Aegean is one of the few islands to export wine; the fortified Sámos dessert wines **Anthemis** and **Vin de Liqueur** are esteemed worldwide. The best local *oúzos* are considered to be **Giokarini** and **Frantzeskos**. Ikaría's **Karimali** organic winery, with its reds and whites, is worth trying. On Híos, particularly around Mestá, a heavy, sherry-like but very palatable wine is made from raisins. *Oúzo* is made here too – **Tetteri Penindari** is favoured by aficionados.

Lésvos is the undisputed *oúzo* capital of Greece, producing at least 15 varieties. **Varvagiannis (**or **Barbagiannis)** is the most celebrated, and expensive, but some prefer **Arvanitis**. EPOM is the principal cooperative, marketing among others the "Mini" brand, a staple of *ouzerí* across the country. Island reds are generally undistinguished, with the exception of **Hatziemmanouil** on Kós and superb **Methymneos** winery products from Lésvos.

Like most volcanic islands, Límnos produces excellent whites (especially the oak-aged **Dryiino**), as well as a few acceptable reds and rosés.

Thásos specialises in *tsípouro* – often flavoured with exotic spices or pear extract rather than the aniseed of *oúzo*. You will also find *tsípouro* in

the Sporades, from Thessaly just opposite (**Apostolakis** brand).

Santoríni, a volcanic island like Límnos, is known for its upscale whites like **Sigala**. For recommended wineries to visit on the island, *see page 193*.

In Crete, the quality wine industry is focused on north-facing hill villages just inland from Irákio; names to look out for include **Miliarakis, Zacharioudakis, Lyrarakis** and **Tamiolakis**.

Fish and Seafood

Seafood is generally expensive, except for frozen squid. Scaly fish are usually in an iced tray for you to choose from, and your dish is priced by the weight of the fish of your choice. It is strongly suggested that you watch the (uncleaned) fish being weighed, and reiterate the price you are quoted, as "fingers on the scales" and later misunderstandings are not unknown.

There is so much farmed and frozen seafood (often marked on menus only with a "k" or "kat.", for *katapsygméno*, or just an asterisk) lying in ambush for the inexperienced these days that the best strategy is to eat humbly and seasonally: far better a platter of grilled fresh sardines in August than swordfish frozen since June.

Greek Salad

"Greek" salad is a staple of taverna menus. *Horiátiki*, the full monty with tomatoes, cucumber, green pepper, *féta* cheese and olives, is a lunch in itself with bread – and this is what you'll probably get if you ask for "salad". Some restaurateurs omit one or two of the vegetable ingredients – not all are available all summer – but by law *horiátiki* must contain a generous chunk of *féta*. If all you want is a small side salad, ask for *angourodomáta* (just tomatoes and cucumber).

Coffee, Chocolate and Tea

Whole arabica beans suitable for cafetière or percolator coffee are making steady inroads among locals and tourists fed up with the ubiquitous "Nescafé", which has become the generic term for any instant coffee. The formula sold in Greece is far stronger than that made for Anglo-Saxon markets, and the

most palatable use for it is in *frappé*, cold instant coffee whipped up in a shaker, and an entirely Greek innovation despite its French name. *Gallikós* ("French"), in other words percolated coffee, is synonymous with *fíltrou* (filtered). *Mé gála* means "with milk".

Espresso and cappuccino are becoming nearly as common as in Italy, though not always so expertly made. *Freddoccino*, another resourceful Greek invention, is a cold double cappuccino for the summer months.

Ellenikós kafés is Greek coffee, made from fine-ground robusta beans, boiled and served with the grounds in the cup – the same style as across the Balkans and Middle East. A large cup is a *diplós*. Greeks generally drink this coffee with lots of sugar, which is added at the preparation stage. For those who like

it without, *skétos* ("plain") is the magic word. If you like some sugar ask for *métrios*; if you want it syrupy, say *varý glykós*.

Chocolate drinks *(tsokoláta)* can be very good indeed, served cold or hot according to season. Loumides is the best local brand, Van Houten the best imported.

Tea *(tsái)* is the ragged stepsister of the hot-drinks triad. Quality bulk or bagged tea, whether green or black, is sold in speciality shops, but in cafés you'll usually have to make do with teabags of obscure Ceylonese or Madagascan vintage, served either with milk or with lemon *(me lemóni)*.

Herbal teas are easy to find in shops, and at more traditional *kafenía*. *Hamomíli* is camomile tea, and *alisfakiá* (sage tea) is found on many of the Dodecanese and Cyclades.

RESTAURANT LISTINGS

ATHENS

Bakalarakia (O Damingos)
Kydhathinéon 41, Pláka
Tel: 210 322 5084
Excellent food dished up in a long-established cellar restaurant (look for the photograph of Josephine Baker being served by the present owner's grandfather). Good things to order include *fáva*, *loukánika* and *saganáki*; the house speciality is *bakaliáro skordaliá* (salt cod with garlic – thus the establishment's name). Excellent barreled wine.

Diporto
Sokrátous 9, corner Theátrou; no sign out; metro Omónia
Located at the western edge of the central market district, Diporto attracts a varied clientele, from "suits" to market-stallholders. They're here for the excellent, no-nonsense grub: grilled or fried fish of the day, a stew or two, and mountainous salads. Space is limited, so you're expected to share tables with strangers. Open Mon–Sat noon–6pm.

Fasoli
Emmanouil Benáki 45, Exárhia
Tel: 210 330 0010
Ippokrátous 22 corner Navarínou, midtown
Tel: 210 360 3626
Excellent value and trendy yet utilitarian decor make these two sister restaurants very popular. The food at both is solid Greek with creative twists: lentil salad, *biftéki* roulade, light pasta dishes, good bread, the usual starters. Closed Sun.

Filippou
Xenokrátous 19, Kolonáki
Tel: 210 721 6390
This *estiatório*, founded in 1923, remains a firm favourite with all sorts of diners for its honest, moderately priced fare, washed down by excellent white or red bulk wine. Service is low-key but efficient; the dining room retains a pleasantly retro air with proper table linen. Open continuously noon until late except closed Sat night, all day Sun and part of Aug.

Kalimarmaron
Evforíonos 13, Pangráti
Tel: 210 711 9727
This rustic-decor taverna stresses island and regional recipes. Several daily specials will be recited to you, though the permanent menu – stuffed baked sardines, sausages, and bean dishes – has broad appeal. Decent bulk wine from Neméa. Closed Sun eve and Mon.

Kostas
Ekáli 7, Pangráti
Tel: 210 711 101
Much-loved, long-running local installed in an early 1900s house; the menu combines generic Middle Eastern dishes such as houmous and taboulleh with fine renditions of Grek standards like sausage, *keftédes*, *mavromátika* and lamb dishes. Good bulk wine, and very inexpensive for the area. Dinner only, not Sun or August.

Kriti (O Takis)
Veranzérou 5, *stoá* off Platía Kánningos, near Platía Omónia
Tel: 210 382 6998
Popular little Cretan *stéki*

(hangout) serving regional dishes such as *hiroméri* (smoked pork) and *marathópita* (fennel pie), along with more usual titbits like fresh *bakaliáros* and of course Cretan *rakí*. A bit pricey for the area, but portions are large. Open daily for lunch and dinner.

Rakoumel
Emmanouíl Benáki 71, Exárhia
Tel: 210 38 00 506
Tiny (30-seat) place featuring Cretan *mezédes* and *rakí* at student-friendly prices. The menu (only in Greek) offers platters like skinny sausages, *gialodádika* (greens similar to lamb's lettuce), and *paximádia* (dark rusks) rather than bread. Very much a local bohemian hangout; summer tables out on the sidewalk. Open Mon–Sat 3pm–midnight.

Santorineos
Dorién 8, Petrálona, metro Petrálona
Tel: 210 34 51 629
Cult taverna installed in an old refugee compound and barrel-making workshop from 1926; seating is in

small rooms or the lovely courtyard. There's a limited menu of Santoríni specialities, mostly pork-based (fish dishes only by pre-order), washed down by excellent island bulk wine, thus the extra tag of "krasotavérna" (wine tavern). If some of the dishes are only three-and-a-

half stars, the atmosphere, service and low prices are four-to-five stars. Dinner only, Mon–Sat.

Thanassis
Mitropóleos 69, Monastiráki
Tel: 210 324 4705
Three hotly competing souvláki stalls cluster here where Mitropóleos meets Platía Monastirakíou, but

this is the best. Thanassis's speciality is kebab, minced meat blended with onion and spices. The side dish of chilli peppers will blow your head off. Open daily noon–midnight except major holidays.

Tristrato
Dedálou 34 corner A. Géronda, Pláka

Tel: 210 324 4472
Excellent café/patisserie which specialises in unusual desserts. Drinks include airáni (diluted yogurt) in summer, rakómelo from Amorgós, home-made liqueurs and a wide range of herbal teas. Daily 9am–midnight.

CORFU

Corfu Takeaways

Invisible Kitchen (tel: 26630 98051, 697 6652933; www.theinvisible kitchen.co.uk), based near Aharávi, is not a restaurant per se, but a catering service: young British chefs Ben and Claudia will deliver ready meals for your villa party or caique day out. Nouvelle Italian, French, Thai, Indian, Chinese or Greek menus (€17–30 each, minimum 4 diners) or boat picnics at about €10 each – and the food is to die for. Operates late Apr–mid-Oct; in the winter they do operate a restaurant, weekends only, in the hills east of Aharávi.

Kérkyra Town

La Cucina
Guildford 15
Tel: 26610 45029
You'll usually have to wait for a table outside at this competent Italian eatery, which does excellent pizzas and handmade pasta dishes, as well as antipasti and seafood – though the interior is extremely pleasant in the cooler months. Open Feb–Nov daily 7pm–midnight.

La Famiglia
Maniarízi and Arlióti 30, Campiello district
Tel: 26610 30270
Greek/Italian-run bistro specialising in salads, pasta, lasagne and Italian puddings. Excellent value and efficient service; limited seating both indoors and out, so reservations always

mandatory. Open evenings only, Mon–Sat.

Mouragia
Arseníou 15, north quay, Kérkyra Town
Tel: 26610 33815
A good mix of seafood (with fresh and frozen items clearly indicated) and Corfiot magirevtá such as sofríto and pastitsáda. Inexpensive for any island, let alone Corfu, and affords sea views toward Vídos islet into the bargain. Open daily noon–12.30am.

Tenedos
Alley off Solomóu, Spiliá district
Tel: 26610 36277
French-Corfiot cooking with ample seafood choice and Lefkímmi bulk wine. Locals go especially for the kandádes (songs) in the evening. Open lunch and dinner.

Theotoki Brothers (Kerkyraïki Paradosiaki Taverna)
Alkiviádi Dári 69, Garítsa Bay
By far the best of half a dozen tavernas with tables out in the eucalyptus park here. A full range of magirevtá dishes and grills, plus some seafood, at very reasonable prices. Service can be leisurely, even by Corfu standards. Open lunch and dinner.

Venetian Well Bistro
Platía Kremastí, northwest of Cathedral, Kérkyra Town
Tel: 26610 44761
Tucked away through an arch, with tables around said well, is some of the town's most innovative (and expensive) cooking, generic Aegean with interesting twists. Recipes change

seasonally, depending on the proprietor's winter travels and inspiration, but past dishes have included duck in plum sauce or dolmádes with wild rice. Excellent (and pricey) wine list. Dinner only Mon–Sat, all year.

Around the Island

Agni
Agní Cove, between Nissáki and Kassiópi
Tel: 26630 91142
The romance of the proprietors – she's Greek, he's English – has been the basis of newspaper features and a BBC documentary, but, beyond the media hype, the food is very good, and reflects the meeting of cultures: stuffed sardines, garlic prawns, mussels in wine and herbs. Open Apr–Oct for lunch and dinner.

Alonaki Bay
Paralía Alonáki, near Korission Lagoon
Tel: 26610 75872
Good country recipes, strong on vegetables and seafood – beans, greens, scorpion-fish soup – at shady tables on a terrace overlooking the sea.

Boukari Beach
Boúkari
Tel: 26620 51791
The less commercial of two seafood tavernas at this seashore hamlet, in an idyllic setting, with patently fresh fare at some of the most attractive prices on the island. Open all day Apr–Oct.

Cavo Barbaro (Fotis)
Avláki

Tel: 26630 81905
An unusually good beach taverna, with welcoming service. A few magirevtá dishes at lunch, more grills after dark, plus home-made glyká koutalioú (candied fruit). Seating on the lawn, and plenty of parking. The only thing "barbarous" here can be the wind, as there's no shelter.

Etrusco
Just outside Káto Korakiána village, on the Dassiá road
Tel: 26610 93342
Top-calibre nouvelle Italian cooking purveyed by father, son and spouses, served at a carefully restored country manor with its own farm for organic sourcing. Specialities like timpano parpadellas (pasta with duck and truffles), swordfish carpaccio or lamb in kumquat sauce, and a 200-label wine list, don't come cheap – budget a minimum €45 each before drink – but this has been ranked one of the best five Greek tavernas outside of Athens. Early booking essential. Open Apr–Oct, dinner only.

Foros
Paleá Períthia
Tel: 26630 98373
The less commercial and friendlier of two tavernas in this rather melancholy village, operating in a restored house. Fare is basic – grills, salads, local cheese, píttes, a dish of the day – but so are the prices. Open May–Oct daily.

Ftelia (Elm Tree)
Strinýlas village
Tel: 26630 71454

An almost mandatory stop on the way to or from the summit of Mount Pandokrátor, this taverna specialises in game (venison, wild boar), unusual starters like snails or artichoke pie, and apple pie with proper coffee. Open May–Oct lunch and dinner, weekends only in winter.

Kouloura
Kouloúra Cove
Tel: 26630 91253
Fairly priced seafood or

fish, large selection of *mezédes* and salads, plus unusually elaborate pies at this taverna overlooking one of the most photogenic anchorages on Corfu. Open Apr–Oct daily all day; reservations needed at peak season.

Little Italy
Kassiopí, opposite Grivas supermarket
Tel: 26630 81749
Jolly trattoria in an old stone house run by Italian brothers; fare includes

salmon in pastry parcels, pizza, pastas smothered in made-from-scratch sauces. *Limoncello* digestif on the house may follow. Reservations suggested.

Mitsos
Nissáki
Tel: 26630 91240
On the little rock-outcrop "islet" of the name, this ordinary-looking beachside taverna stands out for the cheerful service from the two partners, as well as the high customer turnover –

and therefore freshness of the inexpensive fare. This includes fried local fish and well-executed *sofríto*.

Toula
Agní Cove
Tel: 26630 91350
Worth a special mention for its professional demeanour, nice line in hot *mezédes* and the house special *garídes* (prawns, shrimp) grilled with spicy mixed-rice pilaff. Excellent bulk white wine; budget about €30 each; lunch and dinner.

THE IONIAN ISLANDS

Itháki

Kalypso
Kióni
Tel: 26740 31066
Specialities here include onion pie and artichoke soufflé with ham and cheese; not too inflated price-wise considering that yachts tie up nearby. Remarkably full Greek beer list.

Kandouni
Vathý quay
Tel: 26740 32918
Strong on *magirevtá* such as stuffed squash blossoms and stuffed peppers; if you want well-grilled fish, select it next door from the fishmonger. Good Kefalloniá bulk wine, homemade dessert of the day, does breakfast too.

Nikos
Inland near the National Bank, Vathý
Tel: 26740 33039
A good all-rounder, with grills, a few *magirevtá* dishes daily, and fish; inexpensive bulk wine. Tourists go 8–9pm, then locals hold forth until closing time.

Rementzo
Frikes
Tel: 26740 31719
This taverna features local recipes like *savóro* (cold fish in raisin and rosemary sauce), and *astakomakaronáda* (lobster on pasta), and supports local producers, such as the

suppliers of their bulk wine and sticky sweets. Portions on the small side, but so are prices; uniquely here, open all year.

Paliocaravo
Around east quay, Vathý
Tel: 26740 32573
This well-established favourite with locals and visitors alike offers a fine range of *mezédes*, salads, meat and fish dishes, which can all be washed down with their light, refreshing bulk wine.

Ulysses
Frikes
Tel: 26740 31733
Dine on reasonably priced fish and succulent meat dishes like rabbit *stifádo* or lamb *kléftiko*, whilst watching the gentle activity in the harbour.

Kefaloniá

Akrogiali
Lixoúri quay, towards south end
Tel: 26710 92613
An enduring, budget-priced institution, with largely local clientele. Tasty food with a stress on oven-casserole dishes (including *giouvétsi*, *kreatópita* and great *hórta*), but also fish and grills in the evening, plus excellent bulk wine.

Blue Sea (Spyros')
Káto Katélios
Tel: 26710 81353
Its speciality is pricey but clearly fresh and superbly grilled fish from the little

anchorage adjacent. Budget about €30 each for a large portion with a share of *mezédes* and their bulk wine.

To Foki
At the head of Fóki Bay
This is a very pleasant taverna, friendly and just opposite the beach. It serves simple but tasty food – *fáva*, *souvláki* and salads – and lovely *milópita* (apple pie). Much better, and far cheaper, than anything to be found in Fiskárdo.

Kyani Akti
A. Trítsi 1, far end of the quay, Argostóli
Tel: 26710 26680
A superb, if pricey, *psarotavérna* whose wood deck juts out over the water. The speciality is fresh fish and seafood, often with unusual items like the delicious *dáktylia* – "fingers" (razor clams in mustard sauce). There is also a range of *mezédes* and salads, and some tasty house wine.

Maïstrato
Far north end of quay, Argostóli
Tel: 26710 26563
Set yourself up at this genuine *ouzerí* with a seafood *pikilía* (medley), some of their abundant hot/ cold *mezédes* and *oúzo* by the 200ml carafe. Pleasant waterside seating beside a pine grove; Apr–Oct only.

Mr Grillo
A. Trítsi 135, Argostóli
A *psistariá*, not far from the

port authority building, very popular with locals for Sunday lunch. The grilled meats are tasty and accompanying *mezédes* fine. All reasonably priced.

Nirides
Asos, the far end of the harbour
Tel: 26740 51467
This little *estiatório* in a great spot overlooking the harbour has the usual range of salads and a few grilled and oven dishes, as well as fresh fish by the kilo. It is all well cooked – especially the fried peppers with cheese and *melitzánes imám*.

Odysseas
Agía Ieroúsalim Cove, 4km (2½ miles) from Mánganos village
Tel: 693 77 14 982
A hidden gem tucked behind this tiny, little-visited northern beach. Delicious home-style recipes like their own olive bread, and lamb stew made with free-range meat and organic vegetables. The proprietors also sell their own preserves.

Paparazzi
Lavránga 2, SW corner of main square, Argostóli
Tel: 26720 22631
Run by Italians who intend to teach the locals what real Italian food is: trattoria dishes, pasta and theatrical pizzas kneaded and twirled before your eyes. Very reasonable for the quality – two adults with two children can eat for under €70. A few

tables outside; open all year lunch and dinner.
Paradisenia Akti/Paradise Beach (Stavros Dendrinos)
Far east corner of Agía Evfimía resort
Tel: 26740 61392
Fair-priced savoury dishes such as *hortópita* and local sausage, though seafood portions could be bigger. Lovely terrace seating under pines and vines overlooking the sea.
Patsouras
A. Trítsi 32 (north quay), Argostóli
Tel: 26710 22779
Popular, inexpensive *magirevtá* specialist just along from the Lixoúri ferry berth. Good rib-sticking food with especially tasty *bámies* (okra), a few grills, big portions and a velvety red house wine. Open all year.
To Pevko
Andipáta Erísou, by the turn for Dafnoúdi beach
Tel: 26740 41360
A serious contender for the best place to eat on the island, with seating outside under a huge pine tree. A mouthwatering selection of *mezédes*, oven-cooked dishes and some grilled meat and fish. Particularly good are the tomato, mint and *féta keftédes*, the *gígandes* (butter beans) and aubergine with garlic.
Romantza
Póros
Tel: 26740 72294
This *estiatório* is in a

charming position, built into the headland at the end of the town beach. You eat on a first-storey balcony which has views over the sea to Itháki. The focus of the menu is on a large range of fresh fish (priced by weight), but there are also good *mezédes* and salads.
Xouras
Petáni
Tel: 26710 97128
The location halfway along the best beach on the Lixoúri peninsula is ideal, and the Greek-American lady owner offers a warm welcome along with a good assortment of meat, fish and veggie dishes, washed down with decent bulk wine.

Kýthira

Platanos
Mylopótamos
Tel: 27360 33397
Venerable village *kafenío* in an old building on the platía; *magirevtá* for lunch, grills in the evening.
Sotiris
Avlémonas
Tel: 27360 33922
The better of two seafood tavernas here, doing perfectly cooked fresh fish. Often closed weekdays.

Levkáda

Palia Apothiki
Sývota
Tel: 26450 31895
A favourite among yachters, this lovingly converted 1710-vintage warehouse is the place to enjoy fare such as giant prawns wrapped in bacon. Good bulk wine.
Pantazis
Nikiána
Tel: 26450 71211
Appealingly set at the far end of the yacht harbour, this locally patronised taverna does fresh seafood at very reasonable prices – though salad trimmings could sometimes be fresher. *Magirevtá* in high-season evenings; open all day.
Regantos
Dimárhou Verrióti 17,
Levkáda Town

Tel: 26450 22855
Dinner-only taverna with a good balance of grills (especially spit-roasted chicken), oven food and fish; inexpensive and colourful. Sometimes hosts live *kantádes* sessions.
Sapfo
On the beach, Agios Nikítas
Tel: 26450 97497
Innovative, deftly executed recipes such as seafood lasagne and cheese-and-courgette pie, decent bulk wine; not overpriced for the quality and arguably the best view in the resort.
T'Agnandio
West hillside, Agios Nikítas
Tel: 26450 97383
Tucked away up a lane with views to rival Sapfo's, one of the friendliest, least expensive home-style tavernas on the west coast. The stress is on *magirevtá* and fresh seafood such as *garídes* from the Amvrákikos Gulf. Creditable barrel wine; dinner only low season.
Ta Platania
Central platía, Karyá
Seating under the giant plane trees of the name, and fresh wholesome grills, salads and beers at budget prices. Tables for two other eateries share the square.

Paxí

Alexandros
Platía Edward Kennedy, Lákka
Tel: 26620 30045
The most authentic *nisiótiko* cooking and most atmospheric setting in town; own-produced grilled meat (especially suckling pig) and chicken, specialities like rabbit *sofríto* and mushroom pie, and a few seafood dishes – but avoid the barrel wine.
Lilas
Magaziá
Tel: 26620 31102
Inexpensive little meat grill with good bulk wine in an ex-grocery shop at the centre of the island. Usually live accordion or stringed music at weekends.
Vassilis
Longós quay
Tel: 26620 31587

Now often known as Kostakis after the son who's taken it over, this has grown from a grilled-fish specialist to an all-round taverna with imaginative recipes for *magirevtá*, like stuffed mushrooms and peppers, baked meat dishes and various oven pies.

Zákynthos

Akrotiri Taverna
Akrotíri, 4km (2½ miles) north of Zákynthos Town
Tel: 26950 45712
A pleasant summer-only taverna with a large garden. Grilled meats are a speciality here, but they also bring round large trays of very tempting *mezédes* from which you pick and choose. The house wine is very acceptable.
Alitzerini
Entrance to Kilioméno
Tel: 26950 48552
Housed in one of the few surviving 17th-century Venetian village houses, this little *inomagerío* offers hearty, meat-based country cooking and its own wine; *kantádes* some evenings. Evenings only: Fri–Sun Oct–May, daily June–Sept. Reservations essential.
Andreas
Paralía Beloúsi, near Dhrossiá
Tel: 26950 61604
A no-nonsense fish taverna serving fresh catch at fair prices. During summer there is terrace seating by the sea. To go with the fish there is good bread, wonderful *kolokythákia* (boiled courgettes) and decent wine.
Arekia
Dionysíou Romá, Zákynthos Town
Tel: 26950 26346
A smoky and unpretentious hole-in-the-wall, fitting perhaps 70 diners cosily on bench seats; open evenings only all year round. The food is decent – maybe even wild artichokes in spring – but incidental to the main event: *kantádes* and *arékia* singing after 10pm.
Fanari tou Keriou
1.5km (1 mile) beyond Kerí village
Tel: 26950 43384/69726 76302

Watch the moon rise over the Myzíthres sea-stacks below the Kerí cliffs. The food's on the expensive side, but portions are a fair size and quality is high – try the daily-made *galaktoboúreko* or vegetable-stuffed *pansétta*, redolent of nutmeg. Reservations essential.

Kalas
Kambí
By far the best taverna in Kambí, Kalas is set in a pretty garden, shaded by large trees, and serves up all the usual favourites (*fáva*, *loukánika*, *horiátiki* and *patátes*), all tasty and freshly cooked. Good bulk wine as well.

Komis
Bastoúni toú Agíou, Zákynthos Town
Tel: 26950 26915

A lovely *psarotavérna* tucked into a rather unlikely spot behind the Port Authority building. The emphasis is on pricey but fresh and inventive fish and seafood dishes; but there is a good list of *mezédes*, decent wine and tempting desserts.

Malanos
Agíou Athanasíou 38, Kípi district, Zákynthos Town
Tel: 26950 45936
Deservedly popular and inexpensive all-year shrine of *magirevtá*: mince-rich *yiouvarlákia* and *fasolákia yiahní* are typical offerings. Unusually good bread as well as the expected barrel wine.

Mikro Nisi
Kokkínou, 1km (½ mile) beyond Makrýs Gialós
Standard, but reasonable, taverna food – *horiátiki*,

kalamarákia, *souvláki* and other such offerings – but the situation is lovely, on the edge of a headland overlooking a tiny harbour.

Porto Limnionas
Pórto Limniónas, below Agios Léon
Location can count for a lot. The food here is relatively expensive, standard taverna fare, but it is served on a promontory overlooking an idyllic rocky bay and facing west to the sunset.

Roulis
Kypséli Beach, near Drossiá
Tel: 26950 61628
Popular with islanders, Roulis gets very fresh fish – one of its main attractions – but also does the usual salads and vegetables well. The house wine is drinkable, and the generally fresh ingredients make it

worth the detour from the main coast road.

Theatro Avouri Estiatorio
North of Limodáïka near Tragáki
Tel: 26950 62973
A peaceful, stone-built open-air theatre complex set in lovely countryside. Local food (including excellent bread) is cooked in a traditional oven. Open every night from around 7pm.

Theodoritsis
Just past Argássi in Vasilikós municipal territory
Tel: 26950 48500
Where the beautiful people of Zákynthos go at weekends. The stress is on *magirevtá*, but grills and *mezédes* are also served up. Moderately pricey with a summer terrace overlooking town, plus a tasteful interior; open all year.

THE SARONIC GULF

Aegina

Agora (Geladakis)
Behind fish market, Égina Town
Tel: 22970 27308
One of the oldest (founded c.1960) seafood outfits here, offering good value without airs and graces – you'll likely have to wait for a table. Summer seating on the cobbles outside, winter tables inside. Bulk wine or *oúzo* for refreshment.

Lekkas
Kazantzáki 4, northerly waterfront, Égina Town
Renowned for its good vegetable platters and hygienic meat grills, washed down by excellent bulk wine made from sun-dried grapes. Very inexpensive for Égina.

Angístri

Parnassos
Metóhi hamlet
Besides the usual grills and *mezédes*, this friendly, rustically decorated spot, with Kyría Katína at the helm, serves its own-made cheese, a few dishes of the day and good bulk wine.

Hydra

Gitoniko (Manolis and Christina)
Hydra Town
Tel: 22980 53615
Popular with locals and foreigners alike, To Gitoniko offers discreet rooftop dining as well as indoor dining downstairs. Lunch-hour *magirevtá* run out quickly, by 2pm; in the evening there are also grills, especially fish. Excellent draught wine.

Koutouki tis Agoras
Rear of market hall, Hydra Town
The most genuine of the island's various *ouzerís*, with rickety tables and unpredictable hours. It's usually got going by early evening, though, with well-priced meat and seafood titbits.

To Steki
Hydra Town, near Miranda Hotel
Tel: 22980 53517
A simple taverna with a lovely, tree-shaded courtyard. The food is simple, well-priced and unadorned, consisting in the main of slightly oily ready-cooked dishes with a

smattering of grills and *mezédes*. Good bulk *retsína*.

Póros

Taverna Karavolos
Póros Town
Tel: 22980 26158
Meaning a type of snail in Greek, Karavolos is a very popular backstreet taverna. Yes, the restaurant does serve snails, accompanied by a rich sauce, and there's a selection of ready made *magirevtá* dishes as well as grills. Dine indoors or on a leafy patio. Reservations recommended.

Taverna Platanos
Póros Town
Tel: 22980 24249
High up in the backstreets under a plane tree (*plátanos*), the speciality here is grills ranging from regular steaks to *kokorétsi*, mixed offal on a long skewer. The atmosphere is relaxed; evening is the best time to enjoy this place.

Spétses

Exedra (Tou Siora)
Old Harbour

Tel: 22980 73497
High-quality *magirevtá* like *mousakás* and vegetarian *laderá*, as well as some fish dishes, are the stock-in-trade here. Outdoor quayside seating, and a very small price premium considering the quality, compared to neighbouring establishments.

Liotrivi
Old Harbour
Tel: 22980 72269
Upmarket restaurant in an old olive press (*liotrívi*) specialising in both scaly fish and shellfish. Mainly Greek clientele; best for evening dining.

Patralis
Kounoupitsa waterfront
Tel: 22980 75380
Going since 1935, this is the most upmarket, white-tablecloth venue away from the Dápia, with excellent service. Their *psári à la Spetsióta* (fish in ratatouille sauce) is made with fresh fish, not frozen as in many other places. The bulk wine is satisfactory, and baked-apple dessert rounds off the experience. Open all year.

THE CYCLADES

Amorgós

O Nikos
Langáda
Tel: 22850 73310
Polished taverna specialising in platters like beets with greens, dips, goat-based dishes, fish and some *magirevtá*. Not cheap for Amorgós, but the quality is high, with seating on perhaps the island's loveliest vine-shaded terrace.

To Hyma
Hóra, main commercial street
Tel: 69747 86376
Excellent, genuine *ouzerí* in an ex-grocery store, where miracles are worked over a small camp stove. Strong points are salads and seafood dishes, plus a few meat casseroles. *Hýma* (in bulk) is your wine. Open all year, off-season by arrangement.

To Limani tis Kyra Katinas
Órmos Egiális
Tel: 22850 73269
Strong contender for best all-round eatery on the island; strengths are seafood, pulses, vegetable casseroles and local cheese. Very reasonably priced for the quality. Open from just before Easter–mid-Oct.

To Santouraki
Tholária village
Tel: 22850 73054
In a village with at least three decent eateries, this stands out for its good *mezédes*, own-reared meat grills and elevated terrace. Open most of the year.

Anáfi

To Steki
Hóra
Simple, friendly all-round taverna with a terrace, *rakómelo* and bulk wine; in spring you might get flash-fried *hános*, a bony but tasty fish typical of the Cyclades.

Mýkonos

Cavo Tagoo
Hóra, a 15-minute walk out towards Agios Stéfanos

Tel: 22890 23692
The expensive diner of the eponymous luxury hotel, where contemporary Mediterranean cuisine makes the most of seasonal Greek produce; a sushi corner provides an alternative taste sensation.

Chez Catherine
Agios Gerásimos district, Hóra
Tel: 22890 22169
Since the 1980s, Greek cuisine with a French accent – sole, coq au vin, rack of lamb – has made this restaurant, on a back alley, extremely popular. Fairly pricey, reservations recommended.

Efthimios Zaharoplastio
Flórou Zouganélli, Hóra
For nearly 50 years, Efthlmios has sold his almond-flavoured *kalathakiá* ("little baskets"), *loukoúmi* and *soumáda* (almond milk) from this immaculate sweet shop. Takeaway only.

Nikolaos Taverna
Agía Anna Beach (after Platýs Gialós)
Tel: 22890 23566
A locals' favourite: an authentic Greek taverna serving home-style dishes on a pretty, tiny beach.

Niko's
Just off the harbour, Hóra
Tel: 22890 24320
For a quarter-century, Niko's has made fresh fish and lobster a speciality. Also try home-made *mousakás*, salads with capers and rocket. Slow service, moderate prices.

Sesame Kitchen
Platía Tríon Pigadíon, Hóra
Tel: 22890 24710
A nearly all-vegetarian restaurant with good salads and *mezédes*, as well as a couple of token meat dishes. Moderately priced for Mýkonos.

Náxos

Gorgona
Agía Anna
Tel: 22850 41007
This long-time beach taverna has grown more

elaborate over the years, but the prices are still good, as is the traditional Greek food. The fresh fish is bought at the dock out front. Try the *kakaviá* (fish stew). Locals eat here year-round.

Meltemi Restaurant
Extreme southern end of Hóra's waterfront
Tel: 22850 22654
The Meltemi has been here since the 1970s, serving traditional Greek cuisine, including fresh fish. It's authentic and popular with locals. Easter–end October, all day until midnight.

The Old Inn
Boúrgos, Hóra
Tel: 22850 26093
In a charming garden, the German proprietor serves Greek and (mostly) "international" cuisine, and he makes everything too – even the smoked ham.

Páros

Boudaraki
Harbour road, Parikía
Tel: 22840 22297
Well-established *ouzeri* with drinks and *mezédes* such as grilled octopus and sea-urchin roe. Open Easter–early Oct.

Hristos
Opposite the Church of the Panagía Pantanássa, Naoússa
Tel: 22840 51442
Paros's most elegant restaurant (and one of the more expensive) offers Mediterranean food, perfect service and great attention to detail.

Levandis
Market Street, Parikía
Tel: 22840 23613
Inventive Mediterranean cuisine in a pretty, quiet garden. Moderate to expensive.

Porphyra
Parikía
Tel: 22840 23410
Some of the fresh fish and shellfish, including oysters, are caught by the owners themselves. Daily specials include sea-urchin salad. Open off season.

Santoríni

1800
Ia
Tel: 22860 71485
In an old captain's mansion on the main street, 1800 is one of Greece's best for elegant Mediterranean cuisine. Expensive; reservations essential.

Aktaion
Firostéfani
Tel: 22860 2233
This semi-troglodytic taverna, on the caldera edge, has served traditional Greek food since the 1920s. This is how *mousakás* is supposed to taste – Grandma's recipes are still in use. Inexpensive.

Katina's
Ammoúdi port, Ia
Tel: 22860 71280
On the right at the bottom of the steps leading down from Ía. In many people's eyes, the fresh, grilled fish, prawns and Santoríni specialities make this the island's best taverna, all helped along by the excellent, friendly service. Easter–October; from lunch until late.

Nikolas
Erythroú Stavroú, Firá
No phone
Nikolas is Firá's oldest and most traditional taverna, a master of all *magirevtá*. No reservations taken, so be prepared to wait for a table. Open year-round, lunch and dinner. Inexpensive.

Taverna Pyrgos
Pýrgos Village
Tel: 22860 31346
An elegant, moderately priced restaurant with an unusual view. The best plan is to order a table-full of their excellent *mezédes*. Popular with wedding parties and other functions, so call first.

Sífnos

Liotrivi (O Manganas)
Apollonía
Tel: 22840 31246

One of the oldest *koultouriárika* eateries on the island. Maybe resting on its laurels a bit, and not cheap, but good for a special meal in an atmospheric setting.
Odos Oniron
Apollonía
Tel: 22840 32002

Upscale, *koultouriárika* restaurant with eclectic but tasteful decor, featuring mostly baked, strongly herb-flavoured seafood, as well as beef and pasta dishes. There is delicious home-made walnut pie to finish off the meal.

Sýros
Lilis
Ano Sýros
Tel: 22810 88087
Huge place, where the food is almost incidental to the live *rebétika* music at weekends; *rebétika* giant Márkos Vamvakáris was born in this

village and is said to have played here.
Thalami
Platía Tsiropína, Ermoúpoli
Tel: 22810 85331
Upmarket seafood specialist (here the name means "octopus's lair") with great views over the water towards Vapória district.

THE SPORADES AND ÉVVIA

Alónissos

Elaionas
Leftós Gialós beach
Tel: 24240 66066
The better of two decent tavernas here, with unusual platters like *tsitsírava*, *xynógalos*, other chunky dips and daily specials prepared by three generations of ladies toiling in the kitchen. Outdoor seating in a gravel courtyard under the olives of the restaurant's namesake. May–Sept only.
Hayati
Far end of Hóra pedestrianised walkway
Tel: 24240 66244
Café/*zaharaplastío* whose main strengths are savoury turnovers and sweets – from the expected *tyrópitta* to exotic treats like *kazandibí* – and a range of coffees. The view across the straits to Skópelos is to die for, and there will always be a scrum for a prime table. Open 9am until small hours.
Mouria
Harbour end of the access road, Vótsi
Tel: 24240 65273
Friendly, family-run, inexpensive option with big salads, a couple of *magirevtá* of the day, ace squid and bulk wine. They rent rooms upstairs too.

Évvia

Apanemo
Shoreline at Fanári district, Halkída
Tel: 22210 22614
Halkída is famous for its seafood, especially shellfish like *gialisterés* and *petrosolínes*, so

there's no excuse for tolerating the hit-and-miss performance of certain midtown outfits. This seafood taverna has one of the best settings, easiest parking and some of the best food – on the pricey side but worth it.
Hondronastos (To Koutouki)
Sahtoúri 75, Kárystos
Tel: 22240 22406
Terrazzo-floored 1970s-style *estiatório* with just six tables to scoff on bean soup, *lahanodolmádes*, meat grills and *fáva*, plus of course bulk wine, at 1970s prices. The catch is it's only open Oct–May: the owner is off tending his bees in summer.
Pyrofani (Livaditis)
Límni, northwest end of quay
Tel: 22270 31640
Slightly bumped-up prices for average-sized portions at this seafood-strong *ouzerí* are justified by the quality, plus nice touches such as sweet-cabbage marinade as a side dish, and big salads. Stick to their *oúzo*, as the bulk wine is not a strong point.
Smbanios
Opposite ferry dock, Loutrá Edipsoú
Tel: 22260 23111
About the only "normal", and normally priced, taverna in town. Its speciality is grilled sardines, and the bulk rosé wine (a rarity) is good, as are the usual *mezédes*. Pleasant decor includes old photos of the resort.

Skiáthos

Alexandros
Old Town, 2 blocks in from fishing port

Tel: 24270 22431
Good grills (especially the lamb chops) and oven dishes, and home-made crème caramel for dessert – so it's a shame about the poor bulk wine. Greeks in attendance provide singalongs with acoustic *bouzoúki* and guitar. There's winter seating in a small house opposite, otherwise outside under the mulberry trees.
Amfiliki
South edge of town by clinic
Tel: 24270 22839
Good smells wafting out of the kitchen up front are the clue that you've arrived. Out back, limited seating – about 40 places – with unlimited views of Mégas Gialós Bay. The food lives up to the setting, especially off-menu seafood specials like *bráska kípo* (monkfish in spicy tomato sauce), and seafood salad. It's open in winter too, with the fireplace going.
Bakaliko
Airport road, 300 metres/yds past yacht marina
Best of several eateries on a strip better known for nightlife. The decor is a take on a traditional Greek grocer's (*bakáliko*), the fare an unusual twist to traditional recipes, especially fish dishes, and the seating poised over the water.

Skópelos

In Hóra (the main harbour), the west quay is the place to eat and where locals go.
Englezos
West quay near Dimarhío

(Town Hall)
Tel: 24240 22230
The creative Greek menu varies by the year but might include aubergine croquettes with mint and cheese, rock samphire, and a variety of lamb dishes, all done with panache. To drink, bulk wine from the Anhíalos co-op near Vólos, and delicately perfumed brandy.
Klimataria
Right next to Dimarhío (Town Hall)
Tel: 24240 22273
The best place for reasonable (for Skópelos) fish by weight, plus a few cooked dishes and *mezédes* – locals conspicuously in attendance.
Pavlos
Agnóndas port
Tel: 24240 22409
Reliable fish specialist with fair prices, also doing unusual *mezédes* like *tsitsírava* (wild pistachio sprouts); good bulk wine from Apostolakis, a local Thessalian vintner. Pavlos is the best of three choices here. Waterside seating under trees. Open Mar–Oct.
Ta Kymata
Far north end of quay, Hóra
Tel: 24240 22381
About the oldest taverna here, run by an engaging family and renowned for its elaborate *magirevtá* such as lamb and vegetables in *phyllo* triangles. Also, good aubergine salad and real beets with greens attached.

Skýros

Lambros
Aspoús, through road
Tel: 22220 91388

Efficient, polite service, a pleasant interior or the terrace in fine weather, grilled fish, chops and al dente vegetables all make this a natural all-year favourite for locals and visitors.

O Pappous ki Ego
Hóra
Tel: 22220 93200
An ex-pharmacy converted into the island's best *ouzerí*, with signature platters like wild mushrooms (in season) and cuttlefish in anise

sauce. Great sounds on the music system, though this becomes live at off-season weekends when there's a small extra charge. Rather cosy indoor dining area; outside tables in summer. Dinner only.

Perasma
Start of airport slip road
Tel: 22220 92911
The airport staff and seemingly half the air force personnel on the island eat here, knowing a good thing when they see it: succulent own-raised meat and

ABOVE: dining out in Ermoúpoli, Sýros island.

cheese, at reasonable prices. Seating outdoors or

in, according to weather. Open all year.

THE NORTHEAST AEGEAN

Foúrni

Koutouki tou Psarrakou
Market high street
Tel: 22750
You'll get the best, and best-priced, all-round feed – *magirevtá* and meat roasts rather than fish – at this local hangout as opposed to the overexposed waterfront tavernas. Cretan bulk wine and home-made liqueur from the Peloponnese (one of the managing couple is from there).

Híos

Fakiris Taverna
Inland between Thymianá and Neohóri
Tel: 22710 32780
Home-marinated aubergine and artichokes, goat baked in tomato sauce and excellent wood-fired pizzas, along with pork-based *bekrí mezé* in big portions. Open all year, weekends only winter.

Hotzas
Georgíou Kondýli 3, Híos Town
Tel: 22710 42787
Oldest and (usually) the best taverna in the city. Fare varies seasonally, but expect a mix of vegetarian dishes, sausages and fish. Open all year, dinner only (not Sun).

Makellos
Pityós
Tel: 22720 23364
On the west edge of the

village, this is a shrine of local creative cuisine; daily June–Sept, Fri–Sun eve Oct–May.

Mylarakia
Tambákika district, by Híos Town Hospital
Tel: 22710 41412
All eight brands of Hiot *oúzo* available to accompany starters, seafood and some meat dishes. Romantic setting. Dinner all year; lunch on occasion.

Stelios (Tou Koupelou)
Langáda harbour
Tel: 22710 74813
One of the best places on the island for a seafood dinner. Best ring in advance with your party's special requirements, otherwise it will just be the standard *kalamári, barboúni* and *gávros*.

Tavernaki tou Tassou
Stávrou Livanoú 8, Bella Vista district, Híos Town
Tel: 22710 27542
Superb all-rounder with creative salads, better-than-average bean dishes, good chips, *dolmádes*, snails and a strong line in seafood. Open lunch and dinner most of the year, sea-view garden seating in summer.

To Mageirio tis Kyrarinis
Kipouriés
Tel: 22740 22016
The more accomplished of two tavernas here on this oasis-hamlet's square, with home-style casserole dishes, sweets and starters.

June–Sept daily, winter weekends only.

To Talimi
Central Thymianá
Tel: 22710 32940
A lodestar for unusual *magirevtá* and home-style platters, dished up by a very pleasant family. The name recalls a local sword dance representing the medieval locals' ambush of pirates. Open all year.

Ikaría

Delfini
Armenistís
Tel: 22750 71254
Across the way from Paskhalia; more traditional, less polished, but popular for the sake of the waves lapping the terrace – and the sustaining cooking (fish, meat grills and a few *magirevtá*).

Kalypso
Ftema, 2km (1 mile) west of Évdilos
Tel: 22750 31387
Basic but friendly shoreline place with excellent, reasonably priced, own-grown vegetable dishes and fresh fish. Daily May–Oct, otherwise by arrangement.

Kelaris (tis Eltherías)
Gialiskári
Tel: 22750 71227
The best of a trio of tavernas here for *magirevtá* and the freshest fish locally, at moderate prices.

Paskhalia
Armenistís
Tel: 22750 71226
Ground-floor diner of a small *pension* that does good breakfasts (for all-comers) plus reasonable fish with good bulk wine later in the day. Open May–Oct.

Thea
Nás
Tel: 22750 71491
Returned Ohio-Ikarian lady oversees the best *magirevtá* this end of the island, with lots of vegetarian dishes like *soufikó* (the Ikarian ratatouille) and squash-stuffed turnovers. Daily June to September, weekends in winter too.

Lésvos

Anemoessa
Skála Sykaminiás, closest to the harbour chapel
Tel: 22530 55360
Tops for fresh fish, and good *mezédes* like stuffed squash blossoms. Open all year (weekends only Nov–Apr).

Balouhanas
Yéra Gulf seafront, Pérama
Tel: 22510 51948
Seafood *ouzerí* with wood-kiosk seating overhanging the water. Interesting *mezédes* and home-made desserts (like *gioúzleme*) too. Open all year.

Captain's Table
Fishing harbour, Mólyvos
Tel: 22530 71241

As the name suggests, a strong line in seafood but also meat and vegetable specialities, such as their "Ukrainian" aubergine dip, and excellent own-label wine (both white and red). Open May–late Oct, dinner only.

Ermis
Kornárou 2, corner Ermoú, Mytilíni Town
Tel: 22510 26232
The best and most atmospheric *ouzerí* of a cluster in Páno Skálo district, with two centuries of claimed operation and indoor/outdoor seating. Special strengths: sardines, sausages, Smyrna-style meatballs.

Iy Eftalou
By Eftaloú thermal baths, 4km (2½ miles) from Mólyvos
Tel: 22530 71049
Well-executed, reasonably priced grills (fish on par with meat), *magirevtá* and salads. Seating under the trees or inside by the fireplace according to season. Only black spot is the sometimes glum service. Open all year except Nov–mid-Dec.

Taverna tou Panaï
Agios Isídoros, north edge of village
Tel: 22520 31920
Plainly presented but tasty food: vegetarian *mezédes*, grills, cheese and so on. Mostly Greek clientele; open all year.

To Petri
Petrí village, in the hills above Pétra/Mólyvos
Tel: 22530 41239
Friendly, family-run tavernas serving salubrious *magirevtá* and a few grills; unbeatable terrace seating. Open May–mid-Oct.

Women's Agricultural Tourism Co-op
Central platía, Pétra
Tel: 22530 41238
Upstairs restaurant with lots of simple grills – including seafood – *mezédes* and rather fewer *magirevtá*. Indoor and (weather permitting) outdoor terrace seating. Open May–Oct.

Límnos

Glaropoula
Néa Koútali

Tel: 22540 92325
This is *the* place in southern Límnos for a seafood blowout, with bay views from the terrace. Reasonably priced, simple presentation.

Kali Kardia
Platía of Tsimándria
Tel: 22540 51278
Very cheap, very cheerful, with a calm location. From amongst grills and a few *magirevtá*, tick your choices off on the menu-bill combo. Open all year.

Man-Tella
Sardés centre
Tel: 22540 61349
Cult taverna doubling as the central *kafenío* (thus open all year) of this highest hill village on Límnos. Big portions off a meat-strong menu; good service, indoor/outdoor seating by season.

Mouragio
Kótsinas port
Tel: 22540 41065
The better of two seafood tavernas here, worth the slight price premium in terms of execution and service.

Platanos
Mýrina bazaar
Tel: 22540 22070
Traditional, long-established purveyor of *magirevtá* under two plane trees; best at lunch on workdays.

Sozos
Main square, Platý
Tel: 22540 25085
Though Sozos himself is gone, this is still the best and oldest *tsipourádiko* grill here, with steamed mussels, chops and *orektiká* all supervised by his daughter. Usually there's a wait for a table.

Tzitzifies
Rihá Nerá beach
Tel: 22540 23756
A proper taverna at Mýrina town's north beach, with tables on the sand. Good *ímam baïldí*, dips and baked dishes.

Sámos

Aeolos
West end of quay,
Agios Konstandínos

Best-value fish and grills here, plus a few oven dishes of the day. Unbeatable seating by the pebble shore.

Ammos Plaz
Start of west beach, Kokkári
Tel: 22730 92463
Top outlet here for *magirevtá* – especially *mousakás* or *pastítsio* – and fish. You have to book days in advance in high season for their popular beach-facing conservatory.

Artemis (Tou Karathanasi)
Kefalopoúlou 4, ferry dock, Vathý
Tel: 22730 23639
Currently the best taverna in town, with good *hórta* and *fáva*, excellent seafood platters, plus standard meat mains. The smooth red bulk wine from Manolátes won't leave you hung over.

Delfini
Avlákia
Tel: 22730 94279
Tables are right at water level in this tiny, Greeks-only resort, giving the best view on the north coast. Come here for fresh fish platters, large veggie starters, and Kyría Alexándra, the colourful proprietress. The bulk wine isn't good – choose a bottle instead.

Glaros
Iréon
Tel: 22730 95457
Cult taverna off at the west edge of town, barely signposted, equally popular with locals and foreigners. Mama is ace with *magirevtá*, and the fish is also excellent. Portions are big and prices low, so there is a temptation to over-order.

Kryfi Folia
Platanákia district of Kérveli
Tel: 22730 25194
Near the east tip of Sámos in an isolated olive grove, a 1970s-style taverna in the best sense possible, presided over by Stávros your host. Starters precede the finest (and cheapest) lamb chops on the island; otherwise swordfish or *kalamári* are reliable. Open Easter–mid-Oct.

Loukoulos
Above Fournáki beach, west end
Votsalákia resort
Tel: 22730 37147

In what's otherwise a very touristy spot, Loukoulos is genuinely characterful, reasonable and devoted to quality *magirevtá*, with home-made apple pie for dessert on the house. Best in the evenings, as the terrace is unshaded and many dishes aren't ready until then.

Pera Vrysi
Approach to Vourliótes village
Tel: 22730 93277
There are main courses, but the strength here is imaginative *mezédes* like spinach-cheese croquettes, sweet pumpkin turnovers, and chicken livers in bacon. Excellent bulk wine, don't order bottled water – you're next to one of the best springs on the island. Open all day Mar–Oct.

Psarades
Agios Nikólaos Kondakeïkon
Tel: 22730 32489
Long reckoned the best fish taverna on the island, at surprisingly reasonable prices, plus the usual *orektiká*. In season you have to book. Open Easter–Oct.

Psili Ammos
Psilí Ammos
Tel: 22730 28301
The taverna on the far right as you face the water and the most consistent one in the area, though fare's restricted to seafood, meat grills and salad. Booking advised for large parties. Open daily Easter–Oct, weekends winter.

Tarsanas
Little lane 100 metres/yds in from west beach, Kokkári
Tel: 22730 92337
The stock-in-trade here are the pizzas, seafood *mezédes* and perhaps two *magirevtá* of the day at bargain prices. Catch the sea breeze on the tiny terrace or at tables out in the lane. Own-made wine varies in quality.

Tria Alfa
Manolátes centre
Tel: 22730 94472
Unusually, all of the tavernas in this popular hill village are good, but this one just pips the others for culinary innovation (at a

TRANSPORT
ACCOMMODATION
EATING OUT
ACTIVITIES
A – Z
LANGUAGE

slight price premium) and quality bulk wine from Stavrinídes village. Open winter weekends too.

Samothráki

Fengari
Loutrá Thermá
Tel: 25510 98321
Using an outside wood oven to cook most of the dishes, the Fengari (named after the island's mountain) serves a range of traditional island dishes as well as meat and fish grills. Very pleasant ambience and very good value for money.
Klimataria
Kamariótissa
Tel: 25510 41535
On the waterfront some 100 metres/yds north of the ferry quay, this unassuming taverna puts out a range of good *magirevtá* (ready-cooked) dishes and grills to order. Twice a week the chef makes *gianniótiko* – a rich dish of pork, egg, potatoes, onions and garlic.

Thásos

ly Pigi
Central platía, Liménas
Tel: 25930 22941
Old stand-by dishing out dependable *magirevtá* next to the spring of the name; best at dinner.
O Glaros
South end of the beach, Alykí hamlet
Tel: 25930 53047/31547
Oldest, least expensive and most authentic of several tavernas here. Usually has a modest breed of local fresh fish. Open late May–Sept.
O Platanos
Under the central tree,

ABOVE: trays of sticky sweets tempt at this confectioner's *(zaharoplastío).*

Sotíros village
Tel: 25930 71234
Summer-only taverna run by a sympathetic couple from nearby Rahóni village. Elaborate *magirevtá* when trade justifies it, otherwise simple grills and powerful home-made *tsípouro* if you ask.
Simi
East waterfront, Liménas
Tel: 25930 22517
Despite the touristy cadre, this makes a decent fist of fish and *mezédes.* Seating, weather permitting, under trees on a raised terrace. Open all year.

Thessaloníki

Aristotelous
Aristotélous 8
Tel: 2310 233195
One of the older *ouzerís* in the city centre, this serves classic northern Greek cuisine with a twist alongside *ouzerí* standards. Excellent wine list, bulk *tsípouro.* Closed 1 month summer and Sun afternoon.
Myrovolos Smyrni (Tou Thanassi)
Modiáno Market, entrance from Komninón 32

Tel: 2310 274170
Doyenne of several *tsipourádika* at the market hall's west entrance: top-notch food like stuffed squid, grilled sardines and Smyrna-style meatballs, and bags of atmosphere. Booking recommended. Open all year.
Toumbourlika
Kalopotháki 11
Tel: 2310 282174
Yet another of the city's famous *ouzerís,* hidden away in a narrow street off Platía Dimokratías, this consists of a couple of small, cosy rooms with a few outside tables. It specialises in fish *mezédes.* Some live music at weekends.
To Yedi
I. Paparéska 13, Kástra
Tel: 2310 246495
High up next to the Yedi Küle former prison (thus the name), this laid-back and friendly *ouzerí* serves up large portions of *mezédes* from a daily changing menu. Choice of *oúzo, tsípouro* or house wine. Dinner only.
Vrotos
Mitropolítou Gennadíou 6, Platía Athonos

Tel: 2310 223 958
This *platía* is home to many of the city's cheaper central *ouzerís,* and this is probably the most ambitious – and popular, despite being a bit pricier. A good mix of vegetable dishes, meat platters and seafood specials (including smoked eel). Limited seating, especially inside, so book for groups. Open daily except 1 month in summer.
Zythos
Katoúni 5, Ladádika
Tel: 2310 540284
This was apparently the first bar to open in this old warehouse district at the very beginning of its gentrification in the 1980s; the beam-and-brick decor harks back to its original industrial incarnation. It's still one of the best (and most popular) all-rounders here, with an astonishing variety of draught and bottled beers both imported and Greek, as well as a reasonable menu of daily generic-Mediterranean specials (with lots for vegetarians). Very mixed crowd; on the expensive side.

RHODES

Rhodes Town

Marasia
Agíou Ioánnou 155, New Town
Tel: 22410 30745 or 69325 86983
Creative *ouzerí* operating in the courtyard and interior of a 1923-vintage house. Aubergine turnovers, grilled oyster mushrooms and

stuffed squash blossoms precede mains like butterflied *savrídi* (horse mackerel), snails and cuttlefish in wine, and meat grills. Ample wine list as well as *oúzo* to drink. Open all year.
Marco Polo Café
Agíou Fanouríou 42, Old Town

Tel: 22410 25562
The Marco Polo Mansion courtyard sees some of the Old Town's more creative cooking. Platters change seasonally but might include pilaf with lamb and raisins, or pork medallions in *manoúri* cheese, fig and red peppercorn sauce. Save

room for desserts such as chocolate frozen with strawberries or white chocolate mousse. Co-proprietor Spýros is a wine fanatic, so you can dip into his cellar if the bulk wine fails to appeal. Open mid-May–mid-Oct dinner only; last orders 11pm.

Meltemi
Platía Koundourióti 8, east end of Élli beach
Tel: 22410 30480
Unbeatably set, locally attended beachside *ouzerí* specialising in crayfish nuggets, octopus croquettes, grilled red peppers in balsamic vinegar, chunky humous, and superb roast aubergine with beans and onions. Pleasant wintertime salon lined with old prints and photos. Open all day for food and drink, all year.

Sakis
Kanadá 95, Zéfyros district
Tel: 22410 35626 or 21537
An old favourite with pleasant patio and indoor seating, popular with Rhodians and foreigners alike. Known for its shellfish (such as limpets and snails), meat (chops, Cypriot *sheftaliés*) and the usual starters. Daily all year 5pm–1am, also Sun lunch.

Sea Star
Sofokléous 24
Tel: 22410 22117
The least expensive quality fish outlet in the Old Town. A limited menu – only scaly fish and a few shellfish and simple *mezédes* – is all to the good. Inside seating during cool weather, otherwise out on the square under the vines.

Steki tou Tsima
Peloponnísou 22, 400 metres/yds south of Old Town
Tel: 22410 74390
Likeable seafood taverna with seasonal fish; shellfish like *foúskes*, *strídia* (oysters) and cuttlefish grilled with their own ink; a few *mezédes*; and excellent chips, all accompanied by a variety of well-priced *oúzo*. Open daily except Sun dinner.

Steno
Agíon Anargýron 29, 400 metres/yds southwest of Old Town
Tel: 22410 35914
Welcoming *ouzerí* with indoor/outdoor seating according to season, attracting a mix of locals, expats and some savvy tourists. The menu encompasses chunky sausages, *pitaroúdia* (courgette-based croquettes), *hórta*, pulses, stuffed squash flowers, green beans with garlic, and simple seafood platters. Daily all year, dinner only.

Around Rhodes Island

Mavrikos
Líndos
Tel: 22440 31232
Founded in 1933 in the fig-tree square, and owned by

the same family ever since, Mavrikos ranks among the best on the island for its extensive menu of exquisite oven-cooked dishes and seafood (with less prominent meat dishes). *Gígandes* under carob syrup, sweet marinated sardines, and beets in goat's-cheese sauce precede fishy mains like skate timbale with sweetened balsamic vinegar, or superior interpretations of standards such as *dolmádes* or *tyrokafterí*. Excellent (and expensive) Greek wine list. Open Apr–Nov.

Palios Monolithos
Opposite church, Monólithos
Tel: 22460 61276
A favourite weekend lunch venue for grills, several oily *magirevtá*, unusual starters like wild mushrooms or mixed-leaf *dolmádes*, and superior (own-made) wine. Indoor/outdoor seating (and a distant sea view), and always a warm welcome from owners Manólis and Déspina. Open all year, weekends only winter.

Perigiali
By fishing anchorage, Stegná
Tel: 22440 23444
Locals throng the shady patio at weekends for the

sake of excellent seafood, savoury, hand-cut round chips, home-made *yaprákia* (stuffed vine leaves) and copious salads (the "Perigiáli" has caper greens and grilled aubergine) washed down by good bulk wine. The travertine-marble-clad loos are certainly unique on Rhodes. Open Apr–Nov.

Platanos
Lahaniá village
Tel: 22440 46027
Arguably the most exquisite setting on the island, with outdoor tables between two gushing Ottoman fountains under the plane tree of the restaurant's name. *Mezédes* are top-drawer and inexpensive, as are meat entrées, but the fish is relatively pricey. Open all year, weekends only winter, inside a new (2009) purpose-built premises.

Plimiri Beach
By Zoödóhou Piyís church, Plimýri
No phone
On any round-the-island car tour, you're likely to fetch up here at lunchtime. Some excellent fish plus vegetarian *mezédes*; basic presentation, but also fairly basic prices for the location, and willing service. Excellent chips, and maybe a cherry digestif on the house.

THE SOUTHERN DODECANESE

Hálki

Ftenagia
Tel: 69459 98333
Good seafood platters, vegetable *mezédes* and of course *oúzo* served above its own patch of pebble lido at eponymous Ftenágia cove.

Remezzo (Takis)
Emborió waterfront
Tel: 22460 45061
Excellent for *magirevtá* and pizzas.

Kárpathos

L'Angolo-Gorgona
South end of quay, Diafáni
Tel: 22450 51509

A versatile café run by Genoese Gabriella, with offerings including real Italian-standard coffees, *soumáda* (almond drink), lovely pies and limoncello liqueur.

Blue Sea
Main bay, Paralía Lefkoú
Tel: 22450 71074
Reasonable, if basic, fare served up by kindly management in a resort rather given to poor value. Strengths are *magirevtá* and pizzas; also pancake breakfasts.

Dramoundana
Mesohóri
Remarkably reasonably priced for Kárpathos, this

features local caper greens, village sausages and marinated fish.

Ellinikon
One block inland from quay, Pigádia
Tel: 22450 23932
A *mezedopolío* that caters all year to a local clientele with hot and cold *orektiká*, meat and good desserts.

Orea Karpathos
Southeast end of main quay, Pigádia
Tel: 22450 22501
The best all-round taverna, with palatable local bulk wine, *trahanádes* soup and great spinach pie. The locals treat it as an *ouzerí*, so it's OK to order just a few

orektiká to accompany a *karafáki* (small pitcher).

Kastelórizo

Akrothalassi
Southwest corner of quay
Tel: 22460 49052
The most consistently salubrious fish and meat grills. Reliably open at lunch too (unusual here), owing to shade from its arbour.

Ypomoni
Mid-quay
Tel: 22460 49224
Dinner-only seafood specialists (plus a few meat grills) with minimalist presentation, minimal prices, minimal seating and

maximum freshness – so expect to wait for a table.

Sými

Georgios
Top of Kalí Stráta, Horió
Tel: 22460 71984
An island institution: Greek nouvelle cuisine (variable in quality) in large, non-nouvelle portions, served in the pebbled courtyard. Informal live music some nights.
Marathounda
Marathoúnda Cove
The beach here isn't among the island's best, but folk come here for the sake of the taverna, with fish at or below town prices, good

mezédes and decent service. Watch out for the mooching goats and wasps, though.
Mythos Mezé
South quay, Gialós
Tel: 22460 71488
Dinner-only terrace venue on the roof of the former summer cinema, serving some of the more imaginative cooking on the island. Chef-owner Stávros's tasting menu might feature psaronéfri (pork medallions) with mushrooms and sweet wine sauce, lamb stifádo, or féta saganáki in fig sauce, and desserts like lemon pie or panna cotta. Open late May–late Sept.

Syllogos
Just south of Platía Syllógou, Horió
Tel: 22460 72138
Cavernous place with indoor/outdoor seating, great for taverna standards like skordaliá, arní lemonáto, fried fish and aubergine imám. The Rhodian bulk wine is good – but food portion sizes could be more generous. Open Apr–Nov.

Tílos

Armenon (Nikos')
On the shore road, Livádia
Tel: 22460 44134
Excellent, salubrious beach-taverna-cum-ouzerí, with octopus salad, white-bean

salad, etc. Alfa beer on tap.
Kastro
Megálo Horió
Tel: 22460 44116
The managing family can be a bit dour, but it's worth putting up with them for their excellent own-raised meat, goat's cheese and dolmádes, served at the best view-terrace on the island.
Omonia (Mihalis')
Just above the harbour square, Livádia
Tel: 22460 44287
Sit under the trees strung with fairy lights and enjoy the closest thing on the island to an authentic ouzerí by night; filling breakfasts in the morning.

THE NORTHERN DODECANESE

Agathonísi and Maráthi

Georgios
Agios Geórgios, east quay
Tel: 22470 29101
A good mix of seafood, salads and a few magirevtá; also about the only establishment of the trio here to open reliably at midday, thanks to the shady courtyard.
Marathi
Southeast end of Maráthi beach
Tel: 22470 31580
The most welcoming of three establishments here, with simple fish and free-range goat served up by piraticallygarbed Mihalis Kavouras, at attractive prices and to the accompaniment of Greek music. Open all day according to Mihalis's whim.

Astypálea

Australia
Just inland from the head of the bay, Skála
Tel: 22430 61275
Kyría María presides over the oldest and most wholesome taverna here, with fresh seafood, own-grown veggies and island wine. Open Apr–Nov.
Gerani
In the stream bed just behind Livádia beach

Tel: 22430 61484
The most consistently good and consistently open (May–Oct) taverna here, renowned for its excellent magirevtá.
Maïstrali (Tou Penindara)
Head of the harbour, Skála
Tel: 22430 61691
The best spot for a local lobster banquet, or less extravagantly a scaly-fish meal or magirevtá from a broad menu. Open all year for dinner, lunch as per demand.

Kálymnos and Télendos

Barba Stathis (Tassia's)
On path to Hohlakás beach, Télendos
Tel: 22430 47953
Warm little taverna doing just a few magirevtá daily, at bargain prices compared to the waterfront. The daughter of the establishment weaves lovely rag-rugs which are for sale.
Kafenes
Platía Hristoú, opposite municipal "palace", Póthia
Tel: 22430 28727
Going since 1950, this hole-in-the-wall purveys seafood mezédes, great local cheese and salads, with laïká music cranked up loud. Throw in very low prices and it's easy to see

why you always wait for a table.
Pandelis
Behind Olympic Hotel, Agios Nikólaos district
Tel: 22430 51508
The menu only mentions the ubiquitous Kalymnian mermizéli salad (like Cretan dákos) and a few grills or magirevtá; you have to ask after scaly fish, and fresh shellfish such as kalógnomes (like big mussels), strídia (round oysters) and foúskes (a bizarre marine invertebrate gathered by sponge divers as a sideline).
Tsopanakos
Armeós
This family taverna specialises in meat and cheese from local flocks, the speciality being mourí (goat or lamb in a clay pot). Open all year.

Kós

Ambavris
Ambávris hamlet, 800 metres (½ mile) south of Kós Town
Tel: 22420 25696
Ignore the perfunctory English-language menu in favour of the constantly changing mezédes pikilía or house medley – six platters for about €25 can encompass such delights as pihtí

(brawn), stuffed squash blossoms, fáva dip, and loukánika. Courtyard seating. Open for dinner May–Oct.
Ambeli
1km (½ mile) east of Tingáki resort
Tel: 22420 69682
The best policy here is to avoid the mains and order a variety of the excellent starters, such as pinigoúri (cracked wheat), bekrí mezé (pork chunks in spicy pepper sauce), sausages and yaprákia (the local dolmádes). Plates are fairly priced and deceptively large, so don't over-order. Seating indoors and out in the vineyard; open daily lunch and dinner May–Oct, winter Fri and Sat eve, Sun lunch.
Iy Palea Pigi
Pylí village
Tel: 22420 41510
Inexpensive and basic (loukánika, fried vegetables, marinated sardines, bakaliáros with mashed potatoes) but nourishing fare at this taverna hidden away beside the giant cistern fountain with lion-headed spouts. Open lunch and dinner, may close Dec–Mar.
Limni (Karamolengos)
Linopótis, below Pylí on main road
Tel: 22420 41579
If you're tired of being

stuffed like a foie gras goose at Greek tavernas, then this *ouzerí* is perfect for you: all items are available in small, medium and large platters. Choose from a huge number of different types of *oúzo*, *tsikoudiá* and *tsípouro*. Open all year noon–11pm except Tue, though best at dinner time when there's less road noise.

Makis
One lane in from front, Mastihári
Tel: 22420 51592
Currently the best – and best-priced – fish on the island outside of Kós Town, and an excellent spot to wait for the ro-ro ferry to Kálymnos. No *magirevtá*, a few salads and dips, and oblique sea views at best mean relatively few tourists.

Oromedon
Zía approach road
Tel: 22420 69983
One of the few tavernas here that doesn't need to rely on picture-menus and other gimmicks thanks to the prime view from its roof terrace, and the good, local food. Open all year.

Platáni village
Central junction
Ethnic Turkish management at several clustered establishments dish out tasty Anatolian-style *mezédes* and kebabs; go in a group so that you can pass the little platters around. The most popular, if touristy, is **Arap** (tel: 22420 28442); if you can't get in, head across the way to **Asklipios** or **Serif** (tel: 22420 23784), which fills with locals later in the evening. Between November and April these close, leaving **Gin's Place** further inland (tel: 22420 25166) – where the food can be even better – as the sole option. In any season, finish off with an Anatolian ice cream, at **Zaharoplastio Paradosi** opposite the three summer restaurants.

Pote tin Kyriaki
Pissándrou 9, Kós Town
Tel: 22420 27872
The town's only genuine *ouzerí*, with fair prices and

patio seating in summer, indoors in the converted old house otherwise. Dinner only, Mon–Sat; winter Thur–Sat lunch and dinner.

Psaropoula
Avérof 17, Kós Town
Tel: 22420 21909
The most genuine and reasonable of three fish tavernas grouped here, with good *orektiká* preceding fair-priced seafood; sidewalk terrace, but also indoor area and thus open all year.

Léros

Dimitris Mezedopolio
Spiliá district, on road between Pandéli and Vromólithos
Tel: 22470 25626
The heartiest food on the island, hands down, and the best view of Vromólithos. Stars include the chunky, herby Lerian sausages, potato salad, *hanoúm bórek* (pastries stuffed with cheese and *pastourmás* or cured meat). Moderate prices and large portions. Open most of the year.

Giusi e Marcello
Alinda
Tel: 22470 24888
Genuine Italian-run spot for pizzas, pasta dishes, a few antipasti and salads, plus top-notch desserts like sorbet and tiramisu, washed down by good Italian bulk or bottled wine. Dinner only; open late Mar–early Jan.

Neromylos Ouzeri
Out by the sea-marooned windmill, Agía Marina
Tel: 22470 24894
The most romantic setting on the island, whether for lunch or dinner. Specialities include *garidopílafo* (shrimp rice), baked four-cheese casserole and *kolokythokeftédes* (courgette patties). Open mid-Mar–late Oct; reservations mandatory July–Aug.

Psaropoula (Apostolis)
Pandéli beach
Tel: 22470 25200/24671
A good balance of fresh seafood and *magirevtá*, especially popular with locals at weekends. Both

open and enclosed sea-view terraces, so open most of the year.

Lipsí

Dilaila
Katsadiá, left-hand bay
Tel: 22470 41041
Incongruously classy in its rural surroundings, with platters such as marinated fish, saffron rice, excellent *fáva*, and salad with balsamic dressing and local cheese. Moderate prices; open June–Sept.

Giannis
Mid-quay, port town
Tel: 22470 41395
Excellent all-rounder, with meat and seafood grills but plenty of salads and *laderá* dishes for vegetarians too. The only taverna open for lunch as well as dinner all season long. Early May–early Oct.

Karnagio
South side of bay, port town
Tel: 22470 41422
Mountainous salads and good *magirevtá* like pork with celery and carrots await you here, as well as fish or pasta. Open all year for lunch, dinner too in season.

Nísyros

Ankyrovoli
Agios Sávvas Cove, Mandráki
Tel: 22420 31552
The reincarnation of the late lamented Fabrika, this *ouzerí* features *pittiá* (courgette and chickpea patties), *boukouniés* (fried pork), grated carrot salad, bulk wine from Attica, good taped Greek sounds and big portions at moderate prices.

Apyria (Triandafyllos)
Emborió
Tel: 22420 31377
The former *kafenío* of this all-but-abandoned village has been transformed into the best meat taverna on island – *gouronópoulo* on the spit during summer, otherwise just a few *mezédes* and select meat platters daily at very fair prices, with local *halvás* for

dessert. Indoor/outdoor seating; open all year (weekends only winter).

Limenari
Eponymous cove west of Páli
Tel: 22420 31023.
Opened only in 2007, this has quickly grabbed a big share of the local market thanks to fair prices and portions for salads, fish, a few dishes of the day, and made-to-order *tyrokafterí* (which takes a while to arrive). Occupies a lovely spot in terraced valley above the bay. Islanders and army conscripts go all year, always a good sign.

Pátmos

Benetos
Sápsila cove, 2km (1 mile) southeast of Skála
Tel: 22470 33089
This eatery has a reputation as one of the best spots on the island for Mediterranean/Pacific Rim fusion cuisine, with a stress on seafood. Count on €35–40 for drinks and three courses, maybe to include bean and salmon croustade, *astakomakaronáda* (lobster pasta) and lemon sorbet. Open June–early Oct, dinner only except Mon; best to reserve in summer.

Hiliomodi
Just off the Hóra road, Skála
Tel: 22470 34080
Vegetarian *mezédes* and seafood delicacies such as limpets (served live), grilled octopus and salted anchovies served at this *ouzerí* with summertime tables on a quiet pedestrian lane. Inexpensive, thus packed and service can suffer. Dinner only; open all year.

Ktima Petra
Pétra beach, south of Gríkou
Tel: 22470 33207
Hands down the best beach taverna on the island. Chunky *melitzanosaláta*, lush rocket salad, *dolmádes*, brown bread and pork *giovétsi* are typical of lunchtime offerings, with excellent *retsína* from

ABOVE: lunch with a view – all part of the island experience.

Thebes; at sunset the grill is lit, and still later the place becomes a full-on bar. Open Easter–Oct 7.

Leonidas
Lámbi beach, north end of island
Tel: 22470 31490
Another reliable beach taverna, going since 1958; food presentation is fairly simple, emphasising grilled fish. Open lunch and dinner, Easter–Oct 10.

Livadi Geranou
Above eponymous beach
Tel: 69724 97426
Doesn't look like much, but this taverna has a cult following for the sake of its coarse-cut *hórta*, roast goat, *keftédes* and seafood dishes – plus views over the entire island.

Panagos
Upper Kámbos
Tel: 22470 31570
A beacon of *magirevtá* for the whole island. The autumn menu might feature baked *palamídi* (north Aegean tuna), chickpea hotpot, good bulk wine, and yogurt dessert on the house. Very reasonably priced, open all year. Holds a museum's worth of old photos inside.

Vengera
Opposite marina, Skála
Tel: 22470 32988
Since 2002, this has established itself as a worthy rival to Benetos, with top-drawer generic French/Mediterranean cooking and polished service. €40 upwards per head. Dinner only, May–early Sept. Must reserve in high season.

CRETE

Agios Nikólaos

Corto Maltese
Aktí Neárhou 15, by marina
Tel: 28410 22916
Opened in 2007 and serving stylish Med-fusion cuisine in a tastefully chic environment. Signature dishes include *oúzo*-flambéed shrimps with saffron, or *psaronéfri* (pork tenderloin) with Calvados and green apple. Open 10.30am (for late breakfast) until midnight. Thursday is wine-tasting night.

Pelagos
Stratigoú Kóraka 10
Tel: 28410 25737
Ensconced in one of the few surviving neoclassical houses in the town, this expensive taverna specialising in fish dishes, and innovative salads like cuttlefish with wild fennel, has attractive garden seating out back for fine-weather dining.

Ano Arhánes

Diktamos
Pérkolo 3 (side street in town centre)
Tel: 28107 51022
A nostalgic decor (musical instruments, photos of Greek musicians and theatre personalities) complements traditional *magirevtá* like *hirinó mé sélino* (pork with celery). Live *rebétiko* music some weekend nights.

Argyroúpoli

O Kipos tis Arkoudenas
On road towards Episkopí
Tel: 28310 61607
Lamb and pork specialists, serving up good food below the trees of its rear garden. This is a better option than the cluster of tavernas at the famous springs in the village.

Eloúnda

Myli
Káto Pinés
Tel: 28410 41961
In the hills above Eloúnda; traditional, tasty, well-prepared Cretan food, at very reasonable prices.

Vritomartes
Tel: 28410 41325
Set on its own little island, moored in the centre of the harbour. Excellent fish, caught by the owner.

Frangokástello

Kali Kardia
Tel: 28250 92123
Old-fashioned taverna where the best tack is to eat what the proprietors are eating: perhaps a fry-up of the very fresh local fish and wild-picked greens such as *stífnos*, washed down with good *hýma* wine.

Haniá

Ask the locals where they eat when they're tired of the scene on the two Venetian harbours and they'll recommend Aktí Papanikolí, just west of the walls at Néa Hóra, with its 10 seafront tavernas. We list a few reasonably priced choices in the Old Town.

Faka
Arholéon 15, set back from inner harbour off Platía Kateháki
Tel: 28210 42341
Because of its location, Faka is significantly less expensive and touristy than waterfront spots. All the traditional Cretan standards made from sound ingredients; occasional live music sessions a bonus.

Karnagio
Platía Kateháki 8
Tel: 28210 53366
Another establishment set back from the harbour, in an old boathouse (*karnágio*) and with terrace seating allowing a glimpse of the water. Especially good for fish.

Katofli
Aktí Papanikolí 13
Tel: 28210 98621
As much *ouzerí* – or rather, *rakádiko* – as taverna, this has local dishes such as *stamnagáthi* (an unusual autumn *hórta*). A bargain, with a €20 note covering a *karafáki* (small pitcher) of *rakí* and three platters of fishy and vegetarian fare. Open all year.

Ouzythino
Aktí Papanikolí 6
Tel: 28210 73315
Down-to-earth *ouzerí* with tables out on the jetty. The seafood is fairly priced and very fresh; three can eat well for under €40. Best in summer; open in winter too.

Tamam
Zambelíou 49
Tel: 28210 58639
Housed in an old hamam (Turkish bath), this emphasises vegetarian food and creative meat-based fusion dishes. The few tables in the narrow lane outside are perennially in demand – even in October – but the interior, while atmospheric, isn't well ventilated.

Iráklio

Giakoumis
Fotíou Theodosáki, in the market
Tel: 2810 284039
The city's oldest taverna, specialising in succulent lamb chops, washed down with bulk wine from the local Lyrarakis vintners.
Ippokambos
Sofoklí Venizélou
Tel: 2810 280240
A superb establishment overlooking the old harbour, famed for its meticulously prepared *mezédes* and reasonably priced fish. It gets busy, so go early. Open lunch and evenings.
Paradosiako
Vourváhon 9, in a *stoa* opposite Goody's fast food
Tel: 2810 342927
Tucked (deliberately?) out of the way, but giving onto a lovely courtyard, this characterful *koutoúki* (neighbourhood joint) specialises in *magirevtá*, grilled meats and local bulk wine at friendly prices.
Syllogos Erasitehnon Alieon (Amateur Fishermen's Club)
Tel: 2810 223812
Despite the name, this seafood *ouzerí* in an ex-cold-storage plant near the harbour is open to all, with parking out front. By city standards, the scaly fish and shellfish are eminently affordable – two can snack for under €30 with a bit of *tsikoudiá* included.
Trata
Ikosipémptis Avgoústou 12
Tel: 2810 284322
A more conventional option for seafood, with partial views out towards the Koulés bastion. All the usual fishy dishes, though sardines and octopus are particular strengths.

Kalathás beach (Akrotíri peninsula)

Kalathas Estiatorio
Tel: 28210 64729
Decent beachfront taverna with friendly service and reasonable, savoury

mezédes platters – pity about the store-bought, defrosted *kalitsoúna* turnovers though. Open Easter–Oct.

Káto Zákros

Akrogiali
By the beach
Tel: 28430 26893
Níkos and Tánia took over this venerable taverna in 1991, and have built up a good reputation for fresh, locally sourced fish and meat. They also do breakfast for the guests in their affiliated rooms and apartments.

Kournás

Kali Kardia
Kournás village, 3km (2 miles) above the eponymous lake
Tel: 28250 96278
Excellent local cooking and fresh meat, especially lamb and sausages. *Galaktoboúriko*, a lemony egg-custard, may be offered for dessert.

Lassíthi Plateau

Dionysos
Magoulás
Tel: 28440 31672
In this tiny (population 89) hamlet, this is a good choice for grilled meats and Cretan *mezédes*; they also have a few basic rooms upstairs.

Makrýgialos

Oasis
West end of strip
Tel: 28430 51918
Taverna known for using only fresh (not frozen) fish and locally sourced meat and veg; they also have good rooms upstairs.

Nída Plateau (above Anógia)

Nida
Tel: 28340 31141
At the base of Psilorítis, Crete's highest mountain, this country taverna serves hearty meat- and chicken-based oven dishes and

grills. Daily Apr–Oct; weekends otherwise.

Palékastro

Kakavia
On Hióna beach, just beyond Palékastro (20km/12 miles east of Sitía)
Tel: 28430 61228
Named after its speciality, fish soup; also good seafood in general.

Paleohóra

Caravella
Harbour quay
Tel: 28230 41131
The top local seafood restaurant, with bulk wine from nearby Kastélli (Kissámou). High-standard apartments upstairs as well.
Third Eye
Between the centre and the beach
Tel: 28230 41234
This excellent vegetarian restaurant, still maintaining a high standard since the 1960s, also offers Asian and Indian dishes. Basic rooms upstairs too; live music once weekly.

Plakiás area

Ifigeneia
Angouselianá village, 10km (6 miles) inland
Tel: 28320 51362
2008-inaugurated taverna at the western outskirts of the village that's quickly become a shrine to Cretan *mezédes* – such as *volví skordaláta* (pickled wild hyacinth bulbs), *stamnagáthi* (a favourite autumn *hórta*), apákia (smoked pork loin) and a boiled-goat main dish with *gamopílafo* (white sticky rice.
Medousa
Plakiás, inland from the pharmacy
Tel: 28320 31521
Fine home cooking accompanied by shots of excellent *rakí*.
Plateia
Mýrthios village, overlooking Plakiás Bay
Cretan cooking and local wine, with good vegetarian options and fantastic views from the balcony.

Réthymno

Fanari
Kefalogiánnídon 16, between old port and Fortezza
Tel: 28310 54849
Good-value seafront establishment specialising in traditional Cretan *mezédes*, plus good fish and meat mains, as well as decent bulk wine.
Kyria Maria
Moskhoviti 20 (behind the Rimóndi Fountain)
Tel: 28310 29078
Low-key taverna with indoor/outdoor seating, and all the standards. The home-made dessert is on the house.
Thalassografia
Kefalogiannídon 33
Tel: 28310 52569
Clifftop, cutting-edge *mezedopolío*-taverna near the Fortezza, with a modern take on traditional Cretan dishes such as *arní stí stámna* (lamb in a clay pot); reserve at weekends.
Veneto
Epimenídou 4
Tel: 28310 56634
Expensive, old-world diner of the eponymous restoration hotel. Its fusion dishes include salmon millefeuille with avocado and *myzíthra* sauce, and stuffed lamb. Notably well-stocked wine cellar.

Sitía

Kali Kardia
Foundalídou 28
Very hospitable *ouzerí* emphasising local wine as much as the stronger spirits to go with its snails, little fish and the like. Some tourist patronage, but still very much a local hangout.
Mikos
Kornárou 117
Tel: 28430 22416
A haven for carnivores with its rotating spit, and Cretan starters feature too. Tables in the street, as well as around the corner facing the sea; cool weather seating indoors under the usual bric-a-brac lining the walls.

A CTIVITIES

THE ARTS, RELIGIOUS FESTIVALS, NIGHTLIFE AND SHOPPING

THE ARTS

Music and Dance

Thanks to Greece's geographical position and the vast number of cultures that have called it home, there is astonishing regional variety in island folk musics. Crete has one of the more vital traditions, characterised by the *lýra* (three-string spike fiddle) and *laoúto* (mandolin-like lute). In the Dodecanese, these are often joined by either *tsamboúna*, a goatskin bagpipe, *violí* (western *violin*) or *sandoúri*, the hammer dulcimer popularised in the islands by refugees from Asia Minor. Lésvos has a tradition of brass bands, imported apparently from the Asia Minor mainland opposite.

Nisiótika is the general name for Aegean island music; that of the Ionians doesn't really count, being heavily Italian-influenced – especially in its vocal styles *kantádes* and *arékia* – and Western in scale.

Contemporary sounds include original compositions or derivations of traditional material. From the islands, worth special mention are the group **Haínides** and the earlier work of **Loudovíkos ton Anogíon**, both originally from Crete.

Each archipelago (and sometimes each island within it) has its own particular **folk dances**. These range from the basic *stá tría* – three steps to one side, followed by a kick (growing gradually faster and faster) – to a frenzied combination of complicated footwork, jumps, slaps and kicks. Troupes, dressed in traditional Greek costume, are most

likely to be performing on public holidays (you may also see them on television, or the artificial surrounds of hotel- or taverna-sponsored "Greek Nights"). Probably the best-known professional group is the **Dora Stratou Ethnic Dance Company** (www.grdance.org), which holds regular shows to live accompaniment from May to September at the Dora Stratou Theatre, Filopáppou Hill (southwest slope), Athens.

Quality music venues in the islands often take advantage of pre-existing historic monuments – good examples are ancient amphitheatres or *odeia* on Thásos, Kós and Sámos; castle moats and baileys, as in the **Théatro Táfros** on Rhodes, the **Paleó Froúrio** on Corfu or (with spectacular, distracting views) **Mólyvos Castle** on Lésvos. Corfu's opera house was, sadly, destroyed during World War II but the **opera house in Ermoúpoli, Sýros** has been well restored, as has **Rhodes's Italian-built municipal theatre**, Corfu's **Ionian Academy** auditorium and Iráklio's **Níkos Kazantzákis open-air theatre**. Unlike in the west, churches are rarely used, the sterling exception being **St George's on Corfu**.

RELIGIOUS FESTIVALS

(* denotes that this is also a legal holiday, with everything closed.)
1 January Feast of Agios Vasílios (St Basil).
6 January* Agía Theofánia, Tá Fóta/ Epiphany: Blessing of the waters – at any island, youths dive for the honour of retrieving a crucifix cast into the port by the local bishop or priest.

Children's Activities

Despite the general child-friendliness of modern Greek culture, there are few activities or facilities specifically aimed at children – certainly nothing in the order of Paris's Disneyland. There are water parks on Crete, Aegina, Corfu and Rhodes, and the growing number of all-inclusive resorts (on islands like Crete, Kós and Corfu) always have child-centred "animation" (entertainment) programmes. Also, any multi-starred hotel is likely to have a separate childrens' pool and (unsupervised) playground.

February–March Carnival season for three weeks before Lent: all over Greece. Some islands with celebrations of special interest are Zákynthos, Corfu, Híos (Mestá, Olýmbi), Lésvos (Agiássos), Agía Anna (Évvia), Kefaloniá, Kárpathos, Iráklio, Réthymno and (best of all) Skýros. Depending on the place, expect masque-ing, more or less obscene songs, floats, pranks, food-fights, and people rapping each other on the head with squeaky plastic hammers. *Tsiknopémpti or "Roast-Smell" Thursday* The last day, 52 before Easter, on which the devout may consume meat. All grill-type tavernas are booked up days in advance for a final binge.
"Clean" Monday* Beginning of the fast for Lent – last day of cheese-eating, four days after *Tsiknopémpti*. Picnics in the countryside and kite-flying, all over Greece.
25 March* *Evangelismós/Feast of the Annunciation/National Day*:

military parades in all main towns, pilgrimage to Tínos.

Easter Weekend* *Good Friday, Holy Saturday* and *Easter Sunday* are celebrated throughout Greece. The date usually, but not always, precedes or follows Western Easter by one to four weeks; for the exact date in any given year, consult http://5ko.free.fr/en/easter.php

23 April *Feast of St George:* celebrated especially in Kaliópi (Límnos), Asigonía (near Haniá) and Pylí (Kós).

1 May* *Workers' Day:* picnics in the countryside all over Greece; also usually demonstrations by disaffected labour in larger towns.

May/June *Agion Pnévma*/Pentecost Monday*, 50 days after Easter. The resulting three-day weekend (*triímero*) is the excuse for the first proper excursion to the holiday islands and the start of the "season".

17 July* *Agía Marína.* A big festival in rural areas, as she is (in one aspect) a major protector of crops. In many parts of Greece, especially where refugee communities from the Black Sea are to be found, it's considered bad luck to swim on this day as the saint in a malevolent guise always claims a victim.

19–20 July *Profítis Ilías*/Prophet Elijah. Almost every island has at least one summit in his honour, where there will be gathering, feasting and music (if only from cranked-up car sound systems) outside the saint's chapel or monastery.

6 August* *Metamórfosis toú Sotíros*/ Transfiguration of the Saviour. Mega food-fight with flour, squid ink, etc on Hálki; big commemoration at Pythagório, Sámos, where Christ is said to have aided the victorious Greek fleet in the 1824 battle of the Mykáli Straits.

15 August* *Kímisi tís Theotókou/ Dormition of the Virgin:* festivals all over the islands, especially Páros, Agiássos and Ólymbos (Kárpathos). Major pilgrimage to Tínos. In Orthodox theology, the "Assumption" into Heaven takes place eight days later, on 23 August.

29 August *Apokefálisis toú Prodrómou*/Beheading of John the Baptist. Pilgrimage festivals at Vrykoúnda on Kárpathos, and remote Agíou Ioánni Monastery on Crete's Rodópou peninsula.

8 September *Yénnisis tís Panagías/ Birth of the Virgin.* The second-biggest Marian festival after 15 August; notable observances at Tsambíkas Monastery on Rhodes, where childless women crawl up the steps

on hands and knees in supplication for conception, and on Spétses, where the day is also the anniversary of a naval victory over the Ottomans in 1822.

23–24 September *Agios Ioánnis Theológos*/St John the Divine. Special celebrations outside Nikiá, Nísyros, and on Pátmos at the saint's monastery, with special liturgies.

26 October *Agios Dimítrios*/St Demetrios. The name-day of possibly a fifth of the male population, and traditionally the first day new wine was ready to drink.

28 October* *Ohi* (No) *Day:* anniversary of Greek leader Metaxás's supposed one-word response to Italy's ultimatum in 1940, prior to Greece's unexpected defeat of the Italian invasion force. Military parades in major cities.

8 November *Tón Taxiarhón Mihaïl ke Gavriïl*/Archangels Michael and Gabriel. Of the many rites at churches and monasteries dedicated to them, the grandest are at Panormítis on Sými – effectively extending that island's tourist season until then – and at the monastery outside Mandamádos, Lésvos.

Christmas season All over Greece. In a dwindling number of places, children sing *kálenda* (carols) from door to door for a small gratuity; mostly nowadays an excuse for Western-style commercialism and an outbreak of plastic inflatable Santas on chimneys, balcony railings, etc. Both 25 December and 26 December are legal holidays; the latter is not "Boxing Day" as in Britain, but *Sýnaxis tís Panagías*, the "Gathering of the Virgin's Entourage".

31 December *Paramoní tis Protohroniás*/New Year's Eve. Many Greeks play cards for money on this occasion, and cut the *vasilópitta* pie

Winter Entertainment

Indoor *ouzerís* and *kafenía*, or at least those with a conservatory, operate through the winter; some of the island's tavernas and bars keep their doors open too, though often only from Friday night to Sunday noon. But if the owner has something better or more profitable to do, like tend a farm or go fishing on an unseasonably mild night, the establishment will remain closed even if it's notionally supposed to be open. Outdoor cinemas, dance clubs and music venues perforce close down, and cultural edification retreats indoors: many islands have a weekly cinematheque showing quality films, and a few tavernas equipped with wooden stages host live music (often *laïká* or *rebétiko*) at weekends.

with its lucky coin hidden in it. Special celebration in the town of Híos.

NIGHT- (AND DAY-) LIFE

Metropolitan nightlife in Greece (on the islands, this means mainly Iráklio, Haniá, Réthymno plus the larger island capitals like Rhodes and Kérkyra towns and the major foreign-dominated resorts) takes the form of *barákia*, theme bars with a recorded soundtrack, most likely trance, house or ambient; live music venues (most likely Greek *laïká*, or a watered-down version of *rebétika* or even Greek rock); dance clubs with a proper *písta* or floor; and musical tavernas where food prices reflect the live entertainment.

BELOW: celebrating to the strains of the *bouzoúki.*

ABOVE: laidback nightlife in Skiáthos Town.

Barákia won't have a cover charge, and in these tough times may offer extended "happy hours" or permanently cheap drink prices (eg €3–4 for a large beer); generally, however, you should expect stiff, Northern European tariffs for hard spirits or cocktails (€7 and up). **Music clubs** typically levy a cover charge (which may include the first drink), whilst live venues cost a minimum of €15 to get in.

A big current trend is the all-day **beach bar** (likely continuing after dark), which won't charge a cover per se but may ask stiff fees for sun loungers. In return you get a soundtrack, possibly a small dance floor and probably ancillary activities such as beach volleyball.

For many older Greeks, however, the **taverna** remains the most popular site for a night out spent eating, drinking and, sometimes, singing and dancing. In general, it's childless Greeks under 30 or younger who frequent the **bars and clubs**.

In Athens, the weekly *Athinórama* (in Greek) has an extensive listing of all venues and events. The English-language events listings of the *Athens News* and *Athens Plus* are by comparison very incomplete.

During the summer (late June–early September) many Athens and Thessaloníki clubs and music halls close down, with musicians of all stripes touring the countryside and islands, performing for the seasonal festivals.

Casinos

For a more sophisticated – and potentially more expensive – night out, there are casinos in Corfu, Rhodes and Ermoúpoli (Sýros).

Cinema

Going to the movies in Greece during the main tourist season is a special pleasure not to be missed, because nearly all the cinemas operating during summer (the others shut down unless they have air-conditioning) are **open-air cinemas**. In town centres these are to be found tucked among apartment buildings; in other areas perhaps perched on a seaside promontory under the stars, or out at the edge of town amongst the fields.

Rising real-estate values are having an attritional effect, but particularly good cinemas survive in Kós Town, in Paleohóra (Crete), Mytilíni (Sámos), in and around Égina Town, in Parikía (Páros), outside Náxos town, in Firá (Santoríni), in Póthia (Kálymnos), in Híos Town, in Mytilíni Town and Mólyvos on Lésvos, in Skiáthos Town, in Kérkyra Town and Levkáda Town (plus, of course, many in Athens).

Tickets, at €6–8, are slightly cheaper than at indoor cinemas and soundtracks are in the original language (with Greek subtitles). On smaller islands there may be only one film showing, at around 9.15pm, while elsewhere there will be two screenings, at 9 and 11pm. There is always a 15-minute *diálemma*, or intermission, about halfway through the feature. The season of operation for outdoor cinemas is dictated by however long it's comfortable enough to sit still outdoors for two hours after nightfall – typically, late May to mid-September.

Island Cultural Events

April–October Sound and Light performances on Corfu at the Páleo Froúrio.

June, late Rhodes Eco-Films Festival.

June–August Corfu Festival: Jazz, Brass bands, local choirs, invited foreign guests.

July Music Festival on the island of Itháki (Ithaca).

July Manólis Kalomíris Festival, mostly classical music, Sámos.

July–August Thásos Festival, mostly in Liménas ancient theatre.

July–August Astypálea Municipal Festival.

July–August Lato Cultural Festival, Agios Nikólaos, Crete.

July–August Rhodes Cultural Festival, with wine festival end August in Rodíni park.

July–August Ippokrateia Festival, Kós.

July, late Réthymno wine fair, followed by Aug–Sept Renaissance Fair of cultural activities at the Venetian Fort.

July–September Sými Festival; mixed classical and Greek pop performances.

July–September Iráklio Festival – concerts, theatre, opera and dance by world-class acts.

August Levkáda International Folklore Festival, with overseas groups.

September Santoríni Classical Music Festival.

Shopping

Greece is generally not a retail-therapy paradise – clothes, despite often being imported from the far East or Central Europe, are often eye-wateringly priced, and only become affordable during the August sales. Shoes are still made locally, however, and with careful fittting can be worthwhile bargains. All the international chain labels are represented, plus there's a local menswear entity called Glou which can be of interest. The best-value purchases are jewellery, often made to ancient Greek themes, and foodstuffs – not just the ubiquitous honey, olive oil and olives – impossible to obtain overseas. Mind the strictures of your home destination, however: flights bound for the US are likely to have checked baggage thoroughly combed on arrival. And enclose all glass containers in bubble-wrap.

A Handy Summary of Practical Information, Arranged Alphabetically

A dmission Charges

Most archaeological sites and museums, public or private, have admission charges varying from €2 for minor affairs up to €12 for five-star attractions. Occasionally (as in Athens and Rhodes) you can get a joint ticket covering several sites and museums at an advantageous price. From November to March, most state-run sites give free admission to EU nationals on Sunday; Monday or Tuesday are typical closure days. Students with valid ID get one-third to one-half off entry fees, as do certified teachers, journalists, archaeology students and people aged 60 or over.

B udgeting for Your Trip

Especially since the advent of the euro, Greece is no longer by any stretch of the imagination an inexpensive country. Travelling as one of a couple in high season, you should allow a minimum of €30 for a share of accommodation (budget €40–50 each in the biggest cities and name resorts), €15–20 for your half of a meal, €6–12 daily for site/museum admissions, and €15–17 for your share of the cheapest, smallest rental car – before petrol costs, which typically match those of the UK. As elsewhere, most things are more expensive for people travelling alone; single-room accommodation often costs almost as much as double.

C hildren

Children are adored in Greece, and many families are still highly superstitious about their welfare – don't be surprised to see toddlers with amulets pinned to their clothes to ward off the evil eye. So expect your own kids to be the centre of attention. Children are given quite a bit of leeway in Greece and treated very indulgently. However, you may have to put your foot down when shop owners offer free sweets or strangers are over-indulgent towards your own children.

Climate

In general, the north coast of each island is subject to more summer-time gales and cooler temperatures than the protected south coast; be sure to check on a map exactly where a holiday resort is before making a final booking. Many travellers underestimate the differences in climate between individual island chains.

The green, cool Ionian islands, for instance, are prone to rainy spells from mid-September through to the end of April. By contrast, Rhodes and Crete's southern coast can offer swimming for the hardy as late as mid-December. If planning to visit any of the islands from mid-September through to the end of April, a good rule to follow is this: the further south the island is geographically, the better the sunshine rate will be.

On the whole, islands are ill-equipped for visitors during the winter months. Heating can be basic or non-existent, boats are infrequent, tinned food may be all that is available on the smaller islands and amenities are scarce. The tourist season is officially "over" in late October, although it extends into November on Rhodes and Crete, but ends early September on northern islands like Thásos or Límnos.

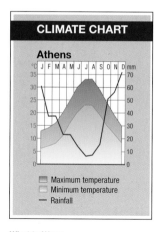

CLIMATE CHART

Athens

- ☐ Maximum temperature
- ☐ Minimum temperature
- — Rainfall

What to Wear

If you visit Greece during the summer months, you will want to bring lightweight, casual clothing. Add a pullover or shell jacket to this and you will be prepared for the occasional cool night breezes, or conditions on open boat decks. Lightweight shoes and sandals are ideal in the summer, but you will also need a pair of comfortable walking shoes that have already been broken in. If you plan to do any rigorous hiking on the islands bring sturdy, over-the-ankle boots with a good tread; leather will be more comfortable in summer temperatures than high-tech synthetic materials. If you visit Greece during the winter months, which can be surprisingly cold, bring the same kind of clothes you would wear during spring in the northern part of the United States or Central Europe.

Crime and Safety

Greece is still one of the safest countries in Europe. Despite the indulgence of the Greek popular press in the luridly publicised antics of certain Albanians and Romanians, violent crime remains relatively rare. Sadly, however, pickpocketing and other forms of petty theft do occur, especially in central Athens, and it is now the norm to lock cars and front doors even in the countryside. Travellers transiting Athens, especially through Sýndagma and Monastiráki, should be highly alert to gangs of pickpockets targetting the heavily-laden, especially in the metro or alighting the airport bus.

Because of tightened security considerations it is unwise to leave luggage unattended anywhere except perhaps in a hotel lobby, under the gaze of the desk staff. However, belongings inadvertently left behind in a café will still usually be put aside for you to collect.

Customs Regulations

There are no official restrictions on the movement of goods within the European Union, provided the goods were purchased within the EU. It is no longer necessary for EU nationals to enter their home-country customs through a red or green channel.

Duty-Paid goods

If you buy goods in Greece for which you pay tax, there are no restrictions on the amounts you can take home. EU law has set "guidance levels", however, on the following:

- **Tobacco** 3,200 cigarettes, or 400 cigarillos, or 200 cigars or 3kg of tobacco
- **Spirits** 10 litres
- **Fortified wine/wine** 90 litres
- **Beer** 110 litres

If you exceed these amounts you must be able to prove the goods are for personal use.

Duty-Free Goods

Since the abolition of duty-free concessions within the European Union, all goods brought into Greece from EU countries must be duty-paid. In theory there are no limitations to the amount of duty-paid goods that can be brought into the country. However, cigarettes and most spirits are much cheaper in Greece than in Britain and Ireland (government duty is much lower), so waiting until you reach your destination to buy these goods will save you money.

For travellers from non-EU countries, allowances for duty-free goods brought into Greece are:

- **Tobacco** 200 cigarettes, or 100 cigarillos, or 50 cigars, or 250g of tobacco
- **Alcohol** 1 litre of spirits or liqueurs over 22 percent volume, or 2 litres of fortified or sparkling wine or other liqueurs
- **Perfume** 60cc of perfume, plus 250cc of eau de toilette

Non-EU residents can claim back Value Added Tax (currently between 6 and 19 percent) on any items costing over €120, provided they export the item within 90 days of purchase. Tax-free forms are available at tourist shops and department stores. Remember to keep the receipt and form. You make your claim at the customs area of the airport when departing.

Currency Restrictions

There are no limits on the amount of euros visitors can import or export. There are no restrictions on travellers' cheques, but cash sums of more than €10,000 or its equivalent should be declared on entry.

Importing Cars

Visitors arriving with their own car are allowed to circulate for up to six months without any formalities; after that the bureaucratic fun begins, and people intending to establish residence will find that it's usually cheaper and easier to buy a Greek-registered car than try to import their own from overseas. Cars detected circulating after the initial six-month period without valid road tax are liable to seizure by customs/tax undercover agents.

D isabled Travellers

Despite nudging from the EU, Greece has some way to go before becoming fully compliant with regulations on facilities for people with disabilities.

Athens, with lifts in the metro, "kneeling" buses on many routes, recorded announcements of upcoming

BELOW: sun, sea and a cold *frappé* – simple pleasures even if you're on a budget.

stops on the metro plus some buses, and ramps (when not blocked by illegally parked cars) at kerbsides, is furthest ahead. The new Thessaloníki metro should also be EU-compliant regarding facilities for the disabled.

Elsewhere, amenities can be poor – there are few or no sound pips for the sight-impaired at pedestrian crossings, and it is common to see the wheelchair-bound tooling down the middle of the asphalt rather than risking the obstacle course of a typical pedestrian pavement.

Electricity

220V. Sockets are the double, round-pin variety. Socket adaptors are easily available at airports if you do not remember to buy one before you leave home. US visitors with 110V appliances will need to buy a transformer.

E mbassies and Consulates
Foreign Embassies in Athens

All embassies are open from Monday to Friday only, usually from 8am until 2pm, except for their own national holidays (as well as Greek ones).
• **Australia** Anastasíou Tsohá 24, corner Soútsou (Ambelókipi metro); tel: 210 645 0404.
• **Canada** Gennadhíou 4, Kolonáki, (Evangelismós metro); tel: 727 3400.
• **Ireland** Vassiléos Konstandínou 7 (by National Gardens); tel: 723 2771.
• **South Africa** Kifissiás 60, Maroússi; tel: 210 610 6645.
• **UK** Ploutárhou 1, Kolonáki (Evangelismós metro); tel: 727 2600.
• **US** Vasilísis Sofías 91, Ambelókipi (Mégaro Mousikís metro); tel: 721 2951.

Emergencies

The following numbers work country-wide:
Police: 100
Ambulance: 166
Fire brigade, urban: 199
Forest fire reporting: 191
For less urgent medical problems, hotel staff will give you details of the nearest hospital or English-speaking doctor.

Entry Requirements

Citizens of EU nations and EEA countries have unlimited visitation rights to Greece; your passport will not be stamped on entry or exit. With a valid passport, citizens of the US,

Canada, Australia and New Zealand can stay in the country for up to three months (cumulative) within any 180-day period, with no visa necessary in advance. To stay longer, you must obtain a permit from the nearest Aliens' Bureau or foreigners' division of the local police station; however, this is lately proving nearly impossible (and very expensive) to do. Citizens of all other countries should contact the nearest Greek Embassy or Consulate about current visa and permitted length-of-stay requirements.

Etiquette

The Greeks are at heart a very traditional nation, protective of their families and traditions. So to avoid giving offence it is essential to follow their codes of conduct.

Local people rarely drink to excess, so drunken and/or lewd behaviour is treated with at best bewilderment, at worse severe distaste (or criminal prosecution, as many young louts on Rhodes, Zákynthos, Corfu and Crete have learnt to their cost).

Nude bathing is legal at only a few beaches (such as on the island of Mýkonos), but it is deeply offensive to many Greeks. Even topless sunbathing is not always sanctioned, so watch out for signs forbidding it on beaches. The main rule of thumb is this: if it is a secluded beach and/or a beach that has become a commonly accepted locale for nude bathing, you probably won't offend anyone. Take your cue from what other people are wearing (or not wearing).

Despite assorted scandals and embarrassing espousal of retrograde issues in recent years, the Greek Orthodox Church still commands residual respect in Greece (more in the countryside), so keep any unfavourable comments about the clergy or even Greek civil servants to yourself.

Greek authorities take the unauthorised use of drugs very seriously indeed; this is not the country in which to carry cannabis, let alone anything stronger.

Dress Codes

The Greeks will not expect you, as a tourist, to dress as they do, but scuffed shoes, ripped "grunge-style" jeans or visibly out-of-date clothing are considered offensive.

In certain places and regions, you will encounter explicit requirements or conventions concerning the way you dress. To enter a church, men must wear long trousers, and women dresses with sleeves. Often skirts or

wraps will be provided at the church entrance if you do not have them. Not complying with this code will be taken as insulting irreverence.

Some specific areas have their own dress codes. On Mýkonos, for example, male and female tourists alike will shock no one by wearing shorts or a swimsuit in most public places. But dresssing in this way would be severely alienating in a mountain village in Crete, or in any other area that is less accustomed to tourists. And while shorts may be uniform male summer apparel at island resorts, when visiting Athens you will notice that *nobody* wears shorts in town, even in roasting temperatures. The best approach is to observe what other people are wearing and dress accordingly.

In general, both Greeks and tourists dine in casual dress. You will only need formal dress if you plan to go to fancy establishments, casinos, formal affairs and so on.

G ay and Lesbian Travellers

Greek society has long been ambivalent about gayness, at least outside the predictable arenas of the arts, theatre and music industry. Homosexuality is legal at the age of 17, and bisexual activity not uncommon among younger men, but few couples (male or female) will express affection in public. Mýkonos, which is the exception to this, is famous as a gay mecca, and Skála Eresoú on Lésvos (where the poetess Sappho was born) for lesbians. Most larger islands have at least one partly gay naturist beach. But elsewhere in Greece single-sex couples are liable to be regarded as odd, although usually as welcome as any other tourists. If discreet, you will attract no attention asking for a double room and will find most people tolerant.

H ealth and Medical Care

There are few serious diseases in Greece, apart from those that you can contract in the rest of Europe or the United States. Citizens of the US, Canada and the EU do not need any vaccinations to enter the country. The most common health problems encountered by tourists involve too much sun, too much alcohol, or sensitivity to unaccustomed food. Drink plenty of water, as dehydration can be a problem in the heat.

Drugs and Medicines

Greek pharmacies stock most over-the-counter drugs, and pharmacists are well trained. The Greeks themselves are enthusiastic hypochondriacs and potion-poppers, and all manner of homeopathic or herbal remedies and premium-ingredient dietary supplements are available. Many formulas that would be obtainable only on prescription elsewhere, if at all, are freely obtainable in Greece. So you should have no problem obtaining most medicines (except on the smaller islands).

Essential drugs, made locally under licence, are price-controlled, with uniform rates all over the country – eg a tube of 1 percent hydrocortisone cream costs about €4 – but discretional sundries and anything imported can be expensive (eg a packet of four water-resistant French-made bandages for €3.50). If you want to be absolutely sure, pack a supply of your favourite remedies to last the trip.

Medical Treatment

For minor ailments your best port of call is a pharmacy. Greek chemists usually speak good English and are well trained and helpful, and pharmacies stock a good range of medicines (including contraceptives) as well as bandages and dressings for minor wounds.

Certain pharmacies are open outside of normal shop hours and at weekends, on a rotating basis. You can find out which are open either by looking at the bilingual (Greek/English) card posted in pharmacy windows or by consulting a local newspaper. In big cities, and major tourist resorts such as Crete or Rhodes, one or two pharmacies will be open 24 hours a day.

There are English-speaking GPs in all the bigger towns and resorts, and their rates are usually reasonable. Ask your hotel or the tourist office for details.

Treatment for broken bones and similar mishaps is given free of charge in the state-run Greek hospitals – go straight to the casualty/emergency ward (*epígon peristatiká* in Greek). You must have with you your European Health Insurance Card, obtainable from UK post offices or online (www.ehic.org) (*see Insurance, below*).

For more serious problems you should have private medical insurance. If you have a serious injury or illness, you are better off travelling home for treatment if you can.

Greek public hospitals lag behind Northern Europe and the US in both

their hygiene and standard of care; the Greeks bring food and bedding when visiting sick relatives, and must bribe nurses for anything beyond the bare minimum in care.

Animal Hazards

Nearly half the stray dogs in rural areas carry echinococcosis (treatable by surgery only) or kala-azar disease (leishmaniasis), a protozoan blood disease spread by sandfleas.

Mosquitoes can be a nuisance in some areas of Greece, but tropical repellents are readily available in pharmacies. For safeguarding rooms, accommodation proprietors often supply a plug-in electric pad, which vaporises smokeless, odourless rectangular tablets. If you see them by the bed, it's a good bet they will be needed; refills can be found in any supermarket.

On the islands, poisonous baby pit vipers and scorpions are a problem in spring and summer. They will not strike you unless disturbed, but do not put your hands or feet in places (such as holes in drystone walls) that you haven't checked first. When swimming in the sea, beware of jellyfish, whose sting is not toxic but can cause swelling and hurt for days.

At rocky shorelines, it is worth wearing plastic or trekking sandals to avoid sea urchins (those little black underwater pincushions that can embed their very sharp, tiny and brittle spines into unwary feet). A local Greek remedy is to douse the wound with olive oil and then gently massage the foot until the spines pop out, but this rarely works unless you're willing to perform minor surgery with pen-knife and sewing needle – which should be done, as spine fragments tend to go septic.

Insurance

British and EU residents are entitled to free medical treatment in Greece as long as they carry a European Health Insurance Card as noted above. However, this guarantees only the most basic health care: you are only entitled to use one of the lowest-grade state hospitals, and will have to pay for your own medicines and special diagnostic tests, so it is advisable to take out private medical insurance. You will have to pay for private treatment up front, so you must keep receipts for any bills or medicines you pay for to make a claim. If you plan to hire a motor scooter in Greece, you may have to pay an insurance supplement to cover you for accidents.

L eft Luggage

Airport At Level 0 of Arrivals at Elefthérios Venizélos Airport, Pacific Left Luggage offers service (tel: 21035 30160).
Hotels Most hotels in Greece are willing to store locked suitcases for up to a week if you want to make any short excursions. This is usually a free service, provided you've stayed a night or two, but the hotel will accept no responsibility in the highly unlikely event of theft.
Commercial offices On the islands there are left-luggage offices in many harbour towns. For a small charge space can be hired by the hour, day, week or longer. Although contents will probably be safe, take small valuables with you.

M aps

Gone are the days when travellers had to tolerate fantastically mendacious or optimistic island cartography, seemingly compiled by people who had never been there. There are three home-grown map companies in Greece whose products are likely to be better and more current than anything you can buy overseas. The two with the most accurate and widespread coverage are Road Editions (www.road.gr) and Anavasi (www.anavasi.gr), with Emvelia (www.emvelia.gr) lagging behind.

Media

Print

Many kiosks throughout Athens and major island resorts receive British newspapers, either late the same afternoon or sometime the next day. *Athens News* in colour (online at www.athensnews.gr) is interesting and informative, with both international

BELOW: get your news fix at a kiosk.

and local news, particularly good for the Balkans, and complete TV and cinema listings. The *International Herald Tribune* contains, as a bonus, the English edition of respected Greek daily *Kathimeriní* (online at www.ekathimerini.com). *Odyssey* is a glossy, bimonthly magazine created by and for the wealthy Greek diaspora, somewhat more interesting than the usual airline in-flight magazines.

Radio and TV

ER 1 and ER 2 are the two Greek state-owned radio channels. ER 1 is divided into three different programmes. The First (728 KHz) and Second (1385 KHz) both have abundant Greek popular music and news, some foreign pop and occasional jazz and blues. Third (665 KHz) plays a lot of Western classical music, and ER 2 (98 KHz) is much like the first two programmes. Additionally, a plethora of private stations broadcast locally from just about every island or provincial town, no matter how tiny.

There are three state-owned and operated television channels (ET1 and NET in Athens, ET3 in Thessaloníki) and various private television channels (Antenna, Mega, Star, Alpha and Alter). Often they transmit foreign movies and programmes with Greek subtitles rather than being dubbed. Several cable and satellite channels are also broadcast, including Sky and CNN.

Money

The Greek currency is the euro (*evró* in Greek), which comes in coins of 1, 2, 5, 10, 20 and 50 cents (*leptá*), plus 1 and 2 euros, as well as notes of 5, 10, 20, 50, 100, 200 and 500 euros (the last two denominations are rarely seen; they, and 100-euro notes, are the most likely to be counterfeit and thus may be treated with suspicion).

All banks and some hotels buy foreign currency at the official rate of exchange fixed by the Bank of Greece, with variable (often stiff) commission charges. Although it is safer to carry most of your currency in travellers' cheques, it is also worth carrying a limited sum in US dollars or sterling. When you can't find a place to cash cheques, there will usually be an exchange bureau to convert those currencies into euros – albeit at a disadvantageous rate. To find the current rate, check displays in bank windows, or the newspapers, or go online at www.oanda.com.

Credit/Debit Cards

Many of the better-established hotels, restaurants and shops accept major credit cards, as do all local airlines and the larger ferry companies or travel agents. The average *pension* or taverna does not, however, so be sure to enquire in advance if that is how you intend to pay. You will find that most types of card are accepted by the numerous auto-teller machines (ATM), upon entry of your PIN number. Surcharges on credit cards, and most debit cards used in ATMs are very high, often amounting to over 4 percent of the transaction value. However, you will find that this is the most convenient and least expensive way of getting funds. Beware,however, the ATMs of the Emboriki/Commercial bank – these do not require you to remove your card to obtain cash, and it is easy to forget and have your card retained.

O pening Hours

All banks are open 8am–2.30pm Monday to Thursday, and 8am–2pm on Friday. But since ATMs are now ubiquitous – even the smaller islands will have at least one –this is how most people obtain cash nowadays. The schedule for business and shop hours is more complicated. Opening hours vary according to the type of enterprise and the day of the week. The main thing to remember is that businesses generally open at 8.30 or 9am and close on Monday, Wednesday and Saturday at 2.30pm. On Tuesday, Thursday and Friday most businesses close at 2pm and reopen in the afternoon from 5pm to 8.30pm (winter), 5.30 or 6pm to 9pm (summer). In resorts, many tourist shops open for part of Sunday, but so far the only mainstream Sunday trading is at some branches of the Carrefour/Marinopoulos supermarket chain.

"Greek Time"

Beware Greek schedules. You will soon learn that schedules are very flexible in Greece (both in business and personal affairs). To avoid disappointment, allow ample time when shopping and doing business. That way, you may also enter into the Greek spirit of negotiation, in which a good chat can be as important as the matter of business itself.

Although shops and businesses generally operate during the hours indicated above, there is no real guarantee that when you want to book a ferry or buy a gift, the relevant

office or shop will actually be open.

Siesta (*mikró ýpno* in Greek) is observed throughout Greece, and even in Athens the majority of people retire behind closed doors between the hours of 3pm and 5.30pm. Shops and businesses also close, and it is usually impossible to get much done until late afternoon or early evening. To avoid frustration and disappointment, shop and book things between 10am and 1pm Monday to Friday.

Since 1994 Athens and the largest towns have experimented with "continual" (*synéhies*) hours during the winter to bring the country more in line with the EU, but this seems to be discretionary rather than obligatory, with some stores observing the hours and others adhering to traditional schedules – which can be rather confusing. So far it has not caught on across the rest of the country.

Tourist shops throughout the country usually trade well into the evening in summer. But butchers and fishmongers are not allowed to open on summer evenings (although a few disregard the law), and pharmacies (except for those on rota duty) are never open on Saturday morning.

P hotography

Although Greece is a photographer's paradise, taking photographs at will is not recommended. Camera use is are not allowed in most museums – at best, you may take pictures without a flash – and you may have to pay a fee to take photographs or use your camcorder at some archaeological sites. Watch out for signs showing a bellows camera with a red "X" through it, and do not point your camera at anything in or near airports – most of which double as military bases – or any site that is remotely sensitive.

Memory chips and spare batteries for most kinds of digital camera are widely available at electronics and computer retailers as well as photography shops.

Postal Services

Most local post offices are open weekdays from 7.30am until 2pm. However, the main post offices in central Athens (on Eólou near Omónia Square and on Sýndagma Square at the corner of Mitropóleos Street) are open longer hours on weekdays, as well as having short schedules on Saturday and Sunday. Rhodes Neohóri post office also has evening and Saturday hours.

Postal rates are subject to fairly frequent change; currently a postcard or lightweight letter costs 70 cents to any overseas destination. Stamps are available from the post office or from many kiosks *(períptera)*, authorised stationers and hotels, which may charge a 10–15 percent commission, and may not know the latest international postal rates.

If you want to send a parcel from Greece, do not try to wrap it until a post office clerk has inspected it, unless it is going to another EU country, in which case you can present it sealed. Major post offices stock various sizes of cardboard boxes for sale in which you can pack your material. They also sell twine, but you had best bring your own tape and scissors.

Letters from abroad can be sent Post Restante to any post office. Take your passport or other convincing ID when you go to pick up mail.

Public Holidays

6 January *Agía Theofánia, Tá Fóta/* Epiphany.
February (Variable) Clean Monday Beginning of fast for Lent.
25 March *Evangelismós*/Feast of Annunciation/ National Day.
March/April (Variable) Easter Weekend *Good Friday, Holy Saturday* and *Easter Sunday.*
1 May *Workers' Day.*
May/June (Variable) *Agion Pnévma*/Pentecost Monday, 50 days after Easter.
6 August *Metamórfosis toú Sotíros*/Transfiguration of the Saviour.
15 August *Kímisi tís Theotókou/* Dormition of the Virgin.
28 October *Ohi* (No) *Day.*
25 December Christmas Day.
26 December *Sýnaxis tís Panagías.*

R eligious Services

Most major towns and island resort areas with significant foreign patronage or a large expat community – most notably Rhodes, Sámos, Corfu, Náxos, Crete and Santoríni – have at least one church dedicated to the Catholic, Anglican or other Protestant (eg Swedish Lutheran) rites, or an agreement for part-time use of an Orthodox premises. There are effectively functioning Catholic parishes on Sýros and Tínos, where foreigners are welcome. Placards posted on the churches themselves, or handouts at the local tourist office,

give current information on service schedules (which may be anything from once a month to two or three times weekly).

S tudent Travellers

In addition to the museum and archaeological site discounts noted on page 347 *(see Admission Charges),* students and young people under 26, with the appropriate documentation, are eligible for discounted fares and youth passes on OSE (the Greek train network) and on some shipping lines, including those operating to and from Italy.

T elecommunications

For local calls, including to Greek mobile phones, buy an OTE (Greek telecoms) phone card from a kiosk and use a (usually noisy) street-corner booth. Cards come in 100-unit, 500-unit and 1,000-unit denominations; the Hronokarta series is slightly better value.

Calls from hotel rooms typically have a minimum 200–300 percent surcharge on top of the standard rates – to be avoided for anything other than brief local calls.

For overseas calls, almost everyone avoids the truly outrageous OTE rates by buying a code-card (Face brand is popular), where you scratch to reveal a 12-digit code, then ring an 807-prefixed number to enter said code, then the number you want. It may all sound a bit of a hassle, but savings can amount to about 70 percent. If you have a laptop, it is worth bringing a Skype headset along to take advantage of wi-fi zones for calling abroad.

Greece has one of the highest per-capita mobile-phone usage rates in the world, and a mobile is an essential fashion accessory for any self-respecting Greek as well as a means of communication. Foreign mobile owners will find themselves well catered for, with thorough coverage and reciprocal agreements for most UK-based services.

Calls within the EU now have capped rates, but beware calling non-EU destinations such as Turkey. North American users will have to bring a tri-band apparatus to have any success. If you are staying for any amount of time, you will find it better to buy either a pay-as-you-go phone from one of the Greek providers (Vodaphone, Cosmote, Wind) or, if feasible, just a SIM card for the apparatus you have brought with you.

Time Zone

Greece is two hours ahead of GMT and, like the rest of Europe, observes Daylight Saving Time from 3am on the last Sunday in March until 3am on the last Sunday in October.

Tipping

Menu prices at most cafés, restaurants and tavernas include a service charge, but it is still customary to leave an extra 5–10 percent on the table for the waiting staff.

Just as important as any such gratuity, however, is your appreciation of the food you eat. Greek waiters and restaurant owners are proud and pleased when you tell them you have enjoyed a particular dish.

Toilets

Public conveniences, often subterranean ones in parks or plazas, or perched on a harbour jetty, are of variable cleanliness and rarely have any paper. Most people just buy a drink in a café and use their facilities. In busy areas, some cafés may post signs reading "Toilets for customers only". Elsewhere, establishments are a bit more lenient about those caught short just popping in.

Tourist Information

Tourist Offices

If you would like tourist information about Greece during your trip, visit the nearest Greek National Tourist Organisation – GNTO, or EOT in Greek. They provide information on public transport, as well as leaflets and details about sites and museums. There are several regional GNTO offices on the islands. The head office in Athens is at Amalías 26; tel: 21033 10392 .

On many of the islands there are semi-official municipal tourist information centres open from June to September. These are usually prominently sited near the centre of the main town, and provide all the local information you might need. Some can even help with finding accommodation.

Tourist Police

The Greek Tourist Police are not really an information source, but a special division of the main police force tasked with intervening when a customer has a serious complaint about an establishment – substandard hotel conditions, for example, or blatant overcharging by taxi drivers. They have separate premises (sometimes seasonal) only on the most heavily visited islands like Rhodes, Corfu, Crete, Mýkonos, Lésvos and Skiáthos.

Greek National Tourist Organisation Offices Overseas

Australia
51 Pitt Street, Sydney NSW 2000
Tel: 02 9241 1663/5
Fax: 02 9241 2174
Email: hto@tpg.com.au
Canada
91 Scollard Street, 2nd Floor, Toronto, ON M5R 1G4
Tel: 416 968 2220
Fax: 416 968 6533
Email: grnto.tor@sympatico.can
www.greektourism.com
United Kingdom
4 Conduit Street, London W1S 2DJ
Tel: 020 7495 9300
Fax: 020 7287 1369
Email: EOT-greektouristoffice@btinternet.com
United States
Olympic Tower, 645 Fifth Avenue, 9th Floor, New York, NY 10022
Tel: 212 421 5777
Fax: 212 826 6940
Email: info@greektourism.com

Tour Operators

Your local overseas branch of the Greek National Tourist Organisation *(see above)* can usually provide a list of that country's tour operators and specialist agents offering holidays in Greece. Otherwise, here are a few suggestions for something unusual:
Archaeological tours
The Traveller
Tel: 020 7436 9343
www.the-traveller.co.uk
Bicycle tours
Classic Adventures, USA
Tel: 1-800 777 8090
www.classicadventures.com
Birdwatching
Limosa Holidays, UK
Tel: 01263 578143
www.limosaholidays.co.uk
Botanical tours
Marengo Guided Walks, UK
Tel: 01485 532710
www.marengowalks.com
Sail-and-trek mixed tours
Explore Worldwide, UK
Tel: 0845 013 1537
www.explore.co.uk
Hellenic Adventures, Minneapolis, USA
Tel: 1-800 851 6349
www.hellenicadventures.com

Walking holidays
ATG, Oxford UK
Tel: 01865 315678
www.atg-oxford.co.uk
Exodus, London UK
Tel: 020 8765 5550
www.exodus.co.uk
Jonathan's Tours, Castillon-en-Couserans, France
Tel: 00 33 5 61 04 64 47
www.jonathanstours.com
Ramblers' Holidays, Welwyn Garden City
Tel: 01707 331133
www.ramblersholidays.co.uk
Writing workshops/yoga holidays
Skyros Centre, Isle of Wight, UK
Tel: 01983 865566
www.skyros.com
Yoga Plus, Brighton UK
Tel: 01273 276175

Websites

Greek weather forecasts are available at:
www.meteo.gr
www.meteorologia.gr
Reviews and sales of books on all aspects of Greece can be found at:
www.hellenicbookservice.com
www.kalamosbooks.com
Seagoing schedules are available at:
www.gtp.gr
For general tourist information and links far superior to official sources, consult:
www.greektravel.com
www.travel-greece.com
The Ministry of Culture site has impressive coverage of most of the country's museums, archaeological sites and remote monuments on:
www.culture.gr
Excellent window into contemporary Greek music, with videos, playlists and artist profiles, maintained by a clued-up lady DJ at New Jersey station WPRB:
http://musicalodyssey.blogspot.com

Weights and Measures

Greece is completely metric. The only exception is that land is measured and sold in *strémmata* (1,000 sq metres/10,764 sq ft).

W hat to Bring

Adaptors

220V AC is the standard household electric current throughout Greece. Shavers and hairdryers from North America that are not dual-voltage should be left at home in favour of versatile travel models – they can be bought in Greece if necessary.

Otherwise, buy a transformer before you leave home. Greek plugs are the standard round, two-pin European continental type, different from those in North America and the UK; plug adaptors for American appliances are easy to find in Greece, three-to-two-pin adaptors for UK appliances much less so, so these are best purchased before departure *(see Electricity)*.

Medicines

See the section of Health and Medical Care regarding essential medicines *(page 349)*.

Sun Protection

A hat, sunscreen and sunglasses are essential for protection from the midday sun, but if you fail to bring them, sunscreens of up to SPF50 are widely available in pharmacies and cosmetics shops, and sunhats and sunglasses can be found everywhere.

Toiletries

Most international brands are widely available, except on the smallest islands. Feminine hygiene products are more likely to be sold in supermarkets than in pharmacies.

Torch

Pack one, as walking home from island tavernas can be tricky if there's no moon. If you forget, Maglites or similar are sold widely.

Universal Plug

Greek basins often aren't equipped with plugs, so if you want water in your sink a universal plug is essential.

Women Travellers

Lone female visitors may occasionally be targeted for attention by predatory Greek males, especially around beach bars and after-hours discos, but in general machismo is no longer any more a problem than elsewhere in southern Europe. Inexorable changes in Greek culture mean that Greek women have much more sexual freedom than previously, especially in the cities, so Northern European tourists are no longer such a novelty. There is now little controversy about Greek women spending time with their male counterparts, up to and including cohabiting before (or instead of) marriage.

However, in remote areas, many Greeks are still highly traditional and may find it hard to understand why you are travelling alone. You are unlikely to feel comfortable in all-male drinking cafés.

L ANGUAGE

UNDERSTANDING THE LANGUAGE

The Greek Language

Modern Greek is the outcome of gradual evolution undergone by the Greek language since the classical period (5th–4th centuries BC). The language is still relatively close to ancient Greek: it uses the same alphabet and some of the same vocabulary, though the grammar – other than the retention of the three genders – is considerably streamlined and is less complicated. Many people speak English, some very well, but even just a few words in their native language will always be appreciated.

Pronunciation Tips

Most of the sounds of Greek are reasonably straightforward to pronounce for English-speakers. There are only six vowel sounds: *a*, *e*, *i*, *o*, *u* and *y* are consistently pronounced as shown in the table below. The letter **s** is usually pronounced "s", but "z" before an *m* or *g*. The sound represented here as **th** is always pronounced as in "thin", not "that"; the first sound in "that" is represented by *d*.

The only difficult sounds are **h**, which is pronounced like the "ch" in Scottish "loch" (we render this as **kh** after "s" so that you don't generate "sh"), and **g** before *a* or *o*, which has no equivalent in English – it's somewhere between the "y" in "yet" and the "g" in "get".

The position of the stress in words is of critical importance, as homonyms abound, and Greeks will often fail to understand you if you don't stress the right syllable (compare *psýllos*, "flea" with *psilós*, "tall"). In this guide, stress is marked by a simple accent mark (´) except for single-syllable words which are, however, still stressed. Greek uses the diaresis (¨) over letters which may or may not have the primary stress as well.

Greek word order is flexible, so you may often hear phrases in a different order from the one in which they are given here. Like the French, the Greeks use the plural of the second person when addressing someone politely.

We have used the polite (formal) form throughout this language section, except where an expression is specified as "informal".

Our Transliteration System

In Greece, most town and village names on road signs, as well as most street names, are written in Greek and the Roman alphabets. There's no universally accepted system of transliteration into Roman, and in any case the Greek authorities are gradually replacing old signs with new ones that use a slightly different system. This means you will have to get used to seeing different spellings of the same place on maps, signs and in this book.

Below is the transliteration scheme we have used in this book: beside each Greek letter or pair of letters is the Roman letter(s) we have used. Next to that is a rough approximation of the sound in an English word.

A	α	a	cat		T	τ	t	tea
B	β	v	vote		Y	υ	y	mildly
Γ	γ	g/y	got *except before* "e" or "i", *when it is nearer to* yacht, *but rougher*		Φ	φ	f	fish
					X	χ	h	loch
					Ψ	ψ	ps	maps
					Ω	ω	o	road
Δ	δ	d	then		αι	αι	(ai)	e	hay
E	ε	e	egg		αυ	αυ	(au)	av/af	have/raffle
Z	ζ	z	zoo					
H	η	i	ski		ει	ει	(ei)	i	ski
Θ	θ	th	thin		ευ	ευ	(eu)	ev/ef	ever/left
I	ι	i	ski		οι	οι	(oi)	i	ski
K	κ	k	kiss		ου	ου	(ou)	ou	tourist
Λ	λ	l	long		γγ	γγ	(gg)	ng	long
M	μ	m	man		γκ	γκ	(gk)	ng	long
N	ν	n	no		ΓΞ	γξ	(gx)	nx	anxious
Ξ	ξ	x	taxi		μπ	μπ	(mp)	b	beg
O	o	o	road					or	mb	limber
Π	π	p	pen		NT	ντ	(nt)	d	dog
P	ρ	r	room					or	nd	under
Σ	σ/ς	s	set *or* charisma		TZ	τζ	(tz)	tz	fads

Communication

Good morning *kaliméra*
Good evening *kalispéra*
Good night *kaliníhta*
Hello/Goodbye *yiásas* (informal:)
yiásou
Pleased to meet you *hárika polý*
Yes *ne*
No *óhi*
Thank you *evharistó*
You're welcome *parakaló*
Please *parakaló*
Okay/All right *endáxi*
Excuse me (to get attention) *Me
synhoríte*
**Excuse me (to ask someone to get
out of the way)** *sygnómi*
How are you? *Ti kánete?* (informal:)
Ti kánis?
Fine, and you? *Kalá, esís?*
(informal:) *Kalá, esí?*
Cheers/Your health! *Yiámas!* (when
drinking)
Could you help me? *Boríte na me
voithísete?*
Can you show me... *Boríte na mou
díxete...*
I want... *Thélo...*
I don't know *Den xéro*
I don't understand *Den katálava*
Do you speak English? *Xérete
angliká?*
Can you please speak more slowly?
Parakaló, miláte pió sigá
Please say that again *Parakaló,
xanapésteto*
Please write it down for me *Na mou
to grápste, parakaló*
Here *edó*
There *ekí*
What? *ti?*
When? *póte?*
Why? *yiatí?*
Where? *pou?*
How? *pos?*

Telephone Calls

the telephone *to tiléfono*
phone card *tilekárta*
May I use the phone please? *Boró
na tilefoníso, parakaló?*
Hello (on the phone) *Embrós/Oríste*

BELOW: Levkáda Town street sign.

ABOVE: a political demonstration in Lésvos says it loud and clear.

My name is... *Légome...*
Could I speak to... *Boró na milíso
me...*
Wait a moment *Periménete mía
stigmí*
I didn't hear *Den ákousa*

In the Hotel

Do you have a vacant room? *Éhete
domátio?*
I've booked a a room *Ého kratísi éna
domátio*
I'd like... *Tha íthela...*
a single/ double room *éna
monóklino/díklino*
double bed *dipló kreváti*
a room with a bath/shower *éna
domátio me bánio/dous*
One night *éna vrádi*
Two nights *dýo vradiá*
How much is it? *Póso káni?*
It's expensive *Íne akrivó*
**Do you have a room with a sea
view?** *Éhete domátio me théa pros ti
thálassa?*
Is there a balcony? *Éhi balkóni?*
Is the room heated/air-conditioned?
Éhi thérmansi/klimatismó to domátio?
Is breakfast included? *Mazí me to
proïnó?*
Can I see the room please? *Boró na
do todomátio, parakaló?*
The room is too... *To domátio íne
polý...*
hot/cold/small *zestó/krýo/mikró*
It's too noisy *Éhi polý thóryvo*
**Could you show me another room,
please?** *Boríte na mou díxete éna
állo domátio, parakaló?*
I'll take it *Tha to páro*
Can I have the bill, please? *Na mou
kánete to logariasmó, parakaló?*
dining room *trapezaría*
key *klidí*
towel *petséta*
sheet *sendóni*

blanket *kouvérta*
pillow *maxilári*
soap *sapoúni*
hot water *zestó neró*
toilet paper *hartí toualéttas*

At a Bar or Café

bar/café *bar/kafenío* (or *kafetéria*)
patisserie *zaharoplastío*
I'd like... *Tha íthela...*
a coffee *éna kafé*
Greek coffee *ellinikó kafé*
filter coffee *gallikó kafé/kafé fíltro*
instant coffee *neskafé* (or *nes*)
cappuccino *kapoutsíno*
white (with milk) *me gála*
black (without milk) *horís gála*
with sugar *me záhari*
without sugar *horís záhari*
a cup of tea *éna tsáï*
tea with lemon *éna tsái me lemóni*
orange/lemon soda *mía
portokaláda/lemonáda*
fresh orange juice *éna hymó
portokáli*
a glass/bottle of water *éna potíri/
boukáli neró*
with ice cubes *me pagáki*
an ouzo/brandy *éna oúzo/koniák*
a beer (draught) *mía býra* (*apó
varélli*)
an ice-cream *éna pagotó*
a pastry, cake *mía pásta*
oriental pastries *baklavá/kataïfi*

In a Restaurant

Have you got a table for... *Éhete
trapézi yiá...*
There are (four) of us *Ímaste
(tésseres)*
I'm a vegetarian *Íme hortofágos*
Can we see the menu? *Boroúme na
doúme ton katálogo?*
We would like to order *Théloume na
parangíloume*

Emergencies

Help! *Voíthia!*
Stop! *Stamatíste!*
I've had an accident *Ího éna atíhima*
Call a doctor *Fonáxte éna giatró*
Call an ambulance *Fonáxte éna asthenofóro*
Call the police *Fonáxte tin astinomía*
Call the fire brigade *Fonáxte tous pyrozvéstes*
Where's the telephone? *Pou íne to tiléfono?*
Where's the nearest hospital? *Pou íne to pio kondinó nosokomío?*
I would like to report a theft *Égine mia klopí*

Have you got (bulk) wine by the carafe? *Éhete krasí hýma?*
a litre/half-litre *éna kiló/misó kilo*
of white/red wine *áspro/kókkino krasí*
Would you like anything else? *Thélete típot' állo?*
No, thank you *Óhi, evharistó*
glass *potíri*
knife/fork/spoon *mahéri/pirioúni/koutáli*
plate *piáto*
napkin *hartopetséta*
Where is the toilet? *Pou íne i toualétta?*
The bill, please *To logariasmó, parakaló*

Food

Mezédes/Orektiká

taramosaláta **fish-roe dip**
tzatzíki **yoghurt-garlic-cucumber dip**
melitzánes **aubergines**
kolokythákia **courgettes**
loukánika **sausages**
tyropitákia **cheese pies**
antsoúgies **anchovies**
eliés **olives**
dolmádes **vine leaves stuffed with rice**
kopanistí **tangy fermented cheese dip**
saganáki **fried cheese**
tyrokafterí **soft cheese seasoned with hot peppers**
fáva **puréed fava beans**
piperiés florínis **red sweet pickled peppers**

Meat Dishes

kréas **any meat**
arní **lamb**
hirinó **pork**
kotópoulo **chicken**
moskhári **veal, beef**
psitó **roast or grilled**

sto foúrno **roast**
sta kárvouna **grilled**
soúvlas **on the spit**
souvláki **brochettes on skewers**
kokinistó **stewed in tomato sauce**
krasáto **stewed in wine sauce**
avgolémono **egg-lemon sauce**
tiganitó **fried**
kapnistó **smoked**
brizóla **(pork or veal) chop**
païdákia **lamb chops**
sykóti **liver**
kymás **mince**
biftéki **small burger (without bun)**
keftédes **meatballs**
soutzoukákia **rissoles baked in red sauce**
giouvarlákia **mince-and-rice balls in egg-lemon sauce**
makarónia **spaghetti**
piláfi **rice**
me kymá **with minced meat**
me sáltsa **with tomato sauce**
pastítsio **macaroni with minced meat**
gýros me pítta **doner kebab**

Seafood

frésko **fresh**
katapsygméno **frozen**
psári **fish**
ostrakaoidí **shellfish**
glóssa **sole**
xifías **swordfish**
koliós **mackerel**
barboúnia **red mullet**
sardélles **sardines**
gávros **fresh anchovy**
marídes **picarel**
mýdia **mussels**
strídia **oysters**
kydónia **cockles**
kalamarákia **small squid**
thrápsala **large deep-water squid**
soupiés **cuttlefish**
htapódi **octopus**
garídes **prawns**
kavourákia **baby crabs**
astakós **lobster**

Vegetables

angináres **artichokes**
arakádes, pizélia **peas**
domátes **tomatoes**
fakés **brown lentils**
fasólia/fasoláda **stewed white beans**
fasolákia (fréska) **green (runner) beans**
hórta **various kinds of boiled greens**
karóta **carrot**
kolokythákia **courgettes**
kounoupídi **cauliflower**
koukiá **broad beans**
kremídi **onion**
frésko kremídi **spring onion**
láhano **cabbage**
maroúli **lettuce**
pantzária **beetroot**

patátes (tiganités/sto foúrno) **potatoes (fried/roast)**
radíkia **chicory leaves**
revíthia **chickpeas**
skórdo **garlic**
spanáki **spinach**
spanakópitta **spinach pie**
vlíta **notchweed**
gígandes **stewed butter beans**
domátes gemistés **stuffed tomatoes**
piperiés gemistés **stuffed peppers**
saláta **salad**
domatosaláta **tomato salad**
angourodomáta **tomato and cucumber salad**
horiátiki **Greek "peasant" salad**

Fruit

míla **apples**
veríkoka **apricots**
banánes **bananas**
kerásia **cherries**
sýka **figs**
stafýlia **grapes**
lemónia **lemons**
pepónia **melons**
portokália **oranges**
rodákina **peaches**
ahládia **pears**
fráoules **strawberries**
karpoúzi **watermelon**

Basic Foods

psomí **bread**
aláti **salt**
pipéri **pepper**
ládi **oil**
xýdi **vinegar**
moustárda **mustard**
voútyro **butter**
tyrí **cheese**
avgá (tiganitá) **(fried) eggs**
omelétta **omelette**
marmeláda **jam, marmelade**
rýzi **rice**
giaoúrti **yoghurt**
méli **honey**
záhari **sugar**

Desserts

galaktoboúriko **custard pastry**
karydópitta **walnut pie**
halvás **semolina-based dry confection**
katlitsoúnia **sweet-cheese-and-cinnamon-filled pastry**
ravaní **semolina and syrup cake**

Sightseeing

information *pliroforíes*
open/closed *anihtó/klistó*
Is it possible to see... *Boroúme na dhoúme...*
the church/archaeological site? *tin eklisía/ta arhéa?*
Where can I find the custodian/key? *Pou boró na vro to fýlaka/klidí?*

At the Shops

shop *magazí/katástima*
What time do you open/close?
Ti óra anígete/klínete?
Are you being served? *Exiperitíste?*
What would you like? *Oríste/ti*
thélete?
I'm just looking *Aplós kitázo*
How much is it? *Póso kostízi?*
Do you take credit cards? *Déheste*
pistotikés kártes?
I'd like... *Tha íthela...*
this one *aftó*
that one *ekíno*
Have you got...? *Éhete...?*
size (for clothes) *número*
Can I try it on? *Boró na to dokimáso?*
It's too expensive *Íne polý akrivó*
Don't you have anything cheaper?
Den éhete típota pió ftinó?
Please write it down for me *To*
gráfete parakaló?
It's too small/ big *Íne pára polý*
mikró/megálo
No thank you, I don't like it *Óhi,*
evharistó, den m'arési
I'll take it *Tha to páro*
I don't want it *Den to thélo*
This is faulty; can I have a
replacement? *Avtó éhi éna elátoma;*
boró na to aláxo?
Can I have a refund? *Boró na páro*
píso ta leftá?
a kilo *éna kiló*
half a kilo *misó kilo*
a quarter (kilo) *éna tétarto*
two kilos *dýo kilá*
100 grams *ekató grammária*
200 grams *diakósia grammária*
more *perisótero*
less *ligótero*
a little *lígo*
very little *polý lígo*
with/without *me/horís*
That's enough *ftáni*
That's all *tipot'álo*

Travelling

airport *aerodrómio*
boarding card *kárta epivívasis*
boat *plío/karávi*
bus *leoforío*
bus station *stathmós leoforíon*
bus stop *stási*
coach *púlman*
ferry *feribót*
first/second class *próti/défteri thési*
flight *ptísi*
hydrofoil *iptámeno*
motorway *ethnikí odós*
port *limáni*
return ticket *isitírio me epistrofí*
single ticket *apló isitírio*
taxi *taxí*
train *tréno*
train station *sidirodromikós stathmós*

Public Transport

Can you help me, please? *Boríte na*
me voithísete, parakaló?
Where can I buy tickets? *Pou na*
kópso isitírio?
At the counter *sto tamío*
Does it stop at...? *Káni stási sto...?*
You need to change at... *Tha prépi*
n'aláxete sto...
When is the next train/bus/ferry
to...? *Póte févgi to tréno/leoforío/*
feribót gia...?
How long does the journey take?
Pósi óra káni to taxídi?
What time will we arrive? *Ti óra tha*
ftásoume?
How much is the fare? *Póso stihízi*
to isitírio?
Next stop please *Káne mía stási,*
parakaló
Can you tell me where to get off?
Tha mou píte pou na katévo?
Should I get off here? *Edó na*
katévo?

At the Airport

I'd like to book a seat to... *Tha*
íthela na kratíso mia thési gia...
When is the next flight to... *Póte íne*
i epómeni ptísi giá...
Are there any seats available?
Ypárhoun thésis?
Can I take this with me? *Boró na to*
páro avtó mazí mou?
My suitcase has got lost *Háthike i*
valítsa mou
The flight has been delayed *I ptísi*
éhi kathistérisi
The flight has been cancelled *I ptísi*
mateóthike

Directions

right/left *dexiá/aristerá*
Take the first/second right *Párte*
ton próto/déftero drómo dexiá
Turn right/left *Strípste dexiá/*
aristerá
Go straight on *Tha páte ísia/efthía*
after the traffic lights *metá ta*
fanária
Is it near/far away? *Íne kondá/*
makriá?
How far is it? *Póso makriá íne?*
It's five minutes' walk *Íne pénde*
leptá me ta pódia
It's 10 minutes by car *Íne déka*
leptá me avtokínito
100 metres *ekató métra*
opposite/next to *apénandi/dípla*
junction *dhiastávrosi*
Where is/are...? *Pou íne...?*
Where can I find *Pou boró na vro*
a petrol station *éna venzinádiko*
a bank *mia trápeza*
a hotel? *éna xenodohío?*

How do I get there? *Pos na páo ekí?*
Can you show me where I am on the
map? *Boríte na mou díhete sto hárti*
pou íme?
Am I on the right road for... *Gia...*
kalá páo?
No, you're on the wrong road *Óhi,*
pírate láthos drómo

On the Road

Where can I hire a car? *Pou boró na*
nikiázo avtokínito?
What is it insured for? *Ti asfália*
éhi?
By what time must I return it?
Méhri ti óra prépi na to epistrépso?
driving licence *díploma*
petrol *venzíni*
unleaded *amólyvdi*
oil *ládi*
Fill it up *Óso pérni*
My car has broken down *Éhi páthi*
vlávi to avtokinitó mou
I've had an accident *Íha éna atíhima*
Can you check...? *Boríte na*
elénhete...?

Numbers

1	énas/mía/éna
	(masc/fem/neut)
2	dýo
3	tris/tría
4	tésseres/téssera
5	pénde
6	éxi
7	eftá
8	októ
9	ennéa
10	déka
11	éndeka
12	dódeka
13	dekatrís/dekatría
14	dekatésseres/
	dekatéssera
15	dekapénde
16	dekaéxi
17	dekaeftá
18	dekaoktó
19	dekaennéa
20	íkosi
30	triánda
40	saránda
50	penínda
60	exínda
70	evdomínda
80	ogdónda
90	enenínda
100	ekató
200	dyakósia
300	trakósies/trakósa
400	tetrakósies/tetrakósa
500	pendakósa
1,000	hílies/hília
2,000	dýo hiliádes
1 million	éna ekatomírio

the brakes *ta fréna*
the clutch *to ambrayáz*
the engine *i mihaní*
the exhaust *i exátmisi*
the fanbelt *i zóni*
the gearbox *i tahýtites*
the headlights *ta fanária*
the radiator *to psygío*
the spark plugs *ta buzí*
the tyre(s) *ta lástiha*

Times and Dates

(in the) morning *to proí*
afternoon *to apógevma*
evening *to vrádi*
(at) night *(ti) níhta*
yesterday *htes*
today *símera*
tomorrow *ávrio*
now *tóra*
early *norís*
late *argá*
a minute *éna leptó*
five/ten *pénde/déka*
minutes *leptá*
an hour *mia óra*
half an hour *misí óra*
a quarter of an hour *éna tétarto*
at one/two (o'clock) *sti mia/stis dýo
(i óra)*
a day *mia méra*
a week *mia evdomádha*
(on) Monday *(ti) deftéra*
(on) Tuesday *(tin) tríti*
(on) Wednesday *(tin) tetárti*
(on) Thursday *(tin) pémpti*
(on) Friday *(tin) paraskeví*
(on) Saturday *(to) sávato*
(on) Sunday *(tin) kyriakí*

Health

Is there a chemist nearby? *Ypárhi
éna farmakío edó kondá?*
Which chemist is open all night?
Pio farmakío dianikterévi?
I don't feel well *Den esthánome kalá*
I'm ill *Íme árostos (feminine árosti)*
He/she's ill *Íne árostos/árosti*
Where does it hurt? *Pou ponái?*
It hurts here *Ponái edó*
I suffer from... *Pásko apo...*
I have a... *Ého...*
headache *ponokéfalo*
sore throat *ponólemo*
stomach ache *kilíopono*
Have you got something for travel
sickness? *Éhete típota gia ti navtía?*
It's not serious *Den íne sovaró*
Do I need a prescription? *Hriázete
syndagí?*
It bit me (of an animal) *Me
dángose*
It stung me *Me kéntrise*
bee *mélisa*
wasp *sfíka*
mosquito *kounoúpi*
sticking plaster *lefkoplástis*
diarrhoea pills *hápia gia ti diária*

Alcoholic Drinks

býra **beer**
krasí **wine**
áspro **white wine**
kokkinélli **rosé wine**
mávro **red wine**
me to kiló **wine by the kilo**
hýma **bulk, from the barrel**
(aerioúho) neró **(sparkling, fizzy)**

Notices

ΤΟΥΑΛΕΤΕΣ	toilets
ΑΝΔΡΩΝ	gentlemen
ΓΥΝΑΙΚΩΝ	ladies
ΑΝΟΙΚΤΟ	open
ΚΛΕΙΣΤΟ	closed
ΕΙΣΟΔΟΣ	entrance
ΕΞΟΔΟΣ	exit
ΑΠΑΓΟΡΕΥΤΑΙ ΕΙΣΟΔΟΣ	no entry
ΕΙΣΙΤΗΡΙΑ	tickets
ΑΠΑΓΟΡΕΥΤΑΙ ΤΟ ΚΑΠΝΙΣΜΑ	no smoking
ΠΛΗΡΟΦΟΡΙΕΣ	information
ΠΡΟΣΟΧΗ	caution
ΚΙΝΔΥΝΟΣ	danger
ΑΡΓΑ	slow
ΔΗΜΟΣΙΑ ΕΡΓΑ	road works
ΠΑΡΚΙΝΓ ΧΩΡΟΣ ΣΤΑΘΜΕΥΣΕΩΣ	parking car park
ΑΠΑΓΟΡΕΥΤΑΙ Η ΣΤΑΘΜΕΥΣΗ	no parking
ΤΑΞΙ	taxi
ΤΡΑΠΕΖΑ	bank
ΤΗΛΕΦΩΝΟ	telephone
ΕΚΤΟΣ ΛΕΙΤΟΥΡΓΙΑΣ	out of order

water
retsína **resin-flavoured wine**
oúzo **aniseed-flavoured grape-
pressing distillate**
rakí, tsíkoudiá **another distilled
spirit from vintage crushings,
unflavoured**
tsípouro **north-mainland version of
*rakí***

FURTHER READING

Books go in and out of print, or change imprints, with such rapidity of late that publishers are not listed here except for websites of obscure Greek presses. For most books, a web search with the author and title should suffice to dredge up its current incarnation.

Ancient History and Culture

Burkert, Walter **Greek Religion: Archaic and Classical**. Excellent

overview of the gods and goddesses, their attributes, worship and the meaning of major festivals.
Cartledge, Paul **Cambridge Illustrated History of Ancient Greece**. Large, illustrated volume by a distinguished contemporary classicist.
Finley, M.I. **The World of Odysseus**. Reissued 1954 standard on just how well (or not) the Homeric sagas are borne out by archaeological facts.
Gere, Cathy **Knossos and the Prophets of Modernism**. Puts the digs

at Knossós in the cultural context of their time, documenting the reciprocal effects of contemporary art and Minoan aesthetics as reconstructed by Evans's assistants, and the "blurry boundary between restorations, reconstructions, replicas and fakes".
Grimal, Pierre, ed. **Dictionary of Classical Mythology**. Still considered tops among a handful of available alphabetical gazetteers.
Hornblower, Simon **The Greek World, 479–323 BC**. The eventful period from the end of the Persian Wars to

Alexander's demise; the standard university text.
Macgillivray, J. Alexander *Minotaur: Sir Arthur Evans and the Archaeology of the Minoan Myth*. Excellent demolition job by an archaeologist, on how Evans manipulated the evidence at Knossós to fit his powerful Victorian-era prejudices.

Byzantine History and Culture

Norwich, John Julius **Byzantium** (3 vols): *The Early Centuries, The Apogee and The Decline*. The most readable and masterful popular history, by a noted Byzantinologist; also available as one massive volume, *A Short History of Byantium*.
Rice, David Talbot **Art of the Byzantine Era**. Shows how Byzantine sacred craftsmanship extended from the Caucasus into northern Italy, in a variety of media.
Runciman, Steven *The Fall of Constantinople, 1453*. Still the definitive study of an event which continues to exercise modern Greek minds. His **Byzantine Style and Civilization** covers art, culture and monuments.
Ware, Archbishop Kallistos *The Orthodox Church*. Good introduction to what was, until recently, the *de jure* state religion of Greece.

Anthropology and Culture

Bent, James Theodore *Aegean Islands: The Cyclades, or Life Among the Insular Greeks*. Originally published in 1881 and reissued regularly since, this remains an authoritative source on pre-tourism island customs and folklore, based on several months' winter travel.
Clark, Bruce *Twice a Stranger: How Mass Expulsion Forged Modern Greece and Turkey*. The background to the 1923 population exchanges, and how both countries are still digesting the experience three generations later. Readable and compassionate, especially the encounters with elderly survivors of the experience.
Danforth, Loring H. and Tsiaras, Alexander *The Death Rituals of Rural Greece.* Riveting, annotated photo essay on Greek funeral customs.
Du Boulay, Juliet *Portrait of a Greek Mountain Village*. Ambéli, a mountain village in Évvia, as it was in the mid-1960s.
Kenna, Margaret E. *Greek Island Life: Fieldwork on Anafi*. Her

1966–7 doctoral research, reflected in her notebooks and letters home, when pre-tourism culture still survived.
Llewellyn Smith, Michael *The Great Island: A Study of Crete*. Before he was a known historian (and twice ambassador to Greece), a young Llewellyn Smith wrote this, with good analysis of folk traditions and in particular Cretan song.
Tomkinson, John L. *Festive Greece: A Calendar of Traditions* (www.anagnosis.gr). Gazetter with lots of photos, of all the most observed feast days of the Church – and the often pagan *panigýria* attending them.

Cuisine and Wine

Barron, Rosemary *Flavours of Greece*. The leading non-tourist-stall cookbook, with over 250 recipes.
Dalby, Andrew *Siren Feasts*. Analysis of classical and Byzantine texts shows how little Greek food has changed in three millennia.
Davidson, Alan *Mediterranean Seafood*. 1972 classic that's still the standard reference, guaranteed to end every argument as to just what that fish is on your taverna plate. Complete with recipes.
Lazarákis, Konstantínos *The Wines of Greece*. An overview, current to late 2005, of Greece's 11 recognised wine-producing regions.

Modern History

Clark, Alan *The Fall of Crete*. Breezy military history by the late, maverick English politician; good on the battles, and more critical of the command than you expect.
Clogg, Richard *A Concise History of Greece*. Clear, lively account of Greece from Byzantine times to 2002, with helpful maps and well-captioned artwork. The best single-volume summary.
Koliopoulos, John and Thanos Veremis *Greece, the Modern Sequel: From 1831 to the Present*. Thematic and psycho-history of the independent nation, tracing trends, first principles and setbacks.
Pettifer, James *The Greeks: the Land and People since the War*. Useful general introduction to politics, family life, food, tourism and other contemporary topics.
Seligman, Adrian *War in the Islands*. Collected oral histories of the caique flotillas organised to raid the Axis-held Aegean islands. Detailed maps and period photos liven up the service jargon.

Woodouse, C.M. *Modern Greece: A Short History*. Spans the period from early Byzantium to the early 1980s. His classic *The Struggle for Greece, 1941–1949* is the best overview of that turbulent decade, and has aged well despite the brief 1990s opening of Soviet archives.

Modern Greek Literature

Beaton, Roderick *An Introduction to Modern Greek*. Readable survey of Greek literature since independence.
A Century of Greek Poetry, 1900–2000. Well produced bilingual volume, with some lesser-known surprises alongside the big names.
Cavafy, C.P. *Collected Poems*, trans. by Edmund Keeley and Philip Sherrard or *The Complete Poems of Cavafy*, translated by Rae Dalven. Long reckoned the "standard" versions in English; 2007 translations by Evangelos Sachperoglou and Stratis Haviaras will also appeal but don't break radically new ground.
Elýtis, Odysséas *Collected Poems, The Axion Esti, Selected Poems* and *Eros, Eros, Eros*. Pretty much the complete works of the Nobel laureate, in translation by George Savidis, Edmund Keeley and Olga Broumas.
Karnezis, Panos. Karnezis grew up in Greece, but lives in London, writing in English; however, his concerns remain Greek. *Little Infamies* is a short-story selection set in his native Peloponnese during the late 1950s and early 1960s; *The Maze* is a darker, more successful novel concerning the Asia Minor War. Both display a penchant for old-fashioned plot twists – or excessive magical realism, depending on point of view. His most recent *The Birthday Party* is based on the Onassis family.
Kazantzákis, Níkos. Nobel laureate, woolly Marxist/Buddhist and voluntary exile, his books bear out the old maxim that classics are praised but unread. Whether in intricate, untranslatable Greek or wooden English, Kazantzákis can be hard going. *Zorba the Greek* is a surprisingly dark and nihilistic work, worlds away from the two-dimensionality of the film; *The Last Temptation of Christ*, filmed, provoked riots by Orthodox fanatics in 1989; *Report to Greco* explores his Cretanness; while *Christ Recrucified* (The Greek Passion) encompasses the Easter drama within Christian-Muslim dynamics on Crete.
Papadiamántis, Alexándros; trans. Peter Levi *The Murderess*. Landmark social-realist novel, set on Skiáthos at

the turn of the 19th/20th centuries. Seferis, George; trans. Edmund Keeley *Collected Poems 1924–1955*; *Complete Poems*. The former has Greek-English texts on facing pages, preferable to the so-called "complete" works of Greece's other Nobel literary laureate. Sotiriou, Dido *Farewell Anatolia*. A best-seller since its appearance in 1962, this traces the end of Greek life in Asia Minor from 1914 to 1922, using a character based on the author's father. Tsirkas, Stratis; trans. Kay Cicellis *Drifting Cities*. Epic novel on wartime leftist intrigue in Alexandria, Cairo and Jerusalem.

Foreign Writers on the Islands

De Bernières, Louis *Captain Corelli's Mandolin*. Heart-rending tragicomedy set on occupied Kefalloniá during World War II which despite dubious politics has acquired cult status. Durrell, Lawrence *Prospero's Cell* and *Reflections on a Marine Venus*. Corfu in the 1930s, and Rhodes in 1945–7, now feeling rather old-fashioned, alcohol-fogged and patronising of the "natives", but still entertaining enough. Fowles, John *The Magus*. Best-seller, inspired by Fowles's spell teaching on Spétses during the 1950s, of post-adolescent manipulation, conspiracy and cock-teasing (the usual Fowles obsessions). Jinkinson, Roger *Tales from a Greek Island*. Stories long and short set in and around Diafáni, Kárpathos, where Jinkinson lives much of the year. Poignant, blackly funny, even revisionist about World War II heroics. Manus, Willard *This Way to Paradise: Dancing on the Tables* (www.lycabettus. com). American expatriate's affectionate summing-up of 40-plus years living in Líndos, from its innocence to its corruption. Wonderful anecdotes of the hippie days, and walk-on parts for the famous and infamous. Miller, Henry *The Colossus of Maroussi*. Miller takes to Corfu, the Argolid, Athens and Crete of 1939 with the enthusiasm of a first-timer in Greece; deserted archaeological sites and larger-than-life personalities. Stone, Tom *The Summer of My Greek Taverna*. Set in a thinly disguised Kámbos of early-1980s Pátmos, this is a poignant cautionary tale for all who've ever fantasised about leasing a taverna (or buying a property) in the islands.

Travis, William *Bus Stop Symi*. Chronicles three years' residence there in the pre-tourism 1960s; fairly insightful, though resented on the island for its artistic licence. Wheeler, Sarah *Évvia: Travels on an Undiscovered Island*. A five-month ramble through Évvia in the early 1990s, juxtaposing historical/cultural musings with adventures on the ground.

Archaeological and Hiking Guides

Burn, A. R. and Mary *The Living Past of Greece*. Worth toting around for the sake of lively text and clear plans; covers most major sites from Minoan to medieval. Hetherington, Paul *The Greek Islands: Guide to the Byzantine and Medieval Buildings and Their Art*. As it says, though there are some astonishing omissions of stellar monuments like Rhodes's painted churches in favour of the obscure. Chilton, Lance *Various walking guides* (www.marengowalks.com). Short guidelets to the best walks around various island charter destinations, accompanied by maps. Wilson, Loraine *High Mountains of Crete*. Almost 100 walks and treks, mostly in the White Mountains but

Send Us Your Thoughts

We do our best to ensure the information in our books is as accurate and up-to-date as possible. The books are updated on a regular basis using local contacts, who painstakingly add, amend and correct as required. However, some details (such as telephone numbers and opening times) are liable to change, and we are ultimately reliant on our readers to put us in the picture.

We welcome your feedback, especially your experience of using the book "on the road". Maybe we recommended a hotel that you liked (or another that you didn't), or you came across a great bar or new attraction we missed.

We will acknowledge all contributions, and we'll offer an Insight Guide to the best letters received.

Please write to us at:
Insight Guides
PO Box 7910
London SE1 1WE
Or email us at:
insight@apaguide.co.uk

also mounts Psilorítis and Díkti, described by the most experienced foreign guide.

Botanical Field Guides

Baumann, Helmut *Greek Wildflowers and Plant Lore in Ancient Greece*. As the title says; lots of interesting ethnobotanical trivia, useful photos. Fielding, John and Nicholas Turland *Flowers of Crete* Massive volume (updated 2008) with 1,900 colour plates of the Cretan flora, much of which is found on neighbouring islands. Huxley, Anthony, and William Taylor *Flowers of Greece and the Aegean*. The only volume dedicated to both islands and mainland, with good photos, though taxonomy is now a bit obsolete.

Other Insight Guides

More than 180 **Insight Guides** and **Insight City Guides** cover every continent, providing information on culture and all the top sights, as well as superb photography and detailed maps. Other Insight Guides to destinations in the region include: Greece, Turkey, Western Europe, Great Railway Journeys of Europe, and Mediterranean Cruises.

The new **Insight Step by Step** guide books contain personal recommendations from a local host, a programme of carefully timed itineraries and a fold-out map. They are particularly useful for the short-stay visitor intent on making the best use of every moment. Titles include Istanbul, Rome, Barcelona and Berlin.

ART & PHOTO CREDITS

INDEX

Main entries are in bold type

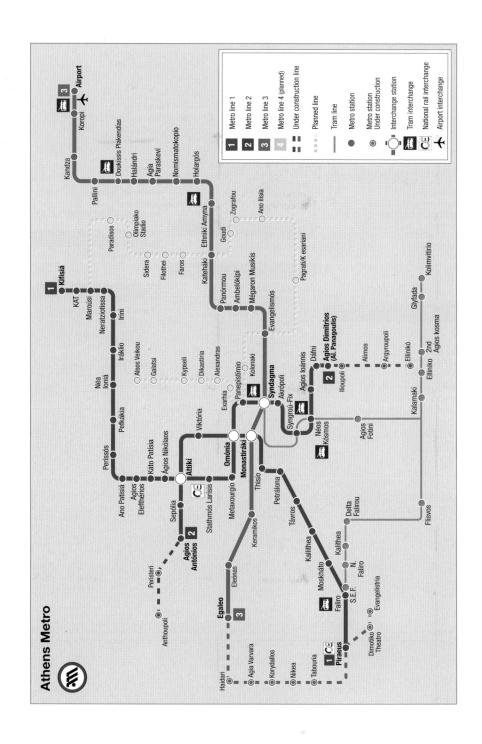

Athens Metro

Greece: Physical and Main Ferry Routes

0   50 km
0   50 miles